GLOCK
DECONSTRUCTED

PATRICK SWEENEY

Copyright ©2013 Patrick Sweeney

All rights reserved. No portion of this publication may be reproduced or transmitted in any form or by any means, electronic or mechanical, including photocopy, recording, or any information storage and retrieval system, without permission in writing from the publisher, except by a reviewer who may quote brief passages in a critical article or review to be printed in a magazine or newspaper, or electronically transmitted on radio, television, or the Internet.

Published by

Gun Digest® Books, an imprint of F+W Media, Inc.
Krause Publications • 700 East State Street • Iola, WI 54990-0001
715-445-2214 • 888-457-2873
www.krausebooks.com

To order books or other products call toll-free 1-800-258-0929
or visit us online at www.gundigeststore.com

Cover photography by Yamil R. Sued
www.hotgunshots.com

ISBN-13: 978-1-4402-3278-7
ISBN-10: 1-4402-3278-4

Edited by Jennifer L.S. Pearsall
Designed by Dave Hauser
Cover Design by Tom Nelsen

Printed in the United States of America

DEDICATION

For those of you who have read my previous books, you know who this is going to be dedicated to; Felicia and the poodles.

Fierce devotion, looking out for the pack, keeping an eye out for trouble, and alertness for opportunity are all traits dogs are supposed to be masters of. Well, as dedicated as the three guys are, they know Felicia is the exemplar after whom to model themselves.

Save for her, I'd be a penniless surfer dude (and probably an only passable surfer, at that), and the world would have fewer firearms books. So, you have her to thank for the need to find more room on your bookshelf.

ABOUT THE AUTHOR

Patrick Sweeney has, in his own words "the kind of work history that could sell mystery novels." With a college degree in chemistry, he never worked a day as a chemist, and viewers of *Breaking Bad* can understand where that kind of education can lead to. What he has done is work for two decades as a gunsmith, and competed for three decades as a practical shooting competitor in USPSA/IPSC, 3-Gun and bowling pin competitions, with some Steel Challenge and Bianchi Cup along the way.

When the thought of yet another Summer and Fall of preparing rifles and shotguns for the upcoming hunting season proved to be too much, he shifted to writing. The result is a large number of Gun Digest titles, including this one.

Continuing his research into ballistics, he has been heard to answer "What do you do for a living?" with "I make once-fired brass."

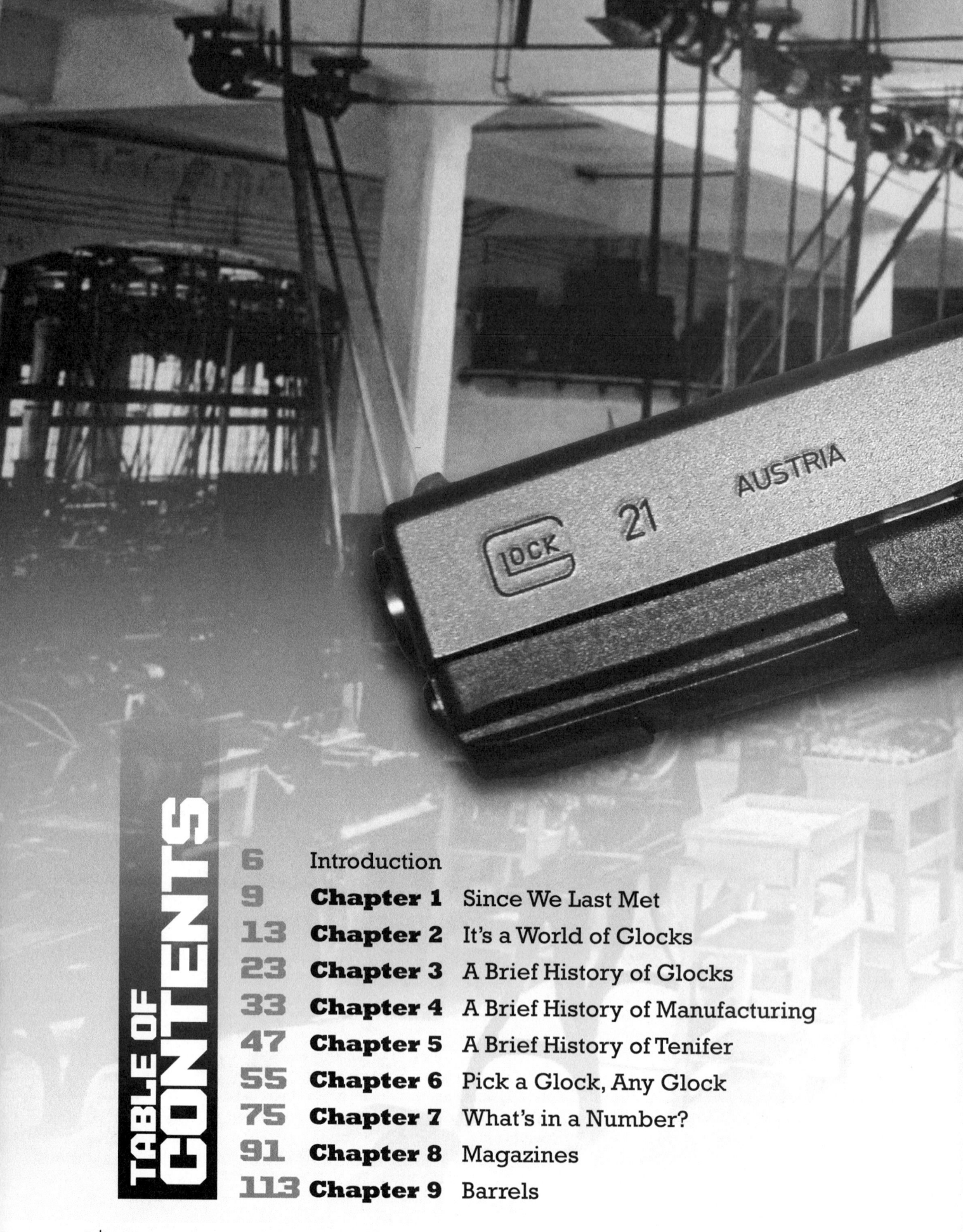

TABLE OF CONTENTS

6		Introduction
9	**Chapter 1**	Since We Last Met
13	**Chapter 2**	It's a World of Glocks
23	**Chapter 3**	A Brief History of Glocks
33	**Chapter 4**	A Brief History of Manufacturing
47	**Chapter 5**	A Brief History of Tenifer
55	**Chapter 6**	Pick a Glock, Any Glock
75	**Chapter 7**	What's in a Number?
91	**Chapter 8**	Magazines
113	**Chapter 9**	Barrels

127	**Chapter 10**	Carbine City
153	**Chapter 11**	Suppressors
173	**Chapter 12**	Tactical Red Dots
185	**Chapter 13**	The G18
219	**Chapter 14**	Single-Stack Musings
227	**Chapter 15**	The Competition
241	**Chapter 16**	Non-Glock Glocks
247	**Chapter 17**	Make Your Glock…Well, What, Exactly?
257	**Chapter 18**	Gen 4: The Evolution?
275	**Chapter 19**	GSSF–The Glock Sport Shooting Foundation

INTRODUCTION

This time, it was going to be different. If you can believe it, Glock actually came to me. Well, a member of the PR company they had hired contacted me with the idea of a new Glock book. "Glock is interested in a new book and is going to support it," they said.

Well, slap me silly and call me rude names. *This* I can get excited about.

To test the waters, I composed a prospective set of questions. Being the clever fellow I am (sometimes too clever by half, if you don't mind the occasional Shakespearean reference), I composed a set of questions that would tell me pretty accurately how much info Glock was willing to divulge and how much assistance they were willing to provide. The queries ranged from simple to the type where I anticipated the answer would be something on the order of "We can't answer this without divulging trade secrets." I covered the basics, like how many loaner pistols they could send and on what schedule, on up to almost certainly secret requests, such as how long the moulding machines cycled to produce a frame or set of frames. And, so, I sent in my queries. I figured that those they'd answer and how they'd answer the ones they did would give me a good read on just what level of support they were offering. To make sure there were no fumbles, I send copies to all involved. I send them to the PR rep, e-mail and snail mail. I send them to Glock, to the address provided. I do everything but semaphore them to Smyrna.

A short detour here. Every year, the firearms industry holds its annual trade show, the SHOT (Shooting, Hunting, Outdoor Trades) show. At this show, everyone who is anyone is in attendance, and all the makers have exhibition booths, with booth being anything from a 10-foot-square patch of carpeting with canvas walls up to a multi-story structure with a footprint larger than the average home. Glock is in the latter camp. Its booth is the size of a parking lot, but it has to be, as it has lots of models and lots of fans. It also need room for the waiting line for autographs to snake around other nearby booths.

The PR rep, on finding out that Glock had not contacted me (nor them) on the matter of answers after a decent amount of time had been allowed, suggested that I talk to the in-house Glock PR guy. Name and e-mail attached, please ask the home office. There is no response.

Were my hopes for a really different book on the Glock firearms gone? You see, what I

wanted to do, instead of simply updating the existing book, the previous *Gun Digest Book of the Glock Volume 2*, I was figuring on starting with a clean slate—well, clean in that I did not rewrite, update, clean up, change, or otherwise massage the existing text. I started with a clean sheet of paper (an interesting turn of phrase, in this digital world), but I was wondering about Glocks: I wanted them to *show* me.

People tell me Glocks are ultra-reliable, durable, accurate, easy-to-use, and easy to maintain. My experience has been not so much. Then again, they don't fit my hands very well. However, Glock sells a lot of them, so they've got to be working for some of you. Now, don't get me wrong. If evil is coming through the door in a short time hence and all I have is a Glock, I won't feel like I'm using a cap gun. (I'll also be doing all I can to get out of there before evil arrives, Glock or no Glock.) But given a choice, I'll pick a lot of other firearms before I pick a Glock. That's me, it's a personal preference.

Still, there is this book, and there's plenty to say about Glocks, both positive and not. And even though I didn't get as much help from the people at Glock as I would have liked, I have a couple decades experience as a gunsmith, more as a competition shooter and reloader, and many, many visits to firearms factories. These basics, combined with earlier work experience in manufacturing, affords me a peek behind the curtain, even if it wasn't an actual tour of the Glock factory.

I did not gush all over the various models of Glocks. I mean, if what you want is breathless recitation of the latest press handout, plenty of writers and PR people can do that for you. There are also plenty of magazine articles about Glocks, though, and I don't mean to dis my brethren gun writers, but there is only so much that can be done in 1,800 words and with a deadline of "next Thursday."

Too, lacking a support team, research laboratory, unlimited budget, and Congressional mandate, I can't serially abuse Glocks pistols, compared to others, to determine which is king of the hill. For those who suggested such, I appreciate your esteem in my abilities to perform such a task, but I really can't do that alone. Plus, statistically speaking, to do so to less than a couple dozen samples is a meaningless exercise. So, no criminally abused Glocks in this volume. Sorry.

Regardless, sit back and enjoy (or grit your teeth) and learn what you can use to hold your own in discussions at the gun club. Have fun.

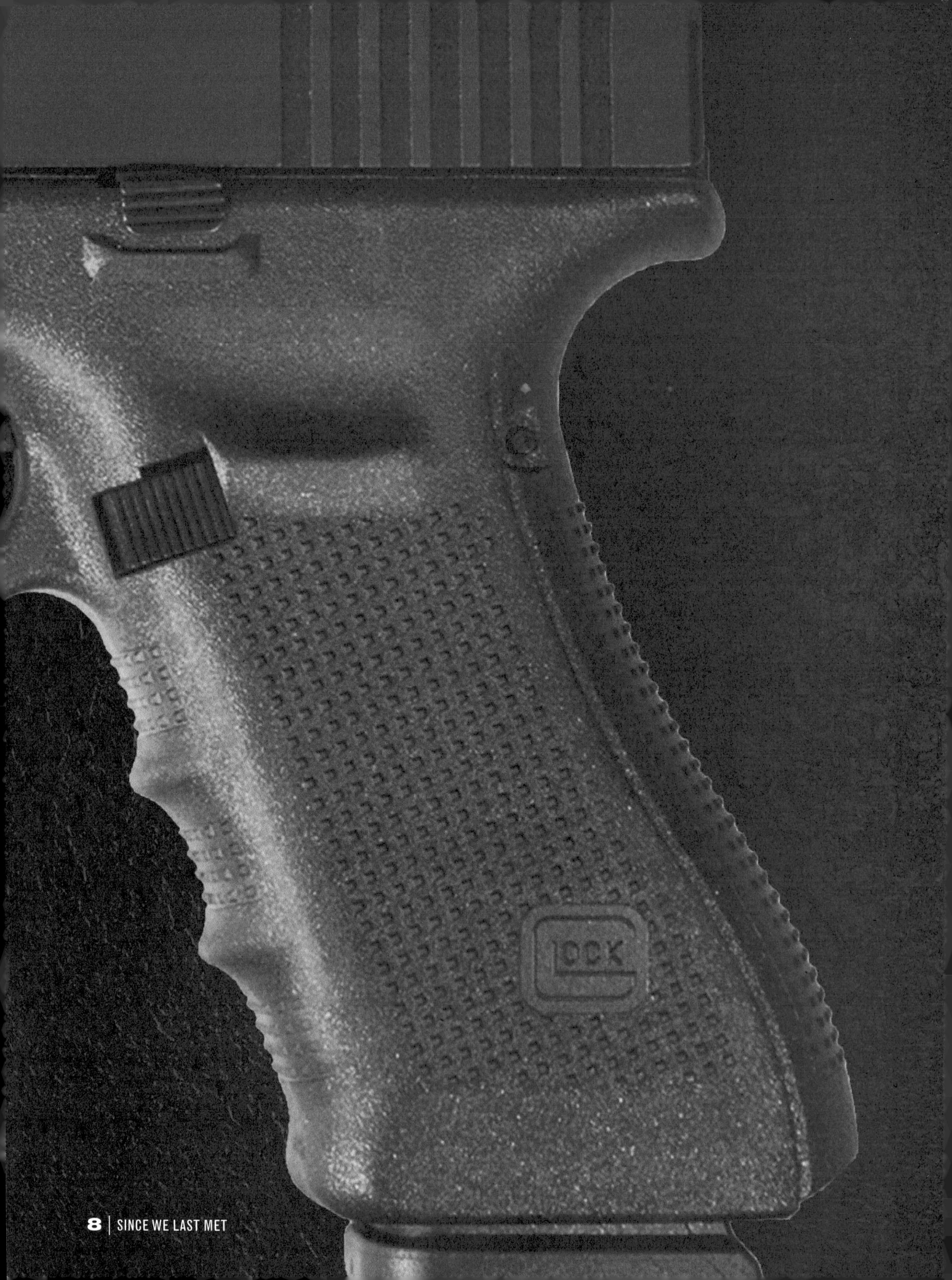

CHAPTER 1

Since We Last Met

Since we last had a chance to talk, back in 2008, in my *Gun Digest Book of the Glock, Volume 2*, a lot has happened. Glock has changed, and yet has not changed. The pistols were changed, then unchanged and re-changed to a different perfection. A lot of competitors have decided that, since Glock makes something almost perfect and people are buying them, then they, too, should make something a bit more perfect and sell lots of them.

Competition improves the breed. If it doesn't, then it brings out aftermarket customizers, who will improve things where the original makers won't. Three different Glock frame modifiers are represented here.

Glock found itself involved in legal wrangling, but, as corporate legal wrangling goes, it wasn't all that unusual. Oh, for those of us who are into firearms, it is always an unnerving proposition, when lawyers get involved. But, in the corporate world, especially in some industries, signing up as a corporate officer or becoming a member of the Board of Directors also involves having a company attorney surgically attached at the hip. That's just a part of modern corporate life.

Glock, after coming out with the original design, stuck with it as long as it could before changing it. The change, one done to make it easier to comply with the silly U.S. import scoring system, gave Glock a chance to change the texturing on the frame. Between origin and the chance to change, shooters had become a lot more interested in a non-slip grip. Wait, let me amend that. There had always been shooters interested in a non-slip grip, but, what with the increase in IPSC competition, there were more shooters who paid attention to that sort of detail. What happened in IPSC (USPSA in the United States), would work its way over to law enforcement. Once enough police officers were paying attention, departments wanted better guns.

Glock stuck with the original design as long as it could before changing it. The change, done to make it easier to comply with the silly U.S. import scoring system, gave Glock a chance to alter the texturing on the frame.

Then there was the RTF2 change. Glock went even further and improved the grip with the RTF2. Then it gave it up for the Gen4 mods, and the guns went back to what looked like the new/old texture. Well, Glock didn't really give it up. If your agency or police department wants the RTF2, you could, for a while, special order it. But, eventually, Glock again dropped it as an option. That move probably made sense. If Glock was going to make the RTF2 available, it would have to keep and properly store the mould blocks for the RTF2 frames and pull them out from time to time in order to produce more inventory as ordered. That has to cost money. Add in the cost and downtime of converting a machine for an agency order, and you've suddenly priced your product out of the running. I mention all this not to give you the history, but to set the stage.

The big thing is, Glock is no longer alone. For a long time, it was the one and only. Then there were a few would-be competitors, companies that were testing the waters and trying out design and marketing strategies. Aftermarket manufacturers have jumped in with both feet, as well. The time of Glock hegemony has ended. Glock isn't even the first in its field, with a small group of wanna-bes tagging along behind them anymore. For a long time, if you wanted a Glock, you went to Glock. If you wanted parts, barrels, springs, etc., you went to Glock. That isn't the case anymore, and I'm not talking about the Glock clones, nor the entire, large, striker-fired market competition. Indeed, it is now possible to buy or build a Glock, where no part in it ever came close to Smyrna, Georgia, just as you can now (and have for a long time), been able to make a 1911 or an AR-15 without having any part so much as come within sight of the Connecticut border.

That's a good thing. Good not because I wish Glock any ill will, but rather because competition is good. Competition, both on the range and in the marketplace, is what got us here. If someone comes up with a better mousetrap, the original mousetrap builder has to either up its game or accept diminished market share. (Or, if you'll excuse a slight divergence back to the legal system, get the courts and legislature involved in hampering the competition. Luckily, we have little of that in the firearms industry, compared to others.)

Since we've last talked, I've had a chance to find and talk to some people who work with Glock, and some people who used to work for Glock. Glock itself remains resolutely uncommunicative. At one point, I mentioned this upcoming book to one of the PR people, how things seemed a lot more promising and that I'd love to drop in on the plant in Austria and see how things are done, even if it meant no camera, and no disclosure of details. There was a pause, and then the comment "Patrick, I've worked for Glock for X years, and I haven't been inside the plant." I do not specify how many years here, but it was many.

On that note, if you think about it, not a whole lot has actually changed in the Glockverse. That said, in the ensuing pages, we aren't going to go all gushy over the various Glock models. Glock does a pretty good job of that, with various annuals and advertising campaigns. You didn't come here to simply get all that with new photos. You want more. So for those who are coming new to the Gun Digest Glock fold, I'll have a look at them, but our efforts will be aimed at the rest of the universe of Glocks and Glock-like and Glock-copy pistols as a whole—and some things that Glock doesn't talk about. I hope thing that make you go *"Hmm?"*

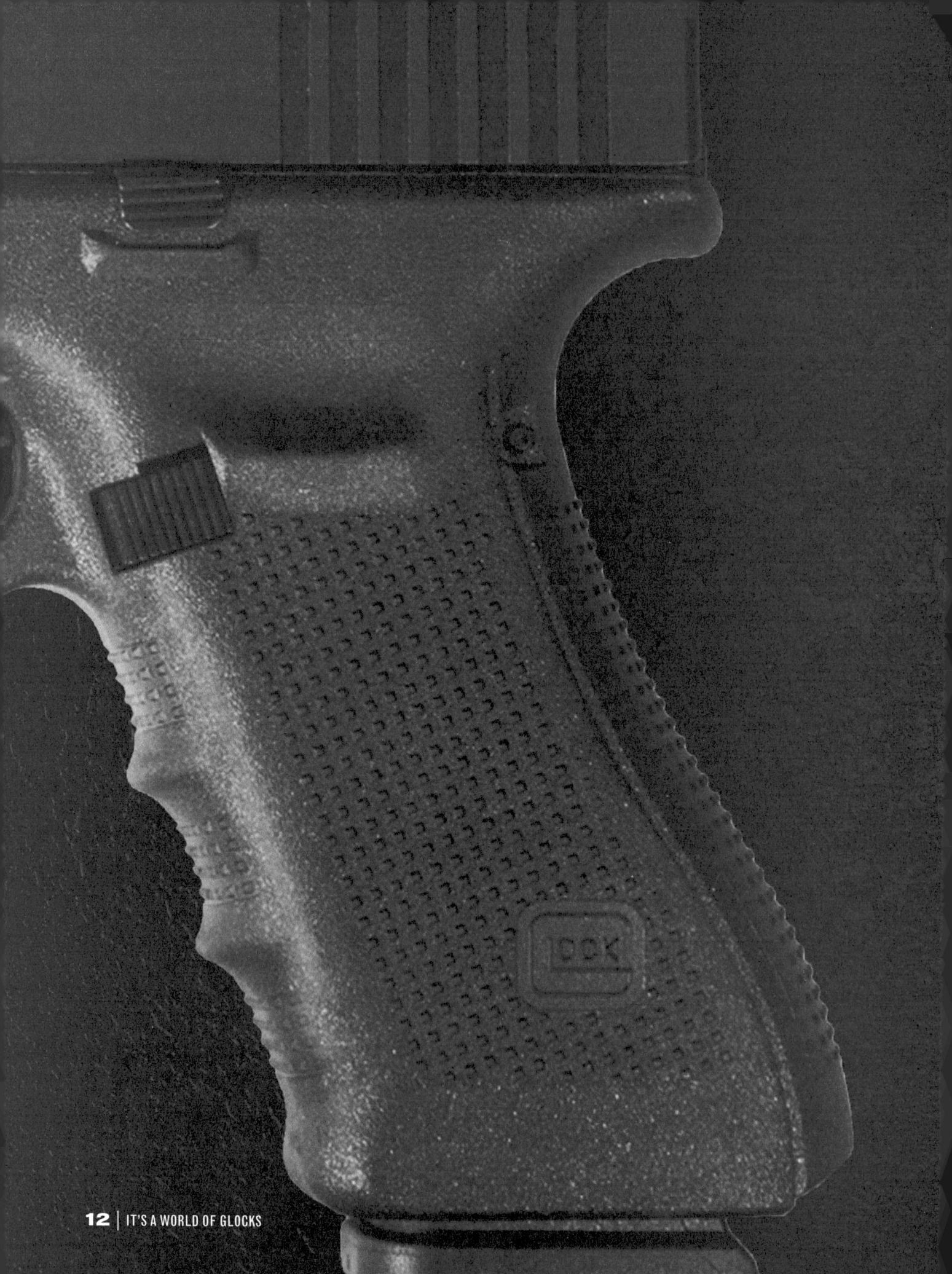

CHAPTER

It's a World of Glocks

A female Iraqi police officer getting pistol instruction. If you are going to equip a brand new police force, starting with Glocks is not necessarily a bad idea. *DoD photo by Staff Sgt. Michael Kropiewnicki, U.S. Marine Corps*

Those conversant in history divide time periods into "ages" and "eras" and the like. As in the Stone Age, the Middle Ages, the Iron Age, the Age of Discovery, the Napoleonic era, the Edwardian period … well, you get the idea. The purpose is to divide time periods according to the span in which an idea, an organization, a material was ascendant. The later ones may be better (iron does have advantages over flint, for instance). Or they may not.

The Soviets may or may not have been an improvement over the Tsars. Depends on where you were in the pecking order. It may well be that future historians will look back and declare the period from 1982 to (pick a date, but don't stop until phasers are general issue), as the "Glock Era" or the "Polymer Pistol Period."

Let's do what Albert Einstein called a "thought experiment." Consider a situation and then explore all the ramifications of that situation. One of the famous ones from good old Al was the elevator. You're in an elevator and you feel the floor pushing up on your feet. Is that push due to a gravitational field or acceleration? (The technical among you will note that gravitation *is* acceleration, but that's a nicety we need not go into here.) Inside the elevator, there is no way to tell. Oh, you know you are in an elevator and you are headed for the twenty-seventh floor, but you are applying knowledge from outside the reference frame.

The problem with using information gathered only from inside the reference frame is you *don't* know. We're still inside a period that may or may not have "Glock" attached to it, so we can't really tell. But given that competitor after competitor has shifted from their metal-framed, hammer-fired pistol designs and now almost all offer at least one polymer-framed, striker-fired model would be a clue.

That's a bit more than we need, I'll admit. Let's try another. You wake up from a nap and find yourself in a strange environment, the gun magazine you were reading still in your lap. A voice asks you about the page open to a color, love-shot photograph of a Glock. "What's that?"

Clearly, you are not where you used to be.

If there is a place on the planet where the image of a Glock is *not* common knowledge, you'd have to be in a grass hut far up the Amazon. The image of the Glock is as common and well-recognized as that of the AK, even though the AK is on some national flags and the Glock is not. So you are either so deep in the hinterlands that you left the sound of banjos a few hours ago, or you are, *hmm*, not on this planet.

Even if your students are familiar with rifles, handguns are a whole new exercise in muzzle safety. Third-world standards are not ours. At least there are earplugs in use. (U.S. Air Force Photo by Staff Sgt. Vanessa Valentine)

The Glock is so common in movies and TV that it is ubiquitous. I could show you many examples, but there is no need. Turn on the TV to any police procedural and odds are, when the time comes to get armed, they will produce Glock pistols. Of course, they will also do the oddest things with them, like draw and then you can hear the clear sound of a safety being disengaged. Or draw, and then the star will work the slide to chamber a cartridge. These are technical gaffes, mistakes, produced by the Foley artist, probably at the behest of the director. The Foley artist (the guy who dubs in the extra sounds) probably knows they are wrong, but he is out-ranked by the director. If the director wants the foot chase to happen in big clown shoes, it happens. So don't blame the actor, the Foley artist, or anyone else for gun flubs like this unless you are sure.

Oh, there's another reason I can't/won't regale you with photos of actors wielding Glocks, and that is money. As in intellectual property rights. The production company hired the actor, the cinematographer, and the stills photographer, and all they produce, on that set, under that contract, belongs to the production company. If I want to show you (fill in big-name actor here) with a Glock in his or her hands, I'd have to ask permission. That permission would come with an invoice. Failing to ask for that permission, I'd find my life to be miserable, hounded by the lawyers to the production company who are all too eager to demonstrate their worth. They, after all, are not licensed to practice law in China, where movie piracy is rampant (or so the newspapers tell us), and even if they were, such lawsuits have in the past produced naught to show for the efforts. Me, on the other hand? I'm sure they'd be happy to savage this writer through the legal system.

How did Glocks get that way, get so famous? Or infamous?

With a great deal of help. When they first came on the scene, the outcry over their being made of "plastic" was so deafening that Glock found itself with millions of dollars of free publicity. The saying "There is no such thing as bad publicity" has been attributed to one or another studio head and famous authors galore, and I'm sure there's some guy on the Internet trying to convince everyone he invented the phrase in 1987. Basically, unless the bad publicity is something that turns off potential buyers, the more your name is out there, the better. Kim Kardashian, good. Ford Pintos, bad. You get the idea. So, with all the politicians claiming Glocks were invisible to X-ray machines and metal detectors and were the handguns of choice of Moammar Khaddafi (I wonder if he then went and bought some, once he'd been blamed for it, just to see what all the fuss was about),

Non-Glock Glocks come in a variety of colors. This one is gray, and I've seen blue, black, red, green, and orange. Really, if you wish to order enough, you can get them in any color you desire.

everyone out there walking into a gun shop had to see one. I know they did at the gun shop I was working at.

Then it just took a movie art director seeing one back in 1986-'87, and the angular black shape and no-nonsense appearance screamed "Put me in a movie!" to them. And so it was. So much so that, today, I'm sure the property master in a movie or TV design meeting has to do a rear-guard action in some productions:

Property master: "Look, this movie is set in the Bicentennial year. Glocks didn't exist then."

Director: "I don't care, nothing else you have shown me is sinister enough. Get one in the shot."

Or:

Property Master: "Our movie is set in [fill in the blank] and that PD doesn't carry Glocks."

Director: "Nonsense, all police departments carry Glocks. Our guy packs a Glock. And the bad guys all have AKs."

And so on. That said, there are a lot of places that aren't movie production sets where Glocks are common, and you can see them in photos if you spend any time perusing the news. With the recent fracas in Iraq, and the ongoing wrangle in Afghanistan, we have been rearming army units, police forces, and the like. This requires serious volumes of pistols, and many, many are Glocks. Indeed, the common 9mm sidearm in many locales is the G19. And not just NYC.

Why that and not the G17? Because the G17 is just too big, that's why. For a western soldier or police officer raised on a modern hi-protein and vitamin diet, the G17 is a normal-sized pistol. Many of us can even pack a G34/35, no problem, because we're simply big enough to hide it.

Lacking that background, a skinny, short—and not to be disrespectful, but five feet, six inches and 135 pounds is not U.S. football stature—trooper/policeman has not much chance

(below) A wall o' Glocks and other pistols, none real.

(opposite top) If it is one-upmanship you seek, then an invite to the annual Glock party at the SHOT show will make your fellow Glocksters green with jealousy.

(opposite bottom) Glocks, other handguns, rifles, machine guns, and none of them are guns. They are all plastic-cast copies for training and movie use.

of handling, packing, and hanging on to a G17. The G19 is just short enough in slide and frame that it is compact enough to easily fit in web gear, holster, or whatever.

Once you accept that, if you're equipping a group, there's no point in having more than one size, unless you need a special-status sidearm for the bosses. So, the default is the G19. The bosses probably get smaller ones, unless they have enough juice to demand and get G18s.

Why Glocks? Well, in some places, Glocks *aren't* common. If you pour through photos of our troops overseas, you'll see scads of Beretta M9s, but nary a Glock. I have it on good authority that Glocks are common in the more selective units, the secret-squirrel groups that can basically use whatever they want. But the general issue in the U.S. Army, Marines, etc., is the Beretta.

The reason for this is simple. Glocks weren't in the U.S. in time to make the cut for the JSSAP tests, the one that lead to the adoption of the M9. You may be surprised at this bit of info, but our government is reluctant to go back and reconsider a decision, just because something better has come along. I know, you're shocked. So, having decided to go with the M9, there was no way, a year or two later, to call a halt to things, drop the M9, and adopt the Glock. No, the system required that the whole process be started over again, the entire years-long process of costs, reviews, etc., and to do so would also get a whole lot of high-ranking officers really ticked off at you. The Generals who ran the previous test are not going to take kindly the suggestion that they screwed up and the whole thing has to be done over again.

The argument before Glock appeared was between pistols, which were viewed with suspicion, and revolvers. And plastic? That was fine for the toss-in-your-truck Remington Nylon 66 .22 rifle and for handgun grips. Glock changed all that, caused a change in attitude, market offerings, and outlook among users. Polished blued steel and hammers are now passé. Striker-fire and polymer rule. All because of Glock.

Having rolled the dice with the M9 back in 1986, the Department of Defense could not go back. And now, by this time, having purchased a bazillion of them, they can change to a new pistol only when there is a seismic change in either procurement or perception. A sweeping change in acquisition law, say, or a new pistol design that DoD can buy for $50 each instead of $500. Or a design that delivers a several *hundred*-percent increase in stopping power, hit probability, or something like that. Short of those or the current stock of M9s spontaneously disintegrating, our armed forces will be using M9s far into the future.

But what about the rest of the world? Surely they aren't locked into the dysfunctional purchasing and procurement system of the DoD, right? Mostly, no. If a foreign government is getting sidearms for the military or police for free as a U.S. State Department or DoD aid program, then they get to pick from what is offered. If the State Department says to the head of the Federal Police of Carjackistan, "You want us to arm your police force? Fifty thousand sidearms? No problem. That's five C17 cargo planes full of Beretta M9s. Where do you want 'em?" then the Police Chief signs for 50,000 M9s. On the other hand, if the State Department says, "Arm your police force? No problem, here's a check for $20 million dollars," Carjackistan's head of police is likely to find suitable sidearms that cost less than market price for an M9. (And the cynical among us will consider the possibility that the police get armed with as many used TT33 pistols as $5 million dollars will buy and the rest of the money goes into various secret accounts in the Caymans.) Even if the price is the same, the purchase of Glocks instead of M9s is highly likely.

As for Glocks versus other designs, Glock has certainly proven its pistols are durable enough, are easily fixable, that training armorers is a snap, and that teaching recruits to use them is also easy. From talking with those who have been there, the biggest problem in third-world small arms instruction is safety, as the cultural obstacles to teaching often illiterate and non-industrial recruits is that they need to keep their finger off the trigger and the muzzle pointed in a safe direction. Doing so is often more work than actually teaching them how to hit targets. But it would be perhaps culturally insensitive of me to delve too deeply into that arena.

If you go the U.S. State Department and ask for free handguns, they'll ship you as many M9 Berettas as you can take. If you want a Glock, you have to figure out how to get cash or credit from them and buy your own.

Movie Glocks

Not to spoil your viewing pleasure, but, you have to keep in mind that, on the screen, not all Glocks are Glocks. Glocks of all sizes appear, but some are "rubber" guns, plastic copies, and solid-block facsimiles so that no one need get their panties all knotted up over the local laws. What, you think the big-name movie star on set in New York City has a local permit for a handgun? No, he doesn't. So he gets handed a plastic replica to keep everyone involved out of jail.

You also have to remember that real Glocks, especially the ones modified to fire blanks, are expensive. A rubber gun costs a hundred bucks at most (probably leased and invoiced to the production company at a couple hundred dollars a day), compared to a real one at $600 and a blank-modified one at over $1,000.

Besides all this, given the track record of movie people with real guns, no one wants to risk letting them get their hands on anything more dangerous than a pointed stick, not even a blank-adapted one. Sure, there are some who are squared away and can be trusted, but, for the most part, it's "Hand him the rubber gun, it's time for the shootout." Nothing is

lost. With today's digital wizardry, it is entirely possible to produce all the excitement of a movie shootout via computer. Muzzle blast, flash, cycling slides, brass flying, bullets hitting walls, cars, and bad guys, all can be done post-production. And more safely, too. The list of movies in which Glocks appear is almost endless and, if you really want to know, the Internet is your friend.

Glock Parties

For a firearm that is flat black, has no bling quotient, and is from a company that keeps confidential everything it does, Glock throws one heck of a party. Each year the firearms industry has a trade show. Heck, every industry has a trade show. For the firearms industry, that is the SHOT Show—Shooting, Hunting and Outdoor Trades Show.

Once a year, in Las Vegas, in January, the industry gets together and we have what seems like a square mile of display booths and something like 40,000 people on hand. The show has gotten so big it is now nearly impossible to walk every aisle. It is *impossible* to walk every aisle, loiter and look at interesting products, and get through it all. Getting into the SHOT show is not easy, and despite the obstacles, it has reached the famous Yogi Berra quote, "No one goes there any more, it's too crowded." Anyway, there Glock throws an annual party. Even more so than the SHOT show itself, the Glock party is difficult to get into. You need an invitation and, trust me, when Glock says "by invitation only" it means it. One year I had not planned to go and had not asked for an invite. At the last minute, an editor wanted me to attend, so I went there and used all my powers of persuasion to get the security at the door to get one of my contacts off the floor to talk to them.

"Patrick, you know better … . Just this once, but, next time, no way." I was in.

If you do go and you do qualify for an invite, what can you expect? Well, for starters, imagine a room large enough to be an aircraft hanger. Were the ceiling high enough to accommodate the vertical stabilizer, you could taxi a 747 in there for maintenance. No, I kid you not, I paced the room at larger than 100 yards on a side. Free food, drinks, prizes awarded, impressively tall, skinny, and gorgeous models walking the stage, music, and several thousand die-hard Glock fans, users, sellers, and the occasional writer wandering the floor. This is when the profit margin of half a million handguns sold a year sinks in. And those half a million are *U.S.-only*—there's no telling how many Glock sells worldwide. At a thousand here and there for police departments, five

Of course, when dealing with foreign governments, there is always the risk that the money sent to buy Glocks ends up buying Tokarevs, with the rest getting deposited in Cayman Island accounts.

thousand for this Army, another batch for that National Security Directorate, plus civilian sales, is it possible that Glock could be selling a million handguns a year worldwide? Such a figure is not beyond the reasonable.

Oh, I did get a really cool Glock pass to get into the latest party. If your intention in life is to make jealous the Glock guys at your gun club, wrangling an invite to the party and showing off the bling will net you a whole lot of points.

Glock's Legacy

There is one thing that is certain, and that is the design and construction of Glocks has caused a change in attitude, market offerings, and outlook among users. Try as they might, no matter how much the traditional double-action pistol makers refined their products, the buyers wanted Glocks or Glock-like pistols. I began working in gun shops and gunsmithing before Glocks came to our shores. Back then, the argument then was between pistols, viewed with suspicion for reliability, and revolvers.

Wheelguns were more powerful, dependable, and accurate. They had a bit of a learning curve, but were a known entity. Pistols were faster to shoot, but not always reliable, were dependent on good magazines (not easy to find), and, if you wanted any kind of capacity, you had to "settle" for 9mm. Double-action pistols were the worst combination of both types, while single-actions were "unsafe" because of the cocked hammer. And plastic? You had to be kidding. Plastic was okay in something like Remington's Nylon 66, a .22LR self-loading rifle, because it was "just" a plinker tossed into the truck for a range trip to blast some tin cans. Plastic was acceptable for grips on a pistol, but that was *it*.

Glock turned all that upside down. Now, to find a handgun done in polished blued steel, you need to scour the used counter at a gun shop or search for the retro, classic offerings by some makers. Hammers on pistols are passé, found only in the holsters of those 1911 loonies. Striker-fired is the future and polymer rules. All because of Glock.

As for the possibility of this being the "Glock Era," I find one aspect of this intensely curious. Having pioneered the polymer-framed pistol (there were others before, but they did not succeed), Glock seems intent on not advancing the design; its guns have been surpassed by others in material, design, and marketing. I mean, Glock was last to the replaceable backstrap party, and its design is the weakest of any. Glock pioneered the use of Tenifer, but others have advanced further with alloys that allow through-hardening and, thus, stand up better to ballistic inadvertences. What if the Glock Era has as its start the introduction of Glocks, and as its end not replacements with lasers, phasers,

phased plasma rifles or such, but the replacement of Glock by all of its competitors, those others overwhelming it with their improvements? Do I really think all the others are going to put Glock out of business? That they will do to Glock, what Colt's let everyone do to it in the 1911 market? Not hardly. But it is an interesting thought experiment.

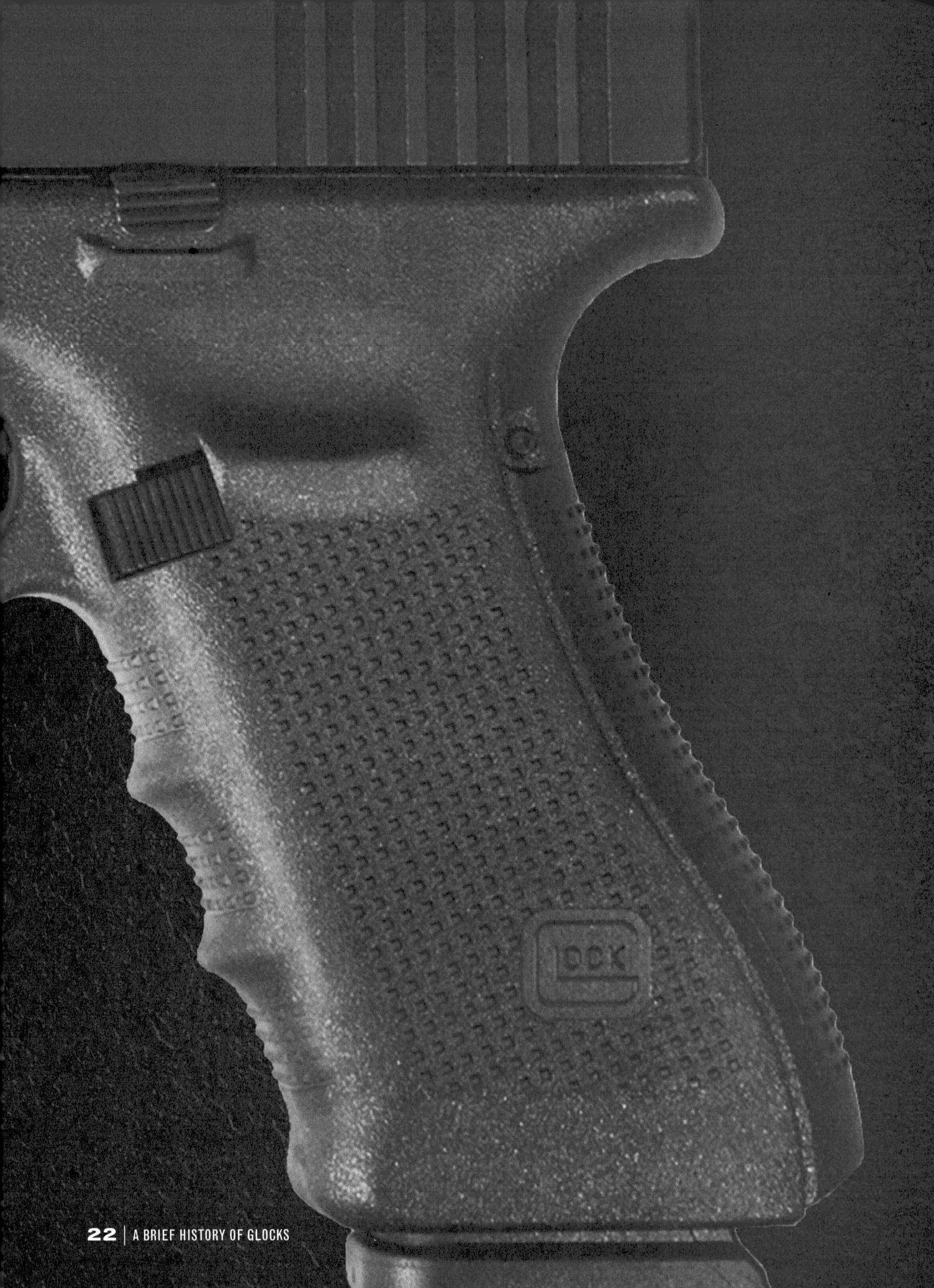

CHAPTER

3

A Brief History of Glocks

Two G19s, two different approaches to making the grip actually fit the human hand. The one on the left has an added tang.

Given the average age of Glock owners, most of you were not around when Glock was new. Even if you were, a significant percentage of you were not old enough to own a firearm and, thus, may not have memories of that time.

A BRIEF HISTORY OF GLOCKS | **23**

Here you see the lack of a tang/extension. This design can see the slide graze the hand of the shooter, if their hands are large. The author says this happens to him.

Once you do this, the Glock warranty is null and void. Oh, a Glock armorer at a GSSF match won't pay much attention to these mods, but if you send it back to Smyrna for work, they will probably kick up a fuss.

The time is the late 1970s, verging on 1980. Jimmy Carter was President and life was not fun. Inflation was actually down a bit, but was still in the 11- to 12-percent range. That meant, simply put, that, if you did not get a raise to keep up, at the end of a year you were actually making only 90 percent in December of what you had been at the time the Super Bowl happened. (And for those who are not NFL trivia buffs, the 1979 Super Bowl was won by Pittsburgh, 36 to 31, over the Dallas Cowboys.) The average price of a new house was "only" $55- to $60,000, but there were several factors that offset that apparently really good price. One, the average U.S. income was only about $17,000. Second, the Federal Reserve rate, the prime rate that banks get on loans, was over 15 percent. That meant you could offer to sell your soul and a kidney to your banker, and you'd still only be able to get a mortgage at 17 percent. Ouch.

The math worked out this way. A 30-year mortgage on $50,000, at 17 percent, came to monthly payments of just over $750 and a whopping total of $275,000 paid to your bank when you were done, in 2009. And, yes, when interest rates came down, everyone with a lick of sense re-financed their houses.

Gas cost 85 cents a gallon, and an efficient car got miles-per-gallon in the high teens. Most US-made cars were not what we'd call "fuel efficient" back then. I owned a typical boulevard cruiser of the time, a 1978 Ford LTD II, a monster of a car that had a hood about an acre in size, a back seat you could throw a duffle bag and a chihuahua into, and its 351 cubic-inch Windsor engine (that would be a 5.75L engine, in today's designation), was rated for 20 mpg highway, 14 mpg city. What it delivered was a consistent 16 mpg, regardless.

That LTD was the biggest "mid-sized" car ever made, and mine, the two-door model, had doors the size of billboards, and if the parking spot was the least bit uphill, you had to be built like Schwartzenegger to get them open. The car was typical of its time, and were you to see one on the road today you'd gawk at it.

The Soviets had invaded Afghanistan, the Iranian "students" took the U.S. Embassy personnel hostages, and the Three Mile Island reactor had a small "oops," which has produced lots and lots of money for film producers ever since. We were at the tail end (although we didn't know it), of "stagflation," a phenomenon in which we have both economic stagnation and inflation. Economic growth was marginal, unemployment was high, and the inflation rate eroded everyone's position.

Rhodesia changed governments, and the new country is named Zimbabwe, starting a decades-long spiral of government kleptocracy, inflation, misery, and staged buffoonery. The Vice President of Iraq took over when the then-President resigns; Saddam Hussein holds the position until December 2003. On the bright side, Menachem Begin and Anwar Sadat sign a peace agreement between Israel and Egypt. Just to keep things uneasy and give us an eerie heads-up of the future, a research laboratory in Ekaterinaburg, Russia, has an accident and, as a result, the first anthrax epidemic breaks out. For weird, there is a recorded snowfall in the Sahara.

On the technology front, the Sony Walkman, a portable tape player (think the iPod, but with only sixteen songs on it) is the hottest thing to own, at $200 each. Adjusted for inflation, that is $595 for a music player that fits (barely) in a jacket pocket. It was immediately knocked off, and you could buy competitive models for the same or less.

The 1970s were known for Disco, a music genre that was polarizing to the point that rock 'n' roll stations would schedule anti-disco concerts, until everyone got tired of it all. The Bee Gees made more money than could be printed, then shifted music genres and continued making money hand over fist. Disco also

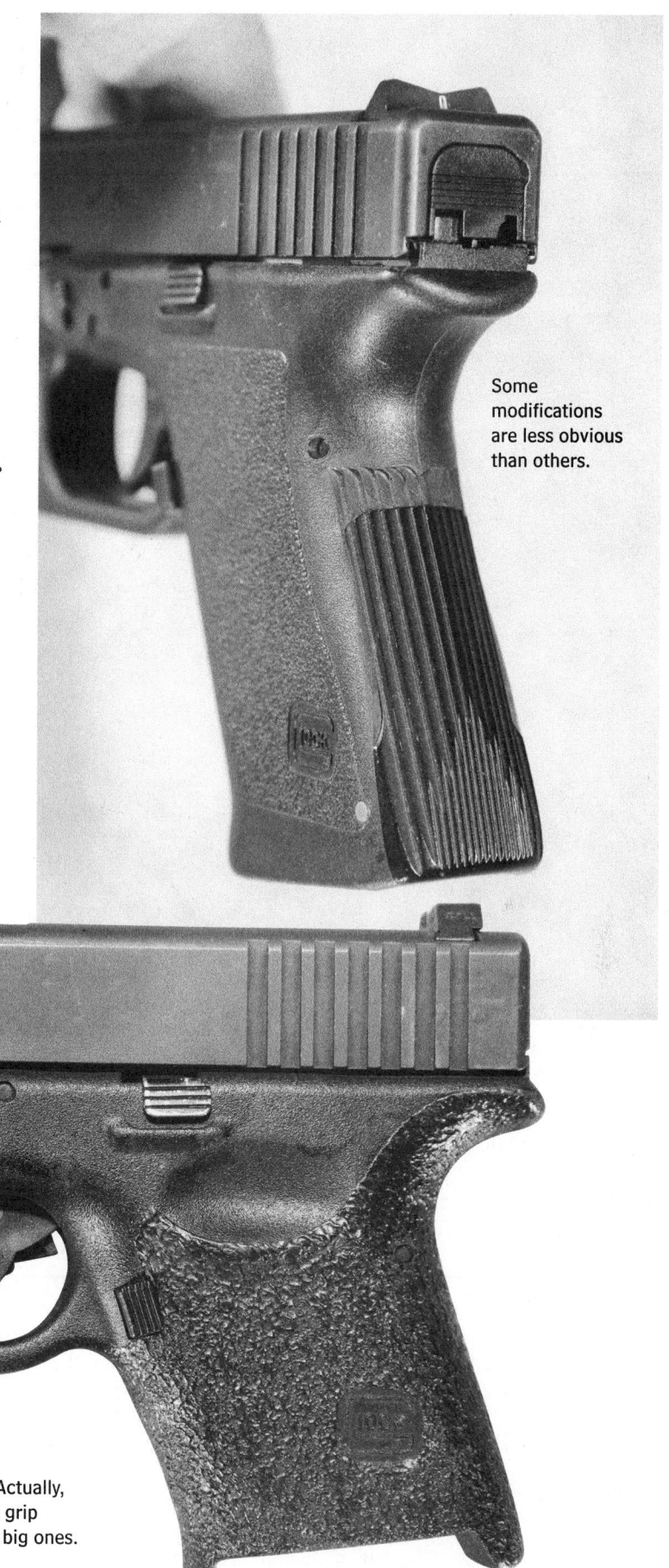

Some modifications are less obvious than others.

Little Glocks need love, too. Actually, the little ones probably need grip modifications more than the big ones.

(above) The good news is it's plastic and you can make it any way you want. The bad news is it's irreversible.

(left) The Parthenon: that's perfection in design. A little the worse for wear right now, but perfect. Glocks? Perhaps not.

brought about hideous fashions, with skin-tight shirts (on men) that were worn unbuttoned to the waist, bell-bottomed trousers in eye-searing colors and patterns, and platform shoes.

It was also a time of great tension. Would the Soviets use their nukes? If not, would the economy spiral out of control, leaving us all worse off than during the Great Depression? People prepared by stocking their homes, basements, and country cabins with food, water, medical supplies, and firearms. Today we call them "preppers." Back then, they were "survivalists." Over it all, Europe waited for the day when the massed Soviet Divisions would mount up, start their tanks, and move West.

Technology? Ha. In 1980, I began work in a research lab. Our lab was still transitioning from punch cards and paper tape programs. For those who have never seen one, punch cards are about the size of an envelope, made of stiff card stock, and had rows where the card could be punched out to create a pattern of open spots. Each card carried a line of instruction in programmers' code. A "program" was a stack of cards, fed into the card reader in sequence. A normal program might have a couple hundred lines of code. Paper tape was another punched-pattern code entry system that made it marginally easier than dealing with a program with a thousand cards in it.

We soon got upgraded to a system with hard drives. Each hard drive was the size of a wedding cake and held its own program. To "load" a program, I'd open up the hard disk drive (a washing-machine sized box), pull the hard drive off the shelf, insert it into the drive, close the lid, and turn on the power.

A decade later, I'm buying a personal computer to begin writing. The seller says, "And it comes with a 60Mb hard drive, too." Looking around, I asked, "Where is it?" Pointing at the computer itself, he proudly remarks, "It's in there." That box was smaller than the 5Mb hard drive platter I'd been loading into the research lab's hard drive housing.

As far as handguns were concerned, not a lot had changed since the end of WWII. Colt's had lost the police revolver market to Smith & Wesson, while Ruger had just begun making DA revolvers in .357 Magnum. The Speed Six and Security Six were solid and dependable, but not as well-balanced as S&W revolvers. They also were new and, thus, unknown as to how 'smithable they were. Stainless was still new, though gaining acceptance, and S&W and Ruger had solved the early problems of "galling," a condition where stainless steel rubbing against stainless steel results in the surfaces of each part chewing each other into a sorry mess.

In pistols, Colt's made the 1911A1 in various models, but was losing market share to a new

(top) Party like a Glockster. Me and a couple thousand other Glock invitees, enjoying the festivities in the hanger-sized ballroom Glock rented to celebrate its wares at the annual firearms industry SHOT trade show.

(above) Models, to show off the Glock awards, draw tickets for the door prizes and generally serve as eye-candy to the masses.

When Glock jumped on the .40, everyone tried to create their own. This S&W 4046 was one attempt. It has an aluminum frame, a double-action-only trigger, and holds 11 + 1 rounds of .40 S&W. To say it was not competitive is an understatement.

Glocks work even when the scheduled maintenance is "neglect." You have to give the gun and company props for that.

Lint, dust, petrified oil, and something I really don't want to know about, it's all in there—and this Glock *still* works.

and upcoming company, Springfield Armory. Colt's other products were the Single Action Army, which the schizophrenic management of the company couldn't decide if it really, actually, wanted to be in the business of making, and the AR-15. The SAA was expensive to make, and the old hands who had been making it were rapidly retiring, which meant quality sometimes suffered. The AR-15 was an unloved rifle, viewed with suspicion as an inaccurate, unreliable, under-powered little "plastic toy." Plus, it was disliked by the gun-control crowd, and Colt's couldn't decide if it really wanted to be making *that* one, either.

Pistols for police were relatively rare. Officers had two choices there, both Smith & Wessons, the M-39 or the M-59. Both were traditional double-action pistols with hammer-dropping safeties on the slide. The 39 was a single-stack, with nine rounds, the 59 a double stack with 15.

Serial number on frame, slide, and barrel? Done, and decades before Glock.

Markings? You want markings? Europe is the *originator* of multiple markings.

A BRIEF HISTORY OF GLOCKS | **29**

Every engineering choice has good and bad details. The Glock haste to make a .40 has never been adequately addressed and, as a result, photos such as this exist. *Photo courtesy Nik Habict*

Polymer? There were plastic grips. Remington had a .22 LR self-loading rifle called the Nylon 66. That was about it. Blued steel and walnut ruled the world. Life was good. (Well, good except for the parts I described above.)

The new shooting sport of IPSC was making serious inroads in some aspects of shooting. While the traditionalists still viewed it as a heretical vice, some unholy combination of "run 'n' gun" or "spray 'n' pray," it was gaining participants. And it was putting a new burden on gunsmiths; they had to change from the old two-choice paradigm, that being the philosophy that a pistol could be loose and reliable or it could be tight and accurate. But a reliable pistol was not accurate and an accurate pistol was not reliable. At least not much, before 1980. Well, IPSC competitors had a perceived need and money waiting for a gunsmith who could do both—make a pistol accurate and reliable. Where there is both will and money, a way will be found. And so they did, and today you can thank them by recognizing where your accurate, reliable carry gun came from.

That was the environment into which the Glock came, that period from the late 1970s to the late 1980s where there was so much change, it's hard to grasp just how much. Gaston Glock made plastic household parts. When the Austrian Army decided it needed a new handgun, he figured "Why not me?" and worked on designs. The good news is that because in part he was new to it, he wasn't strapped to the ideas of what had come before. The bad news is that because he was new to it, once he struck on a good idea, he stuck with it. But we'll cover that in more detail in a bit.

(right) Having innovated in the beginning, Glock appears to have stalled. The .45 GAP didn't become a hit, especially at just 10 rounds, and two-round extensions just didn't help enough.

Your choices in the early 1980s were not magnificent. When the G17 came along with 17+1 rounds, people leapt for joy. Compare that to a pair of revolvers for 12 rounds total, or a Browning Hi-Power mated with a 1911 and 21 rounds, at most, between them. It's not hard to see why the sky-rocketed to fame.

A BRIEF HISTORY OF GLOCKS | **31**

(right) A state-of-the-art manufacturing facility from the early twentieth century. These are individual machines, each doing a single cutting function, and each machine needing a trained operator.

CHAPTER 4

A Brief History of Manufacturing

As we accelerate through the twenty-first century and the digital age, the process of manufacturing becomes less and less known by the group as a whole. Where the knowledge of how things were made might have been more common, when one's Dad, uncles, and dads and uncles of friends at school all worked in manufacturing, now many people seem to think that "manufacturing" is either something done by clicking on "copy," or the blueprints are e-mailed to China, and a box full of stuff arrives some time later.

Modern manufacturing. The machining stations run by computer, with robots shuttling parts in and out. The operator still needs to be skilled, but, today, a plant needs a tenth as many people.

Just to make it absolutely clear, so that there is no misunderstanding and no hard feelings, none of the photos you're going to look at are of items used by Glock. Well, Glock may well be using something just like it, but that would be through sheer inadvertence. We've been over this ground before, but I'll remind you: Glock doesn't answer questions, Glock doesn't invite writers to the plant or offices. So the photos you'll see are exemplars, to give you an idea of how things work.

There is a lot that goes into making something, and not all of it is sexy, hi-tech CAD/CAM involved. A quick history lesson.

It used to be that firearms were made in plants full of machine tools, each tool doing but a single operation. One cutting tool, making one kind of cut, operated by one machine operator. If a single part of a firearm (or anything else, for that matter) required 10 cuts, then that meant 10 machines, each with its own operator, so 10 operators, and a supervisor for each group. Each machine needed cutting tools and measuring equipment. The operator had to be trained in its use and, ideally, would already be trained and skilled in the general aspects of machine tool operation so that, if a problem came up, he could solve it without needing a supervisor or the resultant downtime. Each operation had a set of instructions, the relevant dimension, and how the process was done, all laid out in what was called in most shops "the book."

Roll-marking dies. Each one is individually ground and hardened. With Glocks, the roll-marks have to be applied before the Tenifer process, or else the dies would be busted or the slide cracked.

While a particular part or operation may only be a few pages, the specs for the whole firearm would indeed be book-sized.

Flexibility was not a big feature of the old system. If you had to change workers from one part to another, they'd have to read the new parts book and then get in supervised practice time. If you wanted to double the output (parts per hour/day/week) of that particular part, you had to invest in 10 more machines, 10 sets of tooling, 10 operators with measuring tools, and a supervisor.

Changes were cumbersome. If you had to make a change to a part, you had to stop all 10 machines and then pull out the old cutting tools, replacing them with the new cutting tools. Then you'd have to make a set of parts, test them to make sure they changed what you wanted them to, and that the operators all understood what the change was and meant. Then and only then could you get back to making parts.

Changing models was even more of a hassle. Let's do something simple, like (and not to pick on them) Colt's changing its 1911A1 production over from making .45 ACP pistols to a run of .38 Supers for the export market. Stop the lines, swap the cutters for the feed ramp on the frame, from the .45 diameter, angle, and location to the .38 Super diameter, angle, and location. Do the same for the slide line, exchanging the breechface broaching tools for .45 for the ones for .38 Super, plus the firing pin hole drills. Swap the roll stamp dies from .45 to .38 Super. In all, a simple job could take a couple days back then. Plus, the first few parts to go through have to be thoroughly inspected, to make sure everything is correct.

God forbid they do something like swap from 1911A1 Government models to the

The old ways of manufacturing—a machine and an operator for each cut and part—departed, when computer-aided equipment came onto the scene. At first, NC (numerical-control, as it was called in the early days), machines were expensive and, thus, used for expensive parts. As the machines became common, they were adopted into other industries. Costs came down, and it became easier for a firearms manufacturer to afford the lease payments on them.

A BRIEF HISTORY OF MANUFACTURING | 37

The first liar never has a chance. The French were first to adopt a smokeless powder cartridge, but couldn't change when time and technology passed it by. This is the RSC 1917 rifle, and it holds five rounds. To load, you hinge down the bottom cover and stuff in a five-round en-bloc clip.

lightweight Commander. The slides have to be cut shorter, in several locations, and the frame is not dimensionally changed in just some spots. The cutting tools, cutting lube, and fixtures for the aluminum frames are different than those of the steel. The cutting tool rpm is different, the feed rates are different, and the operators have to know that and be reminded. That change could easily take a week or more and, when you consider that, nothing is being made while the change is going on, it is a minor miracle that Colt's made any lightweight Commanders back then.

All that changed when computer-aided equipment came onto the scene. At first, NC (numerical-control, as it was called in the early days), machines were expensive and, thus, used for expensive parts, typically aerospace. As the machines became common, they were adopted into other industries. As the costs came down, it became easier for a firearms manufacturer to afford the lease payments on them. (Machines were leased one, because they were so expensive for so long, and two,

with a purchase, by the time it needed service, your machine would have been made obsolete by the newer machines, and so leasing was the preferred method.)

One example of how, when properly utilized, NC machines could alter the bottom line, comes from the effort to make M14 rifles. After more than a decade of effort and bogus claims on manufacturing (for example, the M14 was going to be "easy" and "inexpensive" to transition to, because most of the M1 Garand tooling could be used for the M14—wrong), the M14 program was behind schedule. It was so behind that the DoD was forced to entertain additional manufacturers. How far behind was it exactly? The M14 had been adopted in 1957. By 1961, when the Berlin Crisis came up, there *still* weren't enough M14s to issue to frontline troops. With the production rate then in effect, it would have been more than another decade before the Army had enough M14s to go around.

TRW jumped in and bid on the contract. Back then, TRW was a multi-industry manufacturing company, not just a credit-score

reporting agency. It used its aerospace NC machines to manufacture M14s and under-bid everyone. Then, because its machines were faster and more precise, it made a profit on the early delivery and QC bonus clauses in the contract. Yes, it actually was in the classic used-car sales pitch: "A loss on each sale, but we make a profit by volume."

One Machine

A CNC (computer numerical-control) machine offers a host of bonuses over the old, one man/one machine system. First, the machine can use many cutting tools. Each tool is in a tool holder, which has a microchip, and the machine knows which one it needs for which cutting operation. The machine also tracks how much it has used each tool. A machine can have as many as 128 cutting tools and cut on many axes.

An axis is a cutting angle. The early ones were three-axis, later four, and now five-axis machines are common. Simply put, the more axes a machine has, the more angles it can reach into to cut.

The parts still have to be held if they're to be cut. However, this also changed with CNC machines. Instead of a fixture holding a single part to be cut in one pass, as in the old days, a CNC machine can have a row or a rack of parts, four or five in a row or more. The newest machines use an upright fixture, called a "tombstone." (Some are horizontal, it depends on the machine and the parts being cut.) It can hold a bunch of parts on its face, on both sides, and even on a cube. So, a tombstone can have 10, 12, 14 parts in place, all positioned to be machined.

Wait, it gets better. The tombstones can be loaded into and out of the machine by the machine itself. If you have an array of machines with a track between them, you could have tombstones shuttled from one machine to the next, each machine performing its own operations.

A company willing to invest in machines, tombstones and racetrack (the path the tombstones shuttle along), can have a near-continuous output. What typically happens in a situation like this is that the morning shift loads the tombstones, "stacks" them on the racetrack, and then presses the start button. The machines whir away for eight hours, producing parts, and the workers on the end unload the tombstones as each is finished. They also load them up again with fresh parts and, at the end of the day, they press the start button again. In the morning, there are a fresh stack of tombstones, loaded with machined parts. The morning shift unloads and reloads and the process repeats.

All the while, the machine tracks what it is doing. This can be direct-connect, where each tombstone, as it settles into the machine in question, makes an electrical connection with a digital network. The central computer then records its arrival and the operations the machine makes as it cuts each parts. Or, the tombstone can be wi-fi connected and simply broadcasts its info to the server. However the manufacturer does it, each part has a detailed record of when and in what machine each cutting operation is done. The manufacturer can track the use of each tool and pull it out to be replaced with a fresh one, the old one sent to be re-sharpened in the tool room.

In a situation such as this, the programmer is king. A good programmer, one who knows what it takes to cut steel or aluminum, can produce top-quality parts at max speeds with the fewest breakages and slowdown. A bad programmer wastes stock, dulls and breaks cutting tools, spends extra time doing it, and puts you out of business. Also, the more precise he is in cutting, the less hand-fitting you need for your gizmo in final assembly and the lower the costs of assembly.

Okay, all good, right? What do you do when your product is being made on single-use machines? Investing in CNC requires a lot of money. Changing means buying/leasing machines, finding trained operators, and hiring programmers. It also means incurring the wrath of the union (if you have one) when you lay off the people who don't know how to use the new machines.

As if all that wasn't bad enough, it may well be that some aspects of making your product simply aren't amenable to CNC-machining. A part designed to be hand-fitted may require some very involved engineering and programming to be CNC-amenable. You may have to do a bit of redesign.

One example may strike a chord. The barrels on revolvers were typically hand-fitted. It took years to train assemblers to file the frame face and/or the shoulder of the barrel so it tightened down with the exact amount of needed torque and with the front sight straight up. As such, it needed to be made with excess length on the forcing cone end so that, once the barrel was fitted, the back end of the barrel could be trimmed to fit the cylinder with the proper gap.

To make the barrels with precisely timed threads and the shoulder at the right spot to torque down wasn't easy. It was even harder to do it and have the forcing cone length stop right where it was needed, so that fitting by hand to clear the cylinder was also eliminated. To solve one hand-fitting problem required that a dozen dimensions be refined, defined, and nailed in place to within a thousandth of an inch.

The Glock design eliminated much of that. With the slide produced with uncomplicated and straight lines and the barrel being a simple rod with a rectangular chamber on the back end, there were no subtle dimensions to keep track of. A counter example to this is the 1911's barrel.

The barrel of the 1911 has its locking lugs on the top, hidden inside the slide. Each of the locking lug slots is an off-center circular cut in the body of the barrel. Not only is the front-to-back locations of those slots critical, the radius of the offset, the depth the cut creates in the barrel, and the width of the trough cut also matter. Doing it badly (and ten-thousandths of an inch can matter) means a bad barrel. If bad enough, the barrel not only doesn't work, it destroys the slide in the attempt. The distance from the locking lug slots to the rear of the barrel, the hood, matters. Then, the bottom lugs add their own complexity to the dance. The lower lugs not only have to be tall enough, but the radius of the face has to be correct. Too little shelf, and the pistol unlocks early. Too much, and the link binds on unlocking. As if all this wasn't enough, everything the 1911 barrel touches has its own set of dimensions, and each must be closely monitored or the system suffers.

The Glock barrel? You could file one from bar stock by hand and, if it was "close enough," it would be close enough. Clearly, closer is better, and closer also means better accuracy, but if you wanted something in an emergency, close enough will work.

Non-CNC

There are two areas where CNC machines don't have much use. One is in assembly. It is still economical to hire trained, experienced people to assemble firearms; machines can't do it. The other is in marking. The Glock design is such that there are three markings on any model: the frame plate with serial number; the moulded markings, which are handled by the die sinker when he/she machines the injection moulding dies; and the roll marks on the slide and barrel. Someone hand-inserts the serial number plates into the injection moulding machine, before the mould closes and the hot polymer is squirted in.

But roll marks? They are so-named because of how they work. The marking die is a steel wheel carved with the negative image of the markings. The die is made of super-hard steel. In process, the operator puts a slide (or barrel, or whatever is being marked) onto the fixture of the machine. The machine then hydraulically lowers the die to the part (the dimensions here have to be exact, or the markings end up looking quite ugly), and the operator then uses a hand wheel to roll the die back and forth as many times as "the book" calls for.

The markings on your Glock slide are roll-marked. They are not laser-engraved or machine-cut by the CNC machines. Someone stood (or sat) there and ran each one through a roll-marking machine. Additionally, Glocks are marked before they are given the Tenifer finish. Tenifer makes the slides too hard to roll-mark, so the work has to be done before hardening. That slightly complicates things, as they have to be serial numbered before they are hardened, and then each slide has to

The markings on your Glock slide are roll-marked. They are not laser-engraved or machine-cut by the CNC machines. Someone stood or sat there and ran each one through a roll-marking machine, and they do this before the slides are given the Tenifer process. Tenifer makes the slide too hard to roll-mark.

be matched to the frame with the same serial number. Of course, you could produce batches of frames, slides, and barrels within sets of serial numbers, then export to the U.S., where they are "married" and assembled into complete pistols. Made in the USA, in much the same way as your car can be, with all the parts imported and assembled here. I'm not passing judgment, just considering manufacturing processes.

"First Liar Never Has a Chance … ."

I first heard that line while working at a radio station, listening to stoned/drunk rockers on tour trying to one-up each other with tales of "life on the road." Life on the road was hilarious, at least as recounted by professional musicians. It was also scary, and this was when albums made money, tours made bands rich, and everything was obtainable, deductible, or curable by penicillin. The experience was quite eye opening and convinced me that no amount of money could induce me to go on the road with a band, even if I suddenly, overnight, learned how to play a musical instrument.

Too, and to the great regret of some musicians who'd had a hit early in their careers, that hit so defined them that they could not escape. You know of them by the somewhat disparaging moniker of "one-hit wonders." A hit, back then, could be a retirement. A million-dollar song, properly invested in 1978 (that's when I was getting this revelation), could mean a comfortable life for as long as the musicians could wait, be prudent, and stand to tour. Improperly invested (the great example: Willie Nelson) could mean a lifetime of hard work to pay back debts and tax liens in order to get back to square one.

For some, the early hit was an albatross, simply because no one cared about their *new* work. All the fans wanted was to hear the hit and, once they heard it, they were done. What the one-hit-wonder musicians had done since that hit, years or even decades before, was just concert-time filler until they played the hit at the end of the gig. It made some bitter, it made a lot of them alcoholics, and it made me want to do something else.

What does this have to do with Glock? Well, the problem with having an ongoing firearms manufacturing firm is that you are locked into making the firearms you know how to make. If the market doesn't change much and you have a handle on costs, life can be good. If things suddenly change and you aren't ready, you could be in a world of hurt.

Let's jump into the way-back machine and travel back to the dawn of smokeless powder. The French are still smarting after the drubbing they received from the Germans in the Franco-Prussian War. That war was fought with single-shot, breechloading, blackpowder cartridge rifles. Almost all references mentioned that the French Chassepot rifle greatly out-ranged the Prussian Dreyse, 1,500 yards to 600. The idea of an infantry unit armed with single-shot blackpowder rifles, successfully engaging another unit at 1,000-plus yards is absurd. And the fact that *that* fact would be tactically relevant today is even more so. Someone came up with it as an interesting fact, and lots of history bloggers are just copying (I'm being kind, the actual term is plagiarizing) like mad. But I risk digressing.

Way back when, smokeless powder, invented in 1884 by a French chemist, is the big secret the French army is pinning its hopes on in a longed-for rematch. But in its eagerness to adopt it, they make a couple of fatal mistakes. First, the 8mm Lebel cartridge is created by simply necking down the 11mm blackpowder cartridge then in use. This creates a round with

Forging has been the traditional method of creating firearms, and for good reasons. However, just as not all alloys can be forged, not all alloys can be treated to Tenifer. Knowing which is which is why people go to school and get degrees in mechanical engineering.

a severe taper and a big rim. ("Does this rim make my cartridge look fat?" Yes.) In a single-shot rifle, taper and rim is not a big deal. But single-shot rifles in 1886 are an endangered species, at least in military use.

The first French Ordnance attempts used a round- or blunt-nosed bullet, in a tube magazine under the barrel—think a bolt-action rifle with a Winchester Model 94 magazine lashed to it. That is the Fusil Mle 1886. When the use of spitzer (pointed) bullets became the norm, the tube magazine posed a problem. A bullet point resting directly on a primer in front of it in the magazine tube could detonate that primer under recoil. I kid you not, it has happened, often enough that it is an ever present worry for rifle makers whose designs use tube magazines.

The French solution was to make the cartridges with a groove around the primer, to capture the bullet point. Big problem. To reload, you have to open the action and stuff rounds into the magazine one by one. By this time, every other army in Europe had adopted some sort of packet-loading system, either the Mannlicher, using a five- or six-round clip that went into the rifle whole, or the Mauser system, with five-round stripper clips. With either, getting five (or six) more rounds into a rifle takes a couple seconds.

With the gradual adoption of the Berthier rifle, (the first was adopted in 1890 and, by the start of WWI, the French were still in the process of switching over), the French Army had a Mannlicher clip-fed rifle. Alas, the fat rim made it a three-shot gun. In The Great War, the French modified it to make it a five-shot rifle, but this made things even more complicated. You see, the two (three-shot and five-shot) rifles would not work with the other clips. If you were an infantry company in the trenches with three-shot Berthiers and your ammo resupply had the five-shot clips, you were in a bad way.

All this early adopting and modification kept the French locked into a bad start with a tapered rimmed cartridge. The British also adopted a tapered, rimmed cartridge in the late 1880s, but, unlike the French, they doggedly kept at the rifle, modifying, adjusting, upgrading, and replacing, until they had a design that would feed properly and could be topped off with stripper clips. That was the Short Magazine Lee Enfield.

The smart and obvious thing for the French to have done would have been, when spitzer bullets became the norm, to have redesigned the case, remove the taper and rim, and started over. But they did not. Failing that, they could have gone at it again with a new rifle. But again, they did not.

What kept them from doing either? One was a peculiarly French attitude, and the other is a universal one. The French attitude was to keep everything a deep, dark secret, and not let the world at large see anything. After all, if they were going to settle accounts with the Germans, they wanted every advantage, so there was no point in letting secrets out, right? As a result, they did not apply for patents on anything they developed and, as a secondary result, they never had a real chance to compare what they were working on with what others were working on.

The second and universal roadblock was economics. With warehouses full of rifles and ammo for them, it's unlikely someone would be bold enough to say, "We made a mistake, we have to start over again, we have to spend as much money again to get back in the lead." Simply put, they couldn't bring themselves to spend the money. As a result, the French entered WWI with a three-shot bolt-action rifle. Yowza. Millions of francs for fortifications, but not an extra penny spent on infantry rifles.

What does this mean for us? Glock, being first, has subsequently been late (or sometimes completely negligent), in changing and upgrading its designs. Yes, some very early things were changed. The first, thin barrel in the G17 was made larger, but other than that, changes were less than minor; tweaks of extractor design, magazine follower shapes, that sort of thing.

One aspect of the Glock that many complain about—and I realize, in writing this, that there are people who will complain about anything and everything—is its pointability. For all of the modern-as-tomorrow aspects of the Glock, this is something that was definitely stuck in the past. I know the point-shooting fraternity will hate me for this, but *you do not merely point a handgun if you wish to hit.* Point-shooting advocates will demonstrate this or that level of hit probability, usually on very close targets. But if pointing worked, people would win matches by pointing. (To which the point-shooting advocates usually fall back on, "Competition isn't a reflection of reality." Maybe, maybe not. But people win matches—and gunfights—by hitting. Hitting is improved by aiming.)

Now, how a handgun points depends on a number of factors, not limited to the angle of the grip to the bore, the shape of your hand, and what you are used to. In the U.S., the default "point" is the 1911. And lest you think this is a new thing, when S&W first came out with the M59, it, too, pointed "off" from what shooters expected. S&W changed.

So, the "pointability" of the Glock suffers in comparison to the 1911. Why not adjust when that became possible? Wait. A change was possible? When was it possible?

With the Gen2 Glocks, when the new finger grooves and thumb rests were added for the importation of compact models. If you're going to make new molds, then you can adjust the angle of the grip. Yes, the angle of the magazine is a

---

In the CNC world, especially with CAD/CAM, change cost is low. One machine in the R&D shop can have special cutter paths programmed to make a part any way you want it made. In fact, if the R&D guys aren't experimenting, testing, and seeing what works, even when you don't have a specific task for them, you've hired the wrong R&D guys. You should have hired the people who are hardwired to experiment, fiddle, test, and break things.

a limiting factor, but it would be interesting to see how much the frame could be altered and still accommodate the magazine. If not, then bite the bullet, make a second-generation magazine, make it so they won't fit with the old ones, and get on with it.

That experiment has been going on for more than two decades now, with various companies such as Robar offering grip alterations and angle changes to Glocks. If an aftermarket company such as Robar, which has a fraction of Glock's resources, can find a way to change the grip angle of a Glock and still use the original magazines, then you have to wonder why Glock engineers haven't done the same.

Now, one of the obstacles the French (and any other manufacturer pre-CNC machines), faced was the staggering monetary cost of change. As we've discussed, to change a part "only" requires the swapping of fixtures, gauges, and tooling for that part, but that is still a lot of money. To change an entire rifle essentially meant scrapping the entire toolset of a factory, so the cost of change was high in the old days.

In the CNC world, especially with CAD/CAM, change cost is low. One machine in the R&D shop can have special cutter paths programmed to make a part any way you want it made. In fact, if the R&D guys aren't experimenting, testing, and seeing what works even when you don't have a specific task for them, you've hired the wrong R&D guys. You should, in fact, have hired people who are hardwired to experiment, fiddle, test, and break things. If you haven't, you need to fire the accountants responsible who steered HR into hiring non-active roles. Let me be clear about this: if you do not have an R&D person or department, your company is destined to fail. If that person or shop is not regularly bringing you new things, whether you ask for them or not, your company will fail.

Now, the changes would, in many cases, be cosmetic, but even cosmetic changes can be fun and useful and good for the bottom line. One example would be STI, the hi-cap 1911 maker. (Oh, quit complaining, you knew there were going to be 1911 comparisons.) When it comes to designs, style, features, and finishes, STI is absolutely fearless. If they think there are enough people who want 27.6 lines to the inch checkering, they'll program the cutter paths and give it a go. If it works, they'll make more. If not, they won't.

In comparison, in the whole time of the Glock, we have seen two cocking serration patterns, the original and the short-lived curved grooves. Bo-ring.

Now, given the great secrecy of Glock (hmm, can't help but consider the comparison to the French Ordnance department a century ago, can you?), for all we know, they have an R&D department and that department does regularly bring new items to the Board of Directors for their consideration. If so, given the utter lack of new product, they have to be feeling pretty frustrated by now.

Other Parts

Okay, the frame is injection-moulded. The slide and barrel are CNC machined and Tenifer-hardened. The rest? They are stamped, for the most part. The striker is a machined part, but one top-notch CNC lathe to produce it can probably keep up with an acre of CNC machines doing nothing but slides. Stamping is an old and mostly well-understood process.

Take a sheet of metal, in this instance, steel. Slide it over a flat plate with a hole in the plate and bring down a hardened steel die that closely matches the outline of the hole. The result will be a part punched from out of the sheet.

A refinement of the stamping process is called "fineblanking." Here, special engineering jiggery allows the designers to produce a part that has crisp, clean edges and does not require much, if any, handwork to clean up and fit to the assembled design. I do not know if Glock uses fineblanking in its production. Some of the Glock parts show clear signs of straightforward stamping, with rough edges and rounded corners. If the part doesn't need it, you are wasting money using fineblanking to produce parts that regular stamping could make.

A component of stamping is the bending of parts. Once stamped from flats, the parts have to be bent to precise angles and shapes. Bending

metals produces a condition known as "work-hardening." The point of going to engineering school is so you can calculate how much hardness the work creates, if that is good or bad, and what, if any, annealing you have to do to relieve the work-hardening. A good designer makes the work-hardening work for him, not against him.

Stamping is a fast, efficient method for producing parts, and it might make the production cost of some of the parts as high as a few cents each. It comes as no surprise that Glock armorers hand out parts like breath mints, when overhauling Glocks at GSSF matches. All the parts in their bag didn't cost as much to produce as it cost Glock to send the armorer to that match. As a means of building customer loyalty, it is a breathtakingly efficient and cost-effective step.

For a CNC machining station to cut anything, it needs an array of cutting tools, each in a holder, each with a chip by which the computer tracks use.

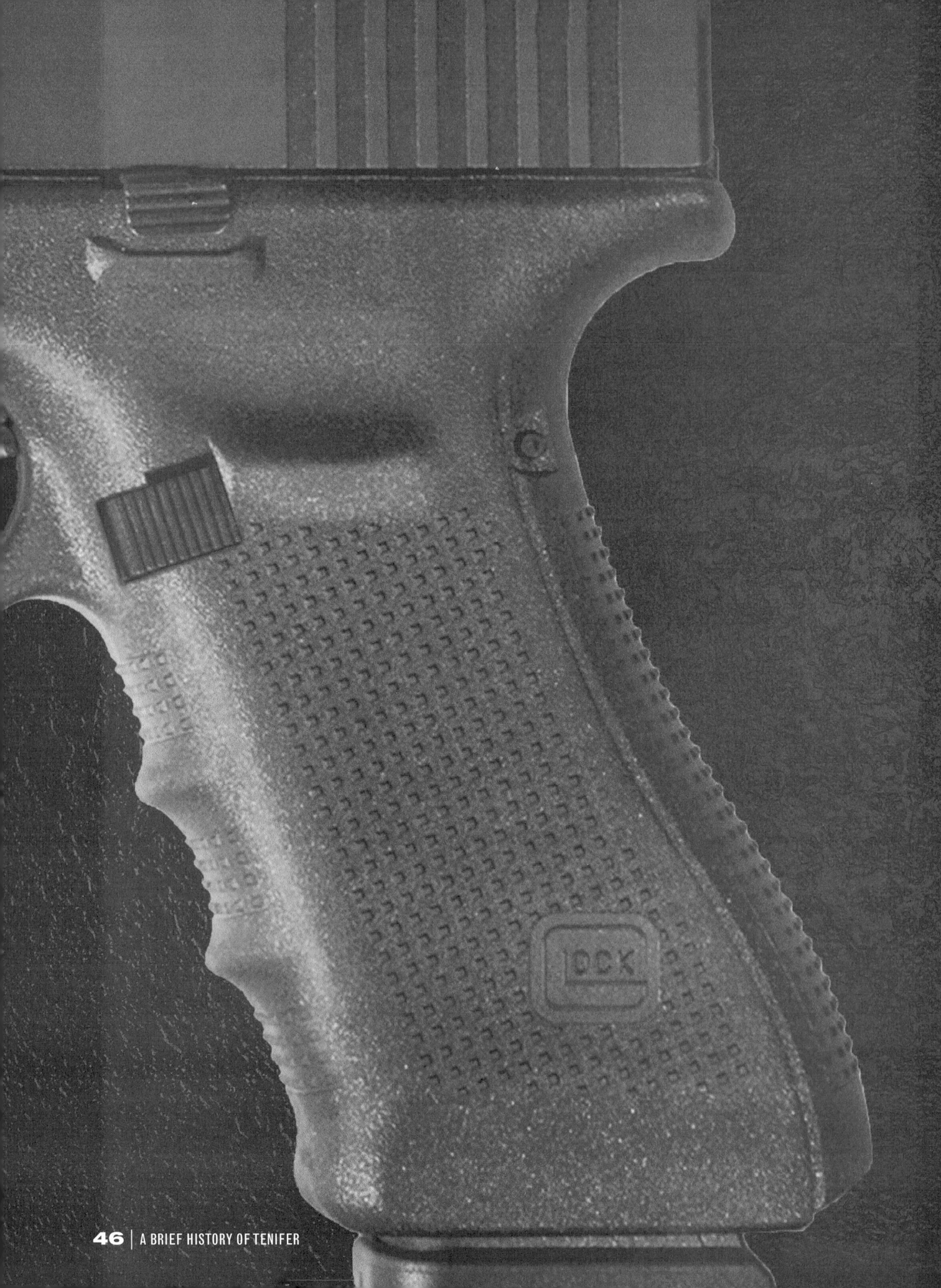

CHAPTER 5

A Brief History of Tenifer

Tenifer makes for a very hard skin. However, if the force acting on a part breaks through the skin, the substrate cannot hold unless it is the proper alloy that had been through-hardened. *Photo courtesy Nik Habicht*

A bit of metallurgy here: steel is iron with carbon in it. Iron, in its natural, un-alloyed state, is too soft to be of much use in firearms. That didn't keep it from being used, but what was called "steel" back in the blackpowder era often wasn't much more than work-hardened iron. Steel, a steel, was too expensive to see much use.

Why does steel come in so many alloys? Because a small change in alloy can have big affect on performance. For example, early in his career, Henry Ford learned that French automobile makers were using Vanadium-alloy steel. By weight, it was stronger than other steels then commonly in use. Not only was it stronger, in one of those quirks of alloying, it was also easier to machine. So advantageous was this steel in the process of automobiles that Henry Ford built his own steel plants, just to make a supply he could be assured was his.

It wasn't until the Bessemer process was developed, in 1855, that the purification of iron on an industrial scale was realizable. Iron, with impurities, can't be made into steel, as the impurities interfere with the desired alloying agents added. Once pure, the molten iron can then be alloyed by adding carbon, manganese, etc. Alloyed iron, or alloy steel (iron with carbon), has much greater strength, durability, resistance to stress, and is the basis for modern construction and fabrication in the twentieth and twenty-first centuries.

Steel, regardless of the alloying materials, is a crystalline structure, and it is the size, shape, and composition of those crystals that determine a steel's characteristics. Some steel is easy to machine, while others make good springs that resist bending and return to original form. Other alloys resist corrosion, and others have great shock resistance. What you use depends in part on what the job calls for, in part how you will shape the resulting components, and in part what you are accustomed to using. For instance, take a common alloy, 1050. A "carbon" steel, with a half-percent of carbon in it and no rust-resistant alloying aspects, it is low-cost and common as dirt in steel circles. It will machine like a dream, but it will not take much in the way of heat-treatment and, if you do harden it, it won't have much shock resistance. So don't use it if you want something to take a beating and not peen-deform or break. Wear resistance it has, but not shock/impact resistance. It also would make a pretty lousy spring, as it would easily deform and decline to return to its original shape.

If you want to make it stand up to shock better, give it a hard surface. Known as "case hardening," a hard surface over a soft core is an old solution to the problem. You probably know of it from cowboy guns and their colorful frames, known there as "color case hardening." The color is a side effect and, actually, to create colors, the old-timers didn't make the parts as hard, nor the hard skin as deep as the process would allow. A deeper, harder "skin" produced a part that did not have color. Great for machine tools, but not so much for firearms.

Cowboy guns like the Colt SAA were made by machining the frames to shape, then packing them in charred leather and bone meal (to create carbon for the process), which was then heated in furnaces. Once heated and soaked to full temperature, the parts were yanked out and dumped into baths of water to harden and color them. You see, no one would buy bare, gray-framed pistols (they were all "pistols," back then), if they could have color.

Why does steel come in so many alloys? Because a small change in alloy can have a big affect on performance. Early in his career, Henry Ford learned that French automobile makers were using Vanadium-alloy steel. By weight, it was stronger than other steels then commonly in use. Not only was it stronger, in one of those quirks of alloying, it was also easier to machine than regular steel of the time. So advantageous was it in the production of automobiles that Henry Ford built his own steel plant, just to make a supply he could be assured was his.

Firearms are not so critical in the steels they need, at least not most designs. (The bolt of the AR-15 is one example of very strict steel requirements.) So, any one of a bunch of relatively common steels will do, and the problem then becomes more a matter of how to shape it. Ruger casts many parts, although even it goes with forgings, MIM'd parts, and parts cut "from billet," that is, parts machined from bars, rods, and plates. In the modern engineering world, how much it costs to make a part becomes part of the design consideration. Yes, you could make parts from forged steel, but if that makes it more expensive with no added operational advantage, why would you? One good answer: because the company already has forging machines and years of experience in producing forgings. Lacking the machine or years of experience, you'd be silly to insist on more-expensive forgings for parts that would work just as well made another, cheaper way.

After forming, the next steps are heat-treatment (and, again, some alloys respond well, others not so much), and surface finish. Heat-treatment uses one of two processes, air-cooled and oil-cooled. (Actually, the difference is a little more basic. It's air or *liquid*, as some alloys use a fluid other than oil as the quenching medium.) The process has been investigated so thoroughly, for so long, that it is possible to specify exactly what you want. For instance, you can order "one-inch square bars in eight-foot lengths of SAE 1040 hot-rolled, air-cooled and Rockwell C-tested to 20." (The "SAE" part is the Society of Automotive Engineers, the group that organized the description of various steels.) And that is what you'll get once you pay and the delivery arrives. If, on the other hand, you want something exotic, like SAE 8620, with an off-the-charts Brinell hardness, high tensile strength, miserable machinability, and larded with lots of alloying materials (manganese, phosphorus, sulphur, silicon, chromium, nickel, and molybdenum), you will probably have to give a better description of your needs to the steel supplier.

Various alloys respond to normal firearms finishes differently. There was a time when Ruger revolvers turned purple. Silicon in the alloy being cast did it, and until it was determined just how much silicon could be shrugged off by the blueing process and what blueing methods handled it best, Rugers were purple. All these considerations go into determining just what alloy you select as a design and production engineer.

So, what steel does Glock use? Short of stepping into the buyers' office and seeing the invoices for steel delivery, I don't know. But the various processes Glock is so proud of tells us a lot.

First, the steel is machined in CNC machines and is obviously fabricated from bar stock. That is, Glock slides are billet-cut. The steel probably arrives in long bars, depending on the mill, eight, 10, 15 feet in length. Once the bars have been tested—no one takes for granted that the steel is actually as ordered, not until the QC department has done a full analysis—they are lopped into segments just long enough to fit the next step. Each section of steel bar is clamped into a CNC tombstone, and the CNC machine then spends however much time it spends (minutes to hours) machining each of the sections.

Why can't we be more precise on the machining? Simple. A tombstone can hold as few as two or four slides-to-be or as many as a dozen. The CNC machine can contain as few as a dozen cutting tools or as many as 128. (Clearly, a Glock slide doesn't need 128 cutting tools.) I would be stunned to find out that a Glock slide needs more than a couple-dozen cutters in order to be shaped and finished.

The smart way to do things, albeit expensive in capital costs, is to run them on what we've described before, a "racetrack," The operation would run something like this:

The machine operator would load tombstone after tombstone, clamping cut bars into the slots. Each tombstone, in turn, would go to the first machine. That machine would be programmed for big, deep, ferocious cuts, hogging out lots of steel. There would be lots of cutting lube and many, many cutting tools. (Each cutter would be tracked for wear and replaced or re-sharpened when needed.) Each tombstone, in turn, would then be shuttled out of the first CNC machine and on to the next. In a shop dedicated to QC, the tombstone would stop in between CNC machines, and an automated gauging machine would measure the relevant surfaces to make sure things are within spec. Then, the next machine would make finer, cleaner, cuts. The last CNC machine would make ultra-precise, to-the-blueprints cuts, leaving the parts to simply be heat-treated and given the surface finish.

But, to machine slides that way, it works best if you have a relatively low-alloy steel. Fast cutting, dimensionally stability, and not prone to warpage when the heat-treatment is done steel. So, you need something to harden the alloy steel and resist corrosion. The traditional method was to use a steel good enough for the task of being a firearm, and then deal with the other problems in assembly, with trained fitters. Glock got around that with Tenifer. Tenifer is the brand name. The process is known as "ferritic nitrocarburizing."

A quick change of focus. Iron and steel have been investigated quite thoroughly for

Glock, when it added the G22 and the .40 to the lineup, was first there. Alas, it has not made the changes that other manufacturers did when it adopted the .40 and, while not common, this is not an unknown sight. (Photo courtesy of Nik Habict)

a century and a half. In that time, many of its secrets have been ferreted out. There is a chart known as a "phase diagram" that shows the temperatures and crystal-shape conditions of iron and steel. Each alloy has its own phase diagram and, with a known alloy, you can consult the phase diagram and see how much heat you need to apply to change the steel to a different condition. Once heated into a given state, it can then be quickly cooled, in a process known as "quenching," and the crystal state of that particular temperature is locked in, as it were.

Ferritic nitrocarburizing is a particular state of low-carbon, plain steel. To treat an alloy to ferritic nitrocarburizing, it has to be a low-carbon, mild steel. You cannot use this process with high-carbon, nor with high-alloy steels. To do so is not to get double your money, but to produce parts that shatter under use or partially dissolve in the treatment process.

In ferritic nitrocarburizing (can we sidestep the trade name, and apply our own? Let's just call it "FNC" for right now), the ferritic-phase steel is subjected to a gas or fluid solution at the correct heat that diffuses extra nitrogen and carbon into the surface of the steel. The extra nitrogen and carbon greatly harden the surface of the steel, without over-hardening or warpage.

The bonuses are many. First of all, the temperature at which this happens is quite low by steel standards. The temperature, depending on which process is used, can be as low as 800 degrees Fahrenheit and only as high as 1,000 degrees. The process also does not require a quenching, so there is minimal distortion of the treated parts.

I mentioned warpage, so let's go back to the heat-treatment process. We heat steel to a particular state in the phase diagram. Once there, we pull it out of the furnace and either lay it out to cool (air-hardening) or toss it into a bath to cool (oil-hardening). It does not cool evenly. As the first part of it enters the quench, that part begins to cool, but the rest is still hot. The quenching process passes through the part and, as it does so, the part can bend from the uneven cooling. That bend is called "warpage."

When Colt's was doing this, it would find that certain operators were better than others at producing warp-free frames. Even with the best, a certain percentage of frames had to be hand-fitted, and some even rejected, sent back, or otherwise reused. I can easily imagine that one reason Colt's was eager to produce nickel-plated revolvers was that it could salvage warped frames by machining them to dimension, and then the nickel-plating would cover the work done to salvage it. Not all nickel-plated single-actions were warped, heat-treat salvages, but some, anyway.

Other hardening processes, which depend on running steel up into its austenitic phase, require both a higher temperature (1,300-plus degrees at a minimum) and a rapid quench, which can lead to warpage. Warped parts have to be machined to dimension or scrapped.

The FNC process improves fatigue resistance, abrasion resistance, and corrosion resistance. The first two are easy to grasp; a harder part is less likely to be marred or weaken with use. The latter is a bit more subtle. By diffusing nitrogen and carbon into the surface, the process "passivates" the surface, that is, makes it less reactive to oxygen. The bonding sites of the iron, which would be attacked by oxygen (that's what corrosion is), are now bound to the extra nitrogen and carbon that has been introduced. With oxygen having no place to gain a toehold, it can't rust. Or, at least, it can't rust at anything near to its normal rate.

The use of an alloy that is not highly larded with extra metals is good in a couple extra ways, too. The mild steel is faster and easier (in most instances) to machine than a high-alloy steel would be. Also, by remaining relatively soft (by steel standards) on the interior, you have a part that is both hard and resistant, but the core is tough and can absorb shocks. The downside is, once the shock resistance of the surface has been exceeded, the core (known in the biz as the "substrate") can't do much to keep things together. So, when such a part goes, it breaks cleanly at one parting line, and then bends. A high-alloy part will simply bend, and bend less than the surface-hardened part would, given the same catastrophic event.

Those who think "Oh, that's all there is to it?" are not going to fare well when they sign up for engineering school. The particular carbon content and alloying metals in the steel being so treated will affect the hardness and depth of the case hardening. Ditto, things like the max temperature and the heat of the quench/soak and its duration. The chemicals in the bath or vapor will be consumed at a given rate and, if you do not carefully track use and chemical strength, the outcomes will also change over time. Do it wrong and the whole batch is scrap, good only to be melted down and turned into rebar. And since the surface treatment is the *last* step, coming after all the machining, then the company has lost all the time, materials, tool life, and labor that has gone on up to that time, a metric buttload of money.

"Tenifer" is a process that uses a salt bath to treat the parts. The finish-machined and marked parts (they have to be, as the surface will be file-hard once treated), are racked, and the rack is suspended in a salt bath. The soaking in the heated salt bath treats the surface, and then, depending on which particular brand process is being used, the parts then go through quench/soak at a cooler temp, cooling, washing, and pickling, and then off to the blackening. Yes, *blackening*, for you see, the surface so treated is just bare, gray steel. The surface comes out a Rockwell C scale hardness in the mid-'60s, on par with your average bargain-basement Chinese file. The blackening on Glocks is most likely a black oxide, which is a modern form of Parkerizing. The result is a surface that, while lacking traditional character, is certainly durable and shrugs off wear.

While Glock lead the way with Tenifer, it is by no means the only company that uses FNC or some variant of it. Smith & Wesson was one of the leaders in a variant of FNC called "Melonite." The differences between Melonite and Tenifer would fascinate a chemist or production engineer and bore the socks off most shooters. Mostly, they are variations of the chemical solutions, the time and temperature, and an increasingly important consideration—the creation (or, rather, the non-creation) of hazardous by-products.

A BRIEF HISTORY OF TENIFER | **51**

S&W's Melonite

While Glock lead the way with Tenifer, it is by no means the only company that now uses FNC or some variant of it. Smith & Wesson was one of the leaders in a variant of FNC called "Melonite." The differences between Melonite and Tenifer would fascinate a chemist or production engineer and bore the socks off most shooters. Basically, and I'll risk boring you, they are variations of the chemical solutions, the time and temperature, and an increasingly important consideration—the creation (or, rather, the non-creation), of hazardous by-products.

You could come up with a process that turns iron into gold or, better yet, iron into a steel alloy that has all the best properties and none of the bad, but if it produces toxic or hazardous by-products, you won't be able to convince a company, any company, to adopt it. It couldn't. The EPA would crucify the entire Board of Directors for using it, no matter how useful the end product might be. It is important, these days, to come up with manufacturing methods that don't create truckloads of cyanide, heavy metals, acids, or other bad things.

Where S&W and the Melonite process differs from Glock and Tenifer are in hardness and material. Let's tackle material first.

Smith & Wesson uses stainless steel in the slides of its M&P pistols so it can double-down on advantages. Seriously? A stainless slide treated to Melonite and given a black oxide finish has to be just about as impervious to corrosion as anything made by man can be. Well, anything that can be hardened, as gold is non-corroding, but we all know how hard gold is, right?

Second, S&W through-hardens its slides, that is, it uses an alloy that can be hardened by more traditional methods first. Then they get the Melonite treatment. So, instead of a hard skin and a soft substrate, an S&W slide has a hard skin over a hard and tough substrate.

Through-hardening is not new. Before WWII and through WWII production, Colt's made slides for the 1911 that were not through-hardened. This was especially true with the WWII guns, on which you can see the effects of the process it used. If you look at an unmolested USGI gun from then, you'll see that the Parkerizing is darker in a band just forward of the ejection port, and some also have a dark band at the muzzle. That is the spot-hardening Colt's and the other makers did by a process known as "induction."

Induction takes advantage of resistance to electrical flow through a wire or cable. If you want electricity conducted efficiently, you use a high-conductivity metal, such as copper. If you want to create heat, you use a low-conductivity metal, such as the wires in your toaster, made of nichrome. To induction-heat a slide, take a length of somewhat-conducting material and wrap it in a coil large enough to pass a slide into the center of the coil. Then place the slide in the center (not touching, you don't want to weld it to the coil), and pump a huge electrical charge into the coil. The coil will heat and the slide will be heated as a result. Once it is hot enough, turn off the juice and pull the slide out. Depending on the alloy used, you either just let it cool or you dump it into a quench bath. The color change is due to the change in crystal structure from the hardness induced into the steel and the subsequent Parkerizing that adheres to the steel with a slightly different pattern.

After the war, Colt's went to all-hardened slides, a process it could have adopted earlier, but a process that was a bit slower than the induction process. When there's a war on, you can't have firearms or ammo too quickly or in too-great amounts. When S&W began making self-loading pistols in the early 1950s, it never had the induction process to get rid of, and always had hardened slides. Just as it does to this day.

Drawbacks

As a hardening process, FNC has a lot of advantages. The surface is hard, corrosion-resistant, and it leaves a softer substrate that will resist some kinds of impacts. But it isn't perfect. First of all, the alloys that can be FNC-treated are not comprehensive. You have to be careful what you treat, as some alloys don't do well with the process. Steels that can be super-hardened don't take will to FNC, and it has to be at least *some* kind of steel, or the FNC will be wasted.

The big thing to know is that you need a sufficient thickness of substrate to support the hard "skin" of the DNC-treated layer, otherwise you get breakage. Those of you who have used an improper tool to take the striker assembly out of your slide know of what I speak. The thin web can easily be chipped/flaked, if you get too heavy handed.

This also leads to a curious admonition on the part of Glock: don't use "non-toxic"

There's a curious admonition on the part of Glock, and that is a warning against using non-toxic ammo, that is, ammo that does not have lead in it. But non-lead bullets are not what Glock is cautioning against, rather, it's non-lead *primers*. Non-lead primers have a higher "brisance," the rate of ignition of a compound, than primers that produce lead vapors on combustion. This higher rate can make the primer slam back harder into a Glock's breechface, and before the rest of the case slams back.

ammo, that is, ammo that does *not* have lead in it. The a non-lead *bullet* isn't what Glock is cautioning against, rather it is the *primer*.

Our historical, non-corrosive priming compound is a substance called lead styphnate (pronounced "STIFE-nate") Unfortunately, it produces lead vapors when it combusts and, in an indoor range, you can actually get more lead exposure from the primer than the bullet. Rather than actually require firearms instructors to pick up good range habits and provide showers and range-only clothes, law enforcement agencies have gone after the ammo companies, complaining, "Why can't you make ammo that doesn't have lead?" (Actually, the complaining was second-hand, as the agencies were in most instances blissfully unaware until OSHA told them.)

The replacement compounds have an irritating consistency: they have a higher brisance than lead styphnate. "Brisance" is a term of art in the explosives industry, describing the rate of ignition of a compound. Chemicals that ignite faster, burn faster, or produce greater shattering force are said to have higher brisance. The non-lead primer compounds have a higher brisance.

If you consider the ignition sequence of your handgun in microsecond steps, it becomes clear. The firing pin strikes the primer and, once it has been compressed enough, the priming compound ignites. While the desire is a jet of hot gases forward through the flash hole, the various gas laws will tell us that the pressure generated will be expressed against all sides of the container, that is, the gas that jets out towards the powder is matched by gas pressing back against the firing pin. The primer gets pushed out of the primer pocket, or tries to. So the small diameter of the primer slams back into the breechface at the primer's initial pressure, before the case then slams into it at the full combustion pressure. A more-brisant primer will slam harder.

The Glock slide is thin at the breechface where the striker pokes through. I can only surmise, not having seen a slide so busted, that the effect of the greater brisance of the non-toxic primers is enough to chip the slot. If you are an agency that uses or is required to use non-toxic ammo, and use it in large volume, this may be a problem. For the rest of us, not so much.

Summation

When Glock began, back in the early 1980s, the FNC process was rare, used mostly for high-end industrial applications such as bearings, machine shafts, machine-tool connectors and cams, etc. We certainly have to tip our hats to Gaston Glock for seeing that an obscure industrial process such as this could be applied to firearms and improve them greatly.

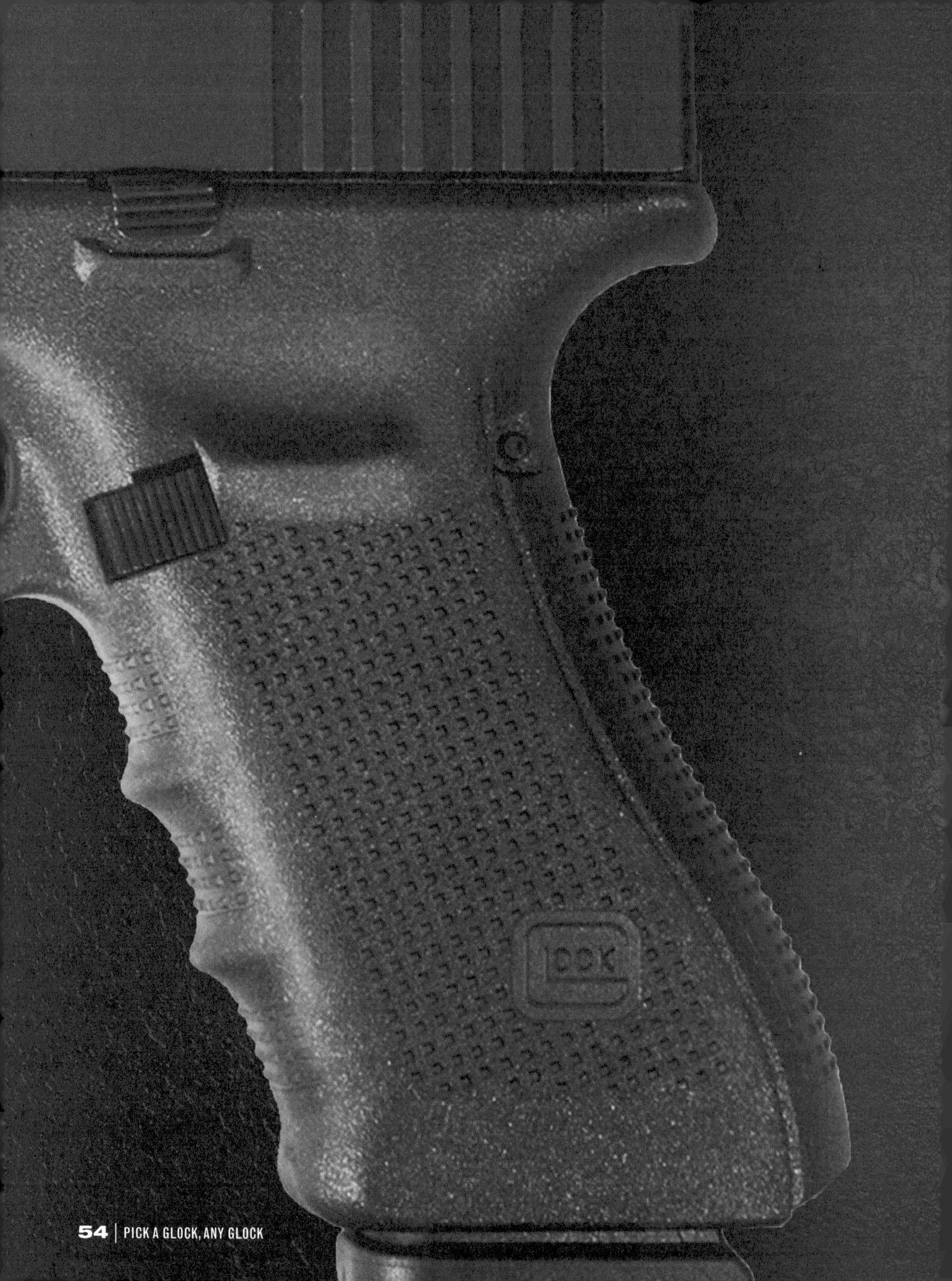

54 | PICK A GLOCK, ANY GLOCK

CHAPTER 6
Pick a Glock, Any Glock

Like the 10mm? You'll love the G20—at least if you can get your hand around it.

On the assumption that there are new readers and soon-to-be Glock owners in the group, I've gone and jotted down my personal impressions of the various models, their strengths and weaknesses, and the best use for each of them. You may find the info useful, and you may find that my impression and needs don't fit with yours. Such is life.

The G30 is a short, fat .45—which describes the cartridge, too. It makes a great backup to a G21.

Still, you have to start somewhere, and unless you find a shooting range that rents all of them (and then go and rent all of them to give them a try), how else are you going to gather enough info to get it all down?

The 9mms

First up, the 17. The original, box-stock, vanilla-plain G17 is a wondrous beast. For reliability, comfort, ease of use, soft recoil, and the ability to find extras like magazines and such, it is hard to beat. If you were going to own only one Glock, only one handgun, and you were not going to be packing it concealed daily, , then the G17 would be the Glock for you. Personally, I'd go with a first or second-Gen G17. At the last GSSF match I was at, the armorer, as he checked out the suitcase full of Glocks I'd brought, commented, "The second-gen Glocks are real workhorses. Replace a few worn parts here and there, and they just keep on running."

You can use whatever 9mm ammo you want, from the softest factory ammo or reloaded equivalent (keeping in mind that using reloaded ammo voids the warranty), to the hottest +P+ factory ammo you can find. As big as it is, and with the mass balance of the slide and recoil spring, it will work forever, work with whatever and, in due time, your skills will surpass the accuracy potential of the G17.

Surpass? Aren't Glocks supposed to be amazingly accurate? Alas, no. Oh, I'm sure that, if you were to clamp each barrel into a firing fixture and fire it on its own, it would deliver brilliant accuracy. But it was designed as a combat pistol, and the very things that make it durable, rugged, and everlasting work against accuracy. Not much, but just enough to keep it from being a bull's-eye-level pistol. If you have doubts, amble off to a local PPC match, the police-only precision shooting competition; most local clubs that hold them will allow anyone to shoot. You will not find many Glocks in the winners' circles of those matches, even at the club level. And you will not find them at all in the winner's circle in a seriously contested match.

Also working against it is the trigger. Yes, you can swap parts to get what you want, even do some tuning, but you're still crushing a sloppy trigger assembly inside of a squishy polymer frame. It is not ever going to be clean and crisp like one in a metal-framed pistol can be, let alone a single-action like the 1911.

The big problem with the G17 as the all-around, does-everything pistol is its size. A G17 is as big as they come, matching a 1911 or a Beretta 92 in size. While it would be just fine for most in a duty holster (the shorter-statured among us would find the muzzle poking the seat cushion in a patrol car), it is just a bit big for daily concealed carry. Which leads us to the G19.

The G19 was the second Glock pistol to see the light of day, and it was made for the exact reason stated above: the G17 was a bit too big for daily carry. Being three-quarters of an inch shorter in the slide/barrel and just about half an inch shorter in height, the G19 is just enough smaller that it is a whole lot easier to carry—so much so that a surprising number of police departments have the G19 as their standard-issue pistol and not the big brother G17.

You see, not everyone is tall. As police departments expanded their recruiting efforts (some because they needed more people than just six-foot tall former Marines, and some because they were told to), the expanded pool included shorter people. And when I say "shorter," I am not using some coded reference to women as police officers. There are short men out there, and when the height restrictions were lifted in police department recruiting, short guys filed

A G17 is as big as they come, matching a 1911 or Beretta 92 in size. While it is just fine for most in a duty holster (the shorter-statured among us would find the muzzle poking the seat cushion in a patrol car), it is just a bit big for daily concealed carry.

for the jobs along with everyone else. So, it is not unusual, in an LEO class (regardless the firearms involved), to see a significant number of officers or deputies under five-and-a-half feet tall standing there.

A duty holster holding a G17 (or equivalent) will, when the short officer wearing it is seated, protrude below the resting surface said officer is sitting on. In plain English, the muzzle pokes the car seat. This goes beyond uncomfortable. With the muzzle poking the seat, pivoting the pistol up

In some respects, the G30 cheats. The frame is short, yes, but the magazine comes with an oversized baseplate to increase capacity by a round. That baseplate also extends the grip length, good for larger hands.

One improvement from years ago, the accessory rail, works great as a place to mount a light.

and levering the duty belt to the side, it doesn't take too many shifts in a patrol car to start manifesting itself as back problems. The shorter slide/barrel length of the G19 makes for a shorter holster and keeps the muzzle off the seat.

The G19, because of the smaller size, is a lot easier to carry, and not just for the police. Those of us who are not sworn officers have needs, too. (And I am both appalled and put off by those who use "civilians" to describe citizens. All of us, police and non-police, are civilians. Unless you are subject to the Uniform Code of Military Justice, i.e., in the armed forces, you are a civilian. Soap box mode off.) We, too, find the G19 comfortable for daily carry. And I found, in talking with those who have been over to the sandbox in a non-reporting job, that the G19 seems to be the sidearm of choice for anyone who is not subject to the UCMJ (that is, private contractors). All the U.S. armed forces folks will have a Beretta plunked into their vest-mounted holster. But with contractors, where decisions are made less through inertia—they're not under the constraints of "We've got a warehouse full of M9s, we have to issue them"—are handed Glocks. They hold as many rounds, they break a lot less often, and the trigger is the same shot to shot. Plus, they fit the crowded tac vest or gear belt better than the larger M9 does.

The drawbacks to that comfort are minor, but you should be aware of them.

First up, you give up capacity. The G19 packs 15 to the G17s 17 rounds per magazine. You can, however, carry G17 magazines as reloads and have the extras if you need them. That would put you at a nice, even 50 rounds total, versus the G17 with 52 rounds on tap. I have to say that, if you find yourself in a predicament where 50 rounds of 9mm from a sidearm wasn't enough and 52 would have made all the difference, you have a tale more than worth the telling. (Unless, of course, you blasted your 50 rounds off quickly and to no avail, in which case having had a bushel basket full of magazines along would not have sufficed, nor a tale worth the telling, except as a cautionary story to others.)

The shorter barrel of the G19 will decrease your muzzle velocity a bit and increase muzzle blast at the same time and for the same reason. However, it won't be a lot. You may not even notice. The ammunition makers have gotten a lot savvier about short-barreled handguns and the problem of velocity loss. Where, in the old days, we might have seen a bigger drop-off from a lower start, they now make defensive ammo that delivers very effective velocities, even from the models shorter-barreled than the G19. I'd love to regale you with charts, graphs, calculations of the fps-per-inch rates, etc., but, in a short time, the ammo makers, which do not rest, will have made it all academic. The loss is measurable over a chronograph, but the bad guys will not notice. A hulking felon is not go-

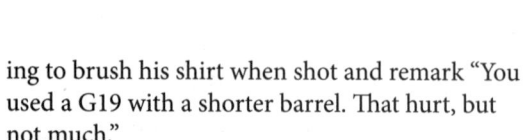

ing to brush his shirt when shot and remark "You used a G19 with a shorter barrel. That hurt, but not much."

From a trigger-pulling standpoint, the shorter slide makes for a shorter sight radius, which will decrease usable accuracy. The difference will be in your ability to determine precise sight alignment, not because a shorter barrel is less accurate. Good eyesight and practice will overcome much of the sighting difference.

The G19, because of the smaller size, is a lot easier to carry, and not just for the police. In talking with contractors who have been over to the sandbox, the G19 seems to be the sidearm of choice. As some told me, they hold as many rounds as the armed forces Beretta 92, but they break a lot less often, the trigger is the same shot to shot, and they fit better on a crowded tac vest or gear belt.

The G21, in .45 ACP, got delayed in production until Glock could get the G22, in .40, out to the public.

One thing to be aware of. If you have both a G17 and a G19, the magazine swaps work only one way. A 17 magazine will fit and lock into a G19, but the 19 magazine will be too short to seat all the way in and lock securely in the grip/mag well of a 17. While it will be mildly annoying at the practice range or a problem for your score and standings in a match, in daily carry you must work to make sure you have the correct match up. Trying to reload your G17 with the G19 magazines on your belt, still there from when you switched from your G19 to your G17, while the bad guys are strenuously objecting to your interference with their "jobs" is a poor way to proceed.

More Compact Still

The G26, introduced in 1995, is getting to the limit of small. You have to have a recollection of where we were in 1995, or maybe a short history lesson. The Assault Weapons Ban of 1994 had passed, and no new magazines that held more than 10 rounds were permitted to be made or sold. Well, they were permitted for police, but not the rest of us. The "full-size" G26 magazines held 12 rounds, and restricting them to 10 didn't decrease capacity enough to complain about. Much. However, a G17 held to 10 rounds because of the law was just silly. So the G26 found a lot of favor among those who wanted a carry 9mm, but didn't want any more bulk than the 10 rounds they were allowed.

The small size came with a big cost. The barrel is now not quite 3½ inches long. That puts a real crimp on fps generation and, as a result, you can easily find 124- or 125-grain ammunition that fails to generate a full 1,000 fps. A 125, trundling along at 975 fps instead of the 1100 fps it was designed for, is not going to expand as designed. That decreases terminal effectiveness, decreases expansion, and increases penetration.

The compact grip can be hard to hold on to for those of us with large hands. Even those with average hands can find the 26 a bit tough to hold. Combine that with the tendency to shift to hotter loads to make up for the fps loss in the short barrel, and it can be a real handful. It is entirely possible that someone who can post a passing score on a police qualification course with a G17 or a G19 falls short with a G26.

The shorter sight radius, now coming in at an inch less overall than that of the G17, adds to the problem. "Only an inch?" you ask. Yes, but that is a 15-percent decrease from the 17 and can

The Gen4 has caught up with the G27.

greatly decrease scores. I've seen it happen; the combination of short grip, sharper recoil, and shorter sight radius can seriously decrease scores. You might object that a theoretical decrease in numerical scores doesn't matter, as most shootouts happen within the length of a car. Still, increased group size can be a problem and, if you need more accuracy than your sidearm and you can deliver, you're out of luck at that moment.

As if all that wasn't enough, there's another problem: the G26 can be too small for some holsters. With the slide and barrel now even shorter, there's less mass and friction between slide and holster to keep the G26 in a holster. To retain it during carry (it is, in many jurisdictions, more than just embarrassing to drop one's carry gun in public), you'll have to either get a holster that rides up higher on the G26 than it would on a G19, or rides lower, deeper, behind your belt. Or has some security strap. Any and sometimes all of those make the draw slower. They can also make you more sensitive to the comfort of a given holster. Comfort matters and, if you do not have it, you can be spotted carrying, as you adjust your holster, squirm in a chair to make it more comfy, or hand-check it in place.

Still, in a pistol that has as much bulk as a snub-nosed revolver (and revolvers have some of the same carry problems as the G26 does), you get now 12 rounds, compared to the five or six of a .38 Special snubby. I'm just glad Glock doesn't make one even smaller, because, if it did, I couldn't shoot it.

Bigger is Better. Maybe.

In the other direction, we have the G17L. The long slide was made as a competition gun, It also had some use as a duty sidearm and backup for police units that operated with long guns, like S.W.A.T. teams. It came out in the halcyon year of 1988 and had a run of a decade. The longer barrel and slide boost velocities a bit, but not a lot, while the longer sight radius is good for precision shooting. With the exact same frame, the 17L had a slide and barrel that were 1½ inches longer than that of the 17. This did, however,

You can't really get much smaller than this G27 and still be able to hold on. For lovers of the .40, those who want compactness, this is a great little blaster. Just don't expect to shoot it as well as your G22.

PICK A GLOCK, ANY GLOCK | **61**

If you load the hottest .40 ammo in your G27, you'll wish for something even more aggressive than the Gen4 nubs to keep the gun securely in your hands. This round kicks hard in this smaller gun.

When I visited, Double Action had shelves full of Glocks. Now, and for a while to come, I suspect the shelves are and will be pretty empty.

call for another change. The Glock, like all self-loading pistols, depends on a certain slide mass to work against the recoil spring and balance the force generated by the cartridge going off. If you make the slide longer by 1½ inches, you increase mass. So Glock cut a rectangular window in the top of the slide, in a location that didn't really need it, to lighten the 17L slide back to the mass that the 17 is. Mass restored to normal, things operate as expected, and everyone is having fun.

Due to changes in IPSC competition, the G17L was replaced in 1998 by the G34. When the Production class was added as an IPSC-recognized division, along with it came the "IPSC box." The box limited the height and length of a pistol, and the 17L was too long. So, the G34 had its slide and barrel trimmed back by three-quarters of an inch, the top window adjusted accordingly, and the result was a match-winning pistol. The G34 exists to fit the box, pure and simple.

Production Division shooters shoot nearly as fast as Open shooters do. Well, on the close-'n'-fast targets, anyway. When the range stretches out and the targets have no-shoots snuggled up against them, the limits of iron sights come in with full force. But, in Production, no one is allowed to shoot (or, at least, declare) Major shooting power factor, so everyone shoots a 9mm. Soft recoil, long sight radius, and lots of practice result in Production shooters going through stages with amazing speed. Glock shooters do very well in IPSC/USPSA Production Division, and they mostly do it with G34s.

.40 S&W, the New Standard

A result of the ever-decreasing power of the FBI 10mm load and the secret project of S&W and Winchester, the .40 S&W surprise was usurped by Glock, which was first to market with a pistol in .40, the G22. So fast did it make this happen that Glock even delayed the unveiling of its own project, work on the 10mm/.45 pistol.

The speed of that unveiling is impressive, but it is also the seed of the struggles Glock has had with the .40 ever since. The G22 was/is, essentially, a G17 with a .40 barrel and breechface—and not even with a stiffer recoil spring. If a holster,

Since the Gen4 makeover requires time to be applied to all models, older Gen Glocks such as this G26 can be had brand new, because Glock keeps making the third-Gen models until it can make the switch.

mag pouch, or other accessory (accept magazines) fits a G17, it fits a G22.

That was the great selling point, but also the weakness of the G22. A police department could switch over from 9mm to .40 and not have the change anything but the pistols, magazines, and ammo. All the holsters, magazine pouches, storage racks, and so on would work just fine with the new pistols.

Glock took full advantage of this in the 1990s, by offering police departments an exchange of G22s and G23s for G17s and G19s, in some instances on a one-for-one basis. This kept the lines rolling, made Glock even more friends in the LE establishment, and expanded the company's reach. "But," you ask, "how do you turn a profit that way?"

If you ever see a Glock overseas, apparently the odds are it will be a G19.

Simple. Remember the Assault Weapons ban of 1994 we talked about? Since hi-cap magazines could not be made new, but the existing ones were still kosher to sell, simple market dynamics raised the price. (The first lecture you get, in your first Economics class, will introduce you to this concept, and, if it doesn't, you should leave and not look back.)

In the early 1990s, a Glock magazine for a G17 cost about $12. If you went through the armorers class, you could by some at a $1.50 each. When the law passed, prices shot up. Twenty dollars? Thirty dollars? At the peak, Glock maga-

If you prefer the .40, then the equivalent to the G19 is the G23—not a bad combo, either.

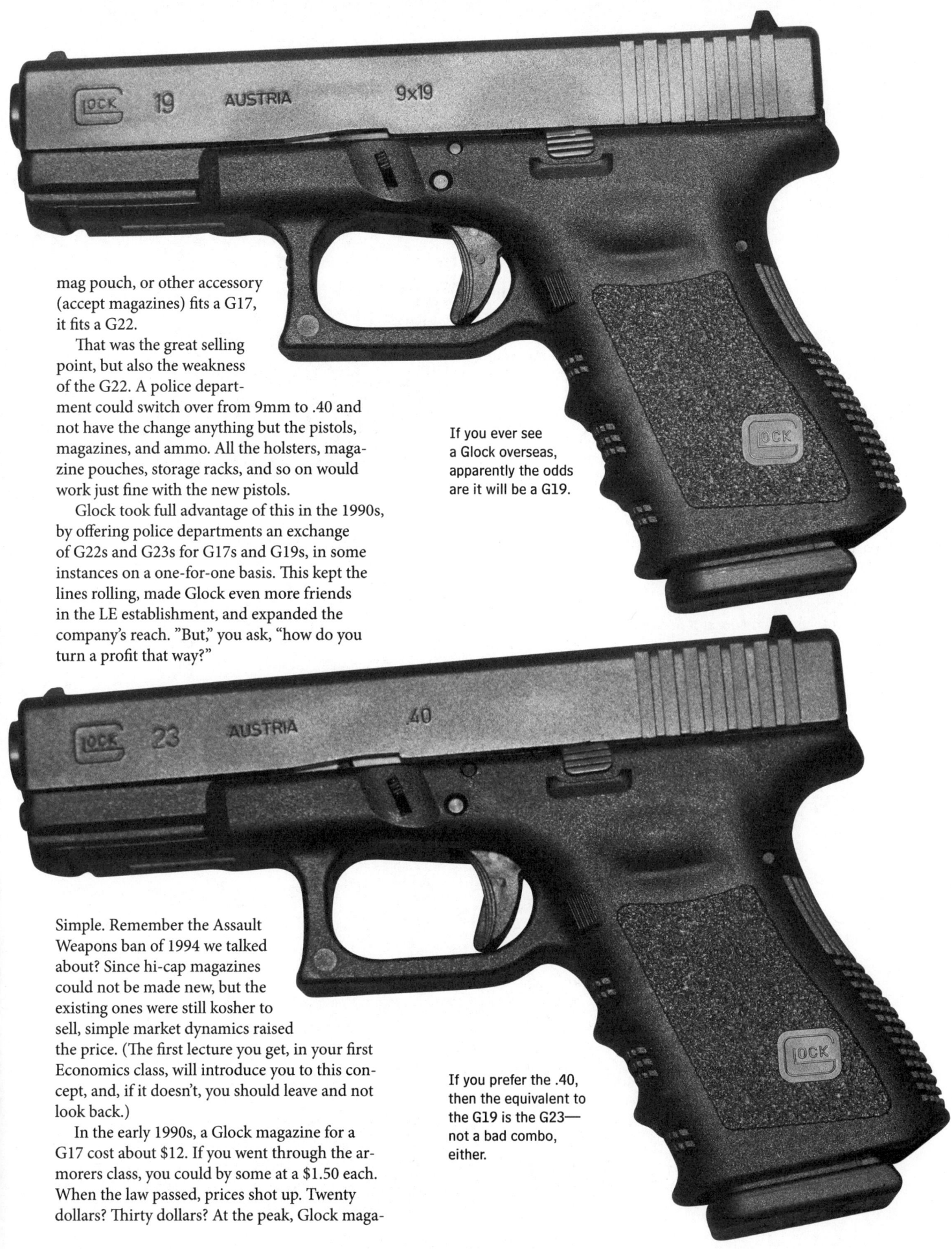

PICK A GLOCK, ANY GLOCK | 65

zines were listed for as much as $120 each.

When police departments bought Glocks, they'd buy in bulk. Let's say we have a police department of 50 sworn officers. If they were adopting the Glock, they'd buy more than 50. They'd get 40-plus G17s (we're talking 9mm, for the moment) maybe 10 G19s and, if they were available at the time, five or six G26s. The patrol officers would be issued a G17, the detectives a G19, and the command officers would score a G26 each. That leaves a few in the armory for issue if one breaks, gets lost or stolen, or ends up as evidence in a shooting. Each Glock would have a minimum of three magazines and, more typically, four or five. Plus there would be extra training magazines and inventory against loss, damage, etc., as with the pistols above. So, our Millville P.D. would have bought on the order of 60 Glocks and 300 magazines.

Glock comes in and swaps out the pistols one-for-one for new .40-caliber Glocks and magazines. Glock then inspects, cleans up, and sells the pistols to a wholesaler at a discount from the usual wholesale price, but still at a nice markup over the cost to manufacture the .40-caliber Glocks it had traded away. Let me repeat that: Glock still made a profit, albeit one that was less than if it had sold the .40s at wholesale.

Now, about those magazines. Inspected, cleaned, and sorted, they were then sold to the wholesaler. However, where it might have sold magazines before 1994 at $8 or $9 each, it could easily sell the pre-ban-manufactured, but post-

When Glock introduced the .45 GAP, you'd have had to wonder if it really thought through the whole "fat as a G22, but only holds 10 rounds" concept. It seems an odd choice, given the market and its competitors.

66 | PICK A GLOCK, ANY GLOCK

Here is a G36 with a more normal capacity, and what Glock should have done to start with. It is a definite improvement over the five-shot magazine single-stack concept.

ban-priced magazines for twice that—or more. It could make a larger profit over the magazines, post-1994, offsetting the decrease in profit from the trade.

This incurred the wrath of the anti-gunners (as if there was anything Glock or any other gun manufacturer could ever do, besides go out of business, that would not incur their wrath), but was entirely lawful. There was much wailing about "adhering to the letter of the law, while breaking the spirit of the law," but the law was what the law was. Oh, and as an aside, if you are in a class on the law and the lecturer tells you it is as important to adhere to the spirit of the law as it is to the letter of the law, leave. You are getting bad legal advice, and paying for a bad education. But I digress.

The compact .40 is the Glock 23. It is the exact same size as the G19 and serves the same purpose, to be more compact while dong what its bigger brother does. It does that, but, where with the G19 the smaller package is not a big deal recoil-wise compared to the G17, in the G23 this becomes a problem. Especially for the new and smaller shooters and those not willing to practice, the G23 becomes a handful, especially when using the hottest defensive ammo available.

More of a handful yet is the G27, the ultra-compact .40. The G27 becomes a real beast for a lot of shooters, and the capacity is limited to nine shots in the magazine. If you are going to carry a Glock for defense, I would steer you away from a G27, unless you are going to practice a lot.

The G17L had a big brother in the G24, introduced at that exquisitely badly timed year of 1994. Wearing a long slide, accurate, and easy to shoot as a result, it went bye-bye with the introduction of the IPSC-sized G34, in 1998, replaced by the G35. The G35 is an IPSC box-sized .40, with no real IPSC division for it. USPSA/IPSC Production Division is a strictly 9mm affair. You can shoot .40, but you don't get extra points for the extra recoil and, in IPSC (unlike the USPSA 10-shot restriction), you lose capacity. If, however, you want a bigger full-sized carry gun and like .40-caliber, then the G35 is just the ticket.

Curiously, even though the G24 was dropped from production back in 1998, it is still listed in the catalog. Apparently it has enough of a following that Glock does occasional production runs (not a very difficult thing to do), and, so, if you want one, you can find one.

Reinventing the wheel is a popular exercise. When John Browning did it, back in 1910, at least he was getting the .45 out of a revolver and into a pistol. Should Glock be considered that innovative some 30 years after it first entered the market?

The G34 is the competition Glock. It fits the IPSC box and works like every other Glock out there. It's also not a bad carry gun, if you can hide it effectively.

10mm & .45

I'm putting these together for one reason: they have the same symbiotic relationship as the 9mm and .40 Glocks do. The frames are the same size and the differences are the barrel's bore and breechface sizes.

In the late 1980s, the FBI was all hot to get a 10mm into the holsters of every one of its agents. Alas, this was not to be. Some test runs with 10mm pistols showed that, for all of these agents' uber-police PR status, they weren't so different than the "regular" police, when it came to shooting handguns. Far too many of them failed to pass the qual course armed with a full-power 10mm. It was that very failure and the subsequent watering down of the 10mm that lead directly to the .40 S&W cartridge.

Glock worked hard to produce a 10mm and its companion .45 ACP. The resulting G20 is a monster of a sidearm. It handles full-power 10mm ammo better than you do and holds 15 rounds of it.

But Glock didn't have a crystal ball and so worked hard to produce a 10mm and its companion .45 ACP. The resulting G20 is a monster of a sidearm. It handles full-power 10mm ammo better than you do and holds 15 rounds of it. The only problem, it's big. You simply can't make a hi-cap 10mm handgun and have a grip that isn't big. If you have the hands for it and the need for the power, have fun.

It took a while, but Glock got around to dealing with the complaints of excessive size. What it did, in essence, was "pull" the backstrap forward and take the volume out of the frame and the ejector block. This was done first in the .45, as part of Glock's effort to get in on the U.S. military Joint Pistol Trials. I might point out, at this moment, that, if there is an organization that is even less resistant to change than Glock, it is the U.S. Army. While the efforts to comply with the requirements of the Joint Pistol Trials lead many manufacturers to produce interesting and useful products, those efforts have not yet, more than five years later, done anything to cough up a likely candidate as a service pistol. Nor even a hint of progress.

The 20SF is smaller. If it is enough smaller to matter to you, great. There is only one way to determine that, and that is to go and shoot one.

The compact 10mm is the G29 and, with full-power ammo, it is as hard to shoot as a G26 with full-power .40 ammo. The ultra-compact is the G30, and you have to be some kind of a masochist to shoot it with full-power 10mm ammo. It doesn't have a lot of grip area to hang on to, and the recoil, muzzle blast, and muzzle jump are rough. Along with the G20SF, you can have a G29SF and a G30SF. Have fun.

Enough about the 10mms. Along with the G20, Glock introduced the G21, in .45 ACP, in 1991. Less obnoxious to shoot than the G20, primarily because the cartridge simply produces less energy, the .45 is still a handful.

Alas, the happy news of a ".45 Glock" was already old hat, because the .40, introduced in 1990, was sweeping all before it. It didn't help that the G21 was as fat as the 10mm, (it uses the same frame). For all that size you got to pack 13 rounds of .45 ACP, compared to 15 rounds of .40 in the G22 and, in those early days, the .40 was touted as being every bit as effective as the .45, in part because all the latest bullet research was going into .40, and not so much into .45.

The Glock .45 offerings are the same size as the 10mm, with one exception. We have the G21, G21SF, G30, and G31SF. Then we have the G36.

Unlike the rest of the .45 Glock lineup, the G36 features a single-stack magazine. "Cool!" you say? Alas, it is a single-stack magazine in an ultra-compact pistol. You see, when the legions of Glock owners and would-be Glock owners back in the late 1980s and very early 1990s were asking for a Glock in .45 ACP, what they had in mind was a single-stack Glock the size of a 1911 or Commander and holding as much ammo, not a wide-body. By the time the G36 arrived, in 1999, the bloom was off the rose, we were soon going to be back to full-sized handguns with full-capacity magazines, and a big-bore micro-gun was not all that appealing. Yes, Glock sells a lot of them. But had it come out with a single-stack right on the heels of the G20/21, it would have sold them like hotcakes.

One recent evergreen speculation involves a hybrid Glock. Allegedly, some Southern Califor-

The .357 SIG is not something we can blame on Glock. What it is supposed to do is equal the .357 Magnum, on the right. What it actually does, except in the G31, is duplicate the performance of the 9mm or .38 Super, but with a lot more muzzle blast.

It is possible and desirable to have a raft of Glocks, all in the same caliber. (It also makes ammo supplying so much easier.) Here, top to bottom, we have a G17L, G34, G17, and G19.

PICK A GLOCK, ANY GLOCK | 71

nia law enforcement agency (or special department/squad in an agency) has been in long, intensive talks with Glock to make a 30S. The special model combines the model 30SF with a G36 slide. The two slides are the same length, the only difference being the width of the slides. The G36 book-spec width is listed as 1.10 inches, while that of the G30 is 1.27 inches. Hmm.

I'd heard the rumors, but I couldn't envision Glock making a small number of non-spec pistols where the difference was so minor, even for a police department. Then, just as I was sending this book off to my editor, Glock and let the cat out of the bag: a G30S *is* going to be available. And, amazingly, with all the whispering that said it would be a G30SF with a G36 slide on top, it actually is that. Glock also had the wit to make the new G30S on the SF frame and to do so without the extra backstraps the make Glocks more portly. If you're going to make an ultra-compact carry pistol, you don't improve things by making it fatter, longer, wider, whatever. Put one in the hit column for the rumormongers.

Size Matters, So Change it

Since the G20/21 is so big, there have been a lot of people looking to reduce the size. One is Robbie Barkman, owner of Robar, who can make a G20/21 almost tolerable. The alterations also change the grip angle, if that matters, so you can have a more 1911-like feel, if you wish.

Robbie isn't the only one. There are people who will do alterations to Glocks of all sizes, so, if you want it, go for it. Just be aware that once you go down that path, Glock won't warranty anything that has been altered. If you bring it to a GSSF match, the armorer probably won't care, but if you ship it to Smyrna for service, it might bounce it back, untouched. That has not stopped a large number of people from shipping off guns to have them re-shaped, sculpted, roughed-up, or otherwise changed from perfection.

The .357 Challenge

One of the drawbacks of the 9mm has always been that it doesn't perform as well as the .357 Magnum. In the early days of law enforcement, the 9mm the argument was always it versus the .357 Magnum. Those who did not like the 9mm would point to the energy charts. There you'd find a 9mm 124-grain JHP doing, at best, 1,150 fps, compared to a .357 with a 125-grain JHP listed at 1,450 fps.

It didn't help that the 9mm was often not even up to the full 1,150 fps, and everyone forgot that not many .357s got to 1,450 and, when it did, it was an awful range time experience. Then, when the "stopping power" statistics were dragged in, where the 125 JHP in a .357 was "shown" to have a 95-percent "one-shot stop" capability, the 9mm fans would walk off muttering.

In the long run, the .357 went away for other reasons—low ammo capacity, marginally improved scores from better triggers in 9mm, the desire for something new and improved—and the 9mm got improved, but there were still limits. While all 9mm defensive ammo now meets or exceeds that 1,150 fps mark, at least from a full-sized gun, it still didn't do what the .357 promised.

SIG changed that. The .357 SIG is essentially (although you can't make ammo that way) a .40 S&W case necked down to hold a 9mm bullet. The extra case capacity allows for more powder (but different powders than a 9mm would use), and, thus, boosts performance up to the .357 Magnum territory. Those of you conversant with Newtonian physics will be ready for what is to come, i.e., you can't get something for nothing.

The .357 SIG is available in a 9mm/.40-sized pistol. That means we have the G37, G38, and G39, which fit the G17, G19, and G26 platforms. Glock does not offer a G34/35 equivalent in .357 SIG, but, if you really desire one, you can simply get a drop-in .357 SIG barrel for your G35.

In the G37, the .357 SIG probably does what it is advertised to do. The 4½-inch barrel is not going to give you all the velocity that, say, a five-inch barrel in a 1911 would, but you wouldn't lose too much. However, as you go down in size, things go from bad to worse. Down to the G38, velocity loss and muzzle blast gains escalate, and you probably are putting up with a ferocious amount of blast and recoil, all to gain a marginal amount over a same-sized 9mm. In the ultra-compact G39, the bargain is no bargain; you get no more velocity than a 9mm would, and the blast is enough to scorch your eyebrows.

The .45 GAP?

This one has had me scratching my head ever since I first saw it, back at the 2007 SHOT show. Basically, the round is an engineering double-down on the .40, as in make a .45 that is short enough to fit into a 9mm magazine tube. Alas, it is an engineering step too far.

Advantages? You have a .45-caliber bullet. In the first loadings, they were only 200 grains, but, with a little wizardry, the ballisticians were

The G17L (bottom, hard-chromed slide) was too long for the IPSC box, when that box was adopted in the early 1990s. Glock then made it short enough to fit the box and, *voilà*, the G34.

get a full 230-grain bullet stepping out at full .45 ACP velocities. Nice. You'd think, being in a G17-sized pistol, that it would be harder to control than a .45 ACP in a G21. Not really. The large grip of the G21 introduces problems of its own, and the end result is that the G37 is actually more controllable.

Disadvantages? The extra bullet diameter cuts into magazine capacity. Where the G22 holds 15 rounds of .40 S&W, the G37 only holds rounds of .45 GAP. The brass is easily mistaken for .45 ACP, so reloaders at your gun club will hate you mightily for leaving your brass. Also, the .45 GAP absolutely cannot be accommodated with a slide of the same weight as a 9mm/.40, so Glock had to increase the slide width. That means your G37 has to have a G37-specific holster, though magazines are the same externally.

The lineup here is G37, G38, and G39. Of the three, the only one to consider is the G38. If you're going to have the size of the G37, you might as well have the capacity of a G22, while the big bullets in the ultra-compact G39 will be an unpleasant recoil experience.

Glock's .380s

These are the G25 and G28, corresponding to the G19 and G26 models. The .380 lacks the energy to work a locked-breech system, so these are simple blowback pistols. For their size you could have a Glock in 9mm, .357 SIG, .40 or .45, so why would you want a wimpy .380? That said, regardless of your desire, you can't own one. They are non-importable, except for LEO, and the few people who have figured one end-around or another have found themselves in hot water as a result. In the Glock universe, they are like supermodels—unattainable and hazardous to try.

So, which one is for you? That depends on your size, experience, needs, and desires, and just how many Glocks you want to own. After all, once you learn how to run a Glock, switching from one model to the next is no big deal. Collect 'em all, complete the set.

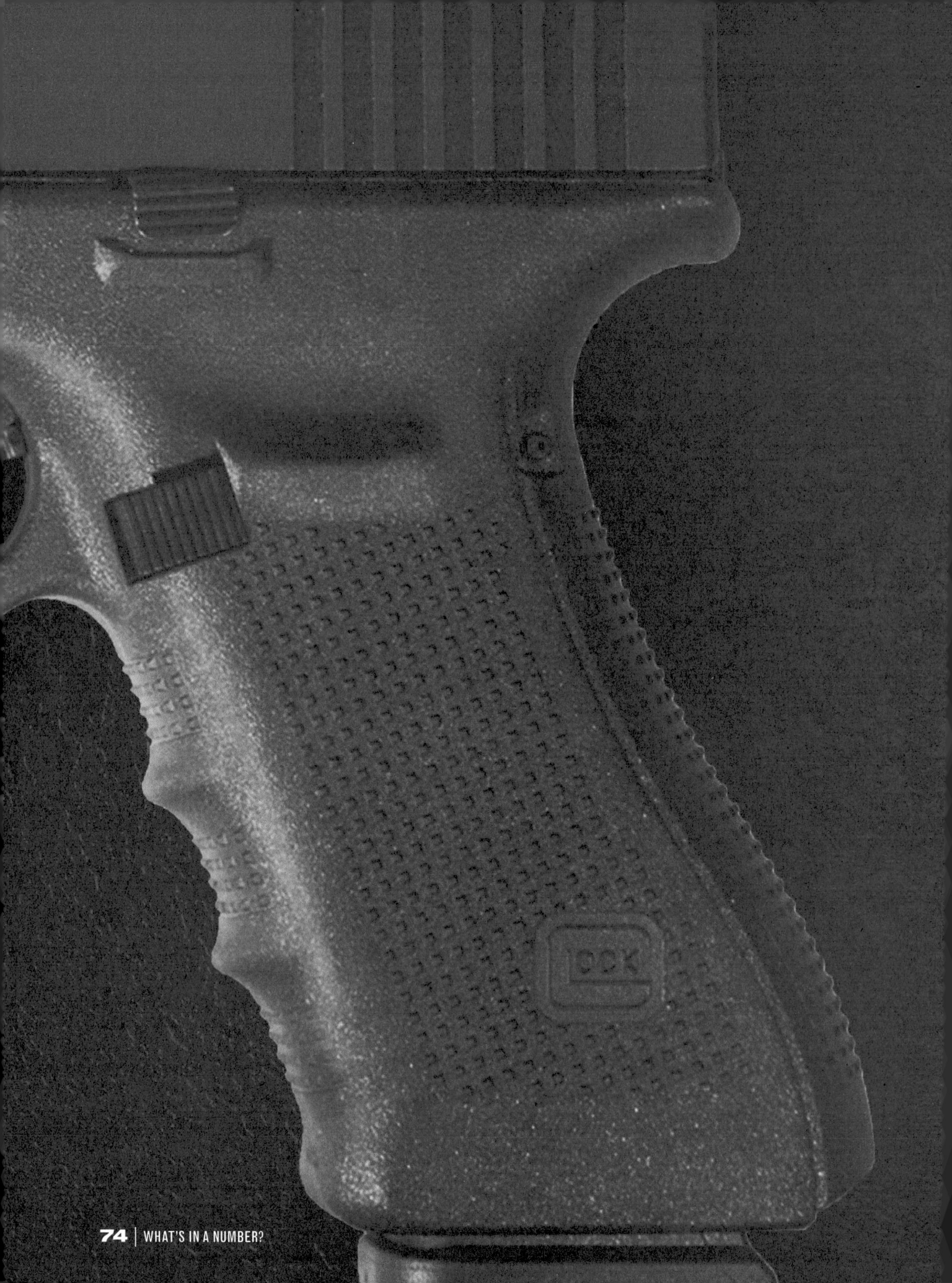

CHAPTER 7

What's in a Number?

The serial number on the frame, slide, and barrel is clear. The letter code in the frame is a mystery.

I have heard bitter complaints from some, concerning the name/numbering system used by Glock. As much as it also drives me crazy, I have to disagree with those who want to complain, because it isn't as if Glock deliberately set out to confuse us.

Glock and Europe were happy with serial numbers stamped into plastic. Then we, the U.S., had to insist on metal. That's us, always making trouble.

Okay, time for a bit of history. Back in the 1950s, a time when cars had fins and "fuel economy" was a phrase unuttered, handguns had names. "Highway Patrolman," "Official Police," and so on. Smith & Wesson had many models (unlike Colt's, its fiercest rival for the handgun market), and finally got fed up with trying to name everything, so they **turned to using just model numbers.** The Highway Patrolman became the M-28, the big .44 Magnum became the M-29, and so on.

With S&W, since everything in the product line was made out of carbon steel, it was easy to keep track. An M-29 could have three different

Quality control in modern manufacturing means you track it all, but you can only track that which is uniquely identified.

barrel lengths, it could be nickeled or blue, and that was pretty much it. The model number was a base descriptor and the extras were, well, extra. You wanted a four-inch nickeled M-29, that's what you told the clerk at the gun shop.

The 9mm S&W pistol got its own model designation, the M-39. (How the company came up with the numbers in question is another matter entirely, and one we need not go into here.) When S&W came out with a hi-cap 9mm, it got a model number that indicated its heritage, but also kept it separate—the M-59.

Then it got messy. You see, by the early 1980s, revolvers could be blued, nickel, or stainless. Pistols could be blued, stainless, nickel, or aluminum-framed. There weren't enough model numbers, and it wasn't possible to keep the parallel models parallelly numbered. S&W went to three-digit model numbers. You could have a 586 and a 686, a 581 and a 681, a 439, 539, and 639. And then the floodgates opened.

Smith & Wesson shifted from a traditional production system—multiple lathes, mills,

> By the early 1980s, revolvers could be blued, nickel, or stainless. Pistols could be blued, stainless, nickel, or aluminum-framed. There simply weren't enough model numbers to go around, and it wasn't possible to keep the parallel models parallelly numbered.

A numerical code such as this can tell the manufacturer all it needs to know about how this frame was molded, including date, machine, polymer lot, machine operator, etc.

WHAT'S IN A NUMBER? | **77**

Even magazine followers have QC tracking numbers on them.

We all know how the G17 got its designation, it being the seventeenth patent for Gaston Glock. The seventeenth patent holds 17 rounds—nice symmetry, eh? Why not go with it? The next one produced, the select-fire, is simply a modified G17, so why not call it the 18, right? Next up, the compact version of the 9mm and, since we're on a roll, it gets the name 19. All very neat and simple, all very easy to keep track of.

and scrapers, each doing one operation, being run by one operator—to CNC machines that did multiple operations. With that came an explosion of options, and the model number designation system went to four digits. For just one example, take a hi-cap 9mm pistol. You could have it with a traditional double-action trigger, a DAO, or a single-action. You could have an aluminum frame, carbon steel, or stainless, and you could have a blued or stainless slide, and fixed or adjustable sights. Add in the options of frame size (regular, medium, or short frame and corresponding capacities), and model naming/numbering became simply unmanageable. Smith & Wesson even made a slide rule-like wheel chart that let you sort out the model names. Without it, you had no way of keeping track what features a Model 6903 had compared to a 5905 or a 4702. We at the gun shop all joked about S&W's "gun of the month" club.

Many of those models did not sell well (big surprise there, as many options were just too off the beaten path for shooters), and are now

This is the old Glock slide marking system, with numbers so small you can hardly see them.

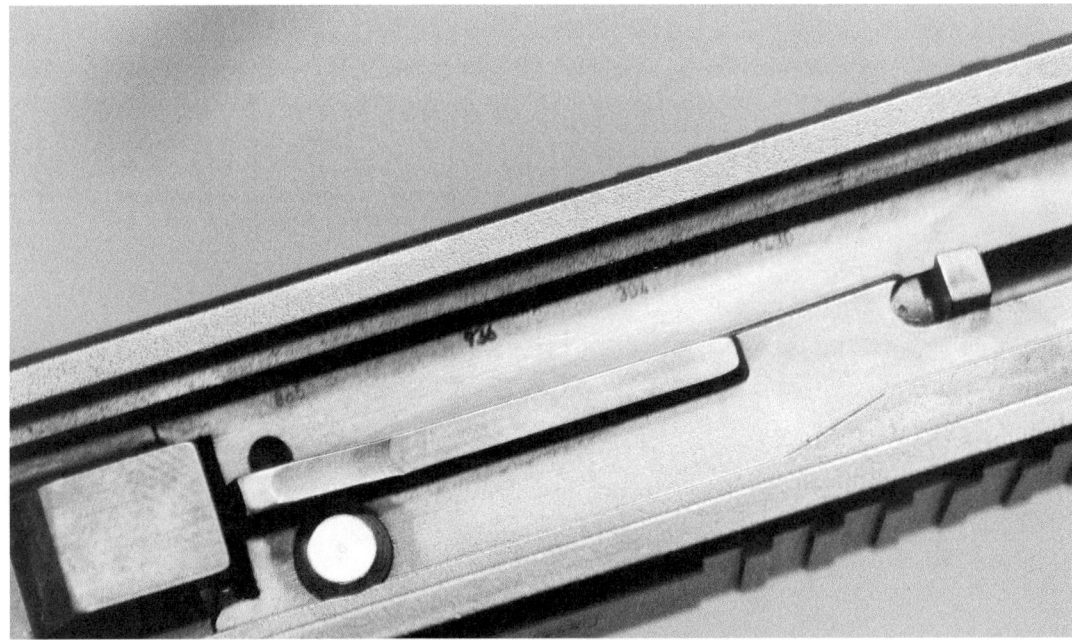

(below) Here is the first four-letter prefix Glock I've come across—as in some 24,000 pistols *after* Glock made the change to using a metal stamp for U.S. importation.

WHAT'S IN A NUMBER? | **79**

This is a replacement slide, as evidenced by the single-letter prefix and the mismatch to the barrel serial number.

collectors' items. Not particularly valuable or pricey collector's items, but give it time. In half a century, the XXXX model of which S&W made only 231 units will become quite valuable.

The lesson here is simple: You can't know ahead of time where the market will take you. So, let's look at Glock.

We all know how the G17 got its designation, it being the seventeenth patent for Gaston Glock. The seventeenth patent, holds 17 rounds—the symmetry is nice, eh? Why not go with it? The next one made, the select-fire, is simply a modified G17 (speaking basically, not of the details that go into it), so why not call it the "18," right? Next up, the compact version of the 9mm, and since we're on a roll, it gets the name "19." All very neat and simple, easy to keep track of.

By the late 1980s, the 10mm round is the hot new round. It looks like the FBI is going to go with it, and, since the round won't fit into the G17, we have to make a new frame for it. So, we'll call the next model the 20 and,

since those crazy Americans are so infatuated with the .45 ACP and it easily fits the soon-to-be G20 frame, we'll call it the "21." Pencil those into the production plans and mark the blueprints.

Oh wait, holy frakkenspiel, we have to stop everything. The Americans have this new, short 10mm called the .40 S&W. Stop the 10mm, stop the .45, switch all the engineers over to this new .40. Wait, what? Our careful plan of model numbers is all shot to hell? We have to introduce the .40 as the Model 22 before we can unveil the 20 and 21? From there it just spun out of control.

I'm sure, had he known, that Gaston Glock would have come up with a different system of designating models. Then again, if you're making money hand over fist, selling an item that everyone wants, do you really care if the model numbering system is a jumble? As long as the customers know which ones they want and the shipping department can keep them straight, does it matter? You could use model number selected by a roll of the dice or (below) The only original part on this Glock is the barrel. The slide and frame broke and were replaced by Glock.

(bottom) A high-mileage Glock, followed up on after years. Despite the tsunami of ammo that has gone through it, the barrel still locks up snugly. A close look reveals that the hood is ever so slightly peened from the million impacts.

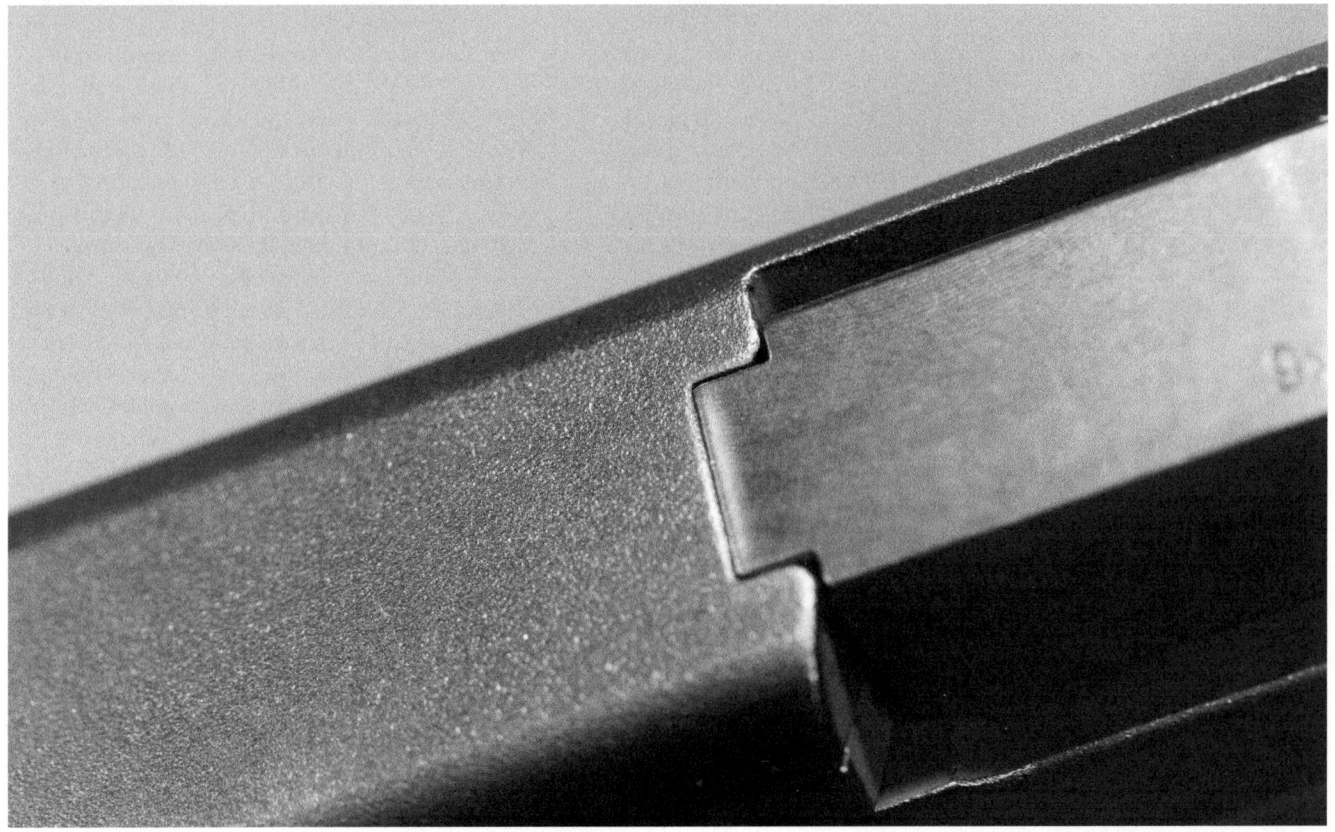

Now, even recoil spring assemblies have numbers.

random street numbers observed on the way to the office and it would work. The numbers are what they are, stop complaining.

In the process of working on this book, I had a chance to visit the vaults of a European military museum. I had a full day to spend, fondle, photograph, and ask questions. One of the curiosities I uncovered was a Glock anomaly—well, at least an anomaly as far as Americans are concerned.

The anomaly in question was a Glock 17, 9mm, serial number AE990. No big deal, right? If we peruse the various serial number lists to be found on the Internet, we'll uncover the detail that good old AE was built around the end of 1985 and could have landed here on our shores in January 1986 (assuming this particular one had gotten exported and hadn't stayed in Europe). There's just one problem: it doesn't have a serial number stamped on a little metal plate in the recoil spring dust cover. The serial number is stamped directly into the plastic, on the right side.

Clearly, this wasn't kosher for the BATFE,

when it came time for Glock to begin exporting to the U.S., and it insisted on a metal plate for the serial number. So, this is a pre-USA Glock 17, and the proof date code on the barrel gives us a clue; the Austrian proofmarks, plus a "ZTF" in the number, point us to a June 1984 production date. If we use the simple math of rolling over serial numbers, by June of 1984, Glock had already made 50,000 pistols and hadn't yet even formed Glock USA for importation.

Hmm, so we then have two Glock G17s with the serial number AE990. Well, close. Somebody out there has a G17 with the serial number AE990USA stamped on its little metal plate. Still, somewhere along the way, Glock dropped the "USA" suffix, and the pistols we now see are simply three (and now four) letters and three numerals.

Curiosity remains. A serial number stamped into plastic? I've seen, even today, proof marks stamped into the plastic as the location of proofmarks in many countries is precisely described by law. If the receiver is metal, plastic, wood, compressed sawdust, it doesn't matter. If the law says you stamp the proofmark on the right side of the frame ahead of the trigger guard, then that's where you stamp it.

Or, rather, that's where the proof inspector stamps it. The big operations in Europe will have an in-house inspector who stamps when firearms have passed proof. Hey, if you are making a hundred or a thousand of something a week or a day, it's easier for everyone to have a proof inspector in-house. After all, even the proof house only has so much room, and the security headache of that many guns schlepping in and out is more than one wants. I had a chance to visit a German proof house recently and, while it had a lot of elbow room, it didn't have enough to handle an operation like Glock's. Even back in 1984, I doubt it had the room, so today? Not a chance. It's a sure bet the Glock factory has an in-house proof inspector.

But about putting the serial number there, in the plastic. Again, on the Continent, it has been customary for many years (centuries, even) to put the serial number on the barrel. The barrel? Sure. Remember that, back when rifles and other firearms were muzzleloaders, there was no receiver. The old saying "lock, stock and barrel" meant just that, a complete musket, rifle, whatever. A rifle, shotgun, whatever, was a stock with a lock or action on it and the barrel up top. If you were the guys in charge and you were going to control and track firearms, you'd serial number or otherwise clearly mark the barrel. There really was no other logical place.

That, in part, is why you see European firearms with multiple serial number markings. It's partly because of Old World craftsmanship and attention to detail, but also because, in some places, the law requiring a serial number on the receiver didn't replace the law requiring a serial number on the barrel. It added to it. So, when Glock made its product, it complied with all the laws and regulations in force at the time and all they could anticipate. That meant serial numbers on barrel, slide, and frame, and that way, no

They may look the same, but the end numbers indicate they are not the same, and you will want to make sure your Gen4 Glock has the correct assembly.

I'm sure, had he known, that Gaston Glock would have come up with a different system of designating models. Then again, if you're making money hand over fist, selling an item that everyone wants, do you really care if the model numbering system is a confused jumble? As long as the customers know which ones they want and the shipping department can keep them straight, does it matter? It doesn't. The numbers are what they are. Stop complaining.

The new Glock slide QC numbering system, using pin-punched numerals. You can read them, though you probably can't decode them.

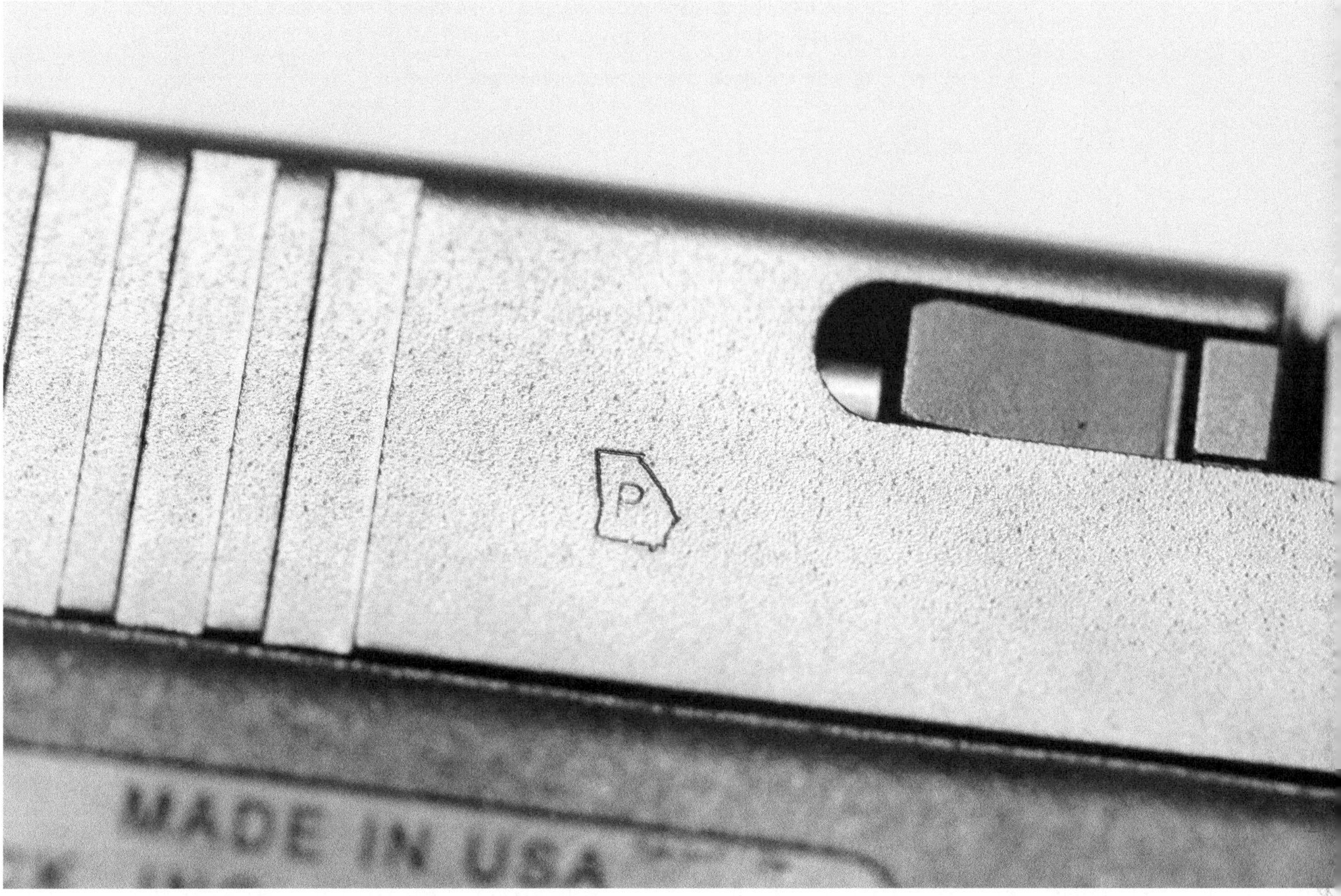

(above) Oh-ho, a new mark from Glock! We can be pretty sure this indicates a Glock actually made in the U.S.A., rather than one imported from Austria.

(left) The mark is also on the barrel, so it looks like we have both barrels and slides made in the U.S.A.

WHAT'S IN A NUMBER?

(below) A pin-punch two-dimensional code, stamped on the barrel foot of a Glock. With a scanner and the Glock codes, you can find out everything you need to know about this particular barrel.

(bottom) Here is the old Glock marking, and a frame made in Austria.

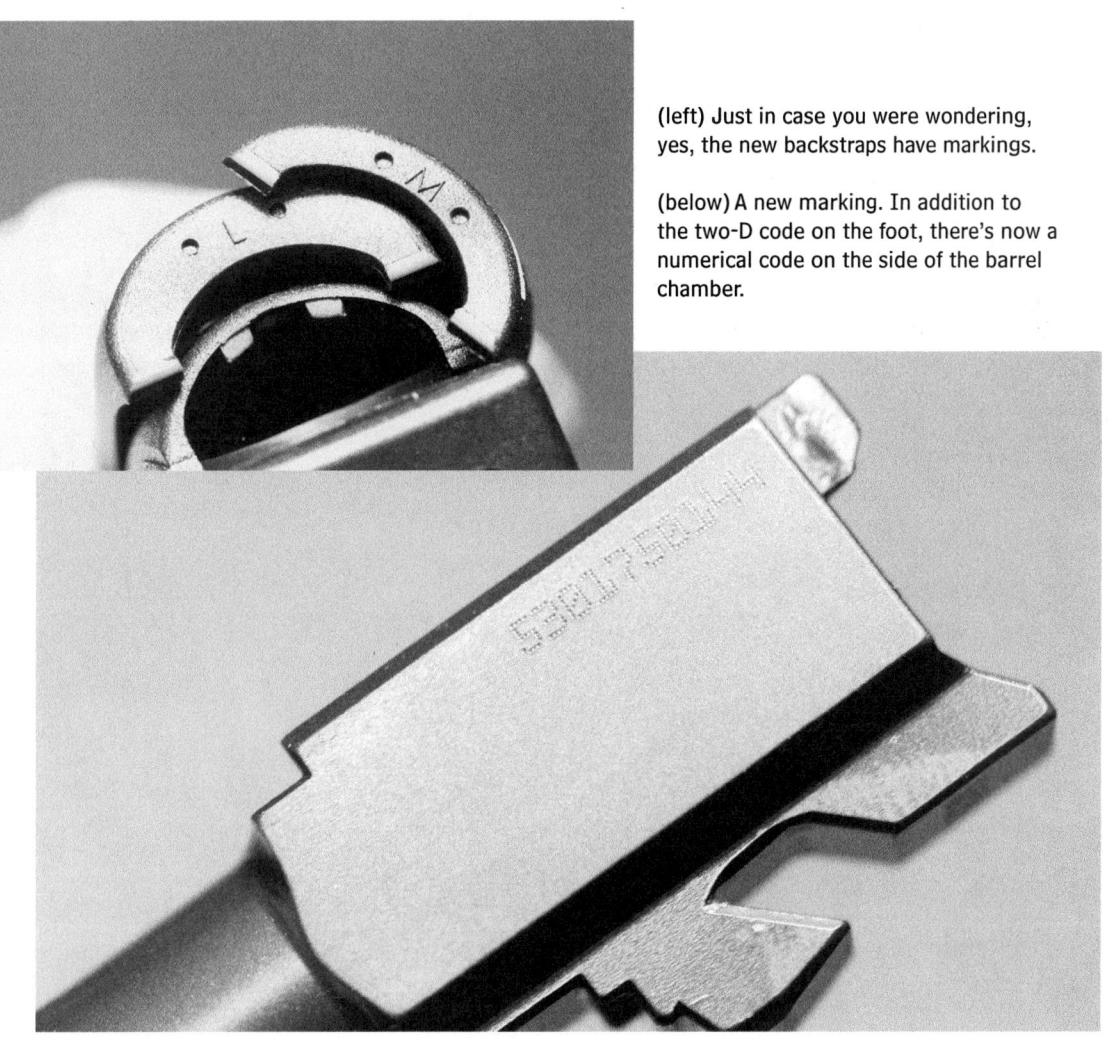

(left) Just in case you were wondering, yes, the new backstraps have markings.

(below) A new marking. In addition to the two-D code on the foot, there's now a numerical code on the side of the barrel chamber.

There are reasons you see European firearms with multiple serial number markings. Part of it is Old World craftsmanship and its attention to detail. But, in some places, a law requiring a serial number on the receiver didn't replace a law requiring a serial number on the receiver—it *added* to it. So, when Glock made its products, it complied with *all* the laws and regulations in force at the time and all it could anticipate.

Then we Americans stuck in our oar.

(above) Glock set aside some prefix blocks for special uses. The cutaways get "J" prefixes. Here is a current-production Glock cutaway.

(right) A very interesting Glock in the collection of a European museum. The frame has the serial number stamped in plastic. There is no metal plate underneath the dust cover—I looked.

88 | WHAT'S IN A NUMBER?

matter what the law called for in a country, a G17 would pass muster.

Then we Americans stuck in our oar. The BATFE adamantly refused to allow importation of a firearm that had its serial number stamped in plastic. Nosirree. U.S. law requires a serial-numbered *frame*, the number stamped or etched into the metal of the receiver. All those other numbers are cute, but they don't meet the law. And plastic? You've got to be kidding. So Glock had to go back and make changes to an already perfect design.

Having made the transition to a metal insert into the frame, I can't help but conclude that Glock, in a correct engineering, production, and regulatory decision, went with the metal insert for all future production. I'll have to query my sources on the continent to see if stamped-in-polymer Glocks are showing up in museums over there. A century from now, Glock collectors are going to have a field day. If they aren't already.

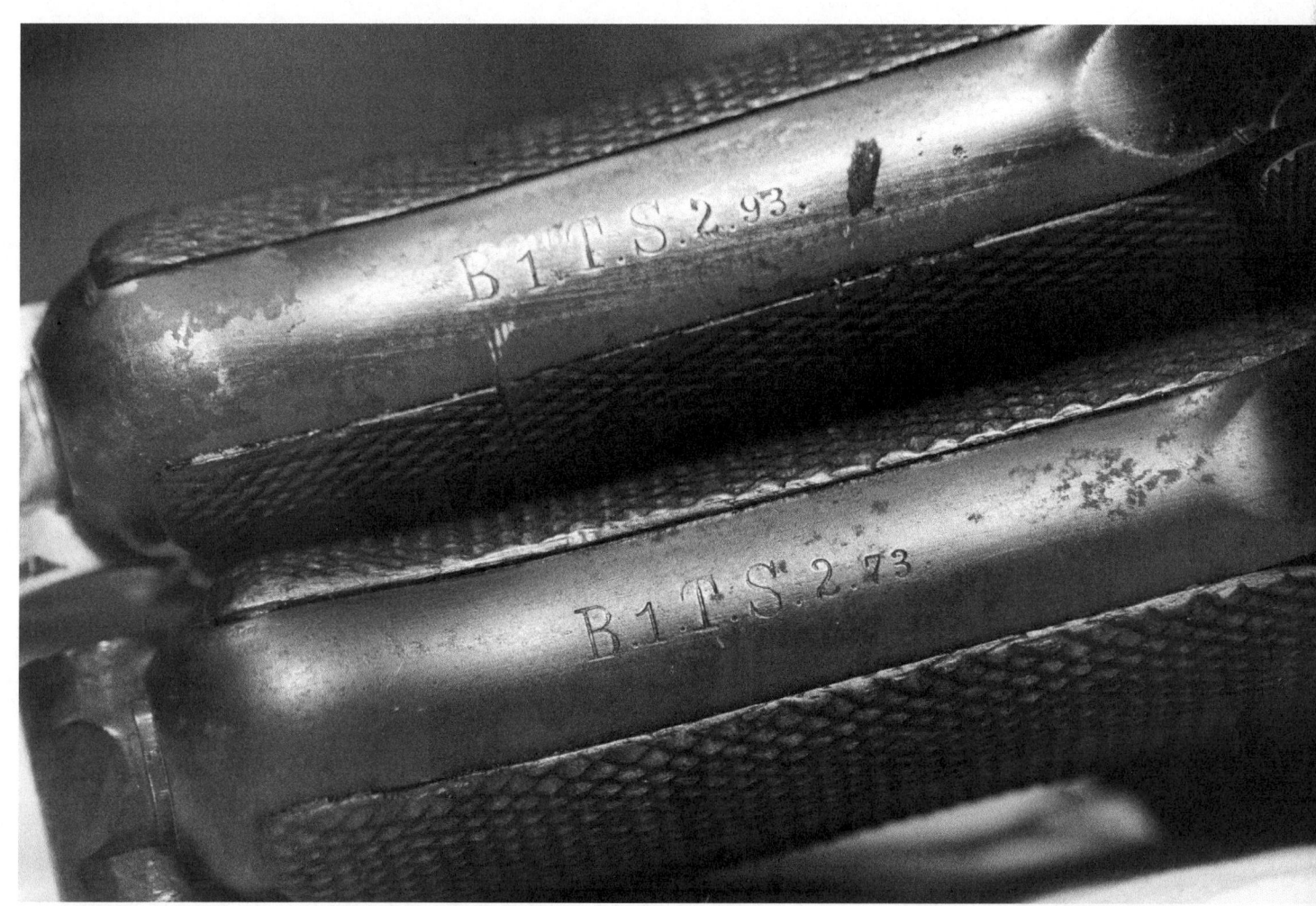

A pair of Lugers, made in 1911. Their factory serial numbers are less than 20 digits apart. The German Army marked them according to the unit they were issued to, and there they got numbers 20 guns apart. Today, they reside in the same drawer, down in the vaults.

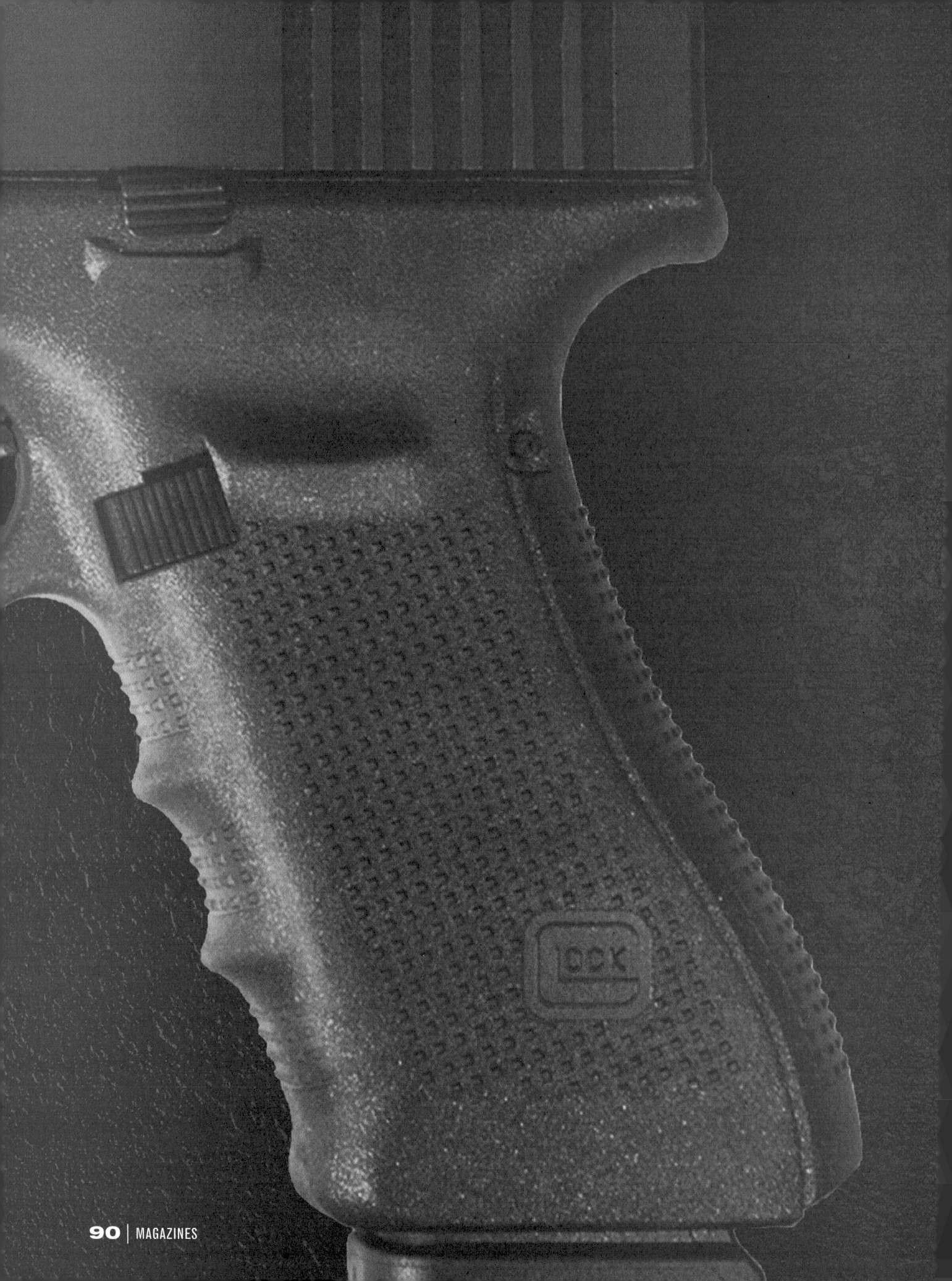

CHAPTER

Magazines

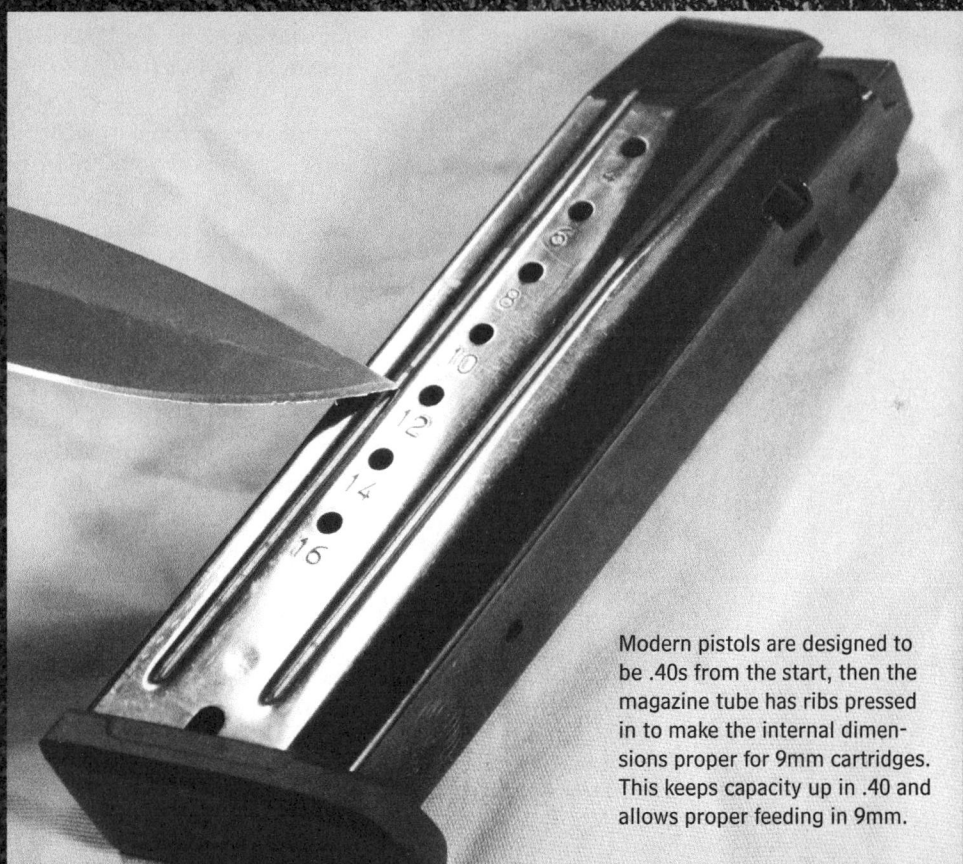

Modern pistols are designed to be .40s from the start, then the magazine tube has ribs pressed in to make the internal dimensions proper for 9mm cartridges. This keeps capacity up in .40 and allows proper feeding in 9mm.

Time to talk mags. If you'll reference the *Gun Digest Book of the Glock Volumes 1 and 2* (you do have them in your library, don't you?), I told the tales of going through a several different Glock armorers course. Basically, these classes were a few hours of learning how to wrestle all the parts off a Glock and put them back, which doesn't fill the eight-hour day set aside for the task.

The Browning Hi-Power magazine, on the right, was designed in the mid-1920s. It holds 13 rounds. By 1980, it was possible to make the same magazine (more or less) hold 17, but notice the G17 magazine is a tad longer. That picks up a round or two from the BHP.

At the end of the first class I attended, the instructors offered us Glocks, mags, and other products at a discount. How much for the magazines? A buck and a half each, a limit of four, *thankyouverymuch.* Even Glock recognized that this was a smokin' hot deal and didn't want us to flood its market with magazines we had purchased at $1.50 each. Seriously, I and everyone else in the class would have cleaned out our bank accounts to buy mags at that price, and that was before the Assault Weapons Ban of 1994.

Let's do a little daydreaming and speculation, shall we? Let's take, just as a starting point, that $1.50 each was the real, actual cost to Glock to produce those magazines. Intriguing, no? Now, with the current retail on Glock magazines at $22 each*, let's crank the math back. If the retailer has a 30-percent markup (and many would kill to have that much margin), they cost the retailer $15.40 each. If the distributor marked them up 30 percent (and, again, kill for that margin), then they paid $10.78 each for them. If it cost Glock $1.50 each, they are making $9.28 for each one of those little plastic rectangular ammo-holding devices.

Now, let's consider details of manufacturing and accountancy. You need a supply of polymer, in this case a basic nylon with some fiberglass tossed in for strength. It typically comes as pellets in barrels of 30, 40, or 50 gallons each (unless your production volume is so great you get it in bulk tanker-truck trailers), and you buy it by weight, with shipping added. You also buy spring steel, which comes in coils. Each coil is three or four feet across, and you buy it either by weight or length.

To put it all together, you have machines that bend the spring steel and cut each to length. Cost for a spring-bending machine varies, depending on how complex the task and how much you wish to produce. Let's budget $100,000 for this machine.

Next, you need sheet steel, the interior stiffening device of the magazine, machines to cut out the blanks, and then other machines to bend them to shape. The steel comes in coils, no wider than you need, and the machine feeds them in and chops and bends. Stamping and bending is old technology and the machines are easy to find, so let's budget only $50,000 for this.

Glock also needs an injection-molding machine, one designed to handle nylon. It can be had with feed hoppers and output conveyors, but those are often custom-built. Since we want a high-volume of output, $500,000 for this. The machine needs a mould, a form into which the melted plastic is squirted. Moulds start at $10,000, and the more complex they are and the faster the machine can produce parts, the more they cost. Let's go high and budget $50,000 for this, and since we don't want any production slowdowns, we'll get two.

Here's the problem competitors to Glock had, when the .40 was introduced. The internal dimensions of the 9mm-intended tube create inefficient stacking with .40 and, thus, decrease capacity.

Early machines held one and fed one, but today you can buy gang machines that take several to many moulds, spitting out product at a dizzying rate. You also need moulds for the follower and the baseplate, as well as the internal retainer. It takes a crew to work this, but, in the scheme of things, that cost just isn't that great, so let's just ignore labor costs for the moment.

With the machine set up, plugged in, and warmed up, you press the button. A minute later, the shell of a magazine drops out. What did that magazine cost you?

Conceptually, it cost you the price of the nylon, a couple of cents worth, and the cost of the encapsulated steel, a few more cents. Your company CPA goes pale at the sound of that and hurriedly tells you that it cost you a million dollars. *What?*

He tells you the honest truth: that first magazine shell costs a million because, in order to make it, you, the owner, had to buy machines, both mould and bending, materials, building, power, get it all installed, set up, and running, and had thus spent a cool million before you produced anything.

Once the second magazine shell drops out, the two of them cost a half-million dol-

The newest Glock magazines are backwards-compatible, with no less than three locking slots.

lars each. And so on. Now the intricacies of depreciation, the tax code, and accounting methodology all transpire to make the "cost" of a magazine an ever-changing number. Make a million magazines a year, and your capital investment cost for each is a buck. However, by then you have a year's worth of employee costs, taxes, electricity, materials, advertising, shipping, packaging, etc. It's easy to see that an efficient production line can make a big difference on the bottom line.

As an aside, let's consider the cost of a Glock receiver. The moulds/fixtures will be a lot more complex. However, we have the same economy of scale entering into it. The bottom line is that the receiver rails are stamped and then heat-treated, and the receiver takes that, the serial number plate, and a few pennies worth of nylon pellets and out pops a receiver. Each box with a Glock and a couple magazines, owners manual, and lock in it really is not an expensive thing to make. At a production cost of maybe $100, the retail price of your G17 at $539 is like dying and going to heaven, as far as Glock's finance guys are concerned. No wonder it can afford to swap parts willy-nilly at GSSF matches. The cost is nothing and the resulting customer loyalty is immense, and for this I have nothing but admiration for the lot of them. Gaston Glock conceived a product that is/was inexpensive to manufacture, priced it competitively, and started raking in the loot. You can't get much more American than that.

(above) Smaller than a big-bore snubby revolver and holding more rounds, Glock has made a niche for itself with its compact models. Here's a G27 magazine. The larger G22 magazines will also fit and work in this gun, giving you 15 on the reload.

(right) The Assault Weapons Ban of 1994, thankfully sunset for the time being, gave us the egregious 10-shot magazines. Still, they work, are indestructible, and are relatively inexpensive.

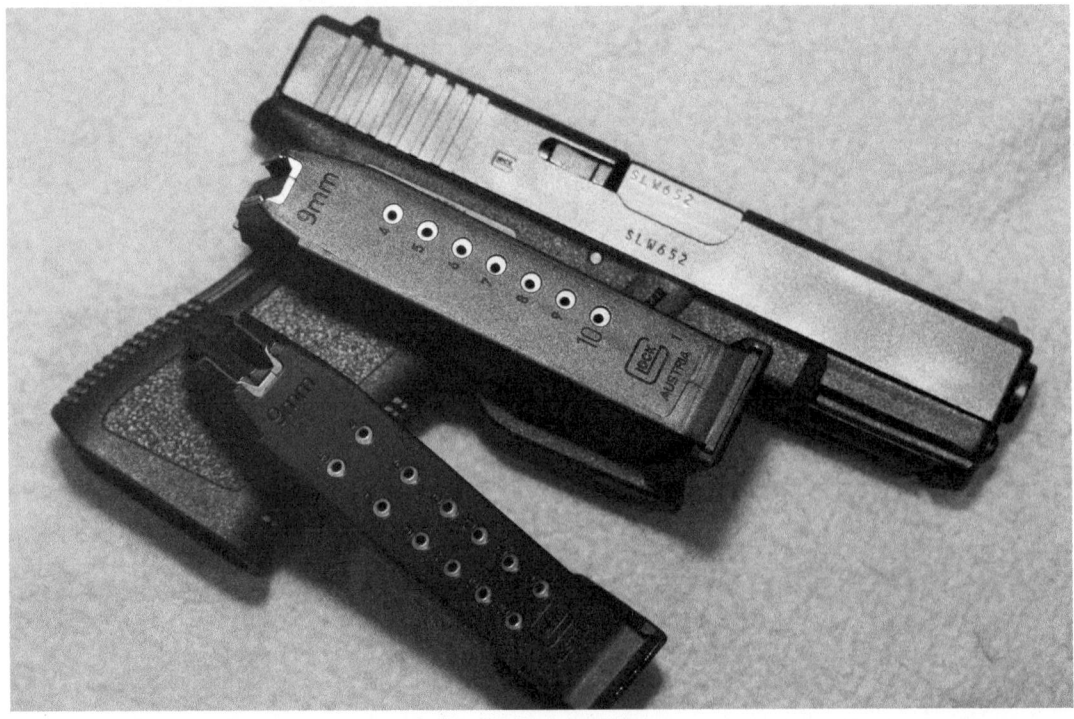

Back to magazines. In the years since their changeover, you still cannot get anyone at Glock to call the magazines "drop-free." They are either "fully metal lined" or they are not. One thing to be aware of is that the proliferation of Glock models and calibers have produced a situation in which you have to be diligent.

The standard length, original dimension magazine in your hands? It can be 9mm, .357 SIG, .40, or .45 GAP. In the case of .357 SIG and .40 S&W, the same magazine could work in either. Still, if your magazine is one of the ones that has not been upgraded since the light-on-a-rail situation, it may not function reliably. In that instance, you'll need a magazine spring of a certain length and a follower with a certain number on it. Which ones? It's quite possible that, in the time it takes this chapter to get from me to the publisher, it will have changed. So, take it to a GSSF match and let the armorer sort it out.

The big problem with Glock magazines is that they were not designed to fall free. In fact, they were designed to not fall out at all, being instead crafted to be pulled out with the free hand when they had to be replaced.

If you care, your magazine followers are marked as to generation and iteration. If yours work fine, don't worry. But a Glock armorer will upgrade that at a GSSF match for free, if you go.

MAGAZINES | 95

(above) Most models come with three magazines, but I have seen some with only two. If you are worried, check with Glock.

(right) With the .45 GAP, Glock found itself in the same position, *vis-à-vis* magazine capacity, that its competitors had been in with the .40, back in 1990. That problem is that Glock can't get enough of this round in the gun to make it worthwhile.

As recounted elsewhere, the unfortunate episode of the nationally ranked competitor who had inadvertently loaded the proper magazines with the improper ammo can happen to you if you aren't careful. While the tubes themselves and most of the internals haven't changed all that much (the various iterations of numbered followers in a given caliber are more for the statistically rare problems, rather than to increase all the magazines), what we put on them has. Back in the early days, we were all so enamored of high capacity that there was no such thing as too much. The Glock plus-two baseplates were topped by non-Glock and durable plus-two, plus-four, and even plus-eight baseplates. Well, now that we're all carrying concealed every day, a plus-eight baseplate or other magazine extension isn't such a hot setup. Oh, we all still crave them, and Robin Taylor of Taylor Freelance still makes them and sells them by the cartload. But now, the hot setup is tactical.

The big problem with Glock magazines is that they were not designed to fall free. In fact, they were designed to not fall out at all, being instead crafted to be pulled out with the free hand, when they had to be replaced. This is a very European approach, where the "abuse" of magazines fulfilling their Newtonian destiny is viewed as a low-class exercise in small arms damage. They consider it bad form, whereas we American prefer to be more vigorous when it comes to

(above) Unfortunately, this design fell **a bit short**. Yes, it's a single-**stack**, but an ultra-**compact one** that is a beast **to shoot**.

(left) If you **want more** rounds in a **magazine or** a better grip, **Pearce can** help you out.

MAGAZINES | **97**

Everything old is new again. The .455 Webley was new in 1887. The .45 ACP was new in 1911. And the .45 GAP does what they do, starting in 2004.

matters of self-defense. Aside from differences in viewpoints about drop-free or pull-out magazine and their subsequent abuse or not, Europeans also tend to view their guns in terms of assuming that all emergencies would permit the use of both hands. Americans, of course, consider that the reason you could be using a handgun at all might be because you have been shot off of your main gun, or that and only one hand/arm physically works.

Anyway, the original Glock magazines wouldn't fall out. The replacements/newer-gen magazines should, but sometimes don't. In any emergency, if you need more ammo, you need it *right now*, and faster *is* better. Glock isn't the only manufacture of guns that don't have drop-free magazines, and, so, many defensive instructors teach "magazine ripping," which is to simply assume the magazine will not fall out regardless its design so, as you press the mag button with one hand, the other, coming off the grips, slides down and rips the magazine out. On a Glock, this is somewhat complicated by the baseplate not being significantly larger than the bottom of the frame. Replacement baseplates give mag-rippers a good grip and so you can perfect this tactic with their addition.

Opportunity Lost

Let's all agree: polymer is great. But even great things have limitations. The idea of a non-rusting magazine is intriguing, but not a world-stopper. Magazines rust, so what? Magazines are practically disposable and certainly cheap enough to replace if they rust. Magazines can be damaged, but, again, see the above. Harder steel rusts more slowly than softer steel and, if you are of a mind, you can plate/bond a non-rust finish to magazine tubes. Magazines have improved through the decades. What was acceptable for magazines back when IPSC was new has not been acceptable for a long time. People expect magazines to be reliable and also expect them not to cost an arm and a leg.

In the scheme of things, magazines are cheap. Well, there have been exceptions. If you'll permit a slight divergence, those of you who are familiar with AR-15s will recognize the H&K high-reliability magazines. They came about when H&K was asked to improve the miserably marginal SA-80 Enfield the British Army was saddled with. It did so (some say they still fell short, but I've never used one in a harsh environment, so I can't say), and part of that was improved magazines. Those magazines also worked in AR-15s. The

> One advantage Glock had by going all polymer was utterly unintentional and could not have been known in 1980: it was the .40 S&W cartridge.

While a standard G22 magazine would be fine, for serious competition you need a +4 or larger extension. In an Open gun such as this, a +8 extension would be cool, but you'd be better off starting with a 9mm and not a .40.

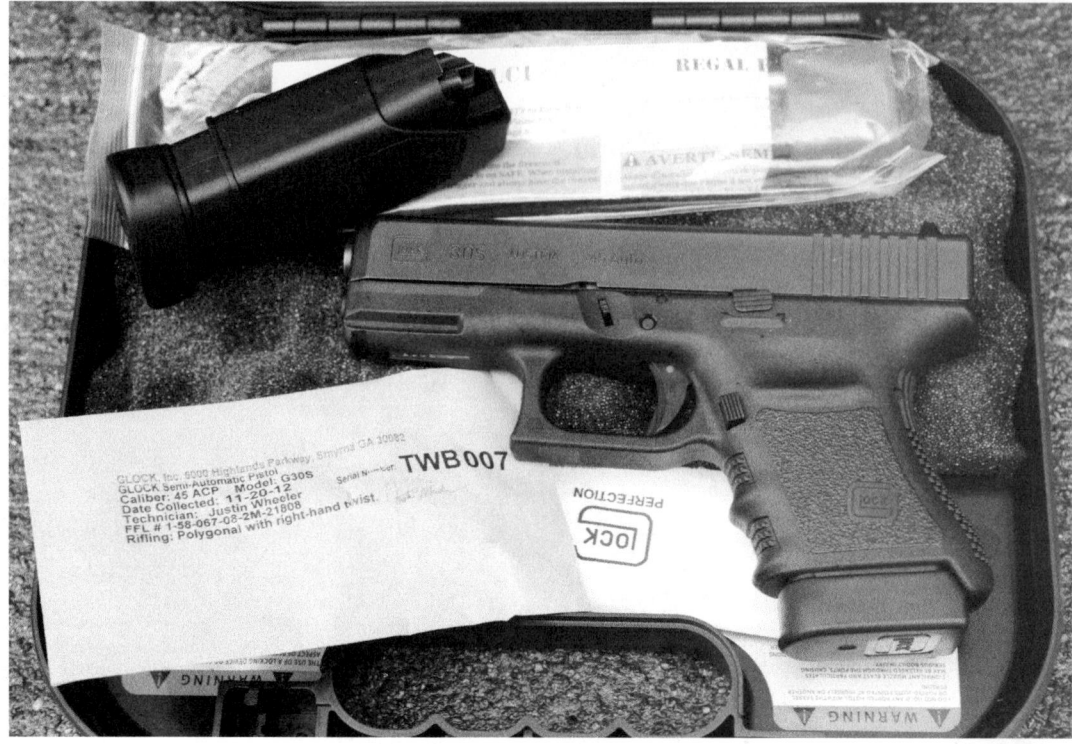

Interesting. A G30S arrived here with but a pair of magazines, and direct from Glock, so no question about the proper inventory.

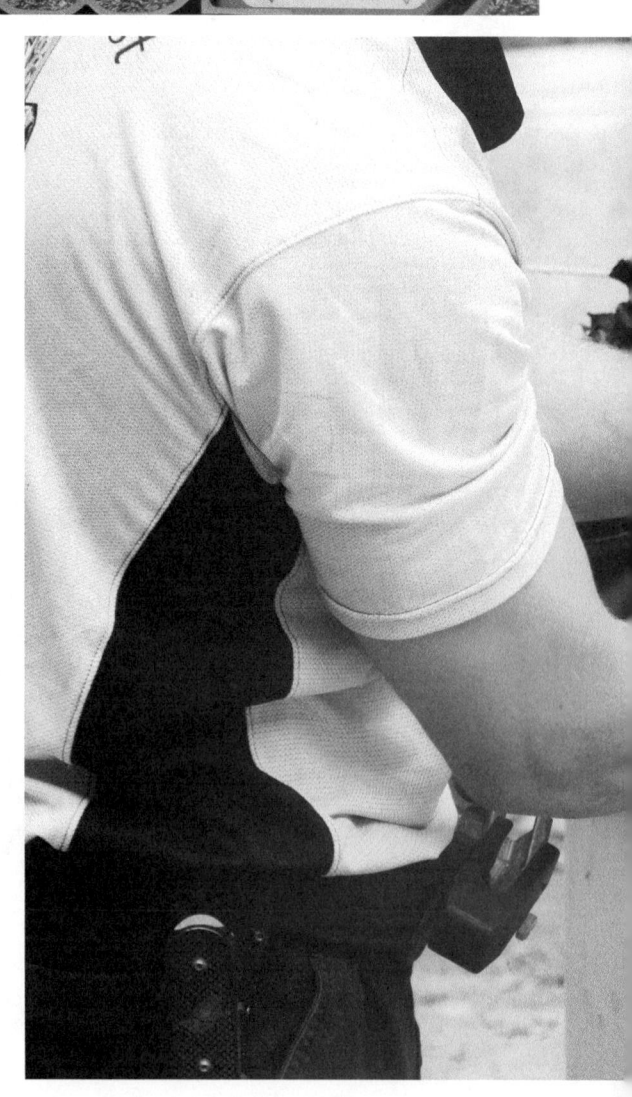

In the scheme of things, magazines are cheap. Well, there have been exceptions. Remember the H&K magazines that worked in AR-15s? Billed as "high-reliability" mags, people got interested in them. When the first mags appeared, they were $45 to $50 each. Ouch. Even worse, they were heavy and, after years of use, they weren't found to be any better than any other mags out there.

H&K reputation was enough to get people interested, the term "high reliability" even more so. When those mags first appeared, they were going for $45 to $50 each. Ouch. In a world where USGI magazines could be had for $15 each, less if you bought in bulk, $45 was outrageous. And they were heavy. After a few years of use, they were found out not be any better than others and so lost their luster. I realized they had hit their "expiration date" when, at an LEO patrol rifle class, I was asked about them. I gave a brief summary of the above and said, "They work. If you have them, use them. If you can't stand the weight, ditch them and get something lighter." The next day, an officer handed me a half-dozen of them. "Here you go, too heavy for me, you can have them." Wow, fallen from grace so fast.

Glock magazines are not appreciably heavier than all-steel magazines in the same application. Yet Glock magazines, starting with the G17, while having interesting technology, are just a tad portly. What do I mean by that? Let's drag out Glock mags, comparison magazines, and the dial calipers.

A double-stack magazine has to stagger the rounds inside at just the right angles or they won't feed. The gap is quite narrow. If you make the interior too wide, they rattle around and won't stay put. Too narrow, and the mag will hold less than it can. So, where is Glock in this? To start, we'll take a look at the Browning Hi-Power, the first hi-cap 9mm pistol. (Fair warning, we're going to be doing a lot of calculating here and throwing numbers around with wild abandon. So stick with it.)

Internally, the BHP magazine is 0.7335-inch wide. This allows the 9mm to stack properly, while keeping the interior as wide as possible. The BHP magazine holds 13 rounds, a big step back from the G17, but there are two reasons for that. One is length. The BHP magazine is 4.28 inches long, while the G17 magazine is 4.75 inches along the same span. The half-inch

If you plan to shoot in a GSSF match, be a sport and bring enough magazines. Nothing annoys other shooters more than watching you hurriedly thumbing more rounds into your magazines while they wait their turn to shoot.

MAGAZINES | **101**

A big pouch (right) for a big magazine (below). This is the 100-round Beta for Glocks. Talk about some fun.

difference easily makes up two rounds (remember, we aren't stacking the 9mms vertically, but rather staggered). Then there's the taper. As the first hi-cap magazine in a pistol, the inventors had to figure it out from scratch. John Moses Browning started the design, but Deuidonné Saive finished it. Why did he use a taper that is more gradual and curved than that of later pistols? I don't know, and we'd have to hold a séance to find out (he died in 1973), but my guess is simply that it worked.

Internally, the Glock magazine is 0.747-inch wide, a difference amounting to 0.0135-inch, hardly enough to matter. That's the thickness of a couple sheets of paper. Externally, it can matter. The BHP magazine, made of stamped steel, welded, heat-treated, and pretty darned tough, is 0.801-inch. The G17 magazine (I have a second-gen, pre-ban to try, it was the easiest to wrestle apart), measures 0.890-inch. Wow, for an extra 0.0135-inch internally, Glock charges us an extra 0.090-inch externally. That may not

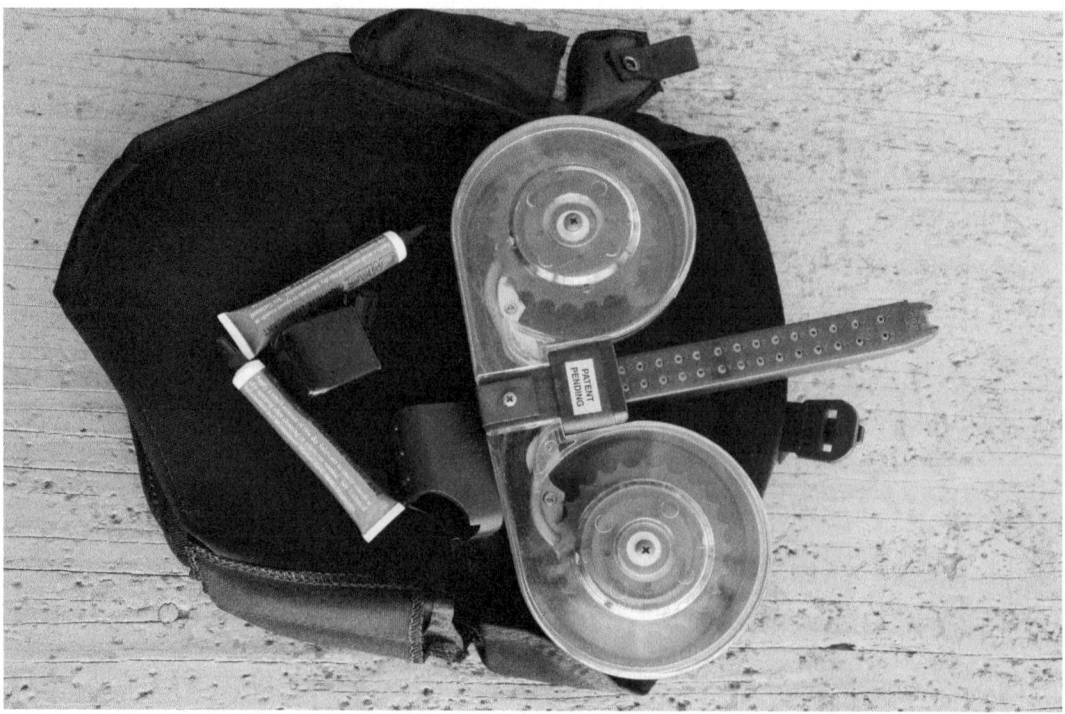

102 | MAGAZINES

seem like a lot, but a couple things to consider.

First, if Gaston Glock had used a steel magazine, back in 1980, he could have taken 0.090-inch off the width of the G17 frame (not that it is overly large). On the other hand, if he had done that, Gaston would have had to give up several things. One was the non-drop-free design. Again, not that anyone at Glock will use these words, but a source of pride in the original design was that the magazines *didn't* drop out. Second, a steel magazine would also have meant not having the complicated Glock magazine assembly system. I'm a big guy, and I have reasonable hand strength from years of shooting, gunsmithing, and hard work. But, when it comes time to disassemble a Glock magazine, even I go in search of pliers. I wondered for a moment how Glock expected troops in the field to disassemble magazines, but then I realized that he probably didn't: soldiers do not disassemble magazines. Armorers back in the barracks/*kaserne* do that.

One advantage Glock gained by going all polymer was utterly unintentional and could not have been known in 1980: the .40 S&W cartridge.

Before 1990, 9mm magazines were designed for 9mm and nothing else. At the dawn of the .40 S&W, all pistols were made as 9mms, with magazines adapted for .40-caliber. That means they all had that .733- to .747-inch internal dimension, despite it being a bit cramped for .40. Designers have since changed their approach. Now all hi-cap pistols are designed as .40s, the magazine tubes proportioned appropriately, and the tubes are modified to accept 9mm.

Let's take a Ruger SR9 as an example. It was designed from the start to be a .40. While the initial offering was a 9mm, that was as much an engineering decision as one of marketing. Making it work as a 9mm took a lot less work and testing, tuning, and adjustment than making it work as a .40. The tube of the SR9 magazine (and the SR40) is 0.854-inch wide externally. Internally, the .40 magazine tube is 0.792-inch, the appropriate dimension to double-stack .40 S&W cartridges.

Internally, the Glock magazine is 0.747-inch wide, a difference over that of the Browning's Hi-Power's that amounts to 0.0135-inch, hardly enough to matter. That's the thickness of a couple sheets of paper. Externally, it can matter. The BHP magazine, made of stamped steel, welded, heat-treated, and pretty darned tough, is 0.801-inch. The G17 magazine measures 0.890-inch, a measurement that results in a larger frame for the Glock.

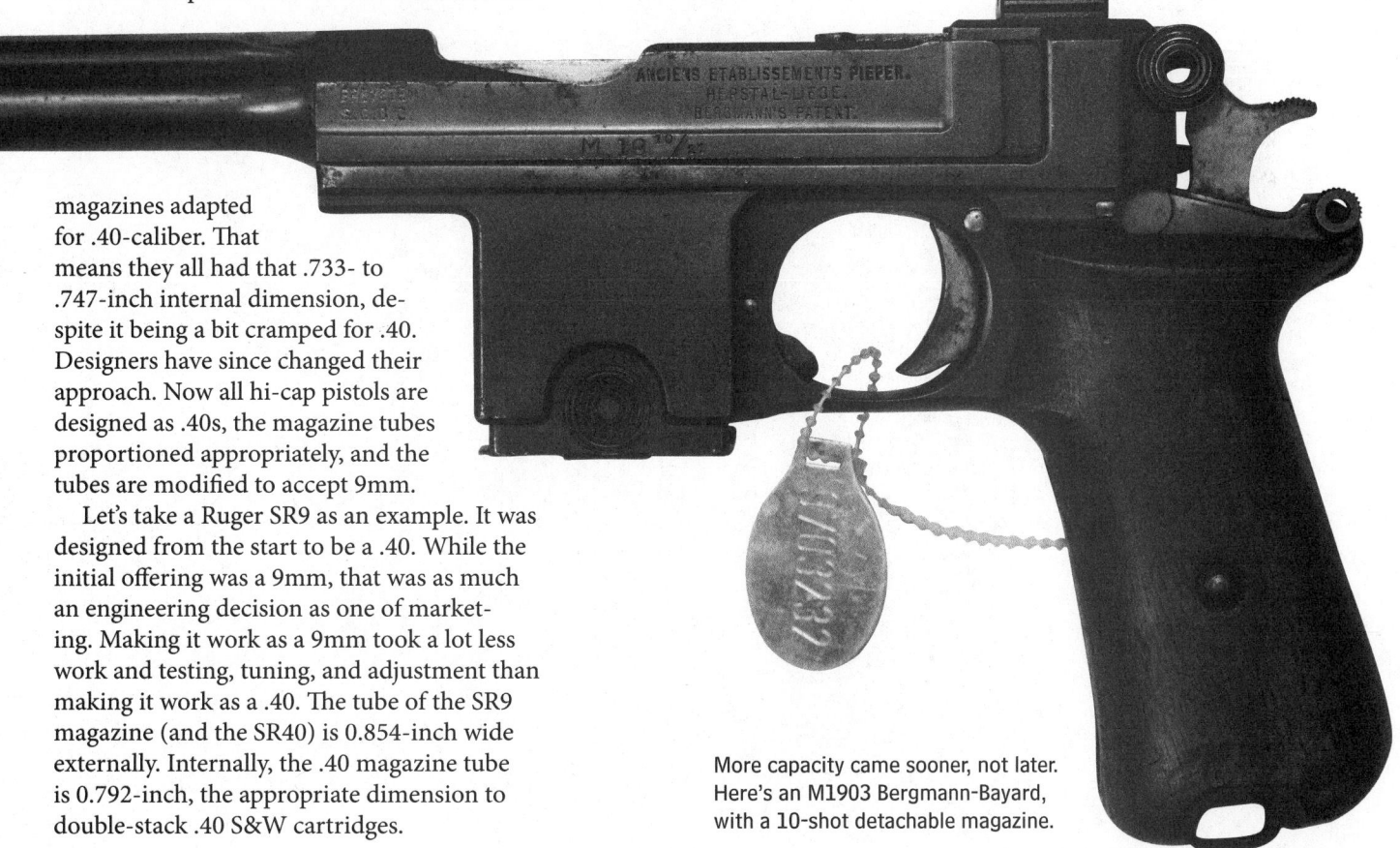

More capacity came sooner, not later. Here's an M1903 Bergmann-Bayard, with a 10-shot detachable magazine.

The hardest part about shooting a Lone Wolf carbine with a Beta mag in it is aiming correctly while giggling.

A Bergmann 1910, with 10-shot double-stack magazine.

To make the tube work properly for 9mm, Ruger took the basic stamping and pressed ribs into it. Also known in the metal-working trade as flutes, spines, grooves, and stiffeners, they act to restrict the internal dimension of the tube and, in essence, make it appropriately small for a 9mm cartridge stack. Across the flutes, the tube is 0.745-inch wide. So, externally, the 9mm and .40 tubes are the same, but the internal difference accounts for the differing case diameter. (The feed lips, of course, are different, but you can't see that just by eyeballing it.)

The most extreme instance of this design comes to us from STI, the hi-cap 1911 maker, though before it was Para Ordnance (now under the Freedom Group banner) and its hi-cap 1911 in .45 ACP. Para started in the mid-1980s, and I ran across its booth at the SHOT show in 1988. At that time, IPSC was of two minds—should we go .38 Super or stay .45 ACP? The competitors wanted .38 Super, the carry-gun guys wanted .45. Para made .45s.

By 1993, when the first Chip McCormick frames came out (to morph into the STI line, among others), the competition world had won, and IPSC guns were to be .38 Super. Recognizing this, (and to risk confusion), Caspian Arms came out with a hi-cap frame with a magazine proportioned for .38 Super only. Chip and his successors used .45-proportioned magazines, fluting the tubes to restrict the interior dimensions to other calibers.

By then, the .40 was becoming a viable choice. The real gorilla in the room was the Assault Weapons Ban of 1994, which caused Caspian to quit the hi-cap market and focus on its core business of 1911 frames, slides, and parts, and caused a frenzy of activity in building, tuning, and increasing the capacity of hi-cap magazines.

Back to Glock. In 1990, when the .40 S&W was unveiled, everyone was using 9mm tubes. Glock had an advantage, in that the G17 magazine tube had enough extra thickness that Glock could make them into .40 magazines, keep the external dimension, and increase internal width, thereby gaining capacity. I disassembled a second-gen .40 magazine (which, I have to note, was able to be disassembled by hand, unlike the 9mm), and measured it.

Externally it came in at .900-inch, a small increase over the 9mm tube. Internally, it measures .800-inch again, close enough to the other tube.

In 1990, Glock was able to make its magazine tubes for .40s thinner walled (different thickness steel plates, different composition polymer, just thinner, who knows), and gain capacity. The longer tubes didn't hurt, but, by comparison, a G22, in 1991, held 15 rounds. A S&W Model 4006 held 11. If you are contemplating increasing your caliber, going from a 17-shot pistol to a 15-shot pistol is a small price to pay to gain nearly twice the bullet weight and nearly a third-again frontal area. But to give up 15 or 17 rounds to then have 11? That was a deal breaker. Smith & Wesson could not increase the width of its 59-series pistols magazine tubes to .40, keep commonality with the 9mm models, and retain the parts interchangeability. Glock could. So that lucky decision and the stubbornness to stick with it paid off for Glock in spades, starting in 1990.

The .45 GAP Dilemma

Alas, Glock's luck ran out in 2004, with the announcement of the .45 GAP. I shot one at the big industry shindig, the SHOT show, in January 2004, in Las Vegas. I'll say that a compact pistol, the same size as a G17/22 but chambered in .45, has a lot of appeal. And making a .45 cartridge that is the same (pretty much) overall length at a 9mm/.40 is a technology feat not to be dismissed. But capacity?

Stuck with the same interior dimensions for a .40 magazine, Glock found it could not stuff more than 10 rounds into the pistol. So

In an interesting twist in the world of magazines, the M1903, while a double-stack, is single-line feed.

When it comes to keeping a pistol running, there is nothing like cleanliness. Powder residue, lint, dust, dirt, and lube that found their way inside, all act to gunk up a magazine and keep it from working. Actually, what all the stuff does is bind the rounds that are in the magazine. The magazine cleaning and disassembly tool from GTul is an essential part of any Glock owner's gear.

Glock was, in essence, right where S&W (and everyone else) had found themselves, back in 1990, with the .40 S&W. That has been a real deal breaker. My friends at Double Action indoor range report that, despite having had a G37 in the rental counter for several years now, it probably has less than a thousand rounds through it. (The .357 SIGs are also just as underutilized.) Meanwhile, all the other rental Glocks get a thousand rounds a week pumped through them, many a lot more than that.

How'd that happen, and why couldn't Glock solve the problem?

The problem is the interior size not being wide enough, which leads to inefficient stacking. Instead of each round contacting two rounds that also contact each other (in an equilateral triangle), the narrow interior leads to each round contacting the rounds above

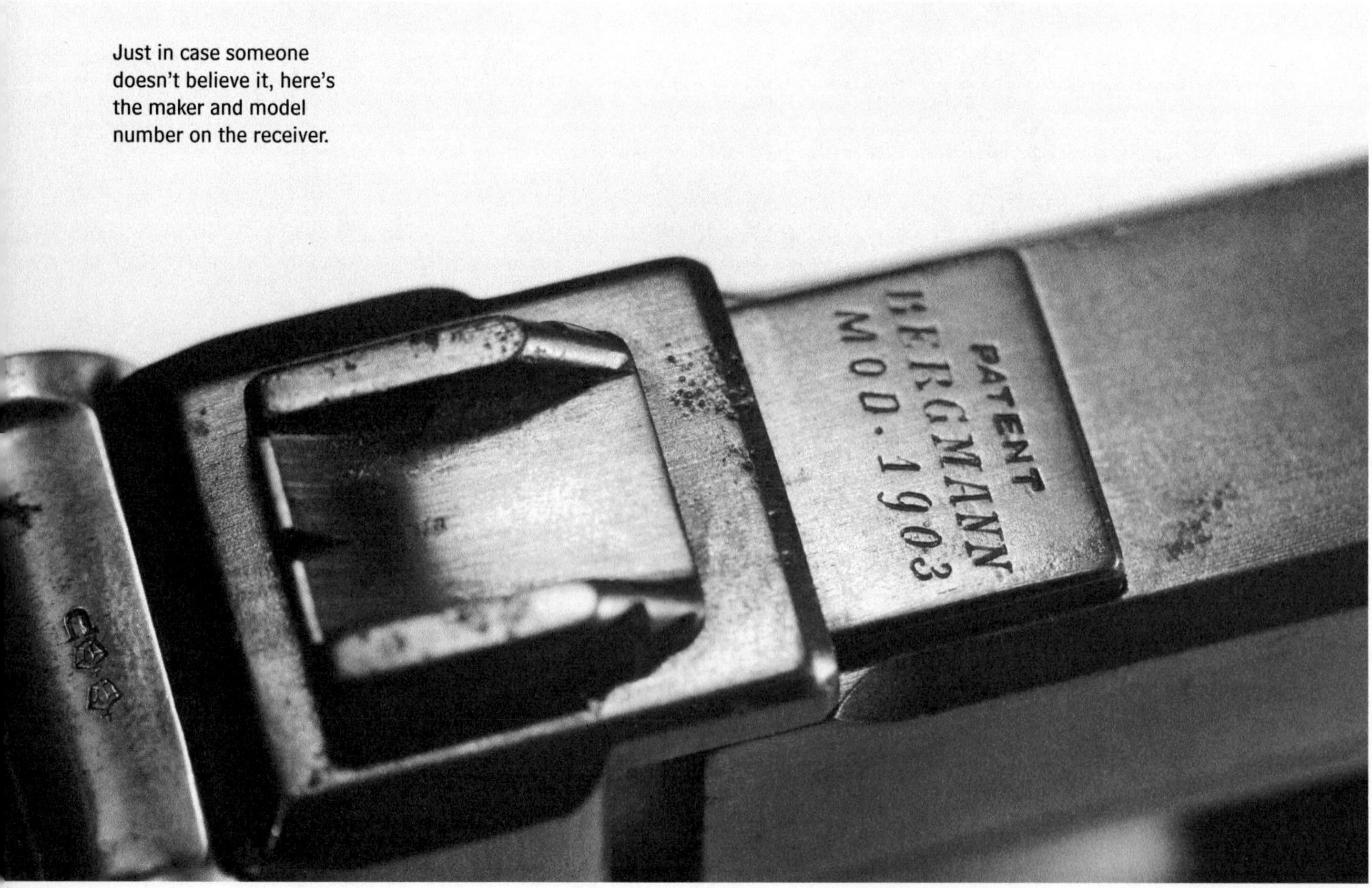

Just in case someone doesn't believe it, here's the maker and model number on the receiver.

Before Bergmann, there was Mauser, a C96, in 7.63 with a 20-round magazine.

and below, but without those top and bottom rounds contacting each other.

Why the lack of room? Basically, Glock had already used up the extra engineering margin in the sidewall thickness of the original frame size magazines. The .45 GAP is (simple arithmetic) 0.045-inch wider than the .40 S&W. To widen the inside of the magazine presents several unappealing solutions.

First, Glock could simply have made it as wide inside as it had to be and lived with the resultant thinner sidewalls. The problem with this approach is that it leaves the company with magazines of un-Glock-like flimsiness.

Second, Glock could have made the magazine solely from steel and gained a bit more efficient stacking and, perhaps, a couple rounds of capacity. But that, too, brings problems. If some Glock mags are steel, why not all? If most Glock magazines are polymer, why would these be steel? Confusing customers does not lead to increased sales. Plus the .45 GAP pistols, if they used steel magazines, would have to have steel magazine catches, just to stand up to use. Again, why steel there and not in others? Also know that, sooner or later (most likely sooner), someone will reassemble their Glock collection so that they end up with a polymer catch with steel magazines and will complain about the wear.

A third correction that was possible? Make the magazines wide enough internally and live with the wider frame. But this solution would be even worse than the others. A wider frame means non-interchangeability with the 9mm, .40, and .357 pistols. Also, it makes the .45 GAP pistols as wide as the G20 and G21, which do not feel the love like the smaller frames sizes do?

In 1990, when the .40 S&W was unveiled, everyone was using 9mm tubes. Glock had an advantage, in that the G17 magazine tube had enough extra thickness that Glock could make them into .40 magazines, keep the external dimensions, and increase internal width, thereby gaining capacity for the fatter new round.

Finally, if you (as a Glock designer) make the .45 GAP pistols wide enough for hi-capacity magazines, but only as short as the .45 GAP allows, you have the oddity of a frame wider than it is long (and a frame that, incidentally, can't be used for any other caliber).

In the end, Glock bit the bullet, accepted the lower capacity, and marketed the .45 GAP for all it was worth. For a while, it looked like it might make it. Other makers that had very compact pistols made prototypes in .45 GAP. I handled and shot some. Alas, the performance was not enough better for the size to make the recoil worth it, and feeding was marginally reliable in those I sampled.

What could Glock have done differently to make the .45 GAP line a success? Pretty much nothing.

Leaving it as a 10-shot frame, the same size as a G17/22, would have doomed it. If Glock had re-proportioned the frame to make it a true hi-cap, it would have made it uncomfortable to handle. On the other hand, if (as more than one person has suggested), Glock had made it a single-stack, it would have been making a new frame, and one for which I surmise everyone would have quickly asked, "When will it be available in .45 ACP?"

Glock had to have been on the horns of dilemma. Keep it in .45 GAP and .45 GAP-proportioned and face the questions every day. Or, make it big enough to be a .45 ACP single-stack, and know that no one would consider buying one in .45 GAP. Thus, the only real solution was to make it as it was and promote the heck out of it.

Magazine Generations

On top of the drop and non-drop magazine generations, we now have the ambi- and non-ambi- generations. The non-ambi- generations are the ones dating before the swappable magazine catches. If you look at a Glock magazine and see the rectangular silver recess on the front, that's an ambidextrous mag. It also has mag catches on both sides, so it works in any and all (in the correct caliber, of course) Glock pistols.

Plenty is Not Enough

Seventeen rounds of 9mm is a lot. A big-stick Glock mag, with a +2 extender, makes for 33 rounds. That would seem to be more than enough, and yet shooters want more. Enter The Beta Company.

The Beta Company folks went to the drawing board and came up with the Glock magazine to make all other Glock magazines jealous: the Glock C-Mag. While it had previously offered 9mm magazines for the Colt AR in 9mm, the H&K MP5, and the Uzi, those are all carbine/SMGs, so the Glock C-Mag is the first for a handgun. (Yes, a lot of H&K "MP5" firearms are really handguns by definition and the Micro Uzi is a handgun, but c'mon. They are stock-less carbines with short barrels. The Glock is a handgun.)

The Glock C-Mag comes with its own pouch, loading assist device, graphite lube, and owner's manual. Loading is simple, if long-lasting. You use the loading assist tool to press the top round down, slide the next one in over it, and repeat. *Repeat 99 times.*

I took the Glock C-Mag and used it both in the Lone Wolf carbine and in my trusty G17. It worked like a charm in that it fed reliably. What it also did was add the bulk and weight of 100 rounds of 9mm ammo to the setup.

Let's be clear on this. One hundred rounds of 9mm and the housing to contain them takes up space and weighs a lot. You will not be carrying this in a holster. You may not even want to have it in a Glock-based carbine, at least not until you need or want to use it, but, if you want to have lots of bullets, this is the thing.

One very specialized application comes to mind. I have a few friends and acquaintances who have spent time in the dustier parts of the world. Those who could get away with it would, when driving, have a 75-round drum inserted in an AK, either 7.62 or 5.45. If they needed to break contact or keep would-be ambushers busy for a bit, they had 75 rounds in a single burst to start the party. Once that was done, they could drop it and get on with the task at hand. Well, a G18 with a C-Mag could serve the same purpose.

It takes a good bit of hand and arm strength to hold up and shoot a whole magazine of 100 rounds. But *doggone* it was fun! Yes, the loading gets to be a real chore. It isn't that you need a mallet to get the last 10/20/50 rounds in or anything, it's just that it takes a whole lot longer to load up than it does to empty. I'm certain there's a metaphor in there for modern life and all, but, at the moment, it escapes me.

Do You Have Enough of Them?

What with the political winds being what they are, the question is asked, "Do I have enough?" Also, "How can I make sure my mags will be kosher in any coming magazine ban?"

The answers, in order, are first, there are never enough, and second, there is no way of knowing.

In a perfectly prepared world, we'd lay in a supply of magazines that would last as long as we needed and until we could get more. Were I headed to a faraway place and had to provide my own gear, I'd calculate it as follows.

The max load would be in an overt mode, where I'd have a pair of Glocks, one on the belt and one on the vest, same caliber, same model. The belt holster would also have magazine pouches, either on the holster or the same belt. That's three to five magazines, depending on whether I have two or four reloads. The vest gun would have another magazine in it and four reloads. So that's eight to 10 magazines.

I would look at it as three sets of mags. I would have the ones on my gear and I'd have the ones that were spares and training/practice mags. Then I'd also have a set, sealed, in my locker at the base, station, wherever. Let's say, for instance, I had to participate in an unannounced water landing and had to ditch everything. I'd be out one-third of my supply. I'd still have another basic load and practice/training mags. Now this is predicated on a year-long contract someplace where getting extras might not be assured. If I could be certain of getting more when needed, I might save the expense, weight, and packing volume for something else.

Do you need 30 Glock magazines for your use? Probably not. A half-dozen would likely do.

What can you do to ensure your magazines will "survive" a future hi-cap magazine ban? Don't vote for people who will ban them and assist those who oppose them. There is no way to predict what would come out of a conference committee concerning a future hi-cap ban. There is no way to predict *anything*, when the two side of Congress get together. The conference committee (the meeting of the House and Senate to hash out the details of competing, passed legislation), can produce anything, even if it wasn't in the original bills passed in either House or Senate. So stop worrying about your magazines as objects and work on the political part of it. The best way to ensure a future bill does not ban your magazines is to see that such a bill never passes.

Magazine Maintenance

A short word here. When it comes to keeping a pistol running, there is nothing like cleanliness. Powder residue, lint, dust, dirt, and lube that find their way inside act to gunk up a magazine and keep it from working. Actually, what all that stuff does is bind the rounds that are in the magazine. The magazine cleaning and disassembly tool from GTul is an essential part of any Glock owner's gear. If your range, like mine, has sand as the floor then you need the tool.

How good is it? I regularly see competition shooters, shooters who are not using a Glock, who have the GTul in their range bag. After a stage, if the range is at all sandy, muddy, or gritty, they'll unload the magazine, disassemble it, give it a quick scrub with the brush, and put it back together.

You say you won't own a magazine that won't work when it gets a bit grubby? Fine. But the only way to be certain your magazines pass that test is to drop them in sand and then test-fire. While you're testing your magazines that way, understand you are also introducing sand into your pistol, and that's not good for it. Save the parts wear and just clean your magazines.

* From page 90. This book was produced prior to the elementary school shootings in Sandy Hook, Connecticut, which pushed hi-cap magazine prices much higher.

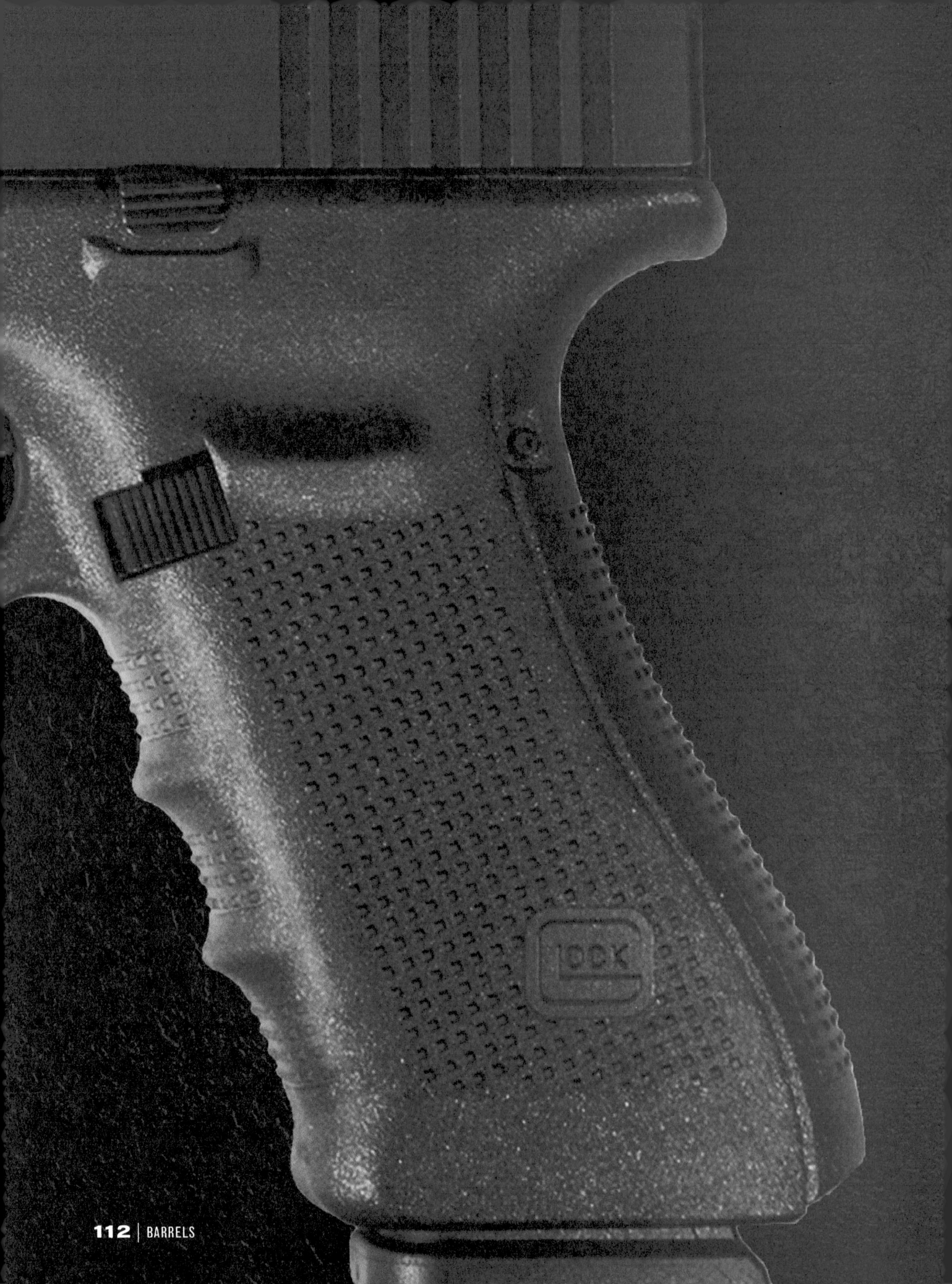

CHAPTER 9

Barrels

Lone Wolf makes barrels. They are not only cool with lead, the threaded ones are ready to go with suppressors.

What's new in the realm of Glock barrels? From Glock, not a thing. New models appear, but, if there's been any change in dimension, materials, rifling pattern, twist rate, or chamber dimension, Glock has been mum about it. So, nothing new there.

But the Glock-verse is not populated solely by Glocks. Other people make barrels, good ones, and they are not the least bit afraid to step up and offer what we want. The two big changes, one of which has been going on for a while now but seems never to fade, are barrels that can handle lead bullets and barrels threaded to accept suppressors.

Lead

So you ask, "Why lead?" Simple. Until the EPA has the handcuffs taken off and can actually and lawfully go after us for using lead, that material is readily available and still the best for many uses. Handcuffs? Well, yes. You see, the EPA is specifically prohibited from addressing lead in the form of bullets. From time to time, one left-leaning environmental organization or anti-gun group will agitate that "The EPA must do something about the lead that poison our water/air/sugary soft drinks!" But the EPA was prohibited by Congress from having any purview in this area, and so it "regretfully" has to let it slide. Make no mistake, the agency would love to weigh in, not necessarily because it is a bunch of lead-hating anti-gun zealots. To quote two famous people. Napoleon Bonaparte once remarked, "One should not ascribe venality to that which can be described by mere incompetence." And Jerry Pournells, in his *Iron Law of Bureaucracy*, simply states that those who are dedicated to the organization and not the mission will gain control of the organization and then run it for the organization's benefit.

If the EPA ever gets control of lead, it will move in because "someone has to" and will promptly screw it up because no one in charge actually cares about lead, only the extra budget and staffing the control of lead would gain them.

Cynical? You are correct. Anyone care to bet against that? Lead as bullet material is here and will be for a long time.

Glock barrels do not like lead bullets. There are several learned engineering treatises on exactly why, but what it boils down to is that the detailed surface level of steel—steel treated by means of Tenifer is rougher than other treatments. And Glock barrels are on

Longer barrels give you a velocity boost. They also provide room to add threads, as in a place to attach a suppressor.

Glock barrels do not like lead bullets. There are several learned engineering treatises on exactly why, but what it boils down to is that the detailed surface level of steel, steel treated by means of Tenifer, is rougher than other treatments.

the small side, to ensure greater accuracy with wartime-dimension bullets. Hey, if there is a war on and your ammunition production has to be upped from a billion a year to a billion a month, dimensions in that ammunition will wander a bit. A tight bore ensures that smaller than usual bullets will shoot reasonably well. The larger ones? Hey, no one reloads ammo, do they? Not in the Army. So no big deal.

But we crazy, non-Army Americans actually reload ammo, expect brass to have a long service life, and desire accuracy, all at less than government-budget ammo prices. Hence the use of cast lead bullets.

The trick, if trick it can be called, is simple. The exterior is of a Glock configuration, while the interior is the same bore and chamber that the barrel maker makes for every other pistol out there. So, no polygonal rifling, just the expected, angular, Enfield rifling. Chambers are a bit tighter than what Glock makes, too, and, often as not, in stainless steel instead of Tenifer-treated carbon steel.

Who? Bar-Sto, Wilson, Lone Wolf, Storm Lake, KKM Precision, and others make replacement Glock barrels, barrels that don't have a problem with lead bullets. You decide what length you want for your model Glock and whether you want a drop-in or a fitted barrel. My suggestion? If you are acquiring a new barrel for less-expensive practice, a drop-in will work just fine. If, on the other hand, you want to use your new barrel for practice and match/competition, get it fitted by the barrel maker or a gunsmith.

For practice, accuracy as good as the factory barrel is fine. If you're going to use it in competition (though you should remember some matches might not permit a non-Glock barrel in your Glock), then you might as well spend a few extra bucks and get all the accuracy you can.

The other use for re-barreling is as a place to mount a suppressor. To attach your "can," you need an extra barrel threaded for the suppressor attachment. That means at least a half-inch of extra length that can be threaded to the thread pitch of whatever suppressor you have.

Now, some shooters are cool with cast lead in suppressors, but me, I'm a lot less forgiving/casual about it. I mean, if I've forked over the equivalent of a couple of house payments for my suppressor, I'm going to take care of it. So, jacketed bullets for me. Of course, you can't get a factory Glock barrel that is threaded for a suppressor, so you go with aftermarket. And guess what? The same people who make the for-lead-bullets barrels also make them for suppressors.

Accuracy

The word among Glock owners is that Glocks are superbly, brilliantly accurate. I haven't seen it at that level. I've shot some accurate handguns, pistols and revolvers, that would put all their shots within an inch or two at 50 yards and under six at 100. (Which is about as good as your average AK, by the way.) I've pasted targets out to 300 meters with handguns, I do not, with my experience behind the Glocks, think I do better with them.

In part it is the trigger. Constructed as it is and housed in a polymer frame just isn't all that helpful, when it comes to placing hits as close together as possible. Don't get me wrong, long and heavy is not a big deal. But I have to consider that in the accuracy-oriented game, PPC, the winners are shooting pistols other than Glocks. There a 600 is perfect and expected to be the winning score in any match, even a mildly contested club match, and your X-count breaks the ties. Few Glocks show up at PPC matches. Regardless your opinion, or mine, of the Glock trigger, a match barrel from any of the high-end barrel makers will markedly improve on the average Glock level of accuracy.

Caliber Change

There is one barrel swap that takes advantage of Glock and the lack of differences between the 9mm and .40 pistols. That is the 9mm to .40 conversion. To accomplish this,

Depending on what model Glock you have, a longer barrel can be just a bit longer or a whole *lot* longer.

first unload and disassemble your G22. Take the recoil spring and barrel out of the slide, put the new 9mm barrel in, replace the recoil spring assembly, slap the pistol back together, and you have a 9mm pistol.

Now, you will, of course, have to be using 9mm magazines to take advantage of this conversion, but since the Assault Weapons Ban of 1994 is dead and gone (at least for now, and good riddance to bad rubbish), finding 9mm magazines is no big deal.

I can see some of you scratching your heads. "Waitaminit, what about the ejector? The extractor? The recoil spring?" Good questions.

The easy one first, the recoil spring. Since the spring assembly is the same for both the G17 and the G22, then there is not only no need to change them, you don't have a choice to change to. You use the same spring for both, and your only concern is mileage. A bazillion rounds later, do you need to change the spring? That change is more dependent on the number of rounds than anything else and, just to be prudent, you'd probably want to be changing the spring every 10,000 rounds anyway, regardless of caliber.

> Since the spring assembly is the same for both the G17 and the G22, then there is not only no need to change them, you don't have a choice to change to. You can use the same spring for both, and your only concern is mileage. When do you change the spring? That's more dependent on the number of rounds than anything else and, to be prudent, you'd probably change it every 10,000 rounds, regardless of caliber.

Next up, the ejector. This, despite the engineering advances the last quarter of the twentieth century bestowed upon us, is going to be a what-works-for-you proposition. Does your pistol kick the empties out? Reliably? Then you're good to go, job over. If it does not, then you'll have the unfortunate luck to have to experiment.

Ditto for the extractor. If it works, then it works. If it doesn't, you'll have to either swap in a 9mm extractor or get a spare and file on the "stop pad," the portion that controls how far the extractor reaches in. In both cases, the situation falls under that classic joke, "Doctor, Doctor, it hurts when I do this," to which the doc replies, "Then don't do that."

Now, why would you want to do this, this conversion? One or more of a host of reasons. First, the 9mm is less expensive to shoot than a .40. You may love your G22, but the price of factory ammo is killing you. Reloads are less expensive, but there's a catch. Actually, more than one.

As noted, there's that lead thing we've been discussing. Second, handloading the .40 is not as easy as falling off a log. In fact, if you are going to take up reloading for fun and decreased shooting expenses, I would not recommend the .40 as your starting point. It is well down the list, and of the calibers available in Glock, perhaps the only cartridge more difficult to reload than the .40 is the .357 SIG. Plus, reloading the .40 for Glocks is more persnickety and less forgiving than reloading the .40 for other pistols. No, you do not want to start here.

The 9mm is relatively forgiving. Where it isn't forgiving, at least it won't bite you. The 9mm will simply deliver miserable accuracy, whereby a bad .40 reload will bust your Glock.

How much difference can reloading make? And how much is the 9mm compared to the .40? A quick search turns up .40 ammunition, 180-grain FMJ, at the cost of $320/thousand, plus shipping. Nine millimeter ammo from the same source is $180/thousand for steel-cased and $200/thousand for brass-cased ammo.

A quick check for reloading components turns up plated 9mm bullets at just under $95/thousand, plus shipping. If you absolutely have to reload for .40, then bullets there are $125/thousand, plus shipping. Primers would be the same for both 9mm and .40, at $20/thousand.

Wilson was an early entrant into the "lead-kosher" Glock barrel business.

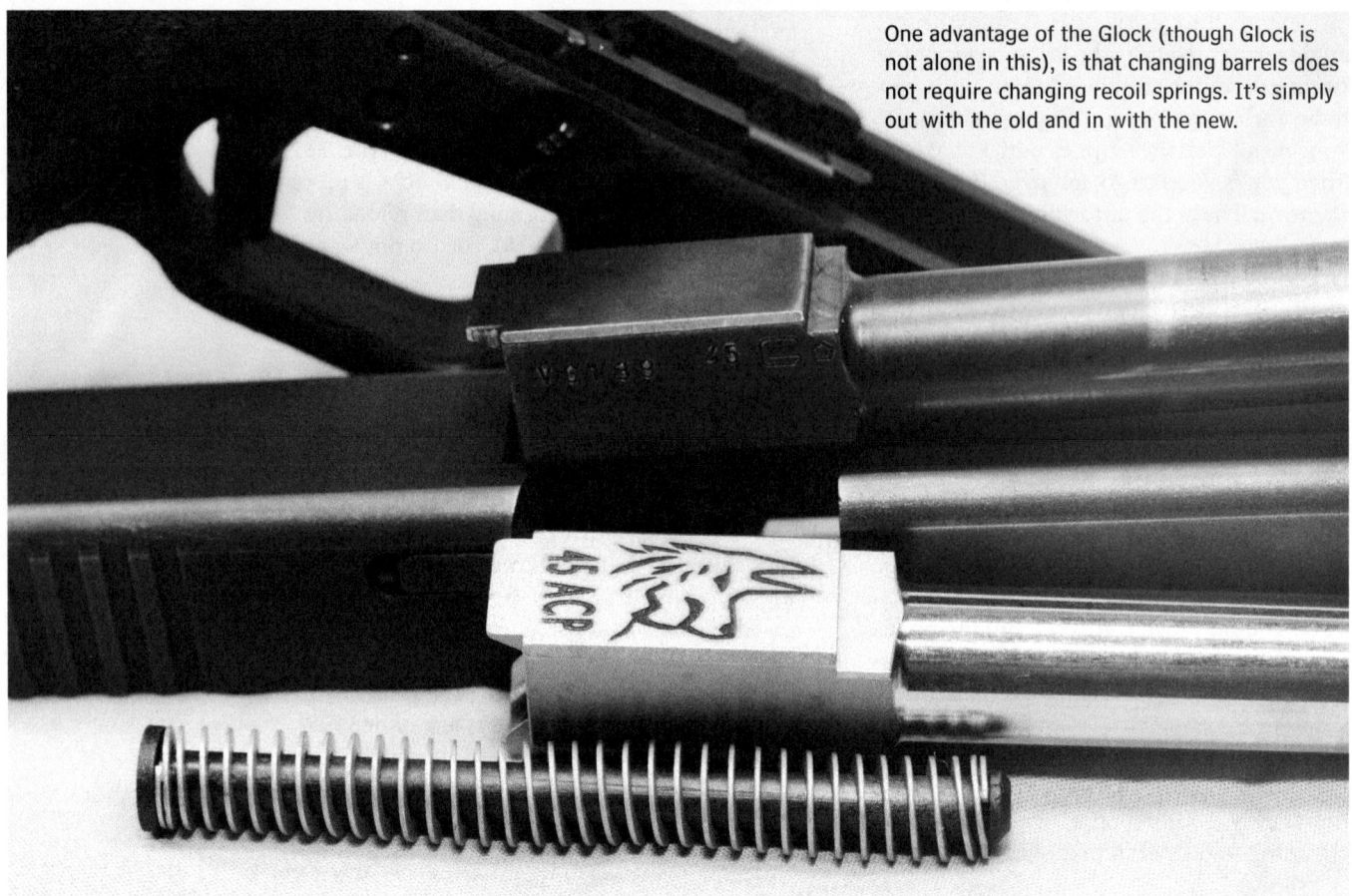

One advantage of the Glock (though Glock is not alone in this), is that changing barrels does not require changing recoil springs. It's simply out with the old and in with the new.

The 9mm is relatively forgiving when reloaded. Where it isn't forgiving, at least it won't bite you. A bad 9mm reload will simply deliver miserable accuracy, whereas a bad .40 reload will bust your Glock.

That leaves powder. Powder is a bit more complicated. First, if you order and have it shipped, you'll be charged a HazMat fee. That fee is $20, regardless of how much you buy. So, if you buy a single pound of powder at $16 per, it actually costs you more like $40—the powder, HazMat, and shipping. So you buy powder in the eight-pound container. At least then you get your HazMat fee down to an eighth of $20 per pound, and you have eight pounds, at $110, plus shipping and HazMat. Since shipping is going to be the same for any purchaser dependent on where you live, we'll just drop that off the calculation.

A pound of powder, then, costs you $16.25. A loading for the .40, to get it up to a proper velocity, will require five grains of powder, the 9mm four grains. Those thousand rounds of .40 will require $11.60 of powder, while the 9mm will require $9.25. We end up with a total cost (assuming we use free, found-at-the-gun-club brass), of $125/thousand for 9mm and $156/thousand for the .40. Overall, with the factory .40 version that is $320 per thousand rounds, we have a cost advantage of $164/thousand reloaded, while the 9mm gives us $195/thousand.

Clearly, reloading saves a bunch of money, as well as provides us a way to tailor our ammunition to the Glock we're using and the game we're shooting. Swapping barrels saves even more, if we also drop down to 9mm while we're doing it. As a last bit of economy, the 9mm bullet we've selected is a plated bullet. If you source hard-cast bullets locally, you can get them (in most instances) for less than $95/thousand.

It is not unusual for an indoor range, an operation that has to dispose of the accumulated lead anyway, to have an arrangement with a local bullet caster. The range will ship off lead, and the caster melts, cleans, alloys, and then casts it. You can go to the range, practice, and pick up more bullets to reload.

Last, the replacement barrel can be what you want it to be. You can have an extended barrel on which to park your suppressor. You can change calibers. You can build a new upper, with a replacement slide and new barrel, and put a compensator on the new barrel. As an extra bonus, a longer-than-normal barrel is likely to give you a boost in velocity. If you're looking for more speed, then this will give it to you at no extra cost. If you, as one club member I knew many years ago, believe velocity is its own reason, then you need a longer barrel. (Just don't come complaining to the rest of us when your six-inch barrel can't boost an 88-grain jacketed bullet past the 1,600 fps mark.)

For all the right reasons, a replacement barrel can give you more options than a factory Glock barrel would. One such is the Lone Wolf 9-40 barrel, extended and threaded. Install it, screw on a suppressor, and have a blast. Or a lack of blast. Another is a barrel I've talked about before, the .400 CorBon conversion I have for my G21.

Drawbacks

There are a few. For the most part, such a conversion requires you to be more detail-oriented, when you pack your gear for a range trip. Since you own conversion needs 9mm magazines, you should probably just have them all in there, both 9mm and .40, everything well-marked. Lest you think this is something from nothing, I once watched a national-level competitor in a USPSA match get it wrong. The competitor (no, it wasn't me), loaded their .40 Glock with 9mm ammo. Yes, the rounds fit in the magazine. Yes, they work, after a fashion. The first shot was a "pop" and no slide cycle. Thinking quickly, the competitor hand-cycled the slide after each

> The replacement barrel can be what you want it to be. You can have an extended barrel on which to park your suppressor. You can change calibers. You can build a new upper, with a replacement slide and new barrel, and put a compensator on the new barrel. As an extra bonus, a longer than normal barrel is likely to give you a boost in velocity—if you're looking for more speed, then this will give it to you.

Since Glock has been so kind (and mechanical-engineering OCD), as to keep the dimensions of its products consistent, it is a simple matter to plug in a replacement barrel.

The differences between a 9mm and a .40 barrel are small. The slide breechface has other dimensional differences, which is why you can swap slides and barrels on a frame, but cannot perform cross-caliber changes in slides—at least, not easily.

Reloading saves a bunch of money, as well as provides us a way to tailor our ammunition to the Glock we're using and the game we're shooting. Swapping barrels saves even more, especially if we also drop down to 9mm from .40, while we're doing it. As a last bit of economy, the 9mm bullet we've selected is a plated bullet. If you source hard-cast bullets locally, you can mostly get them for less than $95 per thousand.

shot and finished before the Range Officer could intervene. It was a short course, maybe 10 rounds. I'm sure, at "Unload and show clear" they palmed the round so the R.O. couldn't see the 9mm. I'm also sure the R.O. knew what had happened, but, since the competitor had finished, no one was hurt, and the shooter hadn't gained an advantage (indeed, they'd shot much slower than the stage time could have been achieved in), there was no need to make a fuss. The lesson, of course, is to keep it all straight and have the ammo, gun, barrel, and magazines you want in the bag and distinctly marked.

The Glock is not the only pistol in which this switch can be made to happen. The other is the Browning Hi-Power, but there the change is for a different reason.

The BHP is a light, compact, handy, even comfortably gripped pistol. It is, also, a relatively fragile firearm. Where a 1911 or a Glock could go 100,000 rounds easy, the BHP in .40 has a reputation for going toes-up in 25,000. I have tested one of the new MkIII Brownings built for me by Wayne Novak, to nearly that—23,000 and it is going strong—but it has

When FN modified the Hi-Power to .40, it changed the barrel and added an extra locking lug. The P35 needed it. However, you can backwards-swap a .40 Hi-Power with a 9mm barrel, and *voilà*, you have an indestructible 9mm Hi-Power.

BARRELS | 121

While this mostly happens with Glocks in .40 and with reloads, this has occasionally been reported with new factory ammo. You might get lucky and have Glock replace parts at cost. Or you might not. *Photo courtesy Nik Habicht*

a limited life compared to the others. Now, drop a 9mm conversion barrel into a .40 BHP and you have a pistol that is the equal of the 1911 or the Glock in durability. Just remember that you'll do so at the cost of size, as the .40 BHP is a bit heavier than its 9mm forebear. The .40 to 9mm Glock conversion has no such drawback.

Want another reason to replace your Glock barrel? Well, a replacement barrel is less expensive than an entire 9mm Glock. Now, if you *want* another Glock in 9mm, don't let me stop you. I'm just sayin'. And, if you get to a GSSF match that has officious Safety Officers, they will complain and bar your .40-converted-to-9mm G22, but most won't care. At most clubs, if you're safe and having fun, everyone is happy.

Gunsmithing

Now, if you have a flair for gunsmithing and a willingness to experiment on expensive tubes of stainless steel, you could do more. For instance, the 9mm Parabellum was derived from the earlier .30 Luger. If you wanted to, you could buy a relatively inexpensive 9mm barrel, bore it out, sleeve it to .30-caliber, and then re-chamber it in .30 Luger and have the world's only .30 Luger Glock. Why? Why not?

More Explanation

Despite being around as a common item for almost three decades now, the ramped barrel is still a mystery to some, so let's discuss it.

The integral ramped barrel comes to us from, ta-da! John Moses Browning. He included it on his M1900 pistols, and it simply is a feed ramp attached to the barrel, rather than existing as the two-piece affair—frame and barrel ramps—as you'd see on a 1911. When the 1900 morphed from the 1905 into the 1911, the ramp got left behind. It was later resurrected, primarily for IPSC shooters and their use of the .38 Super, in the early 1980s.

I know, I know, by the time Robbie Leatham and Brian Enos were shooting .38 Supers in IPSC, the Glock was already in final form, tested, and about to be adopted by the Austrian Army. But, it was not yet here in the U.S., while the .38 Super was, and that is where the confusion comes from. You see, the gunsmiths who were fitting .38 Super barrels to 1911s for the competition circuit were careful to retain the fully supported design of the barrel. Glock did not.

What do we mean by fully supported? In order to get the cartridge from the magazine and into the chamber, there has to be a ramp. That ramp cuts a divot out of the chamber, and so the cartridge case is not completely encircled; there is a gap at that divot. While it is possible to design a handgun where the ramp is separate from the chamber and the chamber completely encircles the case, such a design would be more complicated, make a larger pistol, and provide no useful bonus.

In most instances, the lack of support is not a big deal. Handgun cartridges, pistols in particular, operate at low pressures. Where a low-powered rifle cartridge, say the .30-30, operates in the mid-40,000 psi range, the hottest pistol rounds are only 34,000 psi, and most loadings are less than that. Your typical volume-packed 9mm ammo, a box of 100 loose rounds on sale at the big-box retailers, might have a maximum average pressure of 25,000 to 27,000 psi. At that, an unsupported chamber is no big deal. Even in military use, where the pressures might run 30,000 to 32,000 psi, it's still no big deal, since no military organization reloads empty brass.

However, for IPSC competitors to make Major Power Factor in .38 Super, that is, generate enough energy to be a full-power load, they had to creep into the realm of low rifle pressures. Brass doesn't like that and, when you try to reload your Super brass again and again, it quits on you—a blown case in a 1911, at the very least, trashes a magazine.

One way to prevent blown cases is to make sure the steel of the chamber walls reaches back towards the breech far enough to enclose the case past the thin part at the base. A chamber that does that is said to be "fully supported." A gunsmith fitting such a barrel will take care to not ream the chamber any larger than needed, so that the case doesn't expand any more than it has to in firing. That same gunsmith also will not over-polish the ramp, which would remove metal that would otherwise support the case.

Just because a barrel has an integral ramp does not necessarily mean it has a fully supported chamber. Before you move on, re-read that sentence. *Ramp does not equal support.* So, when someone looks inside a Glock, sees the ramp, and says, "See, the chamber is supported" they are comparing apples to oranges.

The original Glock, the G17, was designed as a military sidearm. The military prizes reliability and durability over accuracy. No one wants an inaccurate firearm, but, if the emergency equipment in your holster is good enough for "minute of enemy" across a room, it's good enough. So the ramp is there to ensure that any and all rounds being fed out of the magazine are gobbled up by the barrel and its chamber. Brass is ejected, never to be seen again and certainly not saved for reloading.

That is not a prescription to handle excessive pressure either deliberate or accidental.

A good reason to use a replacement barrel, one good to use with lead, is if you shoot reloads. A non-Tenifer barrel might blow, but not like this. *Photo courtesy Nik Habicht*

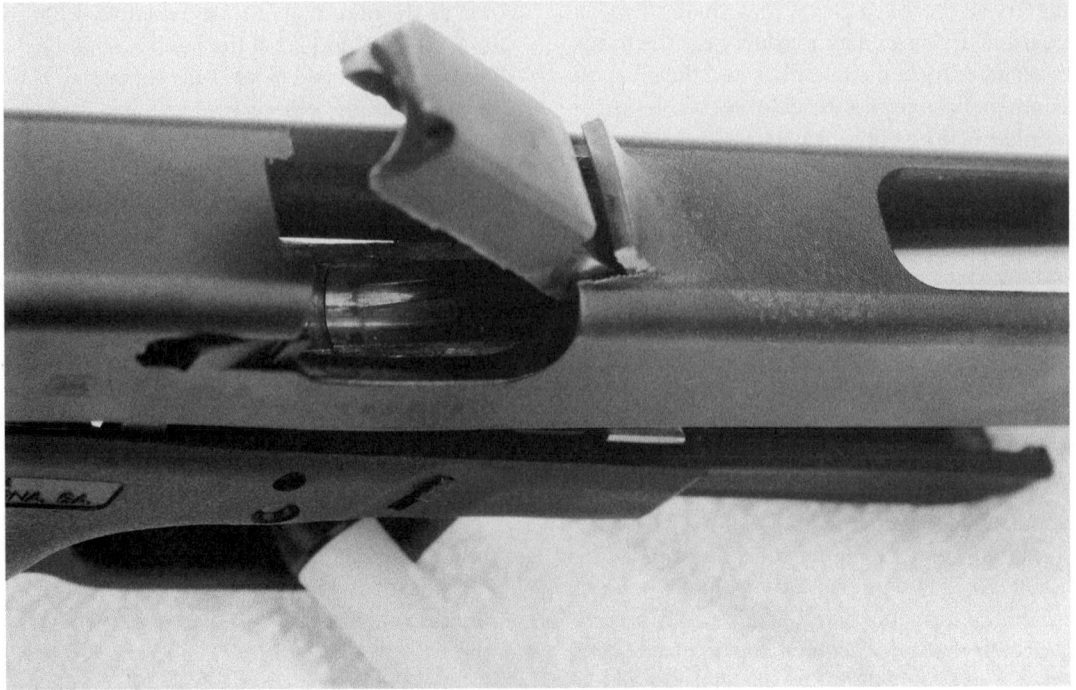

The joy of digital photography. Looking at this photo at 100-percent resolution, the copper residue in the barrel throat is clear to see. No lead here, apparently. *Photo courtesy Nik Habicht.*

Subsequent designs followed that pattern, and the .40, in particular, is known for overly generous chamber dimensions, so much so that .40 brass fired in Glocks is often so bulged it cannot be resized to fit into other pistols unless a special sizing die is used.

So, Glocks do not have fully supported chambers. They come close, they are better than older designs, but they are not the equal of a hand-fitted custom competition gun in that regard. If you have an ammunition "oops" or an excessive pressure event, you will probably have a busted Glock. Glock knows this and tells us not to use reloaded ammunition, rather only factory fresh ammo.

Once More Unto the Breach

Let's get one thing straight right now: Firearms have been breaking or "blowing up," as some put it, ever since there have been firearms. Now, a "boom" can be no big deal. It can be an *expensive* deal, or it can be an end-of-watch event. On the one end, I've blown a few handguns, and the results so far have been a few trashed magazines (though, in some instances, not even the magazines were trashed, and the grips were none the worse for the experience). A few shooters I know of have had "booms" that ended the usefulness of a slide or a frame. One had a "boom" with a .22 conversion kit on an aluminum frame, and the results were enough to turn the frame into an ex-frame.

At the other end, artillery pieces, especially back in the days of muzzleloaders, could burst. The results of those catastrophes were a few spare parts left over for other gunnery crews and a handful of letters back home explaining why the gun crew members involved were no longer listed as active duty on the rolls.

The Glock is in between those extremes. It is *rare* that a Glock experiences a "boom," but, when it does, the pistol is pretty much done. There are a few small parts that can be salvaged, but that's it. Also, rarely is the shooter seriously injured. Mostly they get stung by a few smaller bits of metal, but their hands only feel much as if they'd caught a line drive.

The biggest culprit, if we can use that word, are Glocks in .40. However, I have talked with law enforcement trainers who have an armory shelf dedicated to "boomed" Glocks in all calibers. The inquiry as to why this happens has focused mainly on the bore and the size, shape, surface texture, and the proportions of the chamber. But, in talking with my brother, a licensed Professional Engineer, a few things came into focus. So, let's look them over.

Glock barrels, as we all know, are treated to a Tenifer process to create a hard, rust-resistant surface, one that does not wear readily. (See the measurements I took on the high-mileage G34, elsewhere in this book.) The barrels themselves are either turned, reamed, honed, and broached or they are hammer-forged. The actual process used does not matter for our purposes. Once created, gauged, inspected, and passed, they are then sent off to the Tenifer process.

Tenifer (see the chapter on this), a ferritic carburization process, involves the bonding of extra carbon and nitrogen into the surface of the steel, creating a hard surface layer, but leaving a ductile inner core. This can be done in a gaseous process, but is typically done in a hot bath. (What particular process Glock uses is confidential.) The heat, concentration of chemicals, and the time in the bath all determine the depth of the hard surface.

Barrels go into hot bath. They come out hard. How hard, how deep? Remember, the barrel is a relatively thin-walled cylinder. The Tenifer process works on both the inside and the outside. If the process is allowed to go too far, is it possible to harden the barrel all the way through? Depending on the alloy used in the barrel, that could be a problem—or it could not be a problem. Some alloys will still remain ductile enough, even through-hardened via Tenifer or other ferritic process, and some will become brittle.

Let's look at the chamber. See the hood? Look at where it joins the chamber body proper. Those are sharp-angled corners at the join. In engineering circles, sharp-cornered joins are to be avoided. All parts experience stress in the function of the mechanism to which they are assembled or fabricated for. You can't avoid it, and sometimes you actually can use it, but, what you don't want is uncontrolled stress or focused stress. Sharp-edged interior corners are known as "stress risers," in engineering speak. They act to focus the stress forces, and that is bad.

It gets worse. Remember, we're hardening the barrel, a cylinder, in a hot bath. That means the exterior, the interior, *and* the ends get hardened. The chamber end of the Glock barrel is case-hardened on all three sides, which means that the depth of the hardening on the very end of the chamber is going to be greater than on the sides. It has to be—the bath was hardening it from all three sides.

So, let's take a Glock barrel (or any other, for that matter), and allow it to slip into the too-hard realm. Maybe not hardened all the way through, but the hard shell goes too deep and the remaining ductile substrate is too thin. What happens if we subject it to a shock? It will break, if the shock is great enough.

Let's now add in all the other factors we know create problems. We have a tight, rough bore. We add fouling, either copper or lead (lead builds up faster). We use ammo at the top end of its pressure band. In this, 9mm, .357, 10mm, and .40 would all be tops on our list, as they run in the mid-30,000 psi range. (The .45 ACP less so, as it runs only in the low 20,000s.) And we have a chamber cut/forged on the large size, because that increases reliability, especially when dirty.

Everything is now running on the edge. If one more variable slips to red, over the line, the pistol is toast. What can put things over the edge? A case that has been reloaded too many times. A round that happens to be too much over in pressure. A bullet that has been re-chambered too many times whereby the bullet is set back and spikes pressures. Or, a worn, dirty, or bad-luck slide cycling, where the slide is slightly out of battery when it fires.

"Boom."

The case, unable to support more pressure than it was designed to, blows out. The jetting gases and the impact of the pressure wave seek escape. If the barrel is brittle, it cracks, peels, and forms spectacular shapes. If the barrel is not brittle, it holds, bulges, and the jetting gases wreak havoc on the polymer, now subjected to forces far beyond what it was formulated for.

The hard surface of the steel and the flexible polymer of the frame combine to create spectacular results. In an all-steel firearm, one not using Tenifer, the usual result is a trashed magazine, busted grips, and not much else. On an aluminum-framed pistol, the frame can be marred, distorted, or cracked.

Does this mean we have to avoid Glocks? No. But do recognize that the Glock offers less margin for error. If you really think the factory is seriously under-loading your caliber of choice, please don't experiment with hotter loads and fire them through a Glock. Actually, don't experiment in that area at all. The guys who load ammo for a living, in ammo plants, with a million dollars worth of measuring equipment, know what they're doing. Trust them.

Me, I'm limiting my Glock use to 9mm and .45 ACP. I go with the 9mm because it has thicker chamber walls (and was designed from the beginning as a 9mm), and the .45 because it operates at a much lower pressure. Not that doing so confers immunity on me, there is no such thing. If you shoot enough, you will eventually have a "boom" of some kind, regardless the firearm you're using. Wait for it, expect it, but do everything you can to keep it from happening.

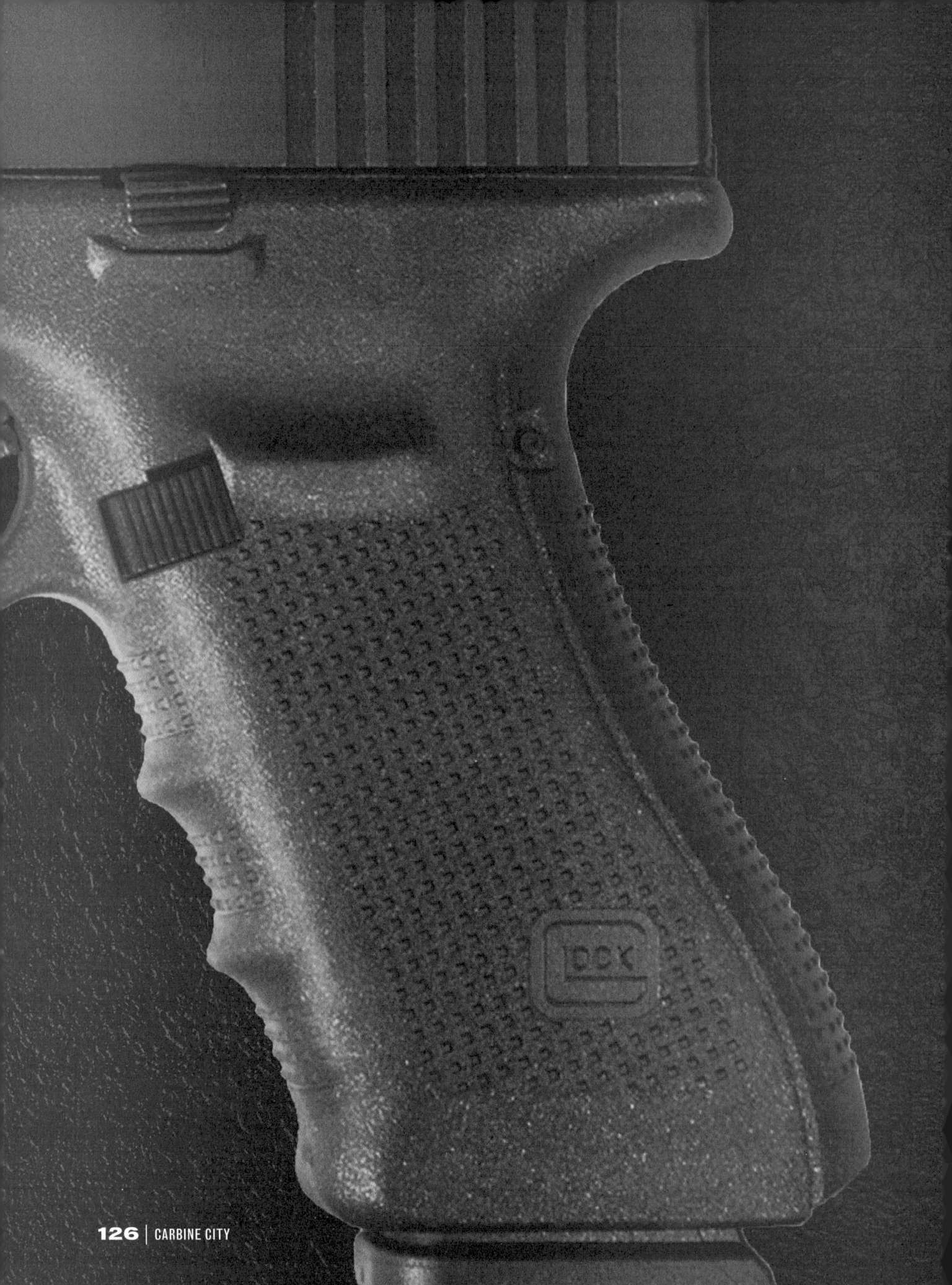

CHAPTER 10

Carbine City

The JR Carbine uses Glock magazines, has an AR-like appearance, and works.

For almost as long as I've been paying attention to Glocks (and I was working in guns shops when they arrived, so that's pretty much from the beginning), there have been rumors of a Glock carbine. Now, back when Glock was new and the world was enamored of 9mm SMGs and carbines, that made sense. Hey, the new guy on the block, the one who has a design that obsoletes everyone else's, making a carbine? Cool.

Let's take a brief jump back then to get a feel for things. It is the mid- to late 1980s. Movies like *Weird Science*, *The Breakfast Club* and *Less than Zero* are raking in the loot. Skinny ties, "popped" collars and a profusion of stick-pin badges are all the rage. We won't get into the hairstyles, except to mention that bigger was better.

The fans of Miami Vice are trying to figure out how to wear silk suits with T-shirts and shoes without socks in climates colder than Miami. They never manage it. We're in the twilight years of the Reagan presidency and soon will have President George Bush, not having a clue that he will after be termed "Bush 1."

A first-class stamp costs $.22, gasoline averages just over a dollar a gallon, and the Dow Jones oscillates just above and below 2,000. The Federal budget just passes a billion dollars a year, and the debt is only 2.6 trillion.

Music? George Michael has hit his peak in 1988, and after that it is all downhill. Radio formats are all over the place, as no one can figure out what will replace Top 40, and we have not yet gotten to the point that rock is old enough to be "classic."

Some things do not change. Even then, shooters complained about the cost of ammo and how "They don't make them like they used to."

The uber-cool carbine of the day is the MP5. S.W.A.T. teams use it, commandos (the pre-operator term for Special Ops) use it, it is all over the movies, and it has a relatively well-deserved reputation for reliability. I say well deserved, because it suffered then, as many products do today, from the less than stellar reputation of H&K's customer service. Specifically, it works like a champ, but you can't get spares. If your department buys MP5s and you are "in the loop," your first act

> It is the mid- to late 1980s. The uber-cool carbine of the day is the MP5. The S.W.A.T. teams use it, commandos (the pre-operator term for Special Ops) use it, it's all over the movies, and it has a relatively well-deserved reputation for reliability.

Yes, SIG is a competitor to Glock, but SIG's new ACP will accept it. That's what is called an "adaptable carbine platform." *Photo courtesy SIG*

will be to order spare extractor springs, because there is a 50/50 chance they will arrive before you need them.

The AR-15 is still getting over its undeserved reputation as a jam-a-matic. While many of the teething problems were discovered in the Vietnam War (which ended a mere decade before the arrival of Glocks), not all its problems had been solved. Those of us with skills and the time to experiment had solved all the problems to *our* satisfaction, but, for many, it was still not a "real" rifle.

Surplus .308 rifles and ammo are still common, inexpensive, and desired. To give you an idea, we had a customer come into the gun shop with a Springfield M1A. He wants to sell it because "the bore is shot out," but the boss isn't interested in A) a military rifle, or B) a rifle that will need work before the shop can sell it. So I get to buy it. Rifle, an ammo can of magazines and one of surplus ammo, all for a price so low I dare not repeat it.

I check with the wholesalers and find magazines for sale: $4.99 for new in wrapper, $3.99 for new but unwrapped, and $2.99 for used magazines. (Yes, be jealous.)Not everyone wants or needs a full-sized battle rifle. For a handier, shorter-range defensive shoulder weapon, the choices are not great. There's the AR, which cannot be depended on, and ammo sucks, too. You could have a shotgun, with the resultant heavy recoil and a choice between buckshot and slugs. Or you could have something 9mm in a carbine, of which the options were few and bad. Unless you had the option to buy an SMG (and not many did back then), you had few options in 9mm carbines.

One that was available was the then-new Colt's 9mm carbine, an AR changed to blowback and 9mm. However, it was tainted by two things. One, it was still an AR, which damned it to many. Two, it used modified UZI mags. The UZI has always had a stellar reputation

The AR-15 has pretty much taken over from the 9mm carbine/SMG in police work. An entire generation of shooters has learned that the AR-15 is not the fragile, unreliable rifle it was thought to be when Barry Sanders was accepting the Heisman Trophy along with a plane ticket to the purgatory of the Detroit Lions backfield.

for reliability, so any change would be viewed with suspicion. Well, Colt's changed the mag to ensure reliable feeding in the AR-based SMG and carbine. That change meant the Colt's mags were prone to spontaneous feeding. To wit, drop a loaded UZI mag and you could pick it up, brush it off, and keep going. Drop a Colt's 9mm mag and watch half your ammo spew out of it. Heck, get clumsy loading it and it would vomit a handful of rounds back out.

In an environment such as that, who would *not* wish for a Glock carbine? After all, we know for sure that it would be reliable, certainly a lot more reliable than the existing designs of other manufacturers. And, unlike the dodgy Colt's magazines or the H&K extractor spring problem, the parts would be durable and obtainable.

Beyond that, I'm not sure anyone really had any expectations. Design, construction, specifications? No one had any or word of any, and no one really knows what they might want. Would we get, or want, something that was a host for a handgun frame, converting the upper assembly into a carbine? Or did we want a carbine design

from whole cloth? Would it even use the existing 9mm G17 or G19 magazines?

In those pre-Internet days, I'm sure there was a lot of speculation, but no real substance. I'm sure there were those who drew up prospective models. Perhaps out there is even a mock-up or two in the hands of a particularly devoted Glockophile. But no, there's no shadow of a carbine at any step of the process.

It is my feeling that the time has passed for Glock to have any impact there. Since those days, we have pretty much gotten over our infatuation with the pistol-caliber carbine in general and the MP5 in particular. A 9mm carbine is nice, but not the uber-weapon we might have thought back then. A 9mm carbine is certainly a good defensive option, and one can make a great training tool. If you shoot a lot indoors, the noise of .223/5.56 can become more than oppressive. It can tire you quickly. Some indoor ranges are touchy about rifle calibers on their backstops and so prohibit anything but handgun calibers and rimfires.

Then there's the issue of lead. Lead exposure, while over-hyped to near-paranoid levels in some circles, can still be a real problem in certain circumstances. The solution, if you aren't going to do as Mom told us to and wash your hands, is to substitute "frangible" ammunition, lead-free ammo. (Yes, there are all-copper hollowpoints that lack lead, but they are more expensive than frangibles, in many instances.) Frangible ammo in 9mm is more durable, and typically more reliable, than that of .223/5.56. Yes, you can tune an AR (or whatever) to work with frangible ammo and have it be 100-percent reliable, but not everyone wants/desires/is allowed to do that.

If you have to use off-the-shelf ammo in out-of-the-box firearms, with frangibles, the 9mm is generally a better bet than .223/5.56.

Now, let's leave the '80s and come forward to today. Glock, were it to unveil a 9mm carbine now, would be facing a lot of competitors. There are already legions of 9mms out there. Every police department in America has at least one MP5, some many, and if Glock came out with a 9mm carbine, the questions would be "Why?" Why spend more money on something just like what we already don't use very often? Why buy a 9mm, when we're already using .223/5.56 a lot more? The AR-15 has pretty much taken over from the 9mm carbine/SMG in police work. An entire generation of shooters has learned that the AR-15 is not the fragile, unreliable rifle it was thought to be when Barry Sanders was accepting the Heisman Trophy along with a plane ticket to the purgatory of the Detroit Lions backfield. The 9mm AR carbine has been tuned, refined, and is now

Love 'em or hate 'em, at least the G17 is a handgun and can be holstered. H&K's MP5, on the other hand, is, essentially, a 10-pound handgun with a stock.

A new contender for the Glock-adapted carbine, from Theuron Defense.

a reliable choice, especially if the .223/5.56 is too expensive or tough on ranges to use.

The time has passed for Glock to own the market there, but that doesn't keep others from trying to fulfill the needs and desires of shooters. Let's take a look.

Mech-Tech Systems

A lot has changed since we last looked at Mech-Tech. First of all, it makes its CCU with options. You can have a CCU (carbine conversion unit) as plain as you want, or you can have it with rails galore, an M4 stock (the basic unit is stock-less, and you'll need to select a stock design as part of the ordering), and optics, iron sights, and lasers and lights festooning your blaster. Okay, that's a bit tongue-in-cheek. You can get your CCU railed, and once railed, you can then add whatever accessories you deem appropriate.

The Mech-Tech CCU, as a barrel and assorted parts, is not a firearm. That means you can order it pretty much anywhere, as far as the Feds are concerned. Local laws might give you more grief, so be sure you know what's kosher in your locale before you gear up and order.

Lone Wolf G9

At first glance, the Lone Wolf G9 carbine is "just" an AR-15 in 9mm converted to take Glock magazines. Uh-huh, and a sports car is "just" a car with a bigger engine in it. It takes more than adapting the magazine well to accept Glock magazines in order to produce a 9mm carbine.

First, the lower receiver is not just an adapted receiver; the magazine well is a dedicated, broached well for Glock magazines. It isn't a .223 AR lower with a set of blocks pinned inside to adjust the magazine angle. Machined from a forging, the broached mag well is pitched for the Glock mags. That means the mag well is not just proportioned for Glock magazines, it is also angled properly. You must have the correct pitch of the magazine feed lips to the chamber so that the bolt can strip off a round and feed it reliably. Which brings us to the next item, the bolt.

(below) Wisconsin, a new center for arms making? Why not? The Theuron Defense carbine is available in all Glock calibers. For those who live in free states, optional integral suppressors are offered, too.

(bottom) Insert Glock, close cover, have fun (after all the paperwork, of course).

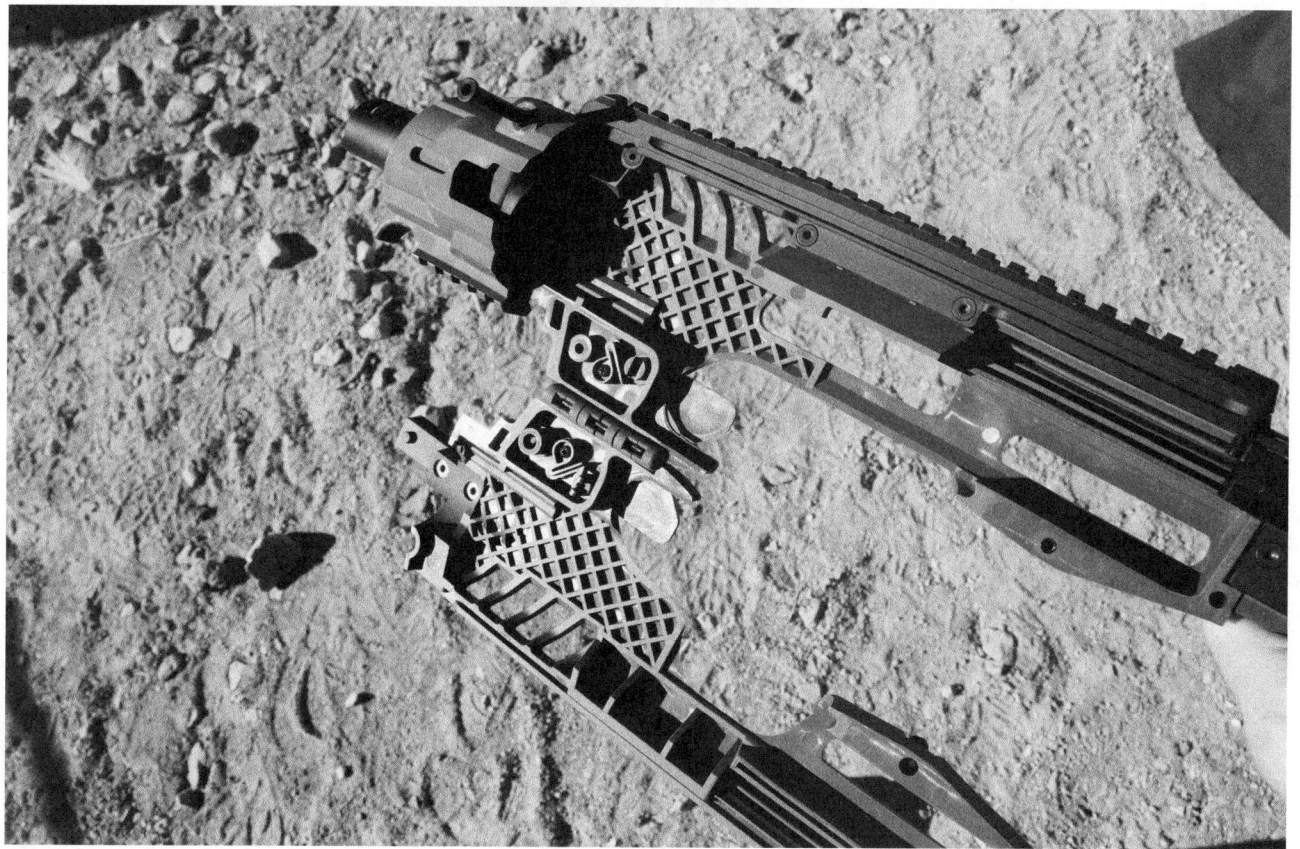

CARBINE CITY | 133

The Roni, opened up.

At first glance, the Lone Wolf G9 carbine is "just" an AR-15 in 9mm that's been converted to take Glock magazines. Uh-huh, and a sports car is "just" a car with a bigger engine in it. It takes more than adapting the magazine well to accept Glock magazines in order to produce a 9mm carbine.

There are two kinds of pistol-caliber AR conversions, those that take a new bolt in place of the .223/5.56 bolt, and those where the bolt is a machined part of the carrier itself. The former is exemplified by the Olympic, the Lone Wolf G9 is the latter.

Now, Colt's approach (the integral boltface design) is proportioned to accept and feed from double-stack, double-feed magazines. Just as with the .223/5.56 magazines for ARs, the rounds feed alternately off the right and left feed lips. That means the "stripper rail," the part that shoves a round out of the magazine, has to be proportioned to strip from both sides. Also, as the Colt's (and all the others, including the Lone Wolf), uses a fixed ejector to pitch the empties overboard, the ejector has to be pinned to the lower. It is a sturdy blade of steel. The bolt has to be machined to provide clearance for the ejector.

The Glock magazine is a double-stack, single-feed design. The rounds are on the centerline of the bolt and feed only and always from both lips each time. Also, the clearance notch on the back of the magazine is shallower on a single-feed magazine, as the bolt doesn't have to have the "reach" of the double-feed design.

The Lone Wolf carbine is an amalgam, but an improved one. It is an AR pistol-caliber carbine that takes Glock magazines.

(below) Note the changed magazine release button. While it is in the same location as one on a standard AR-15, it is bigger—and it holds the Glock magazine in place.

(bottom) A close-up of the Lone Wolf G9 Multical receiver.

The lower receiver is not a modification with pinned-in adaptor plates. The forging is machined to take Glock magazines, only and correctly.

So, getting the Colt's-style bolt to feed from the single-feed Glock magazines takes some work. I was curious to see how Lone Wolf did it. Turns out Lone Wolf took a Colt's bolt (from Colt's or a supplier that makes Colt's bolts, I don't know, and it really doesn't matter), and it machined extra clearance. Someone who knew what they were doing clamped the bolt upside down in the vise of a milling machine, poked a ball-end cutter into it, and cut the clearance needed.

I'm sure some will complain that this is "cheating" or "chickening out" and that Lone Wolf should have done it all themselves. Me, I'm glad to see Lone Wolf did it they way it did. I have this curmudgeonly attitude that the world does not need any more people who reinvent the wheel and expect to be acclaimed as rocket scientists for changing the number of spokes. Well done, Lone Wolf.

Once done, however, the G9 is an AR in that anything and everything AR-15ish you might want to put on it will fit. Oh, and I love the magazine catch. The mag button is in the same location its is on a regular AR, but, since it has to pivot and not be plunger-style, it has a big paddle and a large lever. Really, if you miss this button on a reload, there is no hope for you.

The Lone Wolf G9 cranked through all my magazines and all the ammo I had that was

On the Lone Wolf carbine, the magazine release button is in the same location as on a traditional AR-15. However, since it has to pivot and not work plunger-style, it has a big paddle and a large lever. Really, if you miss this on a reload, there's no hope for you.

suitable for Glocks. Now, as it uses a cut-rifled barrel, I'd expect it to be a lot more forgiving of ammo than Glocks are, but, since we're using it alongside Glocks, it is best to test it with ammo that Glocks would use. Lone Wolf sent the G9 with a red dot sight on it, and the combo was dead-on right out of the box. Pasting plates at absurd distances was easy.

Now, as an AR chambered in 9mm, the Lone Wolf differs from the rest of the 9mm ARs in the one aspect of magazines. Is this enough? To many, yes. As I explained earlier, the AR uses a modified UZI magazine. In order to get the UZI magazine to feed in the AR, Colt's had to account for the differences in feeding geometry. That meant a change in the feed lips.

A dropped UZI magazine is cause for concern, mostly because it will scuff the finish and may allow dirt, mud, sand, or snow to get in, all of which will have to eventually be cleaned out. Dropping a loaded Colt's magazine will usually cause half the rounds to squirt out, never to be seen again. UZI mags work in UZIs. Colt's magazines (and those made for the AR) typically are a "works or it doesn't" proposition. If they don't, all you can do is either sell them off or trade them to someone whose AR in which they do work.

As the Lone Wolf is a blowback system (as it is on all AR-based pistol-caliber systems), the bolted-down part on top of the carrier is just a guide. Plus, the carrier *is* the bolt.

CARBINE CITY | 139

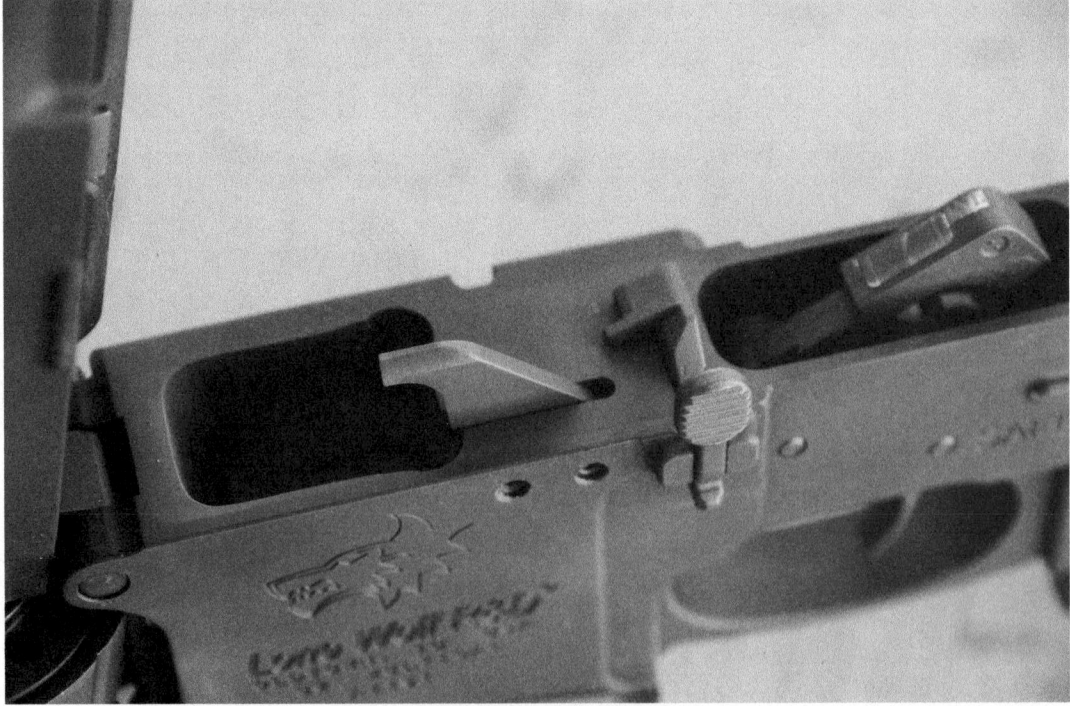

(top) Here you see one reason why rifles and carbines are superior to handguns. It's about the accuracy. This is a five-shot group at 25 yards, aided only by a red dot optic (one without magnification).

(above) The ejector of the Lone Wolf is a pinned-in blade that impacts the cartridge base through a slot machined in the carrier/bolt. Simple and effective, you don't have to worry about spring tension for it to do its job.

One thing we can count on: Glock magazines work. They may be a bit of pain to load, being a single-point feed design, but they work.

Mako/FAB Defense

This one you have to be careful with. Mechanically it is quite simple. FAB Defense makes a conversion chassis that accepts a Glock. So far the conversion will take nine different Glock models in 9mm, .40, and .45. The chassis has a stock on it, so you are stylin' with a Glock in a carbine that is, at its heart, a Glock.

There's a catch. (Isn't there always?) In order to have this and assemble it, you have to apply for an SBR—short-barreled rifle. An SBR is anything that has a barrel shorter than 16 inches (a rifled barrel, else it would be an SBS—short-barreled shotgun) and a shoulder stock. Getting an SBR is simple, if expensive, and requires some waiting. You fill out the application form with the BATFE, enclose a $200 check, and wait. Once your application is approved, the approval being known as a Tax Stamp (because you paid a tax to acquire the new gizmo), you're ready to roll. But that's not the catch. The catch is you have to SBR (it is both a noun and a verb, in this context) a particular Glock.

You don't SBR the chassis, you SBR the pistol. That pistol, and *only* that pistol can go into the chassis. If, however, you have an RDIAS, or a Glock 18, they need not be SBR. The host Glock (and *only* when the RDIAS is installed) can be slapped into the chassis. The G18 can always go into the chassis, as its status as a machine gun trumps the need to SBR the Glock going into the chassis.

There is one other circumstance in which you could do this and not have to SBR your Glock, and that is if you installed a barrel that was longer than 16 inches *before* you installed said Glock into the chassis. As a 16-plus-inch barreled firearm, it would not need to be SBR defined. But wait, there's an exception to the exception—the stock can't fold. You see, the definition of an SBR is two-fold. A rifle with a barrel shorter than 16 inches or an overall length less than 26 inches is defined as an SBR. Sigh. A Mako/FAB chassis, with a 16-inch barrel, comes up short of 26 inches with the stock folded. To be legal, you'd have to have either a Mako stock that doesn't fold or have the stock permanently locked open, as in getting a welder to weld the pivot open.

Cool, yes, but it can be a hassle to get one all set up. And if you do go this route, keep the

It takes a lot of shooting to empty a magazine such as this.

A hundred rounds of 9mm? Of course, with the Beta C magazine installed. It does make the carbine heavy, a tad bulky, and slow to maneuver, but boy is it a blast! Well, at least until the ammo is gone and you have to load it again. Can't get something for nothing.

chassis away from people who don't know the intricacies. If they aren't aware of the law, they could slap their own Glock, a non-SBR unit, into the chassis and have instantly created a technical violation of the law.

SIG Sauer

Another handgun-to-SBR conversion system, the ACP (Adaptable Carbine Platform) is not just a SIG handgun system. The engineers were clever enough to make it adaptable to any handgun, within limits. You will, however, have to have a Glock (this is a Glock book, after all) with an accessory rail on it. That means the SIG ACP will not work for a first or second generation Glock, as only the third and Gen4 models with these rails will work.

The SIG ACP uses an adapter block that locks onto the accessory rail, which in turn slides into and is locked to the ACP. The back plate of the ACP has fitting plates, which allow

it to accommodate the tang of various handguns, curved or flat. For Glocks, use the flat. The assembly of this, since it is adaptable to many handguns, can be a bit fussy and require a bit of range time trial and error. But, once done, you have your Glock encased. And unlike the FAB Defense adapter, which requires your Glock be an SBR in order to be kosher, SIG makes its ACP in two flavors. There is the ACP and the ACP-LE. The ACP lacks a stock, while the ACP-LE has a folding stock.

> The big deal with the Sub2000 is that it folds in half. Opened it is only 29.5 inches long, plenty long enough to keep it from being an SBR. Folded it is 16 inches long, which doesn't matter, as it can't be fired that way. Well, I'm sure it matters somewhere.

The ACP allows you to mount a light, laser, etc., (perhaps too much extra gear). To improve aiming, you use the trick developed by the SAS back in the late 1970s, which employs a single-point bungee sling that is just a bit too short; push the handgun out and, at the end of your presentation, the bungee will tension up and make your aiming a more rigid affair.

The ACP, lacking a stock, does not require you to have and use an SBR Glock for assembly. You can use any or all that fit. The ACP-LE, with its folding stock, requires a dedicated SBR Glock, or else you are committing a felony. Even if you have an SBR Glock, using a different Glock would also be a criminal offense. It may not be rational, but it is clear, so pay attention and keep yourself out of trouble and jail while heading out to have fun.

Kel-Tec

If the Mech Tech is the easiest way to get your Glock to be a carbine and uses the most Glock parts, and the FAB Defense is the coolest, that leaves the Lone Wolf as the one best-suited to competition. As an AR-based carbine, it will accept all the AR accessories out there, and since they are everywhere, you can experiment to your heart's delight, knowing that a replacement doohickey is just an Internet click away.

And then there's the Kel-Tec Sub2000. This is the emergency tool of the pistol-caliber carbine world. A blowback carbine (they all are, there aren't any locked-breech 9mm carbines that I know of), the Sub2000 can be had in 9mm or .40, and the various models of it will use S&W, Beretta, SIG and, for our needs, Glock magazines.

The big deal with the Sub2000 is that it folds in half. When folded, it cannot be operated (in fact, the chamber and bolt are separated from each other, thus it is rendered inert). Opened and ready to go, it is 29.5 inches long, which is plenty long enough to keep it from being an

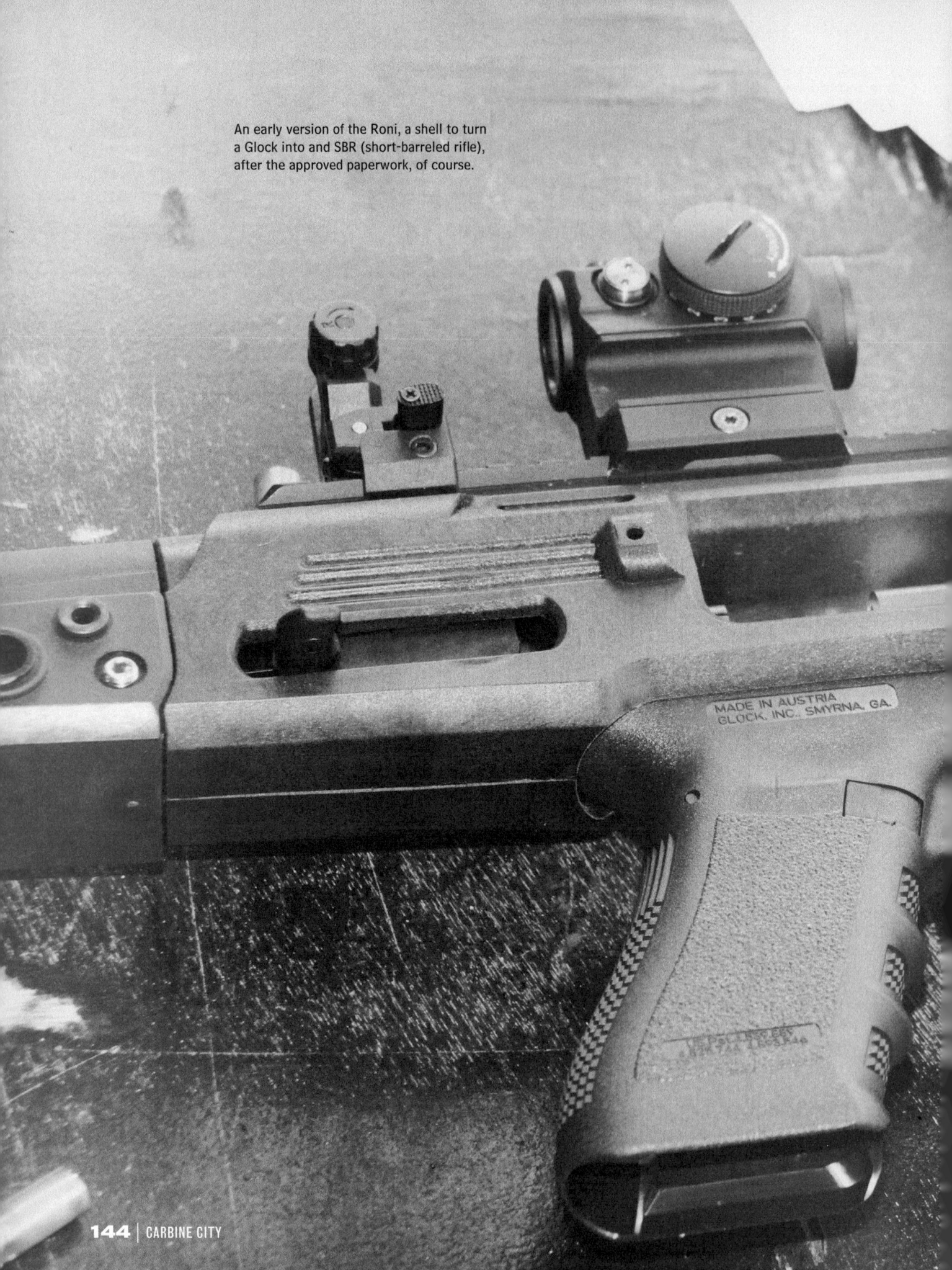

An early version of the Roni, a shell to turn a Glock into and SBR (short-barreled rifle), after the approved paperwork, of course.

The Roni even has a magazine holder in the buttstock.

SBR. Folded it is 16 inches long, but that doesn't matter. Well, I'm sure it does, somewhere, because there is some place with legislators so ignorant of things firearms that being "only" 16 inches folded is against the law. If you happen to live in such a place, my only advice is to move.

Folded, the action hinges up and over and the front sight latches against the buttplate. Kel-Tec makes a model with a railed forearm, but, to me, that negates the biggest advantage the Sub2000 has, and that is its compactness; once you bolt on a red-dot sight, light or laser, you have made it significantly less compact. In fact, with optics on top, you can't fold it enough to make it worthwhile to fold in the first place. As it is, optic-less, it will store, folded, inside an emergency pack or bug-out kit bag. As a 9mm carbine, you aren't going to be engaging targets "out there," but would instead use the stock and better sights (better than on a handgun) to increase hit probability at across-the-parking-lot distances. Since it works with Glock magazines, your Glock in the same caliber—you were clever enough to acquire them in a common caliber, weren't you?—you can use all your magazines for either handgun or carbine. I can see securing a segment of rail to the handguard to mount a light, if needed. I would not fold and store it with the light on it, just to keep things compact. Regardless, whatever bag you are schlepping, the Sub2000 in it can also hold a couple spare magazines, a light, and so on.

The temptation with a pistol-caliber carbine is to gild the lily. (Actually, in Shakespeare's *King John*, it is "to paint the lily, to gild fine gold" but the words changed, and we go with what is current.) The extra barrel length of the carbine gives any load a velocity boost. The temptation is to add a +P or +P+ load to that and gain even more. The problem is, you end up paying for it. For one, the bolt comes back harder and faster, due to the extra energy being generated. On the Kel-Tec, that means it bottoms out harder. The Sub2000 has a bit more recoil than others, partly due to its lighter weight (it tips the scales empty at four pounds even), and partly due to the short travel of the bolt and recoil spring. After all, if you're going to have a folding carbine that has a barrel longer than 16 inches and a folded length of just 16 inches, there is only so much room for the bolt to move. On the Sub2000, I would forego +P or hotter ammo. It isn't worth it.

When you go to order or buy a Sub2000, you have to choose. That is, you can't just swap the pistol grip portion to change from one magazine style to another. When you buy a Glock-mag Sub2000, you have one until you sell it. The Kel-Tec engineers are clever guys, and I'm sure they looked into the design of a magazine-swap folding carbine. And I'm just as sure it was not something that worked as well as they'd have liked, or they would have made it that way.

Pistol Caliber Carbine Uses

In the modern tactical world awash in 5.56 M4 clones and the like, what use or need is there for a 9mm carbine? There are a few, and despite the advantages of 5.56-chambered

The temptation with a pistol-caliber carbine is to gild the lily. The extra barrel length of the carbine already gives any load a velocity boost—the temptation is to add a +P or +P+ load to that and gain even more.

carbines, sometimes those advantages can work against you.

A 9mm (or .40, .45, or whatever) carbine is less expensive to shoot, has less range, less penetration (in most instances—in some it actually has more than a 5.56), is not as noisy, and also not as abusive of targets and ranges.

Cost is nearly self-explanatory: 9mm costs less than 5.56 does. It is also less harsh on the working parts. The DoD, via SOCOM, tell us that the "proper" rotation time, as in service life, of a bolt in an M4 is 7,000 rounds. Of course, that's in a harsh environment, with a liberal application of full-auto fire now and then. Seven thousand rounds through a 9mm

The Roni safety is a two-sided lever that covers the Glock trigger, so you (or others) can't inadvertently get into the triggerguard and cause trouble.

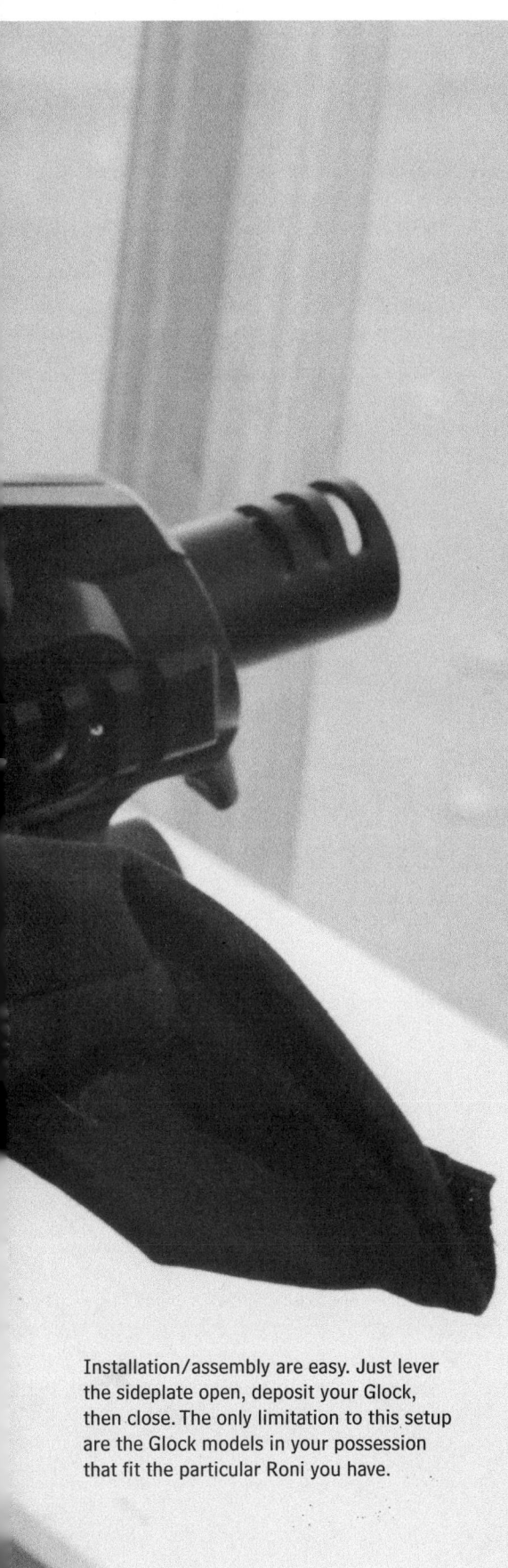

Installation/assembly are easy. Just lever the sideplate open, deposit your Glock, then close. The only limitation to this setup are the Glock models in your possession that fit the particular Roni you have.

carbine? Unless you're firing full auto, 7,000 is nothing. I have a Colt 9mm SMG barrel plugged into one of my pistol-caliber carbines. It was tired when I got it, having seen many bursts and probably more than a few full-magazine giggle sessions. Despite that, it still dings the 100-yard gongs with monotonous regularity.

Less range, as in distance, means that shooting ranges with restricted safety fans (the room behind the backstop for bullets to fall into if you should miss the hill), can use 9mms where they cannot use 5.56-chambered carbines. I recently did an analysis of maximum range for a training facility and used software to calculate the maximum distances of all the usual suspects they might see and how far they could carry to. The 9mm showed a maximum range of some 2,000 yards, compared to the 5.56 with a maximum range of 3,600 to 4,300 yards. If you have limited room in back, a 9mm is a lot friendlier than a 5.56 might be. (If you don't have 2,000 yards, then you can't allow any bullet to go over the backstop, since none will drop fast enough.)

One thing we've learned in decades of shooting on and managing ranges is that, if it's downrange, it will get shot. Don't bother putting something up with a sign saying "Don't shoot this," because it and the sign will get shot (mostly inadvertently, but there are always morons too lazy to put up targets of their own). If you have a falling-plate rack, not only will the plates get hit, but the frame, base, footings, nearby objects, and anything else in the near vicinity of the rack will get hit. While the plates themselves have to be fabricated from armor plate, it would be ferociously expensive to make the entire frame from armor. So, the relatively soft steel frames get chewed apart by 5.56 impacts, where they merely get dinged by 9mm.

As for the noise, a 16-inch barrel combined with a soft 9mm load results in a muzzle blast that is a lot softer than that which a .223 or 5.56 round produces. If you are trying to interest a new shooter, softer is better. Recoil is much the same, but new shooters typically object more to blast than recoil. Plus, if you have a suppressor, then the combination produces a soft sound that is near movie-like when suppressed, and that makes new shooters get all giggly.

The last is the best and the most fun: competition. My home club started it (at least, as far as I know), and what we developed was PCC, a Pistol Caliber Carbine Division. It's a regular USPSA match to be fired with handguns,

> After all this time and despite persistent rumors, Glock shows no signs of ever producing a carbine. Let me clarify that: There's no evidence of Glock producing a carbine, as in manufacture and offer for sale the prototype it has already made. Still, the time might be ripe for Glock to go down this path—and I bet if it did, it'd sell boatloads of them.

but instead of or in addition to the handguns, you shoot the match with a 9mm carbine. The results can be eye opening.

The top dogs in any normal match are the Open shooters, who can, in some instances, shoot a stage in half the time other Division shooters would. Heck, a Grandmaster Open shooter can be done shooting a stage before other shooters in lesser divisions have gotten to their first *reload*. But, with a PCC match, well, depending on the stage design, it isn't unusual for a C or B class shooter to match or beat the times posted by a GM with an Open gun. And that's with *iron* sights. Put a red-dot scope on top of a PCC and you can have some really fun warp-speed shooting.

But Wait, Glock?

After all this time and despite persistent rumors, Glock shows no signs of ever producing a carbine. Let me clarify that: there's no evidence of producing a carbine, as in manufacture and offer for sale the prototype it has already made.

That's right, Glock has made prototype carbines, and I have talked to those who have held them. One remarked, "Yes, it was a very Mini 14-ish looking carbine." That stopped me cold for a moment. I had not thought of a Glock carbine in terms of .223/5.56, I had only been considering a carbine as a pistol-caliber firearm. But no, he was quite clear, it was not in a pistol caliber.

The time frame is important. Without blowing my contacts cover, this was before 9/11, before the massive AR-15 run-up, and before every police department in the land abandoned its MP5s for M4s. When I was teaching law enforcement patrol rifle classes in the 1990s, we still saw a lot of MP5s and even Ruger PC9 and PC40 carbines. Many chiefs, sheriffs, superintendents, and other bosses were still caught up in the mode of a pistol-caliber shoulder weapon not being police heavy artillery, i.e., they were ready to go to rifles. But they were not keen on the AR-15. A Glock

carbine in .223/5.56, back then, would have had the market to itself. With Glocks already in holsters, a Glock carbine for the squad car would have been an easy sell, especially if it didn't look like one of the "assault weapons" that many politically oriented bosses would shy from.

But that was then and this is now. The default rifle for police is now the AR, with a very few departments using something like an H&K G36, SIG 550-series, or an FN of one kind or another. We don't even see Ruger Mini-14s anymore. The police market has been swept by the AR. My insiders were negative on this point, for various reasons, but I believe that were Glock to produce a carbine, even at this late date, I have no doubt it would sell boatloads of them.

Recoil? You've got to be kidding. Right now, the Roni and a G18 would be a seriously giggle-worthy combo.

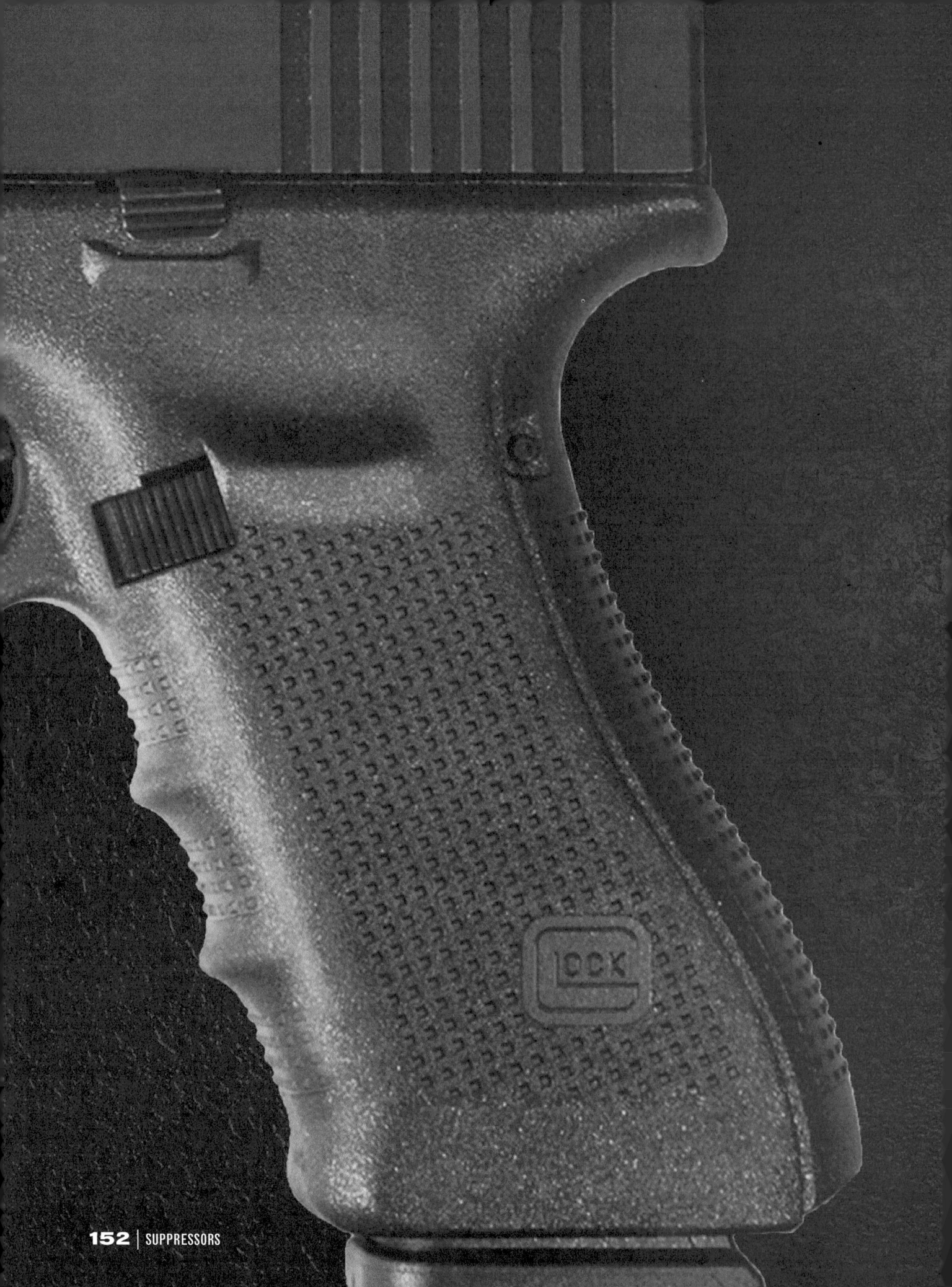

CHAPTER 11

Suppressors

With handguns, it's a simple matter to swap the barrel from the stock unit to a longer one threaded for a suppressor.

The new man-jewelry is suppressors. Well, those and SBRs, but we've got SBRs covered in the previous chapter. So, here we discuss "cans." A suppressor is, for all intents and purposes, a muffler for your firearm. Like the muffler on your car, it diminishes the noise produced by the engine. However, the muffler on your car has a different task and different restraints.

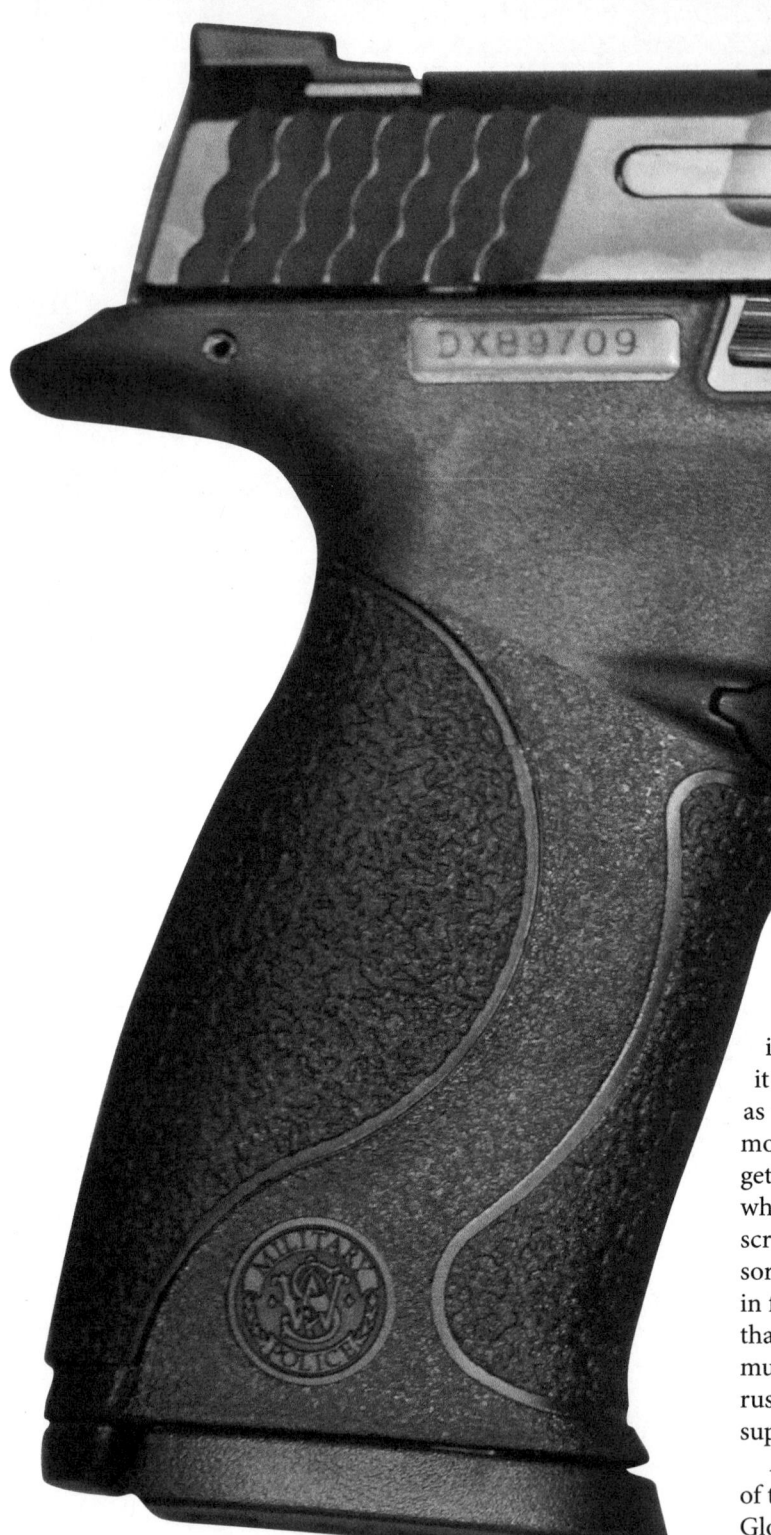

Suppressors are such a hot item, some manufacturers are now offering barrels ready to go.

On a car, the muffler can be, and is, large. Until it becomes too large to fit under the vehicle, size doesn't matter a lot. A designer or mechanic can bend it, contort it this way and that, but, if it fits and works, it works, so muffler makers make them as big as they can, because that allows them to work more efficiently. Also, the muffler on your car gets sprayed by water, road salt, gravel, and whatever road hazard you just hit. If that describes the environment your firearms suppressor has to work in, let me know. I'll not stop in for a visit, as I and my firearms don't need that kind of abuse. Kidding aside, the vehicle muffler, as soon after you drive it off the lot, is rusty. It still works. Rust is very bad for your suppressor, so take care of it.

A suppressor works by delaying the release of the muzzle blast from the bore of your Glock. Noise is a compression wave of the air, traveling at the speed of sound, and the impact of that compressed air on your eardrum is what we call "sound." Sound is measured in units called "bels," and 10 of them is a decibel. The scale is logarithmic, so moving roughly three decibels up or down the scale doubles or halves the energy of the sound. The symbol for decibel is dB. There won't be a test, so you needn't obsess over it. Just be aware that, for instance,

moving up from 100 to 105 decibels is not merely a five-percent increase in noise, but a more than doubling of the energy your ear gets assaulted with.

Noise has been with us for a long time, and a lot of people went deaf as we worked out the parameters of what is safe and what isn't.

This knowledge has been compiled and, while it is fashionable in many quarters to simply dismiss any and all efforts by Federal regulatory agencies, some of them actually know what they are doing. In the area of sound, OSHA knows what it's doing. Sound exposure is like dosage and, in medicine and chemistry, we know that "dose makes the poison." Some of you can shrug off a little. Others of you can shrug off a lot. With some, any is deadly. For comparison's sake we have continuous exposure, momentary exposure, and time.

The maximum continuous exposure for an eight-hour day that OSHA permits is 85 decibels. Some sources list 90 or 95 dB as the limit at which hearing is damaged, so 85 is clearly on the safe side. How loud is 85 dB? There are a large number of comparisons, but the real test

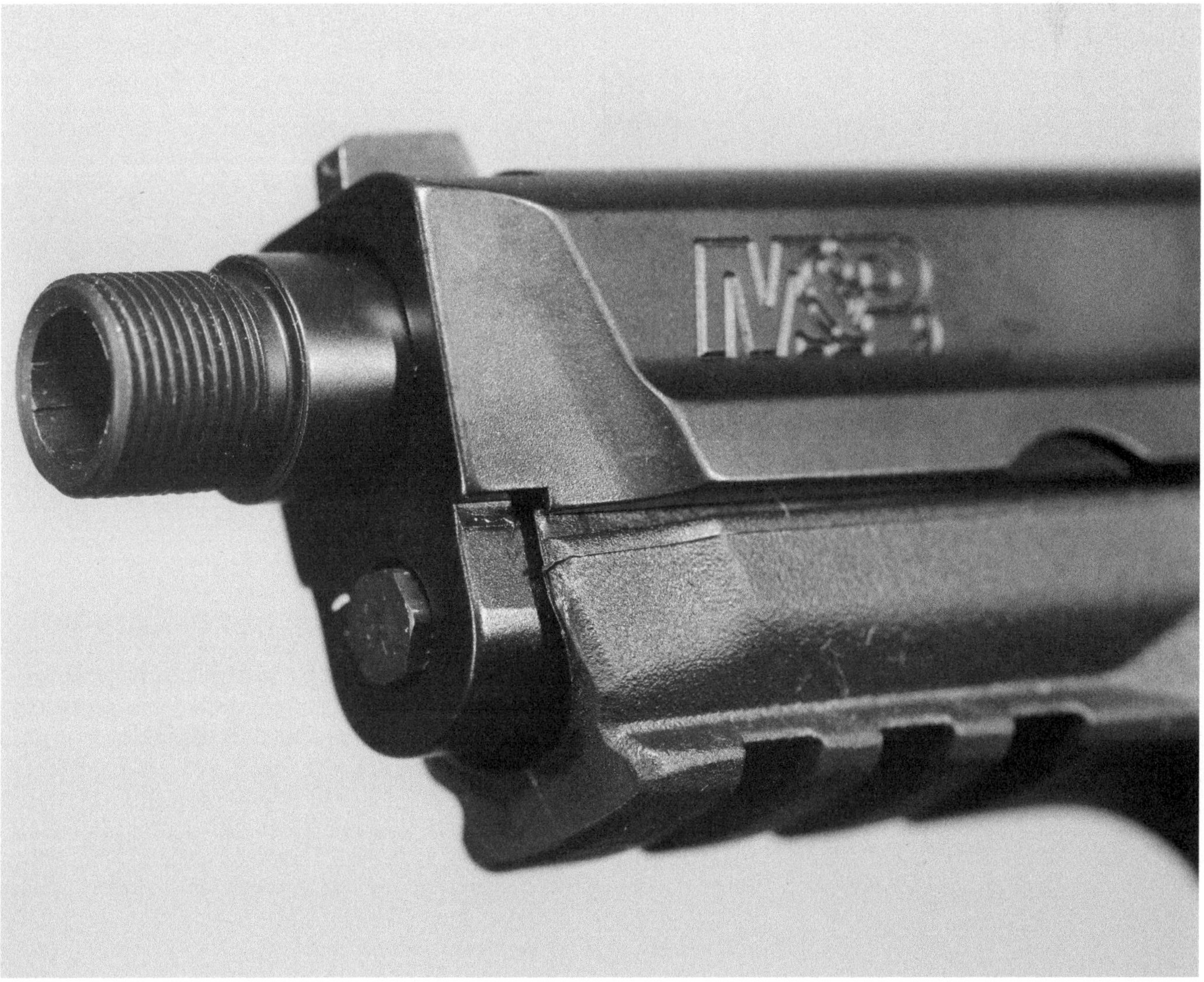

You are correct, S&W makes the M&P, and it offers a threaded-barrel option.

The original method of attaching a suppressor to this MP5 was the "Navy" three-lug setup. Threading is a lot less expensive, and this owner had his so modified.

Watch enough TV and movies and you will have "learned" that suppressors are used only by paid assassins. They calmly walk up to the hotel room they've rented, assemble the "sniper" rifle and, as a last act, install a suppressor. Then they gun down the good guys, with a "*phht-phhtt*" here and a "*phht-phhtt*" there. B-S. I contacted some of my friends in law enforcement and asked about the number of suppressors they seize. I can still hear them laughing.

is that if the person you are talking to has normal hearing, you are at arm's length, and you have to noticeably raise your voice to be heard, you're in the area of 85 dB.

Distance matters. An event that produces an initial sound of 100-plus dB will have the sound decrease to "who cares" given enough distance. The basic equation is known as the "inverse square law," which we need not go into. Basically, you can count on a decrease of six decibels each time you double the distance. So, a sound goes off. You are five feet away and it is 100 dB as it goes past you. At 10 feet it will be 94 dB. At 20 feet it is 88 dB. At the next range, with you 50 yards away, it is down to 70 dB and you don't need hearing protection from it. Confusing things, obstacles, vegetation, humidity, and surface hardness all add to the pluses and minuses of sound diminution.

Time of exposure matters. Eight hours at 85 to 90 dB is bad, but you can probably shrug it off. Eight hours a day, five days a week, for 20 years, in a factory, of 85 to 90 dB? You're probably going to lose some hearing. Now, a power saw or powder drill can easily be 100 dB. A lawn mower cold be 105, a circular saw could go 110 dB. One-time use probably won't hurt your hearing. But, if you use them weekly, in a few years you will have lost some hearing.

My background is illustrative. In the course of shooting, I have personally fired over a million rounds. I've been on the range when several times that number has been fired in classes and matches. I worked in radio broadcasting for eight years. I worked with power tools as a gunsmith for 20. Based on that, you'd expect me to be deaf as a post. However, in all that time, and starting as a kid, I wore hearing protection. My hearing is not just normal for someone my age, it is normal for someone yet to graduate from college. I've met college students who overused earbuds, who have been to only a few concerts, whose hearing is worse than mine.

Protection works and you need it. You need it because sound becomes painful around 125 dB. Short-tem exposure that is pretty certain to cause damage and hearing loss begins around 140 dB. Firearms? They run 145, 150, 160, 165 dB. Pick a number, it doesn't matter, you will lose hearing. A "quiet" 12-gauge load at 140 dB is going to damage your hearing a bit slower than a magnum at 165, but you will go deaf.

A suppressor, by slowing down the release of gases, diminishes the compression wave and lowers the dB of the sound. The best will knock 35 or 38 dB off a sound reading. This, combined with a "quiet" load, can make a suppressor-fitted firearm so quiet you can shoot it without hearing protection. Start at a mere 140 dB, then knock 35 or so off of that, and you have a sound of 105, more or less. While you could go deaf at 105, you're more likely to go broke sooner, trying to buy enough ammo to shoot enough to go deaf.

Assassin Tools

If you watch entirely too much TV or go to the movies enough, you will have "learned" that suppressors are used only by paid assassins. They calmly walk up to the hotel room they've rented, assemble the "sniper" rifle (which, depending on the whims/tastes of the

You can own one! To be legal, you have to live in a state where suppressors are permitted, which, luckily, is most of them. At this moment, you can lawfully own a suppressor in 41 states, and, at last check, I believe the State of Washington had changed its ludicrous policy of ownership but not attachment/use.

(below) If you can't own a G18, then owning a suppressor is the next coolest thing.

(bottom) You may or may not need a "booster," or linear recoil accelerator, to make your Glock function with a suppressor on it.

The booster adds enough recoil to the slide to function your Glock, even with the weight of the suppressor slowing it down. This makes the recoil actually feel harder than it would without the suppressor.

The One Source Tactical TSD pistol comes ready to go for use with a "can."

property master or director, can be anything from fantastic to ludicrous), and, as a last act, install a suppressor. Then they gun down the good guys, with a "*phht-phhtt*" here and a "*phht-phhtt*" there.

B-S. The number of suppressors confiscated by police, discovered in raids, and used by criminals is vanishingly small. I contacted some of my friends in law enforcement and asked. The answers ranged from "Haven't seen one yet" to peals of laughter. Nor had any of them heard of nearby departments arresting anyone with a suppressor. Now that isn't to say it never happens. I'm sure that, if I filed Freedom of Information Act forms with the big Federal agencies and waited long enough, I'd get some kind of answer. Or not. Let's just say they are far from common in the hands of criminals.

You can own one. To do so legally, first you have to live in a state where they are permitted, which, luckily, is most of them. At this moment, you can lawfully own a suppressor in 41 states, and I do believe that, at last check, the State of Washington had changed its ludicrous policy of ownership but not attachment/use.

SUPPRESSORS | **161**

(top) Most suppressor manufacturers produce more than one model. Gemtech makes a bunch of them.

(above) Quick-attach models, and the flash hiders they quick attach to, are too big and heavy for handguns. They work great on rifles, though.

Next, find a Class 3 dealer in your state; they will have to take possession in the mid-step of the transfer. Download the transfer form, BATFE Form 4, a.k.a. 5320.4, in duplicate, and two 5330.20 forms. You'll also have to be fingerprinted, but the local law enforcement agency that handles that (city, county, state police) in your area have the forms, and you need the FBI cards, the form FBI-258LE. Get the two 5320.4 forms signed by the "Chief Law Enforcement Officer" in your area. Once everything is filled in, take the forms and your checkbook to your Class 3 dealer. They will want to make sure everything is correct and will send the forms in for you. Then you wait. Once approved, the manufacturer can ship the suppressor to the dealer, the dealer can transfer it to you (you can pay the dealer the balance), and you get to go home.

There is one stumbling point for a bunch of people: the signature. All the law requires and asks of the CLEO is that they do indeed have jurisdiction over the area in which you reside and that they do not know of any law you would be breaking by owning it. The form does not expose them to any liability, nor does it ask their permission. However, there are locales where the CLEO will not sign. Luckily for you, he/she is not the only one. If your city chief won't sign, ask the county sheriff. (The signature has to be by the head guy/gal or his designated subordinate, not just any officer/deputy you know.) The BATFE has accepted signatures from prosecution attorneys, attorneys general, and I've even heard of coroners singing (something to do with the way the law is written in that particular

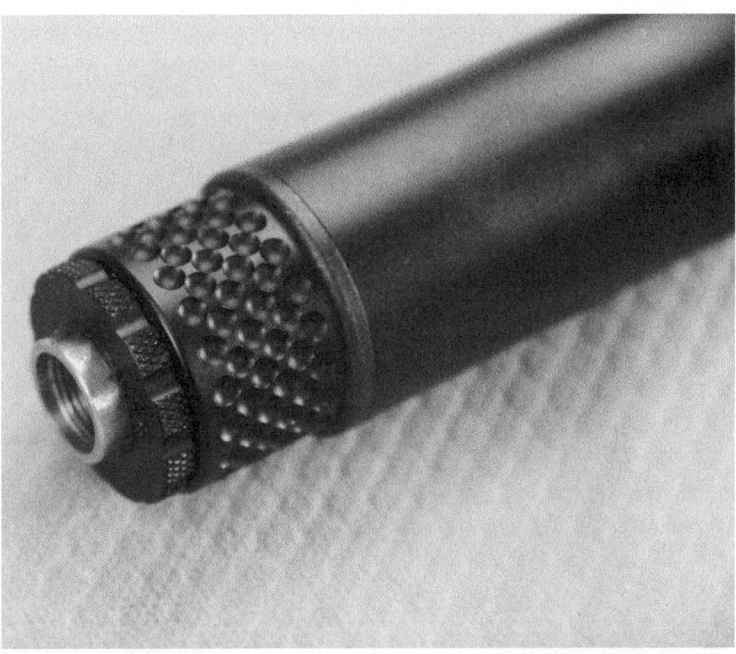

A standard suppressor with a booster attached. Not all suppressors can have the attachment end removed and replaced, so be sure and shop around.

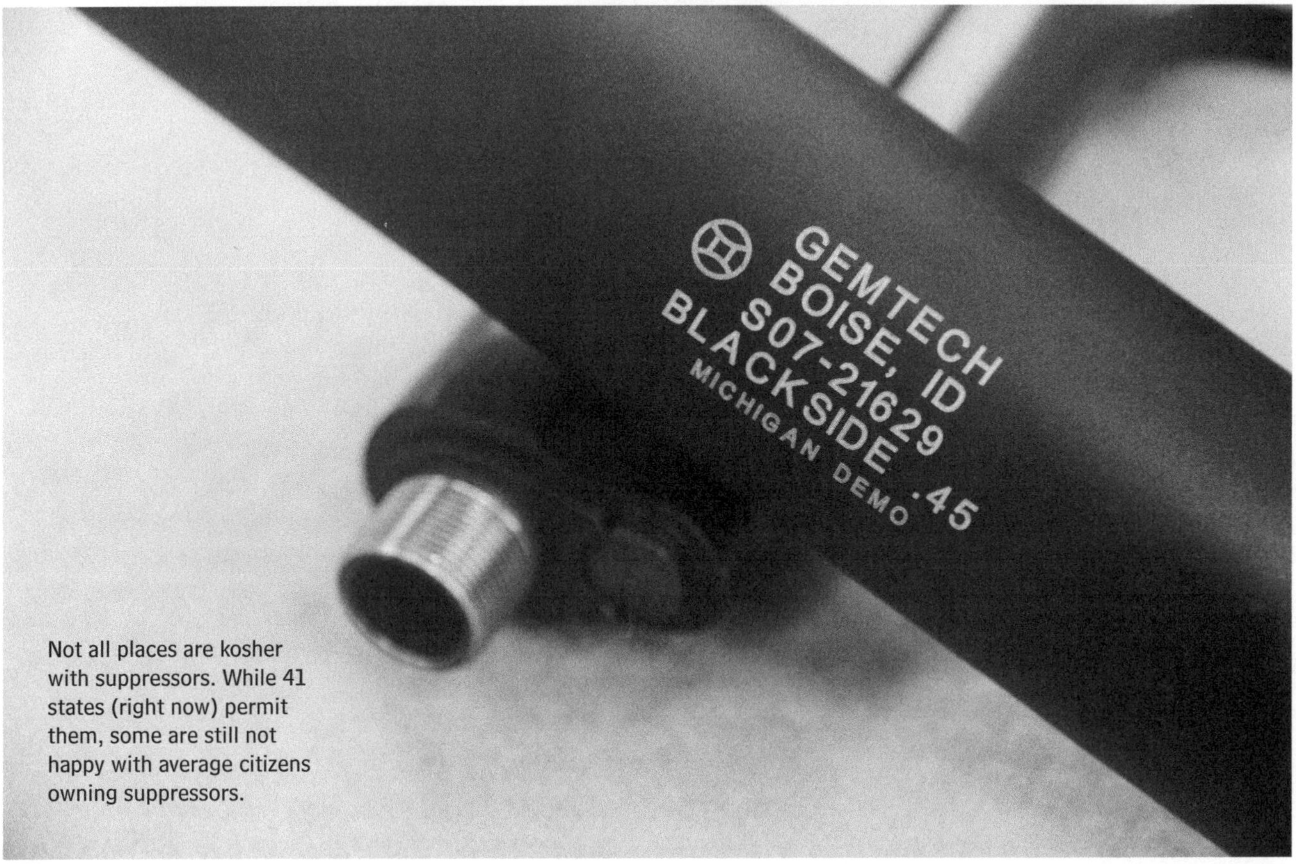

Not all places are kosher with suppressors. While 41 states (right now) permit them, some are still not happy with average citizens owning suppressors.

Handguns suppressors are, for the most part, threaded onto the barrel. To do that, you need an extra half-inch or so of barrel, threaded to the correct pitch, and that means you need a replacement barrel for your Glock. Once you have that, unload and disassemble your Glock. Remove the factory barrel and replace it with the threaded barrel. Reassemble, then screw the suppressor on. Once tight, you're ready to go. Yes, it's that easy.

The insides of a suppressor are both simple and fiendishly complicated—and not easy to make, in case you were wondering.

A bit of Cold War history. This is an utterly unmarked Makarov, with a threaded barrel for a suppressor.

jurisdiction makes the coroner a law enforcement officer, and BATFE has to accept what the laws of the local jurisdiction are). If all that is to no avail, but state law still permits ownership, go to your attorney. Have them form a trust, and the trust will then own the suppressor. The big advantage here is that you do not need the signature. The drawbacks are that you have to conform to the state law concerning trusts, and if that means annual meetings, annual taxes/fees, etc., then you'd better be diligent about keeping up. If you do not, and as a result your trust is voided, you are in illegal possession of NFA items.

Mounting and Operation

To mount a suppressor on a Glock, you have to have a new barrel. Handgun suppressors are, for the most part, threaded onto the barrel. To do that, you need an extra half-inch or so of barrel, threaded to the correct pitch. Once you have that, unload and disassemble your Glock. Remove the factory barrel and replace it with the threaded barrel. Reassemble, then screw the suppressor on. Once tight, you're ready to go. Yes, it's that easy.

Well, more or less. First of all, the extra weight of the suppressor is on the barrel. That means the entire weight of the suppressor is acting on the system before it unlocks. The extra weight can be more than a handgun can take, and some will not have enough operating margin to still work. The Glock, as it is relatively more efficient at staying closed, has less than others. I've seen shooters demonstrate this by putting a thumb behind the slide of a Glock and firing the gun. The slide stays shut, and they suffer no apparent harm.

In order to make sure the pistol works, you have to have a booster of some kind. (Some won't need it, but, if yours does, you have to adapt.) The technical name is "inertial recoil decoupler," but it's generally known as a "Nielsen device." This device takes some of the gases that have been vented into the suppressor and, essentially, directs them to slap a weight back against the front of the slide, giving it a

SUPPRESSORS | 165

The compensator is screwed onto the threaded barrel and provides recoil reduction, albeit at the price of enhanced muzzle blast.

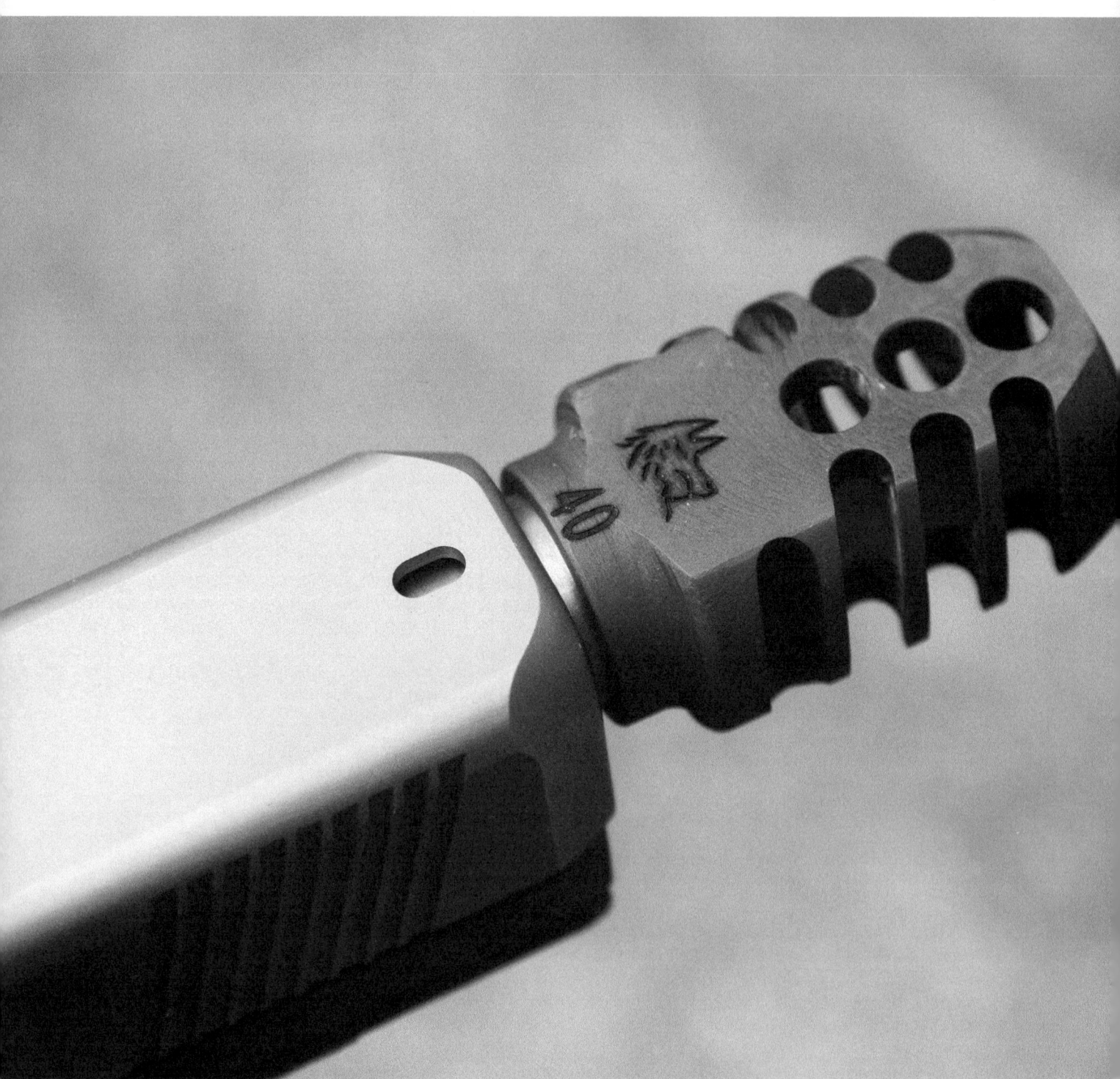

(above) A Lone Wolf pistol needs, nay *requires,* a Lone Wolf barrel. This is an accurate one, no great surprise.

(left) Try not to lose the thread protector. No, it won't be hard to find a replacement, but, until you do, all your friends will know you lost it.

boost in recoil. The result is a curious situation, whereby you have a heavier handgun, one that recoils harder than it otherwise would because of the slide getting an extra boost backwards. The recoil is different also, in that it feels as if the pistol has been slapped, so you have the initial recoil shove (if your hands are sensitive enough to "read" all this), quickly followed by the slap of the booster, and then the slide bottoming out in its recoil stroke.

A simple suppressor will be threaded on the back and won't permit installation of a booster. A takedown or cleanable suppressor, if designed for it, will often be able to accommodate having the rear cap exchanged for one with a built-in booster. So you could, theoretically, have a single suppressor, say in 9mm, that you could use on your Glock pistol with a booster, and on your 9mm carbine without booster. For edification, using the booster on the carbine would be pointless. The booster could not reach the slide (for there is none) but would add to recoil. Indeed, it would probably be bad for the suppressor and booster to use it on a carbine, as the booster would be getting slapped by the gases without the slide to take up the energy.

Sights

Suppressors take up space. They have to, or they wouldn't work. This means that, in a lot of cases, maybe even most, the suppressor is going to be high enough above the bore that it blocks your sights. One solution is to install taller sights, both front and back, so you can see over the suppressor.

Now I'm different. Consider for a moment the process of aiming. Your eyes don't really aim, your brain does. Your eyes simply report what they see to your brain. I've always been able to aim sights, even when they were "blocked" by the suppressor. This does require aiming with both eyes open, something I've never had a problem with. My right eye sees the sights, my left sees the target, my brain combines the two pictures, and I'm off to the races.

This is the "Bindon Aiming Concept," an idea first promoted by Glyn Bindon, the owner of Trijicon. Take a red-dot scope, say, on a rifle. Turn the dot on and close the front cover. Your aiming eye sees the dot, your other eye sees the target, your brain puts the two together. He had a line of sights back in the 1980s that worked that way.

(above) Here is another Mak, this one with its suppressor.

(below) If you thought the Mak was ugly and crude, then the suppressor it came with is even worse. Rubber wipes, a mid-twentieth century method at best, and an incredibly crude internal baffle stack. It would be embarrassing for a spy to shoot or be shot by this.

You'll need a booster with a pistol suppressor. These take some of the gases that have been vented into the suppressor and directs them to slap a weight back against the front of the slide, boosting recoil.

SUPPRESSORS | 169

Anyway, if your brain works with it, you need not raise your sights. However, if yours can't, then raising the sights is not a problem. You'll just have taller sights than normal when the suppressor isn't on your Glock.

Maintenance

How much do you need to baby your suppressor? Good question. Probably no more than you need to baby your Glock. While you do need to tend to them, you don't have to wrap them in bubble wrap between range outings. (You do have to keep track of it—losing a handgun is a bad thing, but losing a suppressor is like losing a machine gun.)

It also depends on how your suppressor is constructed. If yours is a heavy-walled stainless steel tube with welded-in baffles, you could probably use it as a breaker bar when changing a tire or as an impact weapon and not hurt it. I've seen suppressors so built that had gouges in them from military and LEO demos and still worked just fine. On the other hand, if yours is a lightweight unit made from titanium, you may not want to be abusing it in such a manner. There's also the endless debate about designs that can be disassembled and cleaned and those that can't. Me, I don't worry too much. I've been shown suppressors totally packed with powder residue such that there was just a clearance down the middle for the bullet. They still worked just fine.

Is their decibel reduction diminished when they're filthy? Sure, but not so much that you can listen and go "That's the packed one and the other one is the new one." You'd have to get a decibel meter set up and try them side by side to tell the difference. Regardless, keep them looking good, use them, don't abuse them, and worry about how much gunk is in them after you've pumped a few ten thousand rounds through them.

The iconic DeLisle carbine in .45 ACP was very quiet by the standards of the day (WWII) and heavy. It's nearly as heavy as a BAR.

If you have a threaded barrel, it may not always have a suppressor on it. You'll want to hang on to the thread protector it should have come with.

SUPPRESSORS | 171

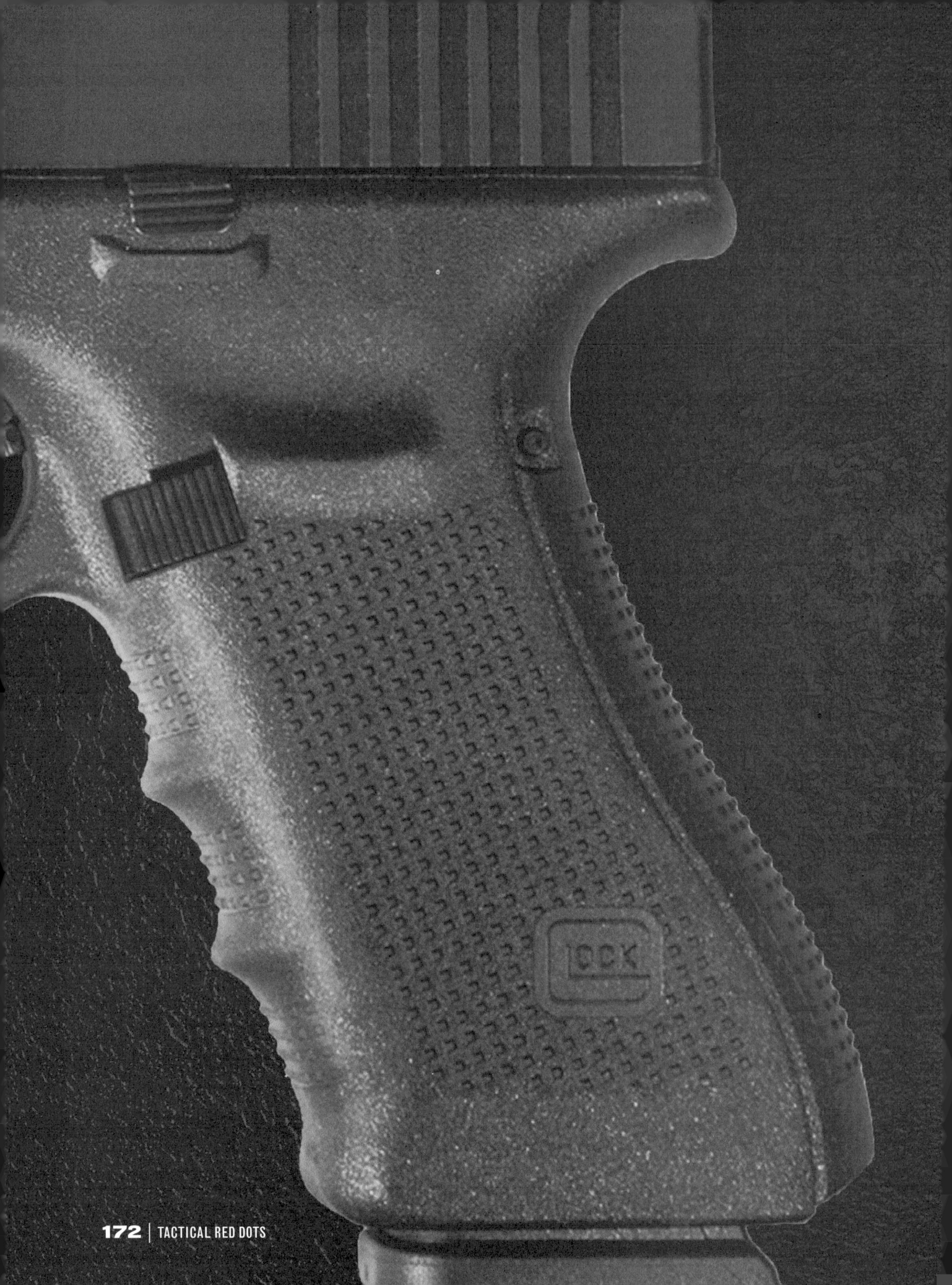

CHAPTER 12

Tactical Red Dots

The Lone Wolf open gun, where no single part ever saw the inside of Glock, in Smyrna.

Fans of the revival *Battlestar Galactica* will recognize this: "This has all happened before, and it will happen again."

In every endeavor, something new comes along, takes precedence, and then is replaced by the new and improved whatever. Be it alloy, tool, process, skill, or even language, the old is replaced. Not in all instances is the replacement an improvement.

Sometimes change is forced. In such cases, the rewards usually go to those doing the forcing, not those who have to do the actual work—at least until the system collapses under the strains of the work-arounds forced by the wrong choice.

One could point to the Soviet Empire, collapsing under the weight of its own economic jury-rigging. A less loaded example would be English versus French.

For a period of nearly four centuries, the international language was French. It was spoken in the royal courts, in many an educated salon, and it was a language that crossed borders and ethnicities. It was the language of diplomacy. Why? At the start of that run, the French monarchy was the big deal in Europe. The Bourbon dynasty, beginning with Henry IV in 1589, was the start of French muscle, economically and militarily. By the time Louis XIV, "The Sun King," was building Versailles, in the 1660s, he was perhaps the richest and most powerful man in Europe. The Czars or the King of Spain might have collected more, but Russia was a technological and economic backwater, and the Spanish spent their New World gold and silver like drunken sailors and netted nothing for it. The Ottoman Empire was larger than both, but so sclerotic that, whatever riches the Sultan theoretically had, most was siphoned off into the pockets of underlings.

France involved itself in everyone else's business and attracted art, literary, and political aspirants towards the court. If you wanted to be with those who were someone or be someone yourself, you had to speak French.

Today, the language is English. Why? One could point to its flexibility, adaptability, and diversity. Or you could simply point out that a lot of big corporations use it and, if you're going to do business with them, you have to use it, too. English is the default language for technology and commerce. Beginning with President Ulysses S. Grant, the U.S. has had the largest economy of any country in the world. Yep, while Victorian England was ruling the Empire, we had a bigger economy. Big means opportunity, and that's how the world came to speak English (well, that and winning WWII).

What does all this have to do with firearms in general and Glocks in particular? For a long time, in organized combat, it was considered bad social form to actually aim. The British Army, in particular, was most put out by the revolutionary colonists aiming, and especially put out by their aiming at officers. Combat in the eighteenth century was risky enough, with lead and iron flying essentially at random. But to have someone, a mere 50 paces away, actually *aiming* at you? By god, send the dragoons to stomp him into a red spot in the mud, sir.

Curiously, aiming artillery was not considered a severe disregard of the proper rules for combat between gentlemen. Oh, artillery officers did their best to aim their cannons, but usually at other cannons, and not at ranges so close they could actually see the combatants at whom they were shooting. Through the period of the American Civil War, artillery sights were pretty rudimentary, but a good gun crew could lay, aim, and fire a 12-pound Napoleon well enough to have a good chance of hitting an opposing gun crew well beyond rifle range.

Actual sights, used for aiming, became common with the use of minié balls, then got quite involved, as rifles evolved to cartridge firearms. Basically, the greater consistency of cartridges made it possible to consider the act of aiming as something other than a four-letter word.

It wasn't long before sights, at least on rifles, became quite sophisticated: ladders, vernier scales, micrometer adjustments and, even on

> For a long time, in organized combat, it was considered bad social form to actually aim. The British Army, in particular, was most put out by the revolutionary colonists aiming, and especially put out by their aiming at officers. Combat in the eighteenth century was risky enough, with lead and iron flying essentially at random. But to have someone, a mere 50 paces away, actually *aiming* at you? By god, send the dragoons to stomp him into a red spot in the mud, sir.

the early Enfields, "volley" sights. Set that sight to 2,200 yards and have the whole rifle company hold on the next ridgeline. "Aim, *fire!*" At least, that was the theory.

Meanwhile, handgun sights remained vestigial lumps on the slide or barrel. I have a selection of handguns from various locations and covering each decade of the twentieth century. For much of that time, sights were pretty miserable, as aiming aids. I blame the cavalry. The cavalry was the elite fighting arm for a long time, right up to the chatter of belt-fed machine guns in France, the summer of 1914. Cavalry depended on shock tactics, the "shock and awe" of its time. You didn't have to hit with every pistol shot. The trooper behind you would, or he'd cut them down with his sabre or spit them on his lance. Too, you didn't ride into an enemy formation or location, you rode *through*. Then you reformed and rode back through in the opposite direction. Do that a couple times, pistols blazing and sabers slashing, and the infantry

(left) TSD has its own approach. It rebuilds Glocks, rather than make new pistols from scratch. They're good pistols.

(below) The tall sights? That's so you can still see your sights over the suppressor you might install on the threaded barrel.

Just like a Glock, the serial number is where you'd expect it. Why make anyone hunt for it?

would break and run. Or the artillerists would abandon their guns. Then the real fun began. Bottom line, at full speed, all you could do was point a pistol, so why have more sight than needed?

The cavalry is long behind us now, and pistols aren't main armaments any more, but rather backups, secondary, and specialty tools. Despite the pant-wetting hysteria of the VPC (very politically correct) crowd, there are no "assault" handguns. One does not mount an assault, using a handgun, unless there is nothing else to be done or for it to be done with.

As emergency tools, we need handguns to be as efficient at the job as possible. It took a while, starting with the efforts of Jeff Cooper and the Bear Valley Gunslingers, back in the late 1950s and early 1960s, but the idea of actually using the sights to be faster at getting hits than you would with "natural" pointing finally took hold. By the time Glock came along, in the early 1980s, and despite the point-shooters who were still putting up a stiff fight, the handwriting was clear: sights win.

What we got in sights on the G17 was state-of-the-art for the time. They were a dot front and an outline rear, big and fixed. Too bad they were plastic, but Gaston came up with a clever way of attaching them. Unfortunately, the clever way precluded any other way, and so we've been stuck with plastic sights on Glocks ever since.

Oh, you can get steel sights into a Glock slide, but it isn't easy. Well, the rear is pretty straightforward, what with the dovetail. You just press out the old, press in the new, and *voilà*, you have steel. But up front? That little sight and its plastic wedge? What a pain in the butt. Not for the sight, because as long as it remains intact, you can pretty much count on it being there. Aye, there's the rub: staying intact.

Polymer has a long list of positive attributes, but how it wears isn't one of them. At least, not when wear is applied to a small part. Steel is better, but how to attach a steel sight to the front? With tiny threaded shafts and tiny hex-head nuts, that's how, and once together you must Locktite the assembly to within an inch of its life or it will loosen and fall off. So, once on, it is permanent. A front dovetail would have been better. Oh, well.

But, we're here for red dot sights. If you've spent any time looking at photos from Iraq or Afghanistan, you'll notice a few things. For one, every rifle you see has an optical sight on it, either a red dot or a low-power magnifier. They also have a lot of other extras, such as double-magazine holders, bipods, and the front handrails (they have railed handguards, not the simple plastic clamshells of old), and some have a laser targeting designator.

All of that, except for the laser, came from practical shooting competition known as

3-Gun. In fact, a current-issue M4 carbine would have made a pretty decent Open Division rifle about 1995. If, however, in 1995, you had suggested that the Army, Marines, etc., would be issuing, *across the board*, optics, railed handguards, and more, you'd have been laughed out of the squad room. However, when the score isn't just numbers posted on a bulletin board, but rather people on your side hurt or killed due to less-effective tools, what is normally done quickly gets jettisoned.

Okay, so red dots on handguns? No big surprise here, as red dots on competition guns have been *en vogue* for 20 years now. Ten years ago, in a Krause Publications book of mine, out just before my first Glock book, I suggested that a red dot-equipped and compensated handgun might make a pretty interesting entry gun. Today, red dots are no longer rare, fragile, and bulky, nor do they have a short battery life.

Advantages

The red dot solves an optical problem that a

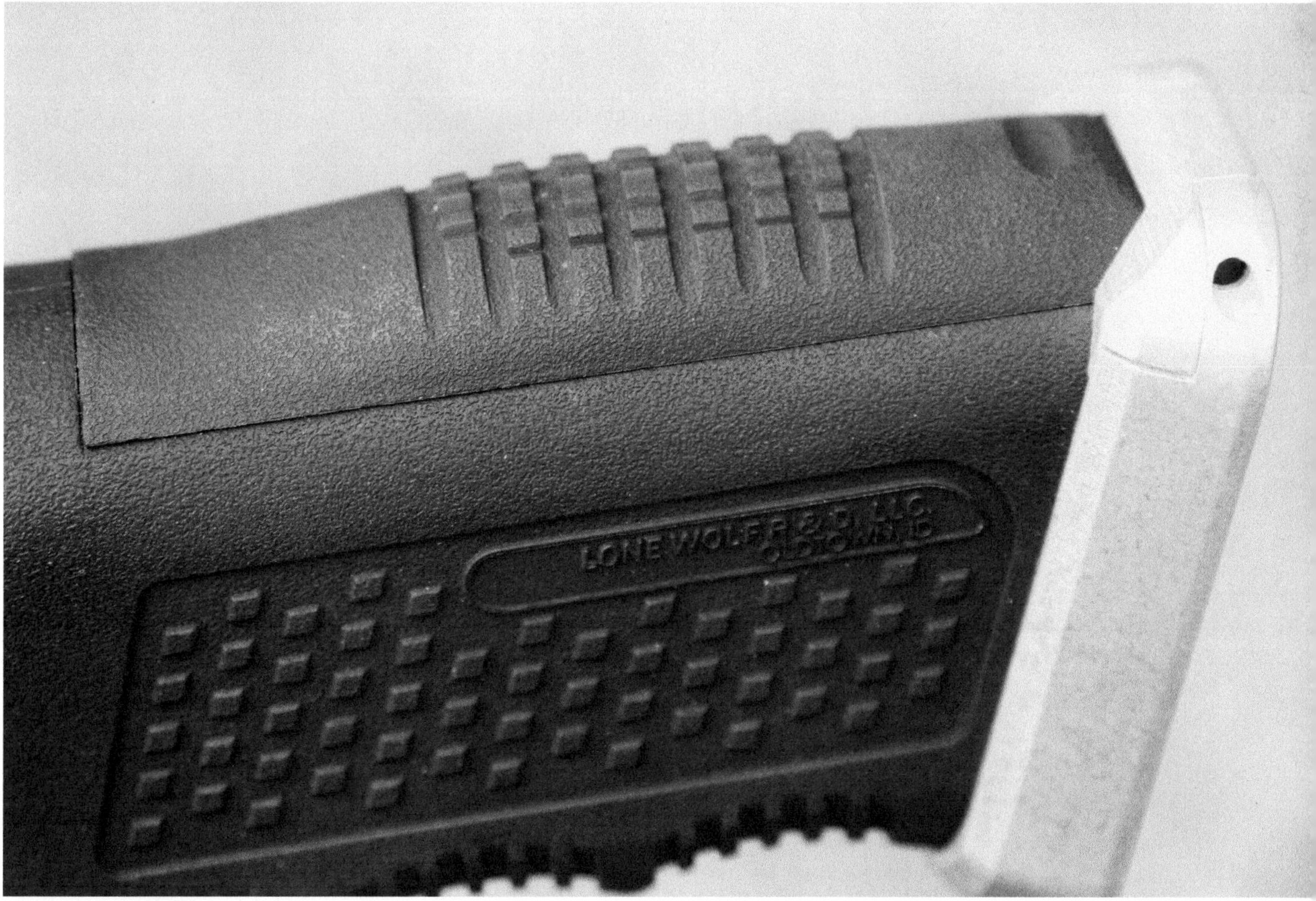

Unlike Glock, which makes its backstrap an add-on, Lone Wolf uses a replaceable panel.

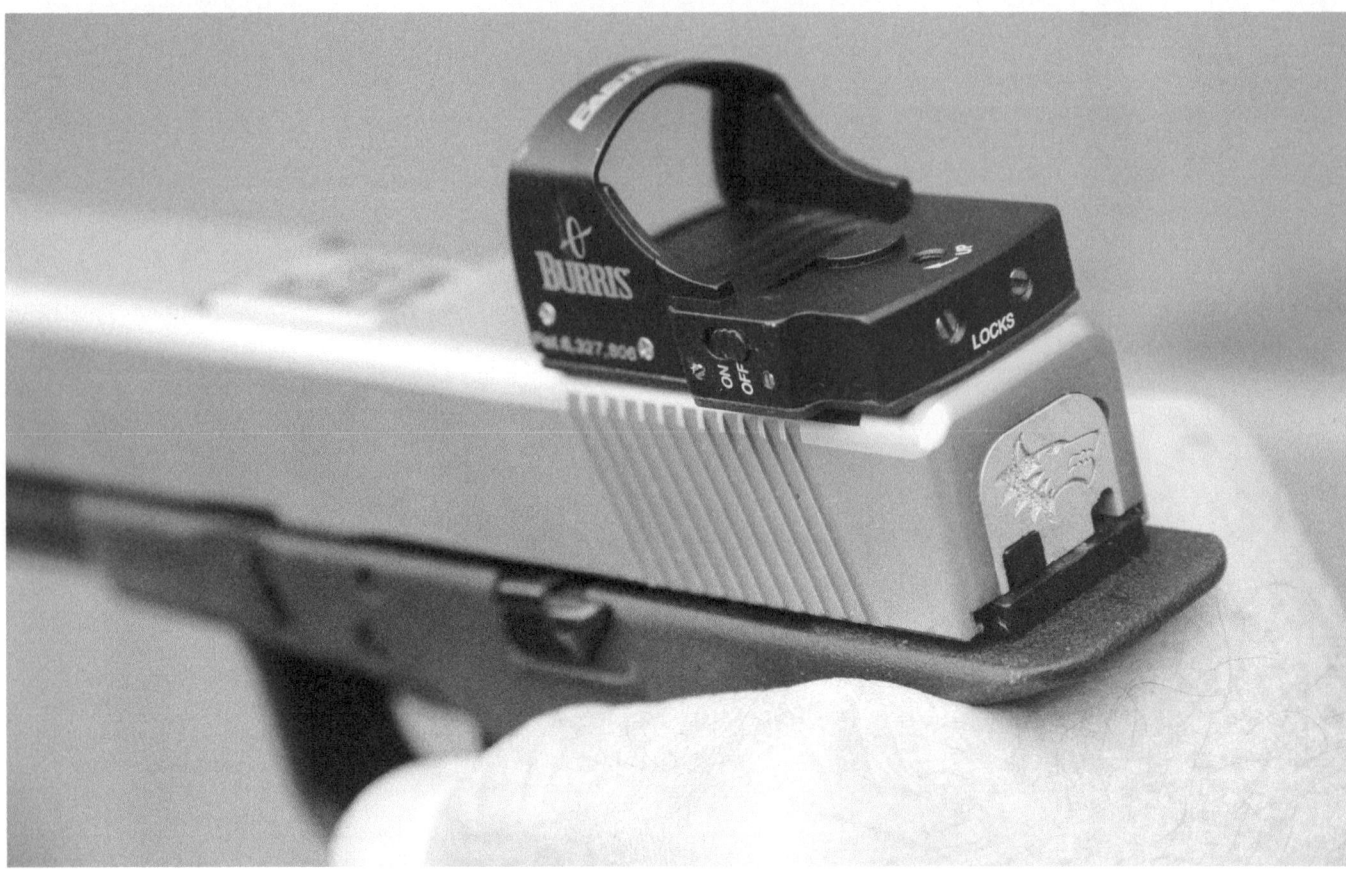

The Lone Wolf has an extended tang, not that you need it, but it can enhance control and improve your scores.

lot of people have to deal with, and one that the NRA in its marksmanship efforts has been trying to properly describe for decades. Basically, to aim a handgun (or rifle) with iron sights, you have to align three things, the rear sight, the front sight, and the target. Get any one or two out of line and you miss. The problem? Your eyes can't do all that. They can focus (mechanically dial in to optical sharpness) just one thing at a time. So, in order to aim, you'd have to have your eye mechanically focus across three spots in rapid order.

The classic marksmanship solution to this is to focus on the two that you control, the front and rear sight, and leave the target blurry. This works just fine when the target is stationary and clearly delineated. A black bull's-eye on a white background is easy to keep track of, while you're mechanically focusing on the front and rear sights. (And just to be clear, until otherwise described, I'm not talking about mental focus at all. Just the optical/mechanical focus of "Is that object clearly outlined?") But, when the target is not black-on-white or is moving, allowing it to be a blurry blob against which you interpose the image of your sharply focused sights doesn't work very well.

A red dot or optical sight with a low magnification solves that problem by presenting the shooter with only two things to focus on, the target and the red dot or reticle of the scope. Place the dot or crosshairs on the target, press and repeat as necessary. If there is time, it is even possible to mechanically focus the scope so that both reticle and target are clearly delineated. By making the aiming process easier in this manner, it is possible to shoot more accurately and faster. Proof of this comes from a common observation: in competition, regardless its kind, if optics are allowed, they are scored separately from iron sights.

Disadvantages

The faults, if faults they be, are obvious. First, it simply isn't possible to make a red dot sight as compact as iron sights are. They will always be bigger and require a special holster, simply to account for the extra bulk. Second, since they are larger, the red dot will be higher above the axis of the bore than iron sights will be. (This can be an asset, if you are using a Glock with a red dot sight and a suppressor. The dot will be above the rim of the "can" and aiming is easy.)

You do have to make a distinction between rifle sights and handgun sights, when it comes

Today, red dots are no longer rare, fragile, bulky, or have a short battery life.

There are now factory models of pistols that come ready for a red dot sight. What used to be for open competition only is leaking over to the practical and tactical side.

TACTICAL RED DOTS | **179**

Even without a muzzle brake, the TSD has little recoil and is fast on the plates.

Your basic G17 Gen4, rebuilt to be a race gun, tactical gun, carry gun, or whatever you want it to be gun.

Basically, to aim a handgun or rifle with iron sights, you have to align three things, the rear sight, the front sight, and the target. Get any one or two out of line and you miss.

Here the Lone Wolf demonstrates how compensators work. Hot gases vent up and to the sides, and the muzzle stays down.

to dots. The rifle sights, exemplified by those that come from Aimpoint and EOTech, are bulky indeed. But, then, they have to be, to be sturdy enough to withstand not just rifle recoil, but rifle handling. While handguns can recoil sharply, they are not exposed to the banging around that rifles can get.

For handgun use, rifle red dots are too big.

That wasn't always the case. In the early 1990s, when red dot sights started to become common in competition, we had no choice. So we figured out ways to mount full-sized optics to handguns. They were sometimes nearly as large as the handguns they were mounted to! To give you an idea of how large they were, at that time it was still relatively common to have Standards in handgun competition. Every Standards stage had to have a weak-hand-only firing string. It was common for shooters to "draw" the handgun out of the holster by grabbing the scope (from the top) with their strong hand, and then transfer the gun to their weak hand before beginning shooting.

As they are larger than iron sights, red dots add weight. As extra weight to carry, the largest are too big, but we've already eliminated the Aimpoints or EOTechs from handgun use these days. The extra half-ounce a JPoint, for instance, adds is inconsequential.

Red dot sights need batteries. We can't get around that, and until someone comes up with an onboard battery that can recharge, you'll have to carry spares and swap them when one gets too weak. When the battery dies, you have a big, open window through which to aim. At very short distances, that could be "good enough," but, for most uses, it isn't.

Red dot sights are more fragile than iron sights. Bang them too hard and they will quit. They also have that big open window to deal with and, if it gets blocked by rain, snow, mud, dirt, etc., you don't have an aiming device.

I was once in a training class, using a red dot on a rifle. It began to rain, and since this was training, we didn't quit. The rain turned into a torrential downpour, and my red dot sight was so rain-smeared I couldn't aim with it. Luckily, it was mounted on a QD setup and I could pry it off and continue.

One solution would be to stick with iron sights. Another would be to install a red dot sight, machine the slide to accept it (instead of an external, frame-mounted scope mount), set it in as low as possible, and to install iron sights, too. Let's look at a pair of Glocks with red dots on them.

TSD

From One Source Tactical, the TSD package on a Glock is pretty cool. The company takes a Glock (yours or its) and machines the slide to accept a Trijicon RMR sight. Or you can have an aftermarket slide, if you wish. The Trijicon RMR also gets companion sights, iron sights that are tall enough to show in the bottom of

That's a standing, two-handed, 100-yard group. On a cold, blustery March day. That's what a red-dot sight does for you.

the window of the RMR so that, if the battery dies, you can still use the irons. However, if the window shatters or gets obscured, you've got a rear sight and no chance of seeing the front sight.

One Source Tactical machines a recess for the Trijicon right in front of the rear sight in the space between the rear sight and the ejection port and bolts down the RMR in there. The front and rear are replaced with taller sights, so you can still see them through the window. As an option, One Source offers extended, threaded barrels, so you can combine all the current man-jewelry items and put a suppressor on your Glock. As another option, it can sculpt and reshape the frame so it points more like a 1911, if that's your wish, or still point like a Glock but have a more aggressive surface texture.

One Source sent me one, built on a Gen4 G17, and I had a grand time reacquiring my skills in shooting an IPSC Open gun, which is basically what this is, absent the compensator. Fast shots at close range were the norm, small groups at normal handgun distances were easy to produce, and dropping the computerized pop-up targets at the National Guard base involved learning the hold for the wind, more than anything else. For the camera, I shot a standing nine-shot group at 100 yards. (By the time I got to that point of the day's range work, there were only nine rounds left in the box.) Eight of the nine were inside of the USPSA target "C" zone, centered about six or seven inches below the center of the aiming circle. The one stray out of the "C" zone was directly to the left, a classic trigger finger push/slap shot out of the group. At no time did the TSD Glock show signs of wanting to quit, failure to function, or disagreement with ammo I fed it.

As an extra, One Source included an in-the-waistband kydex holster sculpted to fit the G17 with the RMR on it. The extra kydex keeps the RMR away from your ribs and lint off the scope. The RMR has a two-year battery life, four years if you put it on brightness setting "4" on the adjustable LED version. Two years makes things simple. Annually, on your birthday, Christmas, whatever day you've selected, change the battery for a fresh one. Sure, you're tossing out a year's worth of run-time, but ,for the cost of batteries, who cares? Skip one flavored latté and you've got the battery cost covered.

> Red dot sights are more fragile than iron sights. Bang them too hard and they will quit. They also have that big open window to deal with and, if it gets blocked by rain, snow, mud, dirt, etc., you don't have an aiming device.

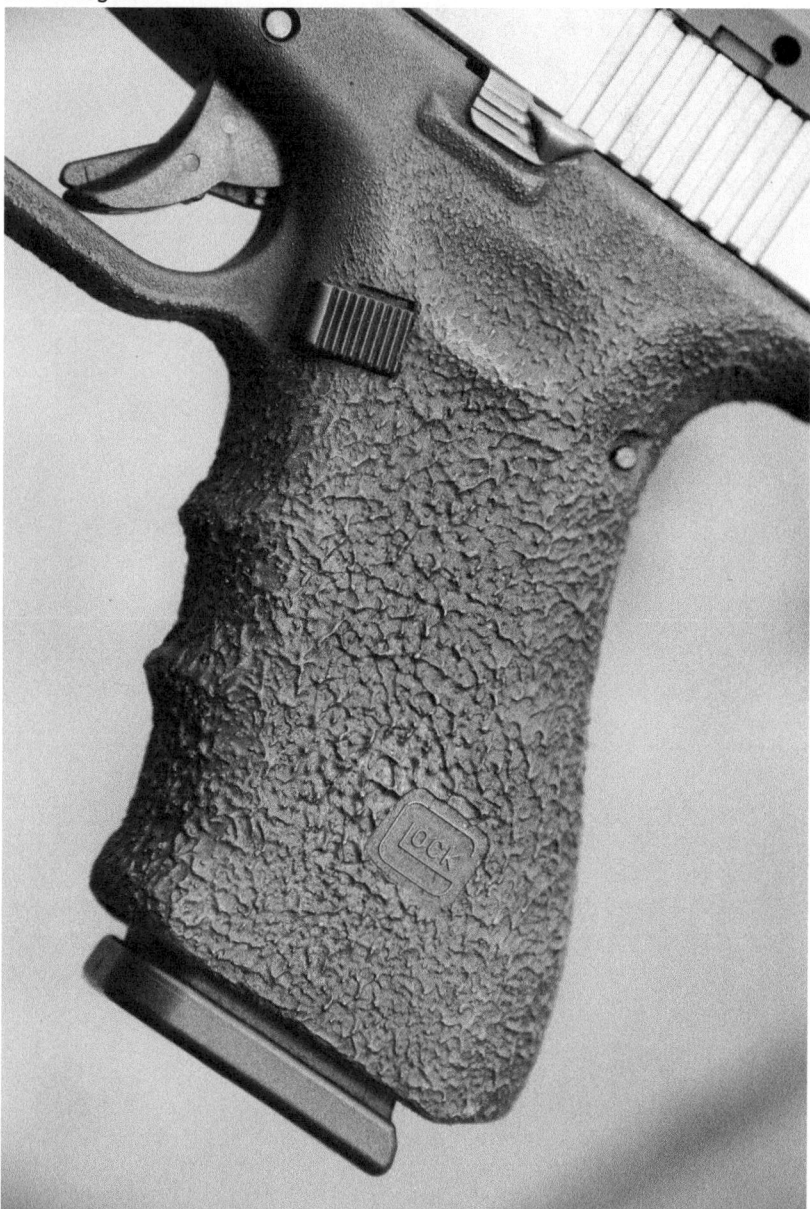

While TSD kept the general contour of the Gen4 frame, it textured it to provide a non-slip surface more aggressive than that of the factory finish. That can come in handy when you top the gun with an expensive red dot sight you don't want to see damaged.

TACTICAL RED DOTS | 183

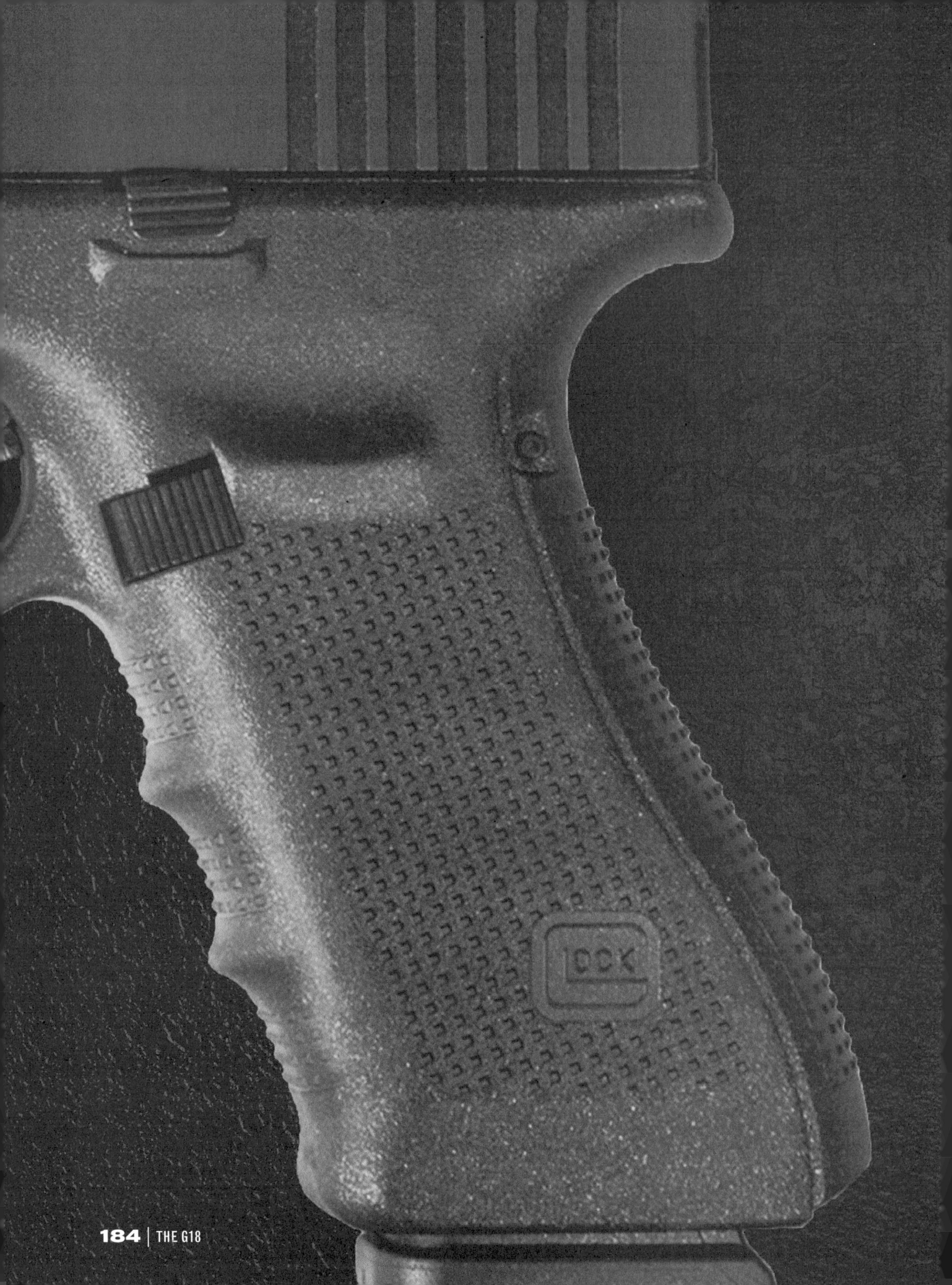

184 | THE G18

CHAPTER 13

The G18

If you didn't know what the lever was for at the top of the slide, you might mistake this for a G17 with a custom safety.

In the pantheon of desirable firearms, the goodie-blasters we can't have but dearly want, the G18 is *very* high on the list. What is the G18? Simply put, it is a G17 with a buzz switch. Select-fire. Fully automatic. One of the fastest ways to turn money into noise. (One of the others being auto racing.)

The simple rollmark that causes so much lust in the Glock-verse.

It was literally less expensive for Gaston Glock to simply buy a warehouse full of ammo (which he had to do anyway, to test-fire each and every firearm before it left the factory), than buy computer time and expertise. The most expensive part of his task: labor. The time it took for someone to stand there on the range and pull the trigger, over and over and over, was the pricey part.

And how did this wondrous beast come about? Well, when I first looked into the matter, all we "knew" was what had been told to us for many years, that the super-secret anti-terrorist agency in Austria, EKO Cobra (and that name alone sounds like someone had spent too much time watching spy movies), had asked for it. Ostensibly, they wanted something with lots of output in a small package. As had been explained to me back then, "A guy standing in an airport, holding an MP5, might as well have a 'Shoot me first' sign overhead. Cobra wanted lots of firepower without the sign."

Select-fire pistol-caliber firearms are nothing new. By then they hadn't been new for more than three-quarters of a century. The archetype was the 1896 Broomhandle Mauser, of which the world had seen plenty during WWII. They had been popular before, but before and during WWII, they were so desired in China, local machine shops made copies. The Germans, needing everything they could get their hands on, while on the Eastern Front, to hose Soviet infantry off the tanks they were riding, produced the *Schnellfeuer*, a select-fire C96 Mauser with a 20-round box magazine.

As a fun toy and a way to turn ammunition into noise, heat, and busted range props, a machine pistol is very cool. As a toy to do more than scare the uninitiated and potentially make you look like a goof, it has no equal. But they are fun.

So, how did the G18 come about? Economics. Gaston Glock wanted to conduct high-volume testing of the G17, to make sure there wasn't some small flaw someplace. Remember, this was before computer-aided design and manufacturing integrated with big business. Too, even in the 1980s and despite the burgeoning revolution in desktop computers, this type of analysis wasn't easy for a small company. To run computer simulations on anything required hiring specialists—specialist engineers, specialist programmers, specialists every step of the way. So, it was literally less expensive for Gaston Glock to simply buy a warehouse full of ammo (which he had to do anyway, to test fire each and every firearm before it left the factory), than buy computer time and expertise.

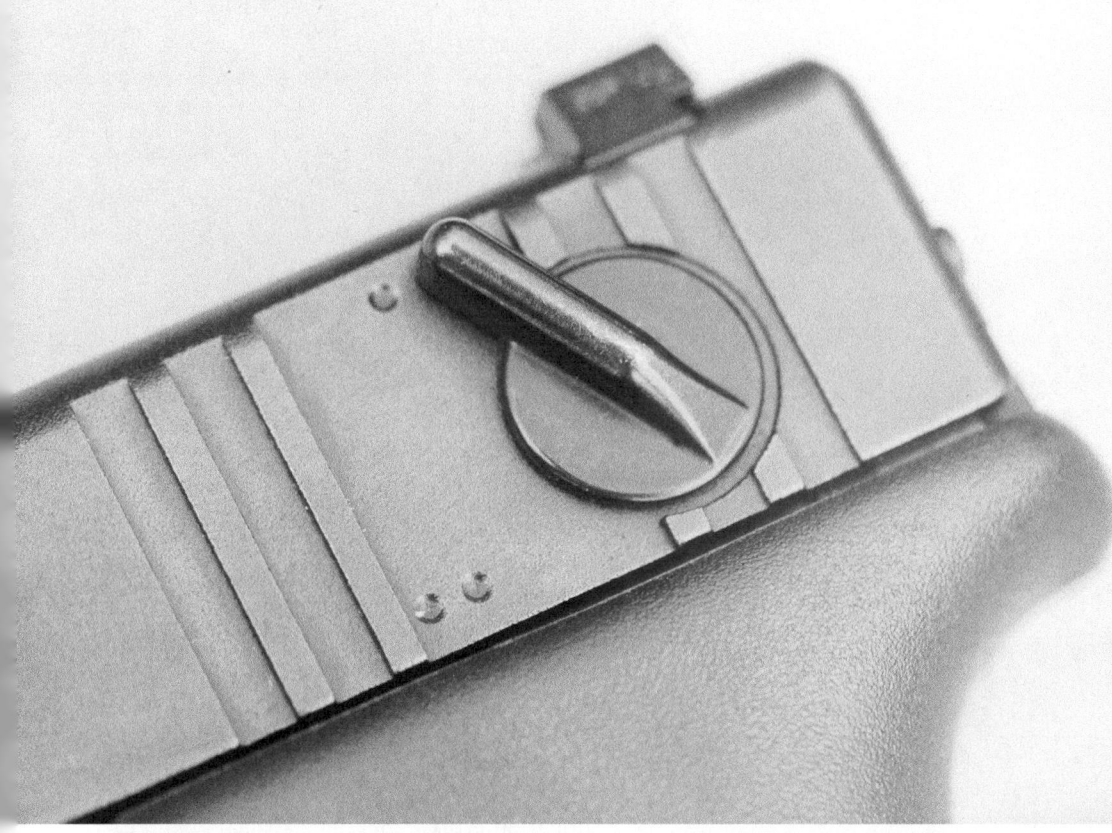

(left) The selector lever is simple—up is one and down is giggle.

(below) The G18 (at least this one, but, for all we know, all of them), was so early in the timeline that it is proofmarked on the polymer frame.

THE G18 | 187

The most expensive part of his task: labor. The time it took for someone to stand there on the range and pull the trigger, over and over and over, was the pricey part. Consider the last time you went to the range. How much time did you spend and how much ammo did you shoot? Even just slapping the trigger and not trying to aim or work on skills, it takes time to consume a pile of ammo. So Gaston Glock devised a conversion for his G17 to make it full-auto. Instead of a company employee standing on the range for days on end, grinding his way through ammo, that same employee could shoot his way through a couple cases before lunch and a couple more before clocking out.

Now, the people present when I learned this tidbit all thought it was funny, but not in a good way. The owner of a multi-million dollar enterprise making a special gizmo to save a few bucks? Me, I was less amused than appreciative. When Gaston Glock did this, he was not the head of a multi-million dollar firearms empire. He had one firearm product, and one client—the Austrian Army. If, in a year or three that army found out there was some flaw in his G17, Glock would have been well and royally screwed. The Austrians would have wanted their money back, Gaston would have been stuck with unsold inventory and, even if he did find a solution, his reputation would have been a total loss. (Think of the firearms makers *you* wouldn't buy from, based on what you've "heard" about their product. See what I mean?)

There is another imperative to this approach besides saving a few bucks, and that is saving time. If you are going to have to make design or engineering changes, the time to find out is before you have made anything. Once you start making things, the price and time lost to go back and correct it add up at a staggering rate.

Finally, hiring an employee in Europe, especially Germany or Austria, isn't like here in the States. Here, you need someone you hire someone. If work drops off or the job is done, you hand them a pink slip and tell them "I'll give you good references."

There, then, in Europe? You hire someone and you have them for the rest of their working days. Glock wasn't going to hire someone who might turn out to be superfluous next year. Remember, *he didn't know he would be a multimillionaire in a few years.*

So, Gaston Glock slaps together a modified G17, and shoots the snot out of it.

And this is where the Cobra guys *do* enter the picture. Apparently, at a time when the modified G17 was being thrashed, there were some guys from *Einsatzkommando Cobra* there to see this new pistol that the Army was adopting and heard the commotion. (Hard to miss, really.) "What's that? Sounds cool. We want some. When can you have

Hi-cap magazines are not new. This set of magazines and leather carrying case date from before WWII.

Simple, durable, and unavailable to Glock owners, this is a common method of stocking a handgun.

them shipped?" In short order Gaston had to take his cobbled-together G17 select-fire handgun and make it into an actual machine pistol. And, to keep everyone happy, he had to throw in some dimensional changes so the new G18 parts would not slap right onto a G17 and turn *it* into a machine pistol.

Today, you can buy a really cool AR-15 for $1,500. A transferable M16 can easily run you *$15,000*. A dealer's sample, since it can only be ordered, sold to a P.D. or another dealer, and re-ordered, runs a bit more than its equivalent AR, and most of that is due to the extra paperwork and hassle of the process, but it's nowhere near $15,000, that's for sure.

A Slight Digression

Now, as a select-fire (or even as a full-auto) firearm, the G18 is covered by the National Firearms Act of 1934 and the Firearms Owners Protection Act of 1986. The NFA-34 (abbreviated even more in firearms-speak to "NFA"), means that ownership requires a lot of hoop-jumping. For a select-fire firearm in general, acquiring such a firearm requires application, a transfer tax of $200 (which was a metric butt-load of money in 1934, equal to about $3,300 in today's dollars), and a wait while they check you out. The FOPA-86 adds a twist. In that enacted law, no newly manufactured machine guns could be purchased by civilians. The existing ones, machine guns manufactured and registered *before* the date of the act (May 19, 1986) and known as "transferables," could be bought, sold, traded, modified, or rebuilt, but no new ones could be made for sale or distribution to anyone who wasn't military or law enforcement, or as test firearms created by manufacturers and some "dealer samples."

Let's propose for the moment that the perfect select-fire firearm has been devised. Let's call it the XYZ-1. It does everything but slice bread and brew coffee and everyone wants one. If your police department wants to see if the XYZ-1 is for them, it has to have a sample firearm brought to them, it cannot simply ask for a loaner to test. Doesn't work that way. So, the local Class 3 dealer gets a demonstration letter of intent from the P.D. and sends a copy along with a check to the XYZ Corporation and another copy to the BATFE. Everyone waits until the BATFE says "Yes," and then the XYZ Corp ships a dealer's sample of the XYZ-1 to the local C3 dealer. The dealer then shows it to the local police department.

"Cool!" you're thinking, "I'll apply for a Class 3 dealer's license. My buddy at the P.D. can cut me a letter, and then we're home free." *That's the kind of thinking that lands people in prison.* No, I'm not kidding, and neither is the BATFE. People have gone to prison over just that sort of thing.

There are other limits. First, dealer samples can be sold only to another dealer; such a sample is not eligible to become a transferable. If you've ever looked into machine gun prices, this explains the two-tier pricing you'd see.

Let's take as a real-world example, the M16.

Since the number of transferables was frozen in 1986, the price has gone up. In 1986, you could buy an M16 for about $100 more than an AR-15. Call it $600 and $700, AR-15 and M16. While economics as a "science"— you couldn't get 10 economists to agree on what pizza to order, let alone what will happen in the future—is a pretty dreary subject, economics as a business subject is pretty clear: Freeze the available supply of a desired object and the price goes up.

Today, you can buy a really cool AR-15 for $1,500. A transferable M16 can easily run you *$15,000*. A dealer's sample, since it can only be ordered, sold to a P.D. or another dealer, and re-ordered, runs a bit more than its equivalent AR, and most of that is due to the extra paperwork and hassle of the process, but it's nowhere near $15,000, that's for sure.

Where does this leave us with the G18? Consider the time line. The Glock comes about in 1982, but doesn't arrive in the United States until 1985. The law is changed in May of 1986, leaving us a very narrow window for

Common in the pre-WWII days, the stock was a holster and, in some designs, also the magazine carrier.

any transferable G18s to have been imported. Toss in the reluctance of Glock as a company to deal in G18s, and the number is even lower. I have heard various estimates of the number of transferable G18s in the USA as being somewhere on the order of two to 10. All the rest are either dealer's samples (D-S) or police property.

Now, if you have done any Internet surfing on machine guns, you've no doubt read of police departments and sheriff's offices selling or auctioning machine guns. Their ability to do so depends entirely on how they acquired them. If they bought them as transferables, they can sell them. If they bought them as PD-only, post-1986 firearms, they cannot. Also to be noted, if they confiscated them and applied to the BATFE for possession, they cannot sell them.

So, what explains all those Glock (and other) machine gun videos you see on the Internet? Simple. They are dealer's samples being test-run while someone turns on their video camera. Or they are manufacturers' test guns, R&D models, being given their moment of fame the same way. You cannot buy them.

Glock got even more reluctant about this particular gun as time went by. I know of one NFA-item manufacturer who owns several G18s and cannot obtain spare parts for them; Glock won't sell them. And that manufacturer is reluctant to send the beasts in for repair, truly wondering if they'd be sent back. Getting a G18 in front of a police department essentially requires a visit by someone from Glock, *not* a local Class 3 licensed dealer with a D-S. Why? Because Glock won't ship a sample to a dealer. Fear not, though, your intrepid reporter has found ways to get you the info you so dearly seek.

A Work-Around

Okay, as a mechanical solution, turning any self-loading firearm into a machine gun is pretty easy. And no, it does not involve "filing the sear" or finding "the magic paperclip that you just wedge in the receiver in the right place." I swear, I've had both of those spouted at me. Hearing it from a newspaper reporter or seeing it on TV is bad enough, and hearing it at a gun shop is troublesome, but having it said in a court of law is blood pressure spike-inducing. Making a Glock full-auto takes an understanding of how things work and a machine shop. And in case I haven't made this point before, the first machine gun that John Moses Browning whipped up was born from a Winchester lever-action rifle. If you have the brains, you can make *anything* go fast. It is today, however, a strictly licensed and controlled exercise in mechanical engineering.

Back when machine guns were "expensive" (as I pointed out, your best investment in 1986 would have been to buy new-in-the-box Colt M16s instead of gold or stocks), guys converted them. Actually, the main reason they converted them—after the proper paperwork was filled out, an allowable thing pre-1986—

Here is the G17 test host, with some light custom work and the RDIAS installed on the rear of the slide.

RDIAS: registered drop-in auto sear. If you own an RDIAS, it *is* the machine gun. Once you are the proud owner of an RDIAS, you can install it into any firearm for which it fits. If you own a dozen ARs and an RDIAS, each and every one of your ARs can be, in turn, a machine gun. And it is all entirely kosher. You can also, *when the RDIAS is installed in a particular firearm*, change the AR to one with a shorter barrel. However, the moment the RDIAS comes out, the short barrel *must also* come off.

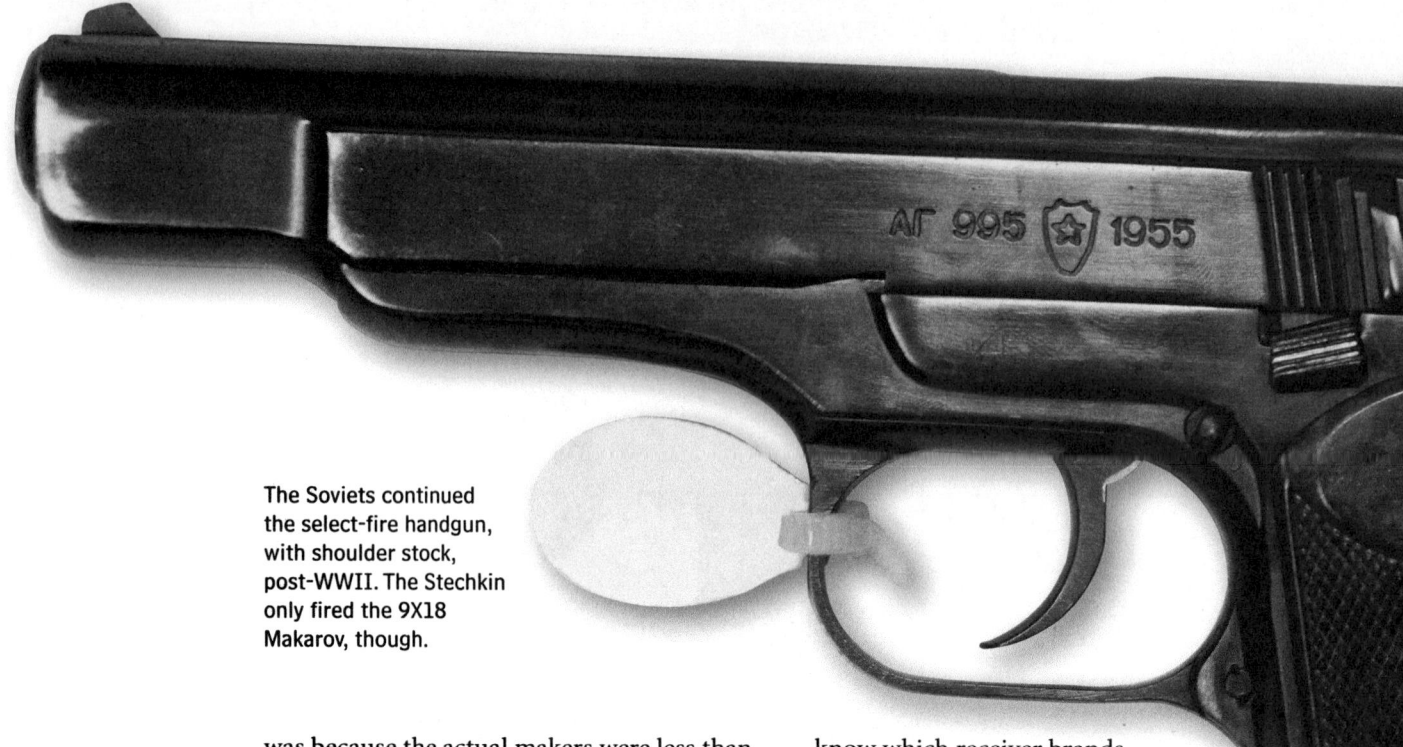

The Soviets continued the select-fire handgun, with shoulder stock, post-WWII. The Stechkin only fired the 9X18 Makarov, though.

was because the actual makers were less than eager to fill orders. Back in the old days, Colt's wasn't all that hot about selling machine guns to anyone but the military. (The police weren't often buying M16s back then, unlike today.) And, since Colt's was "it" for M16s, you'd have to find something else. Except all the big makers were pretty much on the same page, i.e., no machine guns for you. So, guys said, "Screw Colt's/HK/*et al*" and paid more than Colt's would have charged to have their AR-15s converted to M16 status.

Conversions came in two flavors, modified receivers or drop-in auto sears. As our example, we'll use the AR-15/M16. A modified receiver would be one that has had the rear of the lower machined to clear the auto sear, and the receiver drilled for the auto sear pivot pin. Once done, it is forever and always a machine gun. Install the correct parts, adjust for proper function, and you have an AR-15-marked rifle that works like an M16. There is a downside besides the inability to undo the work. If anything happens to bust the receiver, you are out of luck. It is toast. You can't replace it and, unless you can repair it, it is lost.

A drop-in sear nestles in the rear of the receiver, but does not require any receiver modifications. In fact, you *can't* make modifications, or the lower is suspect. (I know, I know, you aren't making any change more than a manufacturer would make, but remember, *you aren't a manufacturer.*) Since you can't make changes, the people in the NFA community who have these sears are the ones who know which receiver brands they will fit into and which they don't. And let's get right to the acronym, RDIAS: registered drop-in auto Sear. If you own an RDIAS, it *is* the machine gun. Once you are the proud owner of an RDIAS, you can install it into any firearm for which it fits. If you own a dozen ARs and an RDIAS, each and every one of your ARs can be, in turn, a machine gun. And it is all entirely kosher. You can also, *when the RDIAS is installed in a particular firearm*, change the AR to one with a shorter barrel. However, the moment the RDIAS comes out, the short barrel *must also* come off.

And so it is with Glocks. If you have a G18 and anything happens to it, you are toast, and so is it. If, however, you have a Glock RDIAS, you can install it into any Glock (known in the NFA parlance as the "host") and rock on.

The RDIAS is a low-wear part. It doesn't do more than trip the sear/hammer/striker/cruciform at the appropriate moment. The parts of it that do wear, properly designed, can be replaced; the one single part of it that has the serial number on it cannot. A smart designer takes a low-wear mechanism and puts the serial number on the no-wear part of it. If the host Glock gets worn to the point of being scrap, no big deal. The expensive part, the RDIAS, just goes on to the next Glock.

Now, the RDIAS arena is one that has great

The Stechkin. Take a pistol larger than a 1911, chamber it in the underpowered 9x18 Makarov (the "magnum" of the .380-class cartridges), use a blowback design because the 9x18 can't power a Browning locked-breech design, and then put a selector switch and stock on it. Then you fit it with a double-stack magazine holding 20 rounds, just to make the grip as fat as possible. The end result was worse than that unenthusiastic description. The Soviets made them by the metric butt-load and issued them, at least as much as they issued any firearms at all to anyone.

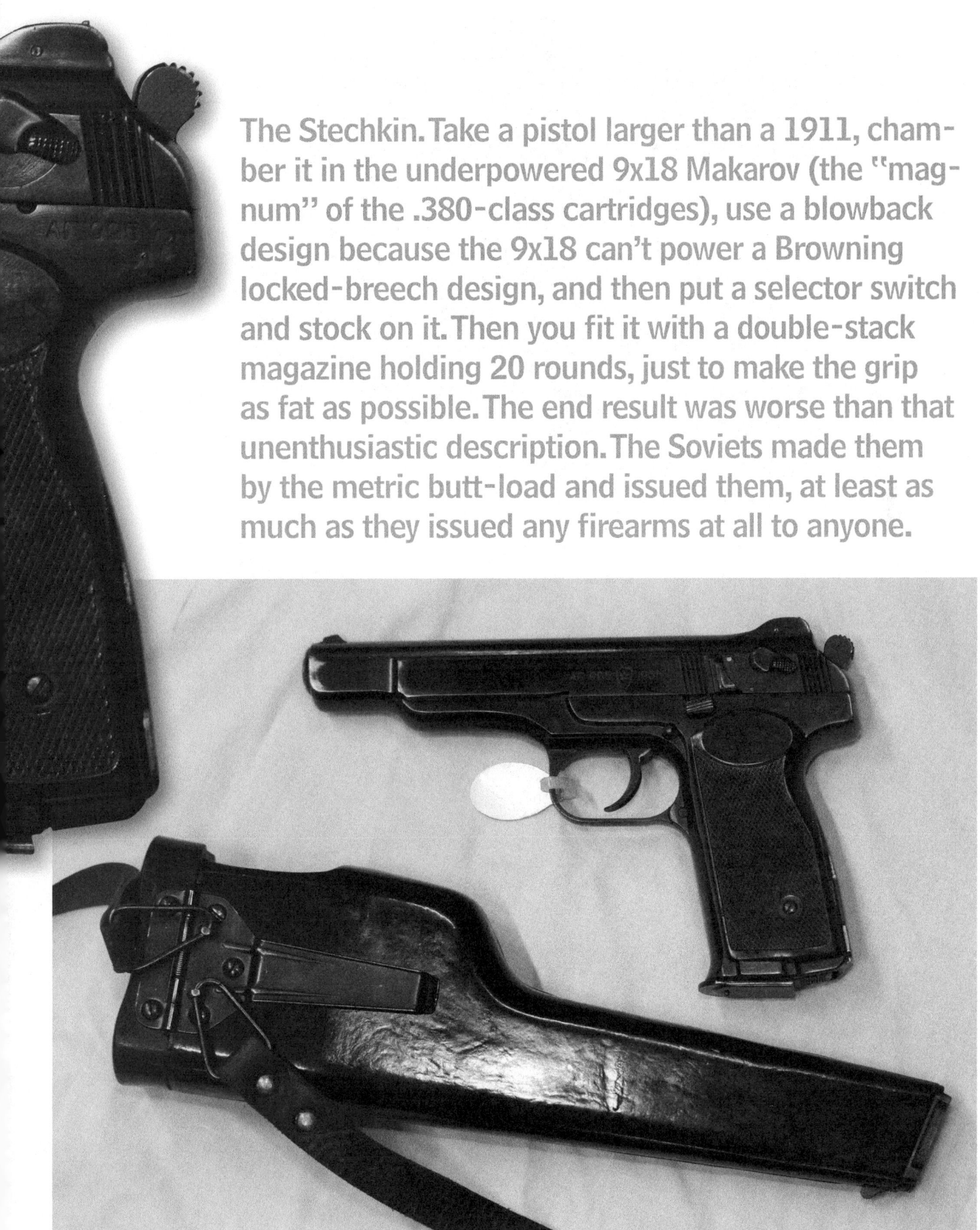

The use of a steel frame makes attaching a stock an easy task.

With stock attached, the Stechkin became a compact SMG.

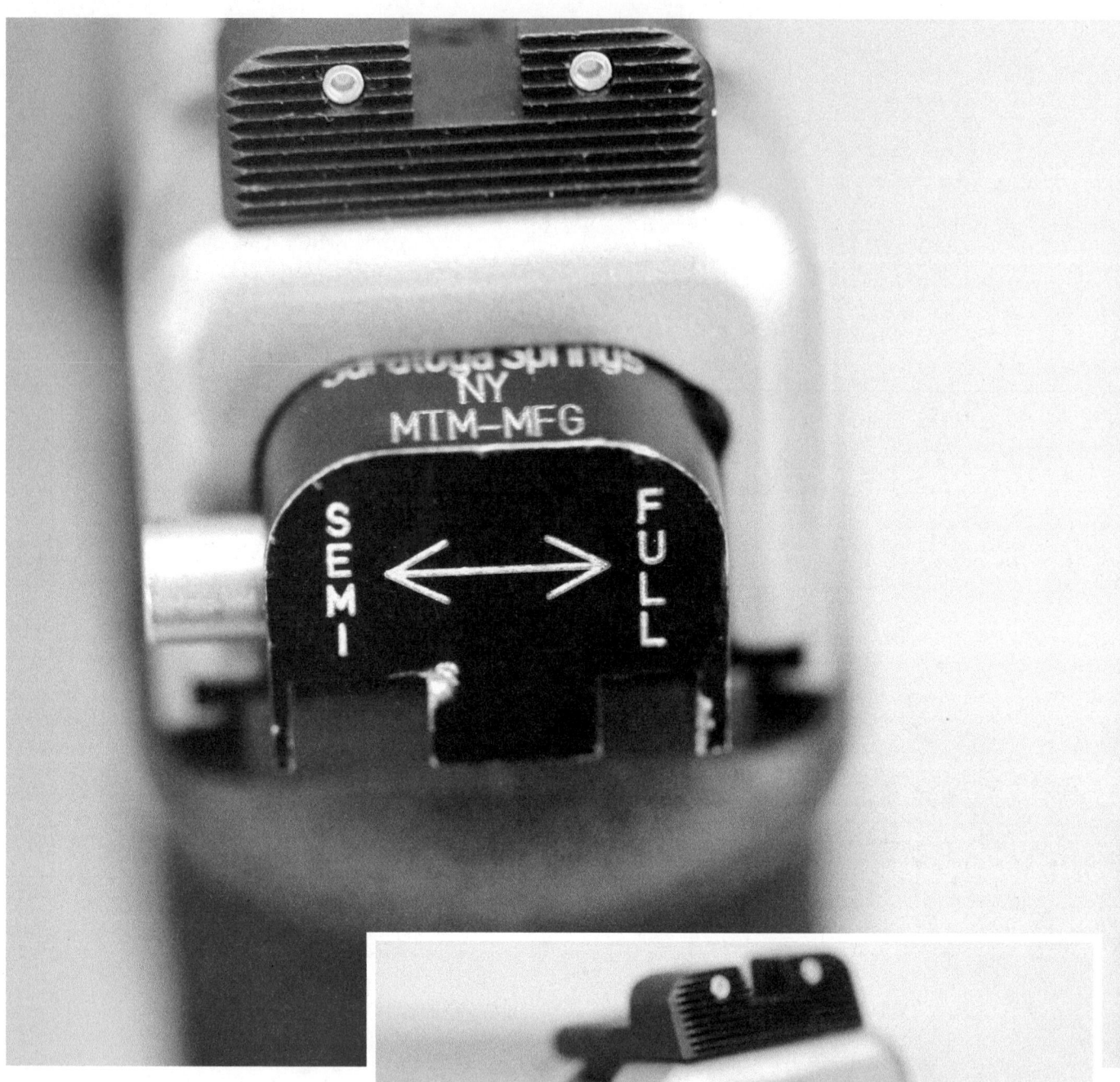

(above) The G17 with the RDIAS installed, here set for "semi."

(right) The RDIAS replaces the rear plate of the slide, and the button indicates what the pistol is set for. Please, no jokes about it "only" being a 9mm. And where's the "stun" setting?

(opposite) There is no burst setting. Your choices are semi or full.

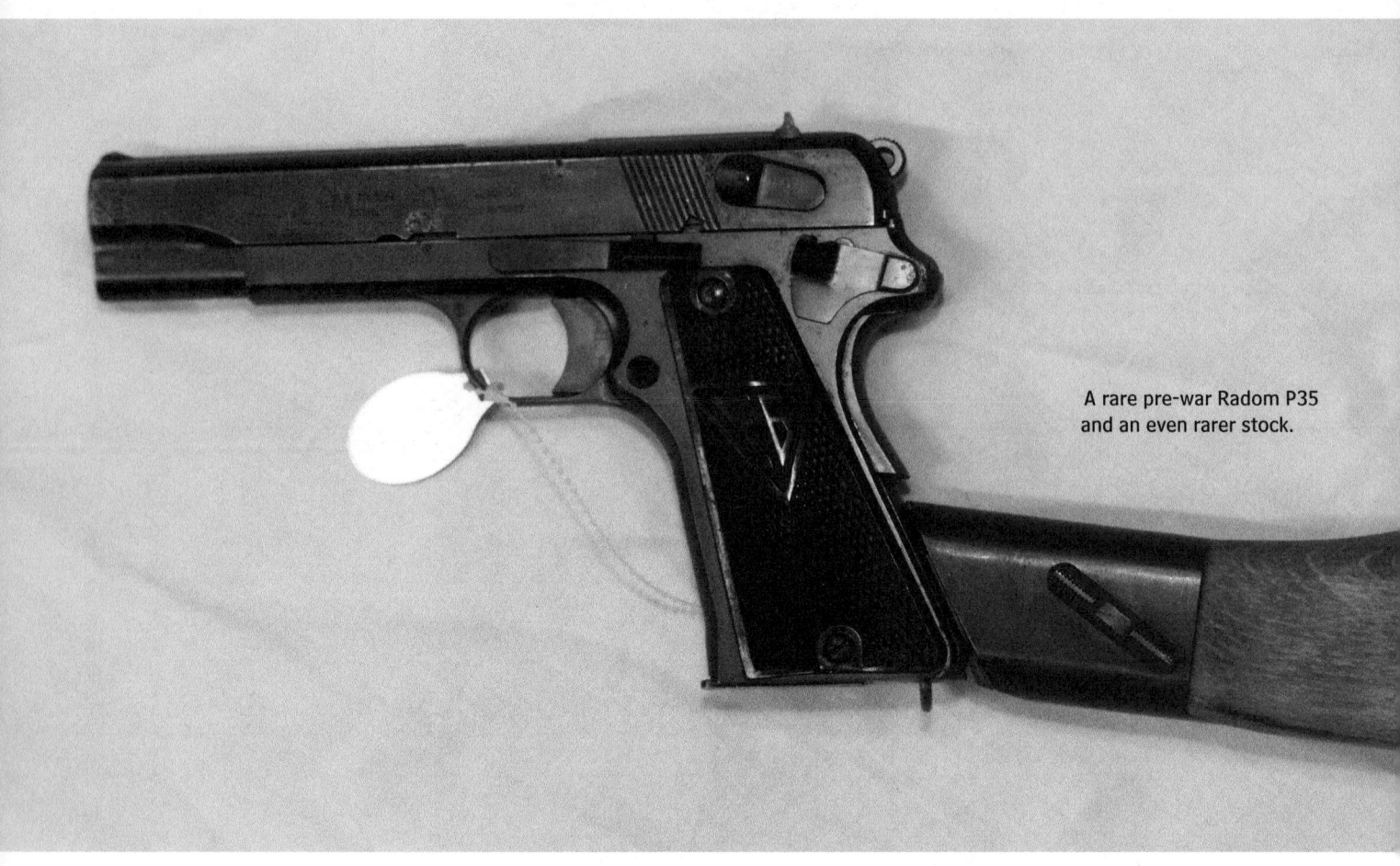

A rare pre-war Radom P35 and an even rarer stock.

I've actually seen people who were almost tipped over by the recoil of 9mm in semi-auto shooting. With the sear-hosted G34, I saw five-shot bursts that, at less than 10 yards, had the first shot in the ground in front of the target and the last over the head of the target. As the berms were a bit low there, I was worried. You've *got* to know what you're doing to be safe. When you do, a full-magazine dump of 33 rounds stays on a USPSA target at seven, 10, 12 yards.

potential to get your butt landed in jail. Remember; it is the machine gun. So you can't just loan it to your buddy, brother, friend, or whomever. Also, while it is installed, you can make it into anything a regular machine gun can be, but in the Glock-verse this is not without its problems.

Again, our comparison to an AR-15. Once the RDIAS is dropped into a host AR, you can then swap out the upper for one with a shorter than 16-inch barrel. The machine gun status of the RDIAS trumps the short-barrel conversion of the AR. However, remove the RDIAS, and you must (and probably first) *must* remove the shorter barrel.

Owners of an AR-15-specific RDIAS typically keep it in a hard case, along with the short barrel or barrels they use when the RDIAS is in a host weapon. (Smarter yet is to keep the RDIAS in the host weapon and the shorter barrel *on* the weapon and don't take them apart.)

Technically, when the RDIAS is installed in a host Glock (and, for the record, the AR and Glock RDIAS units are different, non-interchangeable, and work differently), you could install a shoulder stock on your Glock. The problem is this, however; any stock you install on the RDIAS-equipped host Glock would also fit on a Glock lacking the RDIAS. I can't see any way to avoid having to double-dip. If you want a shoulder-stocked, select-fire Glock, you have to have both an SBR-registered Glock and an RDIAS. I don't see a way to bootstrap your way to the status of both, with just an RDIAS. If, however, you send a letter to the BATFE asking just that and get approval, keep a copy of the letter with your SBR conversion, because it is a valuable letter.

The RDIAS Glock

The sear (easier on the eyes than the acronym) replaces the rear plate on the Glock slide. There are no other changes befitting the intent and requirement of a conversion sear. The sear housing (the assembly is bigger than the regular Glock plate) has a button. If the button is out on the side that says "Semi," then you have a one-shot firearm. If the button is out on the side that says "Full" you have a machine gun. Unlike a selector on an AR or on a made-to-be machine gun, you do not have a safe/semi/full option. If you want to go from one to the other, you have to push the button over. This is not a fast and easy thing to do.

Once set to "Full," the sear works as intended, with a few caveats. Without going into too much technical detail—I'm not trying to hide anything, but if you do this without the proper

In case you think you've got a trick idea, the Radom stock included room for two extra magazines.

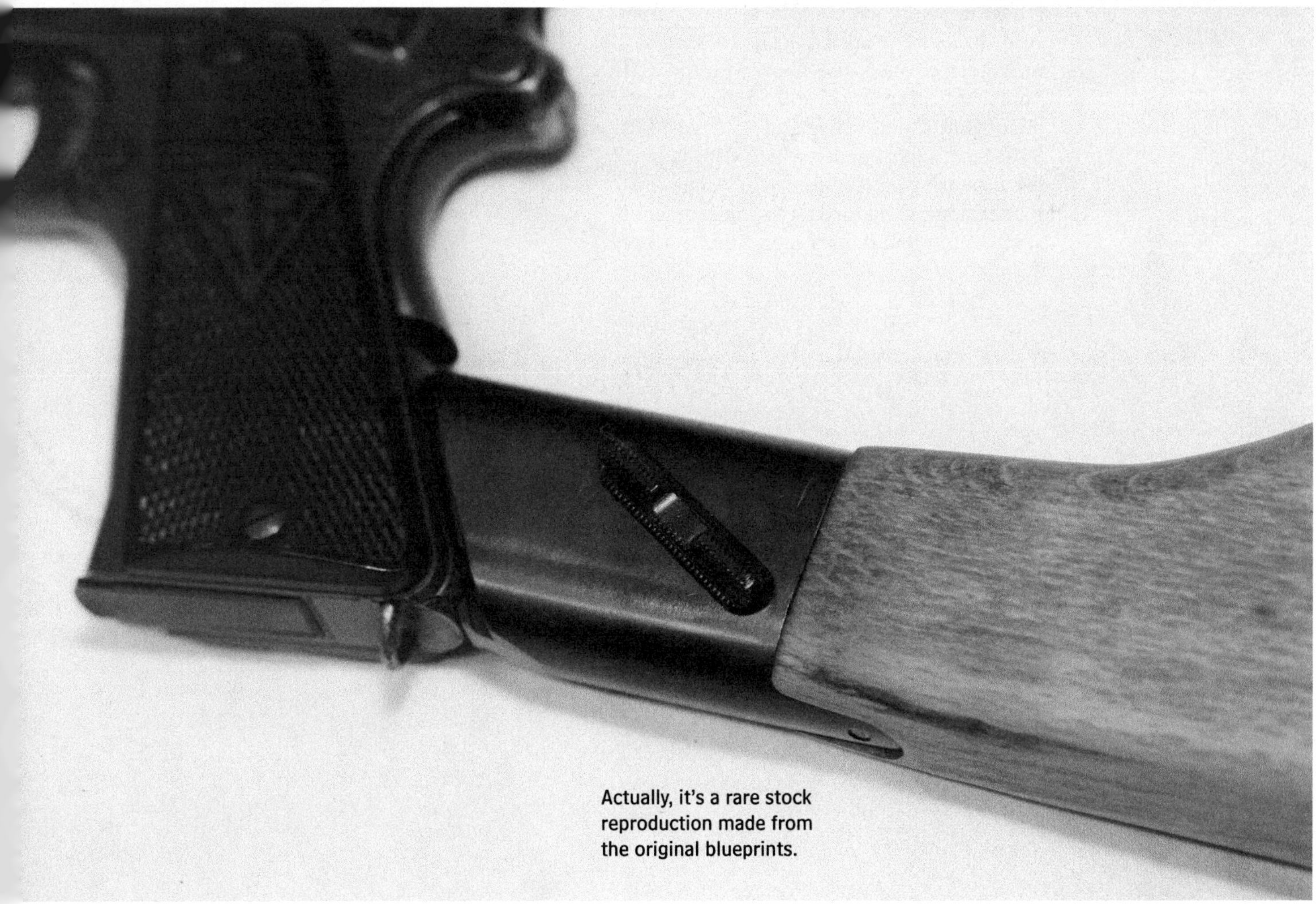

Actually, it's a rare stock reproduction made from the original blueprints.

license you're committing a Federal felony, good for 10 years in prison and a $10,000 fine, plus, if you do it without the proper technical know-how, you could end up hurting yourself—the sear engages in a controlled, precisely timed sear release as the slide is closing, one that has the striker hitting the firing pin after the slide and barrel have had time to close and lock. The difference between working and not working is small, and the minor dimensional differences between various Glock frames, slides, cruciform, and sears can mean the difference between functional and not.

On the first day of testing, we had three Glocks to try, a Gen2 G17, a Gen3 G34, and a Gen4 G17. Of them, two worked. The Gen2 G17 did not, but it was not due to being a Gen2, rather it was simply a luck of the draw. The internal dimensions simply did not line up correctly.

This is *not* a slam against Glock. The Gen2 G17 has worked just fine for many thousands of rounds in semi-auto function. *That's* what it was designed for. Asking it to work full-auto with a random RDIAS dropped in place is asking too much. So, if you buy an RDIAS and it does not work in your Glock, don't despair. And, for heaven's sake, don't go looking to file on, adjust, or otherwise screw with the RDIAS. That thing is *expensive!* Pull another Glock out of your shooting bag and try it. At $400 to $500 each, experimenting with Glocks is a lot less expensive (and easier in the paperwork) than swapping out an RDIAS for another at several thousand dollars each—more, a *lot* more, if they are transferables.

We installed the RDIAS in two Glocks and had a blast. You learn a few things doing this. One, most people have no idea how to control recoil. You've heard the usual objections to full-auto fire, I'm sure, things like "Your first couple shots are on target, then the rest are in the sky," and so on. Well, if you don't know what you're doing, yes, that'll happen. If your marksmanship skills are only to a level deemed adequate for law enforcement or the military, again, yes.

I've actually seen people who were almost

What I found was that the average of four, five-shot bursts was right at 1,100 rpm (the slowest at 1,075, the highest at 1,125). This was with 115-grain factory FMJ, not that the ammunition makes much of a difference, as we found out later. Looking at it from an engineering standpoint, the ammo *shouldn't* make a difference.

tipped over by the recoil of 9mm in semi-auto shooting. With the sear-hosted G34, I saw five-shot bursts that, at less than 10 yards, had the first shot in the ground in front of the target and the last over the head of the target. As the berms were a bit low there, I was worried. You've *got* to know what you're doing to be safe. When you do, a full-magazine dump of 33 rounds stays on a USPSA target at seven, 10, 12 yards.

Fun? You bet, a veritable giggle-fest. And beyond fun, if your task is to turn money into noise, you have a success on your hands. As a truly *useful* weapon, I can't really find a use, with a very few specialized exceptions.

There is one exercise the military does that is hard on firearms. It is known, in general, as "breaking contact." Imagine a patrol goes out and, in the process of checking their assigned area, they encounter a much larger group. Oops. If they stay and slug it out, they will be flanked. If they try to back up, they can be overwhelmed. So, they pump as much firepower as they can, straight at the enemy, while

The selector on a Mauser Schnellfeuer.

So popular were the C96s in China, that local entrepreneurs started making them.

bugging out as fast as possible. Known by various "peel" methods, it is simple. Once the situation is clearly "Okay, they vastly outnumber us, we should leave," the forward-most soldier fires off as much ammo as is in his magazine and immediately gets up and runs back. As he passes the person behind him, he signals—shout, tap, hand signal, whatever. *That* person then does a magazine dump and runs back, signaling the person behind *them*. If a small group is attempting to break contact and are armed with one or more G18s, the shooters would fire on semi- until it was their turn to peel, then switch to full and dump the mag with several bursts or a full magazine dump. The idea is to combine both high firepower with a fast withdrawal, discouraging the enemy with the impression that they are facing more than they are.

Used to discourage attempted vehicle ambushes, a G18 in the hands of a personal security detail also might be useful. But, again, if there is room for people, there is room for people with rifles. Breaking up an attempted vehicle ambush with an M4 is a whole lot more likely to happen than using a G18 for the same purpose. Anyway, from these two examples, you can see that, in theory, the G18 can be useful. In practical use, not so much.

But back to the RDIAS. I had my PACT MkIV timer along for the testing. It allows me to time full-auto bursts and check the cyclic rate. What I found was that the average of four, five-shot bursts was right at 1,100 rpm (the slowest at 1,075, the highest at 1,125). This was with 115-grain factory FMJ, not that the ammunition makes much of a difference, as we found out later. And looking at it from an engineering standpoint, the ammo *shouldn't* make a difference.

Given the mechanical limitations, there is a very short space in which the mechanism can work. Driving the slide harder won't pick up the cyclic rate, because it depends on the slide coming back, very close to rest, before it "trips the sear" to fire again. On many designs, the auto sear mechanism has a larger working window, and the parts can be driven hard to get them to the window faster. On the Glock, that isn't the case.

Words Will Have to Paint the Picture

With the RDIAS out of the way, I had a chance to look at the real-deal G18. I can see that you are disappointed. No photos showing the interior, no diagrams, arrows, and dimensions for each of the parts. I'll tell you why. It is too simple. I mean it! The most difficult part of a G17-to-G18 conversion would be machining the slide to install the selector lever. All the rest a competent gunsmith could do in an afternoon, once you showed him the interior. If you're that clever, you can get into massive trouble all on your own, you don't need my help.

But hats off to Gaston Glock for the simplicity of the design. Another bonus? The design is self-seating. Not self-*setting*, but -*seating*. The G18 parts, once engaged to their purpose of full-auto fire, are arranged so that they work to keep each other in that setting, i.e., it is not going to self-set back to semi-auto on you.

The lever clicks up and down with a secure and satisfying snick and stays there. The frame, as near as I can tell without pulling out the dial calipers and doing bench-top drawings, is a G17 frame. Were you able to slide the G18 upper off and install a G17 (or G34, etc.), I'm not sure you could tell the difference. The G17 slide will fit a bit loosely, however.

7.63, 9mm, long barrel, or short, the C96 was very popular in all guises.

You are not, of course, going to swap parts the other way. While a G17 slide might fit on a G18-specific frame, it will rattle and wobble. The G18 slide will *not* fit on a G17 frame.

Stocks came in various sizes, too.

You are not, of course, going to swap parts the other way. While a G17 slide might fit on a G18-specific frame, it will rattle and wobble. The G18 slide will *not* fit on a G17 frame. Where does it bind? You mean, besides the rails being too wide? C'mon, you expect me to make it that easy? Just leave it at that. Glock has done its due diligence, and you can't mix and match G17 and G18 parts.

Insides aside, the external dimensions were the same and, if the G18 were lying down on its left side, you would not know the difference between it and the 17. Neither would you see a difference in semi-auto setting. The G18 handles and recoils the same as a G17. It's when the lever is flipped down that things get fun. A G18 is not, however, different from the RDIAS-equipped G17 or G34. The cyclic rate is the same—I used the same ammo, saving the opened carton for just this sort of comparison—and recoil is the same.

It may sound heretical, but once we'd gotten over the fun of firing it full-auto, it was kind of boring. I mean, it was fun, but the overriding concern of keeping the muzzle down on bursts, the focus on keeping the firing in short bursts (gun heat and low berms), and the repetitive nature of it was just a bit much. So we took a break and shot a G17 with a suppressor installed, just to get the fun meter back up in the green, and then went back to the G18.

What have I learned, in playing with an RDIAS conversion and a veritable rack of G18s? That the G18, more so than a lot of other buzzguns I've played with, is a firearm fitting the role of Italian sports car. It's a lot of fun, an object that confers great status on the owner, one that is ferociously expensive to buy, maintain, and run and, in the end, is something that wears out its welcome pretty fast. Oh, don't get me wrong, if I won the lottery, I'd certainly be looking to buy a G18. But short of a head-spinning amount of free money, I'm not going to sink the cost of a decent SUV into one.

G18 Extras—What Could Have Been

Casting back to the era of horse cavalry, there's an item of service that hung on for a long time: stocked handguns. The idea was simple, really. You take a pistol, put a stock on it, and you have a handy carbine for the mounted soldier. When all firearms were one-shot muzzleloaders, that approach had some merit. The example that got things started in the modern era—we'll overlook Samuel Colt and his stock cap-'n'-ball revolvers—was the Borchardt, also known as the C93. As the first reasonably reliable self-loading pistol, it was not the world's easiest sell. Combined with its 7.65 cartridge, a high-speed but lightweight round, it just didn't looked like a "real" service pistol, a.k.a. a revolver. By putting a stock on it, Hugo Borchardt expanded the options and caught shooters' interest. Soon after, the Mauser C96, the Broomhandle, came out, and that was a hot number.

Rifles of the time were bolt-action, five-shot, and were viewed as bullet-launching bayonet mounts. A typical military rifle of the time had a 29- to 30-inch barrel, hardly a compact, convenient package. A "carbine" as issued to artillery crews or cavalrymen would have a shorter barrel, but still one of 24 inches. At the start of WWI, there were some military organizations that were going with a compromise, a 24-inch barrel for nearly everyone, but perhaps a shorter carbine for the artillery.

Why all this concern for the artillery? Because back then, artillery wasn't like we know it to be now. Until the trenches of WWI settled down, artillery was a mobile branch of the army. Members were expected to ride with the cavalry or keep

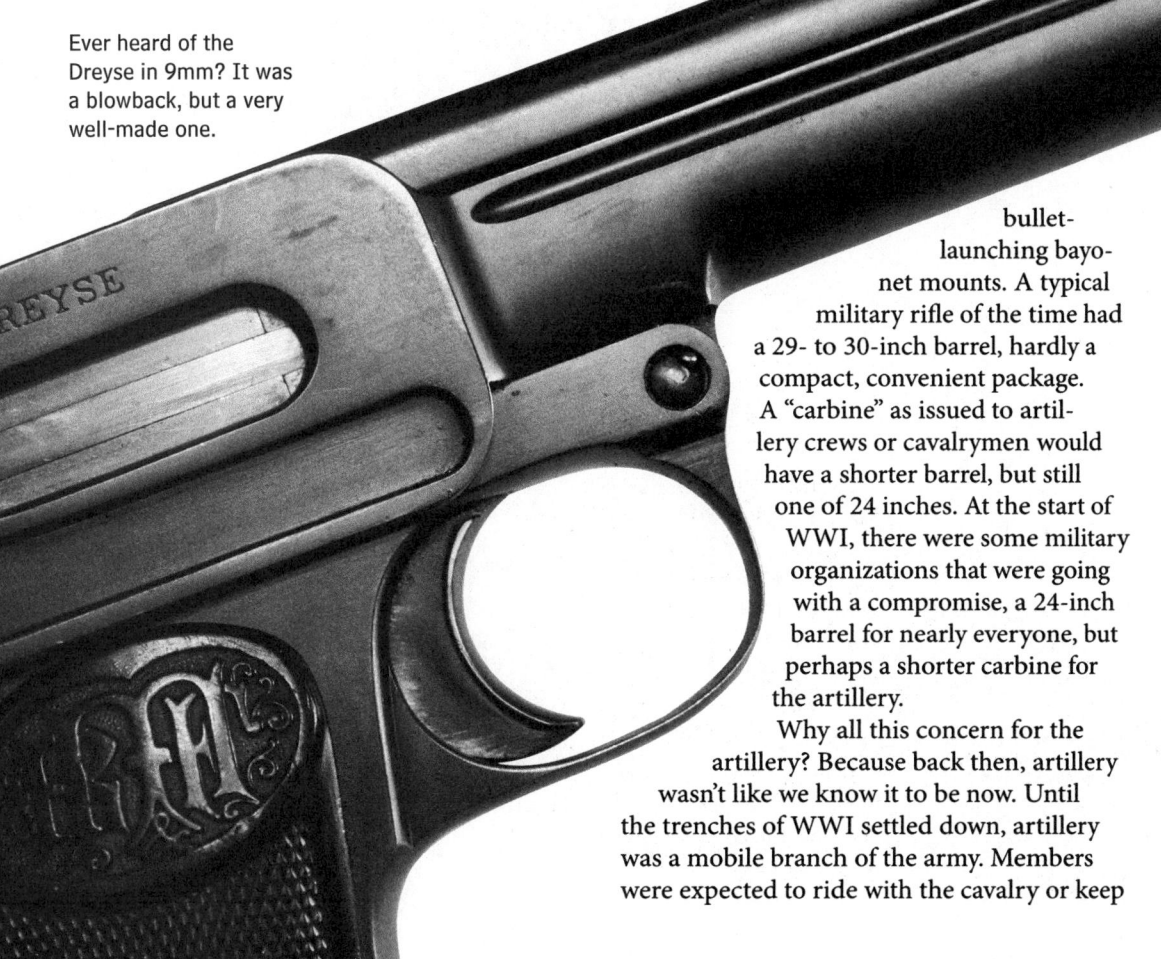

Ever heard of the Dreyse in 9mm? It was a blowback, but a very well-made one.

For those who have never held a Mauser Broomhandle, I'll let you down easy: the thing is an ergonomic nightmare. The grip is round (hence the nickname), the tang does not protect your hand and, so, the hammer will bite mercilessly if you use anything approximating a modern grip, and the bore axis is high enough, even with the relatively low-recoil 7.63 Mauser, that the muzzle rise is impressive.

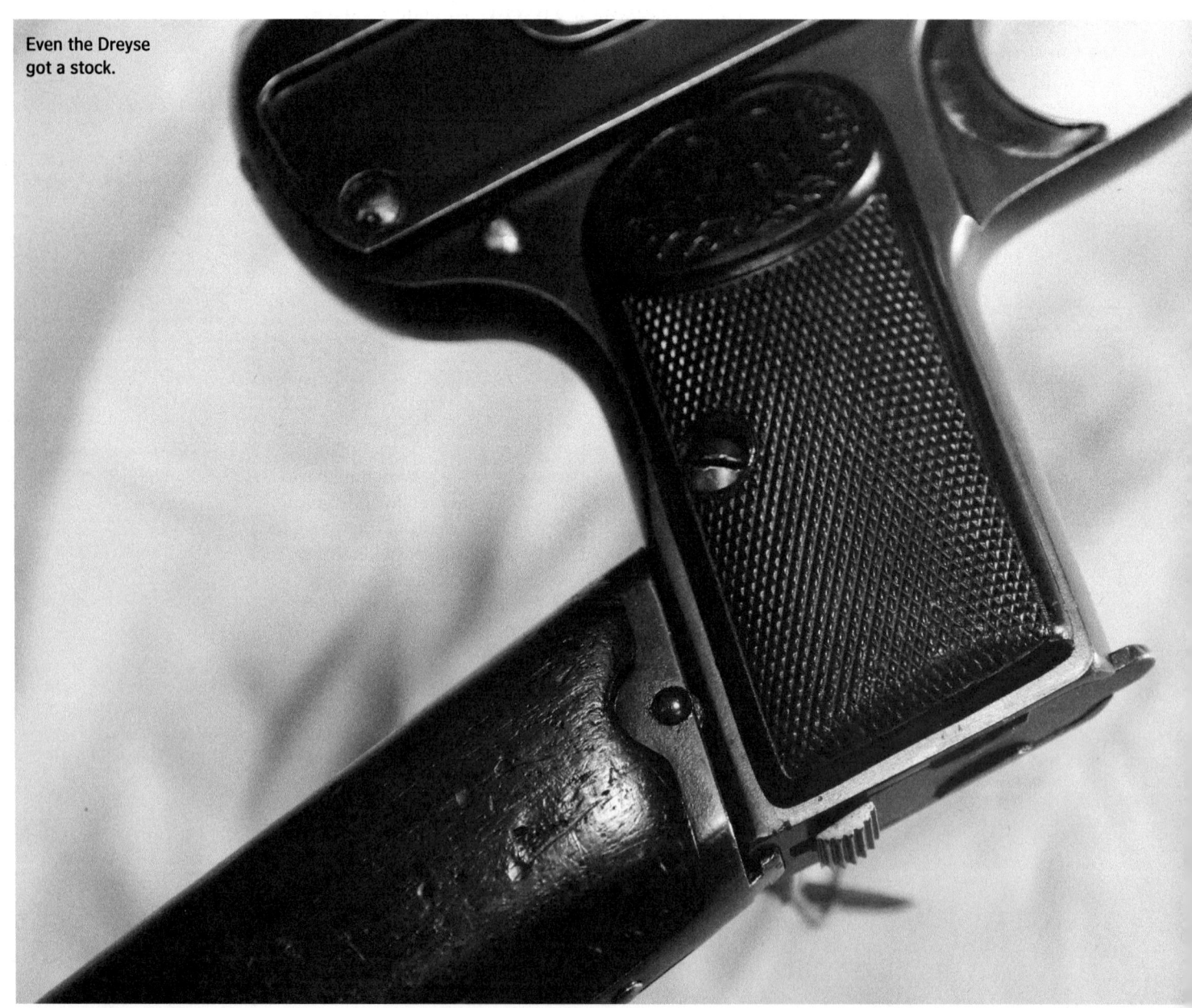

Even the Dreyse got a stock.

Seven empties in the air. With practice, it was relatively easy to get bursts down to three or four rounds. To get two shots per squeeze took a lot more work.

up with the infantry and deliver direct-fire artillery to the enemy positions. Well, if you're close enough to deliver direct fire, so are they, and one of the great joys of being cavalry was to ride through enemy artillery positions, merrily shooting up and sabering their crews. Indeed, for a couple centuries before WWI, this had been an *expected* task of artillery crews, the using of small arms to fight off the cavalry and infantry that your side's own guns themselves hadn't dealt with.

In the first decade of the twentieth century, anyone who made a self-loading pistol for military use made a version of it to also permit a stock, and any army that adopted a self-loading pistol asked for one with a stock. From the Scandinavian countries (I've seen Finish, Swedish, Norwegian, and Danish pistols fitted with stocks), to Europe (there, Belgian, French, German, and Austro-Hungarian Empire models), from before the Great War, side-arms were made to accept a shoulder stock.

Such a design made sense. Imagine yourself an artillery gunner and you suddenly realize that your position is about to receive the unwanted attentions of a troop of enemy cavalry. Would you rather have a five-shot bolt-action rifle or an eight- to 10-shot self-loading pistol?

A C96 Mauser in 7.63 Mauser hurls an 86-grain bullet at some 1,450 fps. This, in a light, handy package. I can't help but make a quick comparison to the M1 Carbine with a 110-grain bullet at 1,900 fps and 15-round magazines in an only slightly bigger and heavier package. That's one of those things that makes you go "Hmm."

Surprisingly, we didn't get a whole lot of muzzle flash photos, even at 1,100 rpm and an afternoon of photography. Still, we got as much as anyone would want.

Before you exclaim that the rifle is more accurate, has greater range, and more stopping power, remember, the enemy are riding straight at you. A 9mm or 7.65 Mauser is not going to have the stopping power of a 7.92/.303/8mm Lebel, but you've got more pistol cartridges and they can be fired more quickly.

In the colonial era, an officer or NCO on the flank of his line of riflemen would be well-served with a stocked pistol. After all, if his unit is the expedition's flank, then he's out there on his own. There's no one to his flank but the colony and the locals.

In WWI, the German Army, in particular, issued shoulder-stocked Lugers to artillery and machine gun crews in large numbers. (At that time, machine guns were considered "pocket artillery," rather than the mobile base of firepower they later came to be.) The evolution of things is pretty interesting. Pistols get shoulder

Any RDIAS can be picky about what pistols it works on. The one we tried worked on some, but not all Glocks. Here is a G34 getting some serious hammer time.

stocks and, in the case of the artillery Luger, longer barrels. And while an eight-shot pistol is nice, more is always better. So, the Luger gets the 32-round "snail" drum magazine. When the idea of a pistol-caliber carbine or submachine gun comes up, what magazine did they use? The snail drum, in the Bergman MP18, all 9½ pounds of it even before it got loaded with most of a box of ammo.

As part of the research of this book, I had a chance to peruse a raft of select-fire handguns, as well as stocked handguns. For those who have never held a Mauser Broomhandle, I'll let you down easy: the thing is an ergonomic nightmare. The grip is round (hence the nickname), the tang does not protect your hand and, so, the hammer will bite mercilessly if you use anything approximating a modern grip, and the bore axis is high enough, even with the relatively low-recoil 7.63 Mauser, that the muzzle rise is impressive. Fired in the stock, the bolt, shuttling back and forth, comes back startlingly close to your face; crawling the stock is ill advised. But, for a fast-shooting, quick-reloading, handy carbine, as long as you left it off "Full," it was quite the gizmo. The Spanish copies, in select fire, were so popular that Mauser had to follow suit. Mauser even went with a detachable box magazine, up to 20 rounds worth.

A C96 Mauser in 7.63 Mauser hurls an 86-grain bullet at some 1,450 fps, all this in a light, handy package. I can't help but make a quick comparison to the M1 Carbine with a 110-grain bullet at 1,900 fps and 15-round magazines, all in an only slightly bigger and

heavier package. That's one of those things that makes you go "Hmm."

The end of the Great War and the advance of SMGs did not dampen the enthusiasm for stocked handguns. Again, if it was made between the wars, there was a model of it made for a stock, the Browning Hi-Power and the Polish Radom being just two. What really did them in wasn't that they were unhandy or clunky to use. It was cost. Compared to the cost of a finely machined P-35, a stamped-steel SMG with only the bolt and barrel needing to be machined was cheaper. For the time and cost of a P-35, a C-96, or other, you could have five or 10 Stens, PPS-42/43s, M3 "grease" gun, and so on.

This did not stop the handgun makers. While various makers had made them between the wars, some also made them during the war. One in particular was Inglis. When the Germans overran Belgium, the FN people who could, fled, and, with the blueprints, ended up setting up shop in Canada. There, in the plant of John Inglis and Company, they produced the P-35 for Allied use. Many of these firearms went to China; collectors will be happy with a Chinese Inglis, happier still with one not Chinese-marked. Meanwhile, the C-96, Spanish copies of it, and many other pistols continued to be made to accept shoulder stocks. But only those already making pistols did so. No one tooled up with a new one to take a stock.

World War II was the end of the SMGs and machine pistols, for the most part. Sure, they worked, but once the pressing need for as many guns as possible had passed, everyone wanted something a little more stylish than a Sten. After all, why go with a heavy, clunky, relatively inaccurate 9mm SMG, when the M1 Carbine, for all its alleged faults, worked better?

In the brave new world of the Atomic '50s, we in the U.S. were going with an all-M14 setup. I kid you not, the M14 was going to replace *everything*—the Garand, BAR, M1 Carbine, and M3 SMG—and some even suggested it could replace the 1911A1. Commies, of course, were going with AKs for all hands. That was until they found it was all but impossible to crawl out of a disabled tank, AK in hand. (Truth be told, if you were over five-and-a-half feet tall, crawling into or out of a Soviet tank at all was a mean feat in and of itself, let alone doing so with gear on and a rifle in your hands.) So, almost solely on their own in the post-war period, the Soviets developed the Stechkin.

The Stechkin. Take a pistol larger than a 1911, chamber it in the underpowered 9x18 Makarov (the "magnum" of the .380-class

In the end, the Stechkin lost out to short AKs, such as this AKS-74U.

cartridges), use a blowback design because the 9x18 can't power a Browning locked-breech design, and then put a selector switch and stock on it. Then you fit it with a double-stack magazine holding 20 rounds, just to make the grip as fat as possible. The end result was worse than that unenthusiastic description. The Soviets made them by the metric butt-load and issued them, as much as they issued any firearms at all to anyone.

Why go to all that trouble? The new Makarov pistol was going to be chambered in 9x18 (this was all back in the late 1940s and early 1950s, as both the Mak and Stech were adopted in 1951), and, after the war experience, there was no way the Soviets were going to adopt handguns in two different calibers. Since the issued-to-every-officer Makarov was going to be in 9x18, the Stechkin, if it was going to get adopted, had to be adapted to the same round. Add to this the fact that tank crews were unhappy with the thought of

World War II was the end of the SMGs and machine pistols, for the most part. Sure, they worked, but once the pressing need for as many guns as possible had passed, everyone wanted something a little more stylish than a Sten. After all, why go with a heavy, clunky, relatively inaccurate 9mm SMG, when the M1 Carbine, for all its alleged faults, worked better?

Even when not full auto, a short-barreled rifle such as this one is more powerful, accurate, and easier to use than a stocked handgun.

having only a single-stack pistol as their arm if they had to bail out and, so, the Stechkin. Don't forget, tank crews don't spend all their time inside their tanks. Even in wartime, they'd spend more time out of the tank than in it. Outside, someone has to stand guard or pull security, while the crews eat, sleep, wrench on tank parts, etc. Sure, a rifle, AK or otherwise, is the proper tool for that, but once everyone "saddles up" and gets inside, what do you do with the rifle? It has to go inside, and it has to be compact to do that.

I've handled Stechkins a few times, fired one once, and was underwhelmed. However, a friend of mine, a real-deal Spetsnaz trooper who served in Afghanistan (and *there's* a sentence that would have seemed really, really, out of place in the 1980s), carried one in Afghanistan, loved it, and is prepared to sell entirely too many things he currently owns if the chance comes about to acquire one.

Next up, the HK MP5K. Take an MP5, shorten the barrel enough to make it handgun-sized (more or less), and then fit a side-folding stock to

it. Why? Because of pants-wetting hysteria on the part of NATO, that's why. It was afraid the Soviets were going to field armies clad in bulletproof armor when they drove West, and NATO needed something it called a PDW, or Personal Defense Weapon. The initial answer from H&K was the MP5K, the short 9mm SMG.

Later, H&K came up with the MP7 in 4.6mm, and FN gave us the P-990 in 5.7. The Soviets? They never could, then or now, afford to equip all their troops in the Crisat-level armor—an absurd number of layers of Kevlar,

Where Do I Get One of Those Things?

Alas, in all likelihood you can't. The first Glocks were imported in 1985. The law was changed in 1986. This means there was a very short window for RDIAS design, manufacture, and sales. Once the law was passed, no new ones could be sold into civilian hands. The number of transferable RDIAS for Glocks is probably less than 100. Again, when you see one in a video or at a range, it is almost certainly a registered dealer's sample. A manufacturer can make one, but it is automatically a D-S.

But even dealer's samples can come out to play. A lettered employee of the company can take it to a range, shoot it, show it off, even let other people he knows and trusts shoot it. When he's done, it goes home (or back to the shop) with him—but, no, he isn't going to let you spend time alone with it to measure, photograph, and make drawings of. It isn't against the law to know these things, but, if someone makes their own illegal RDIAS and the information source was a particular D-S from which the employee of the ABC Corp let people basically draw up blueprints at the range, well, that will not go well in his performance review. And the BATFE might take a closer look at the ABC Corps operations.

In that regard, the BATFE has a lot in common with the IRS: its best deterrent is its reputation. People do not screw around with the BATFE with impunity.

Why didn't Glock have any option for a stock? The logical conclusion is that the Austrian Army didn't ask for one. Remember, Glock wasn't looking to be the everywhere-for-everyone pistol of the future, Gaston Glock was looking to fulfill a contract for the army of his home country. Larding on extraneous features wasn't going to get him more points in the testing, so why bother?

plus a Titanium plate—used as the reference/test target for PDW testing.

As fun as select-fire handguns are to play with, they really aren't all that useful and don't have much of the market. Would I turn down an afternoon to try one out? Nope, but I wouldn't shell out the money it takes to own one, either.

So, what happened to SMGs, the PDW program, the stocked handguns, and all that other interesting, rarely-seen ordnance? Why were they dropped?

I blame Colt's. When the U.S. Army adopted the M16 (with much reluctance) in the Vietnam War, it wasn't enough. Despite being shorter, lighter, and handier than the M14 it replaced, it wasn't light, handy, or compact enough. So Colt's produced the XM-177, or Commando, an M16 with a telescoping stock and a barrel only 10½ inches long (That was too short for reliable function, and it later became 11½ inches in length.) With a rifle that compact and light (I built an XM-177A1 clone, and bare it weighs 5.66 pounds), there was no need for a submachine gun. After all, even a relative lightweight like the Swedish M/45 or the Sten weighed seven pounds, and for that you got a relatively underpowered "carbine" that fired from an open bolt and lacked rifle accuracy. In the Colt's, you could have it all: light weight, accuracy, rifle-like power and, best of all, the ammunition and magazines were the same as those packing "real" rifles. (We'll avoid, for the moment, the arguments that the M16 isn't a real rifle.)

Even modern SMGs suffered in comparison. The hallmark of the submachine gun in modern use, the MP5, comes in at 5½ pounds in its full-sized, bulky-boy trim, and over 6½ in the more compact (but excruciating to shoot), telescoping stock version. The one that actually has a chance in this comparison is the MP5K, which is 4½ pounds, but, with the short barrel you lose even the velocity boost the SMG barrels give the 9mm.

If the 9mm SMG was dead on arrival, then the select-fire handgun, with its stock, was even more dead. (Is that possible?) Since then, the Soviets have made the AKS-74U, a folding-stock, short-barreled version of the AK-74, and everyone else who made any rifle that was competing for a government contract made sure that they, too, offered a short-barreled version for special use.

Back to Glock. Given that Austria asked for the new pistol-to-be in the late 1970s, why didn't Gaston Glock have a shoulder stock option as one of the models? Yes, yes, yes, the area on the grip where a stock attachment would be is but a thin shell of polymer. But that is a design consideration that could have been addressed. In fact, it would have been an amazing irony if Glock, having come so late to the replaceable backstrap party, had, in 1980, made his design to take a replaceable backstrap—a backstrap that could be replaced with a shoulder stock. Instead of a thin shell of polymer we'd have had a robust dovetail with a hand-grip backstrap that, once removed, would be replaced with a shoulder stock that slid right onto the dovetail. To spin this further, it could have been a polymer shoulder stock with room to store the pistol and a spare magazine or two.

It was not unknown, even then. The firm of H&K had done so with its VP70 pistol. Introduced in (you guessed it) 1970, the VP was a design pioneer in that it used polymer and steel stampings, and the stock not only provided a secure firing rest, it also engaged the burst control. That's right, on the burst guns (alas, the ones imported here neither accepted stocks nor had the burst option and were instead named the VZ70), when you installed the stock, you automatically engaged the three-shot burst feature. Woo-hoo! In an emergency, a soldier could haul out the combo stock/holster, yank out the VP70, slap it onto the stock, and have a three-shot burst 9mm SMG. With a magazine of 18 rounds, that gave you six, three-shot bursts and a reasonably quick reload. The VZ/VP stayed in the H&K catalog until the end of the 1980s, both beating Glock to the polymer-framed pistol feature and overlapping it as a plastic pistol (albeit one lacking a stock).

Why didn't Glock have any option for a stock? The logical conclusion is that the Austrian Army didn't ask for one. Remember, Glock wasn't looking to be the everywhere-for-everyone pistol of the future, Gaston Glock was looking to fulfill a contract for the army of his home country. Larding on extraneous features wasn't going to get him more points in the testing, so why bother? And, so, Glock missed a chance to revisit the option of a stocked handgun. Given the popularity of Glocks, had they done so, there would be a lot more interest in them.

Such a design would have been of particular interest here in the States, as the Hughes Amendment of 1986 prohibited new production or importation of machine guns, putting the kibosh on any future for the G18. But, SBRs (short-barreled rifles) have since then become a real hot property, and a Glock SBR in the various models would be really interesting options.

But wait. Isn't that a possibility, what with the new Gen4 Glocks and the replaceable backstraps? Um, no. The new backstraps are just overlays, not replacements, and they are held on by the simple means of hooking on the lip of the backstrap hollow and replacing the top rear pin of the frame. (The extra bulk of the new overlay requires a slightly longer pin.) That arrangement is nowhere near strong enough to stand up to being a stock attachment system. So, having missed a chance to be decades ahead from the start, Glock now has a system that makes it impossible to construct a Glock SBR today.

As a final note, I discuss elsewhere the several clamshell-type SBR enclosures that turn a handgun into a stocked handgun. While they do work, they are not as elegant as the designs that were produced in the first half of the twentieth century. They are better than nothing, but they certainly are not up to the standard set by a wooden-stocked FN Hi-Power from between the wars.

In the end, the small arms horizon moved another way, another direction. The future is in rifle-caliber carbines and not in handgun-caliber adaptations, despite the noise rifles in short barrels produce. Thus, SMGs and stocked handguns are dead today. Which is too bad, because, if you aren't hung up on theoretical body armor penetration, they still get the job done.

The Future

What is the future for the G18? In a nutshell, there isn't one. The tactical application of hand-held ordnance has passed it by—*had* passed it even before it first saw the light of day. Select-fire handguns, machine pistols, were passé by the time automobiles lost their running boards. No military, police department, contractor agency, or other armed organization is going to buy any. That's not to say that operators or agents in the field in places where the oversight might be a bit, shall we say, sketchy, won't avail themselves of one if it passes their way. As a breaking-contact firearm, something you can poke out a window, let loose a magazine on Full, and drop, it does have a certain appeal. But that would be in the next Mogadishu, not in L.A. As for a G18 enveloped in a clamshell stock or some other SBR-like contraption, that would simply make it a high-cyclic-rate SMG, and SMGs have also lost their luster.

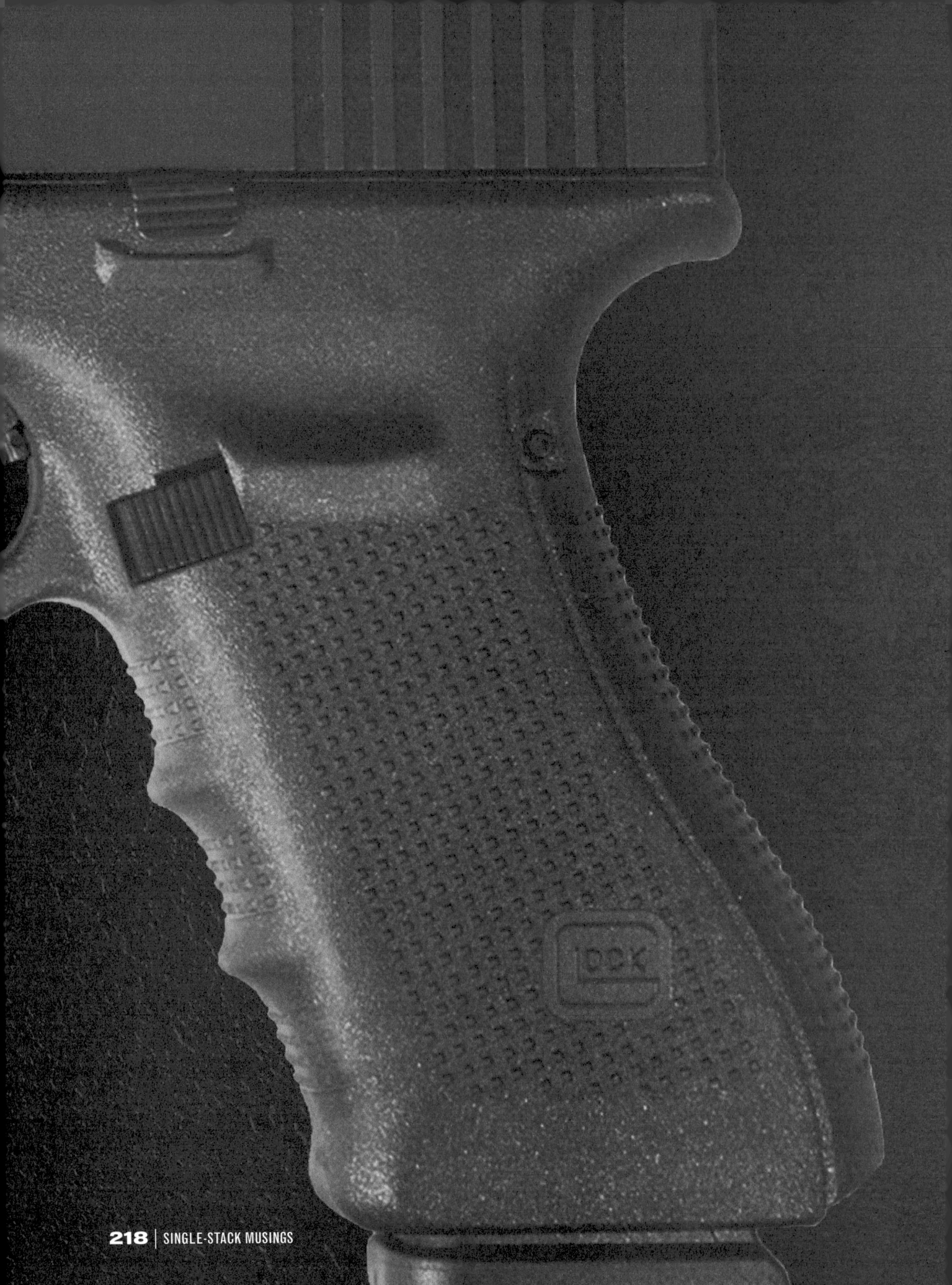

CHAPTER 14

Single-Stack Musings

Let's assume, for the moment, that the world has changed the direction of its spin, that the magnetic field has spontaneously changed directions and North is now South, that Gaston Glock has decided he really will fill everyone's Christmas stockings, or that he has decided "the heck with it all" and retired to an ashram in the Himalayas, the kids are in charge, and they will make the Glock Single-Stack.

The G36. Sigh. It could have been a contender … .

What would it look like?

Well, first of all, we can expect to see the G20/21 slide on top. Which means trouble. The G20/21 was proportioned and built to be a 10mm, which means it is probably a bit on the portly side for being a .45 ACP.

At a bit over 4½ inches (4.61 inches by the book) the length is going to be most like a Commander, which is just fine. A single-stack with the slide length of the G34/35 size, with a 5.3-inch barrel, would be cooler than cool, but, without the perceived need for international competition acceptance, even more unlikely than a single-stack would be to begin with.

Then we have the matter of magazines. The Glock system cannot use steel magazines. The magazine catch would have to be made of steel to withstand the recoil pounding, and that's unlikely to happen. So, we have polymer mag catches and, thus, polymer magazines, and it's here we run into a problem. You see, making a double-stack magazine out of sheet steel-reinforced polymer can get us to a thinner pistol. The main decrease in bulk on a pistol is in jettisoning the frame grips, but, for a double-stack, the polymer mag is no big deal. On a single-stack? *Big* deal.

First, it isn't just the thickness of the slide we have to deal with. The entire upper portion of the G20/21 would have to be retained, in order to house the trigger mechanism. Really. Think about it. No way would Glock, even if it would make my dreams come true and produce a single-stack, abandon the interchangeability of the internal parts. It would have to use the same trigger parts and house them in the same-shape polymer, or it would be adding yet another raft of SKUs to the list. Glock already has more than you can shake a stick at, adding more would just be crazy. Still, only from there down could we slim the frame.

How much? We need a certain minimum inside width in which the cartridges can rattle around. We wrap that dimension in sheet steel reinforcement and then clad it in polymer. The polymer has to be thick enough to provide a recess for the magazine catch. We can't get by with less, or we can't count on the magazine being retained. Then, we have to envelope the magazine with a frame and provide enough polymer thickness to control recoil, prevent material fatigue, and ensure reliable and durable function.

How thick will the frame be where we hang on to it? We can calculate this one of two ways.

The hard and correct way is the engineering way: we determine the cartridge "envelope." The envelope is the collection of internal dimensions needed to contain and control the cartridge without binding as it feeds. We add the thickness of the steel reinforcement. Add the thickness of the polymer cladding. We add the clearance between the magazine exterior and frame mag well interior; we have to have clearance for easy insertion and removal, as well as debris elbowroom. We add the thickness of the current frame around the magazine and then blend it to the existing frame, just below the slide. This is all done in CAD, computer-aided design. If we're a high-tech shop and have all the toys to play with, we then take those prospective dimensions and do two things.

First, we send them over to dimensional analysis and let them do computer simulations on recoil and function, to see if our blending/melding of the single-stack lower and the current upper has created any thin spots or weak locations that would break under use.

Second, we send the dimensions to the 3-D

The question is, would the single-stack Glock be as attractive as we have been thinking all along? Remember, we're working in polymer here, we can't be imagining things as if we were plunking a G21 slide assembly on top of a 1911 frame. Steel and polymer are different.

model shop and have them produce a 3-D model. That model then gets handed around to everyone with a high enough security clearance, to see if it is comfortable to hold and to look for production problems, aesthetic objections, or "this just feels wrong" objections.

If the simulations don't uncover problems and everyone who handles the 3-D model approves, we then go to the next marketing meeting with a 3-D model, the results of the simulations and production cost estimates, and see if marketing thinks they could sell enough to make it worth the investment. If the company is at all properly run, the production team is also in the meeting, and they would be asked if they had the extra capacity to make it, if marketing can sell it.

Has this happened at Glock? Heck if I know. Oh, it certainly has the money to invest, there is no doubt a single-stack would sell—they could sell them like rubber boots in a replay of Katrina—and, if production hasn't the capacity, Glock certainly could afford to invest in more equipment. Employees? Hmm.

In Europe, it is difficult, if not impossible, to let go excess personnel. Basically, once you hire someone, they will be with you until they retire. Even if they aren't working, you are paying a goodly amount to keep them anyway. As a result, companies in Europe are loathe to hire new people, because they can't be shed. However, temporary jobs are easy to hire for, as a "temporary" worker can be let go. But, would you want to be the Glock company that keeps its inner workings confidential and then hire a slew of temporary workers, only to let them go knowing all they know, but no longer beholden to you for a paycheck? Nope. What you'd do is go to double and triple shifts and pay massive overtime to avoid that.

I mentioned that there were two ways to determine the dimensions. For the second, you'd take the inside width of the magazine of a G21 and compare it to the inside width of a 1911. Subtract the extra width of the G21 magazine interior from the G21 frame exterior, and you'd have a rough but good idea of how wide a single-stack Glock would be.

The G21 magazine is a real porker. Double-stacked and with thick walls, it is a wonder any G21 hasn't had an aftermarket frame size reduction.

Yes, it's close to that of a G36, but not the same, as the recoil forces on the full-sized gun would differ slightly. While the G36 magazine would be a guide, it would not necessarily be the exact model. Getting a short magazine to hold five rounds and work is not the same as one that holds eight.

The question is, once Glock did all that, would the single-stack Glock be as attractive as we have been thinking all along? Remember, we're working in polymer here, we can't be imagining things as if we were plunking a G21 slide assembly on top of a 1911 frame. Steel and polymer are different.

To get an idea on how such a Glock might look, I did a quick analysis along the lines of how the magazine chapter in this book looked at magazine tube dimensions. The quick and dirty is that we could, if we were creative, get the single-stack Glock frame down to pretty darned close to that of a 1911 with fat grips on it. But we could not get it down to that of Springfield Armory's XDs, that company's single-stack .45 ACP. Why? The polymer-clad magazine Glock sticks with. In most instances, it is a good thing and, in a few, it's a neutral

SINGLE-STACK MUSINGS | **223**

Ignore the hammer for a moment. Is this really what we want in a single-stack Glock? Heck, I'd buy one.

thing. Here it's a real hindrance. The Springfield, using a steel magazine, doesn't have the extra polymer cladding to add bulk. As a result, it is even slimmer than a 1911. And now, with its new extra-capacity magazine, you can have an XDs with a seven-round magazine, making it the equal of a 1911. The longer magazine can be sheathed in a sleeve, making the extended magazine, in effect, a longer frame to hold on to. So, you've got a striker-fired single-stack slimmer than a 1911, with a compact (3.3-inch) barrel and as much .45 ammunition in the hold as is considered normal.

A single-stack Glock could come close, but even if Glock did it, probably not. No way, retaining the polymer-clad magazine, could it shrink it down to the flat, one-inch width of the XDs. Lose the polymer cladding, and it would have to use a steel magazine catch.

Who knows, they might just decide "What the heck" and go for it.

Oh, that joke about the magnetic field changing direction?

It does happen. Called a "geomagnetic reversal," the Earth's field has swapped directions a number of times. The intervals between reversals range from 100,000 years to a million, with the average about 450,000 years. The polarity swaps themselves take between 1,000 and 10,000 years to happen, but there have been times the fields changed directions more often than an Oscars host changes outfits. That last one was more than 750,000 years ago (or, according to some recent scientific discoveries, as recently as 41,000 years ago, during the Ice Age, in what has come to be known as the Laschamp Event). Either way, I figure we're about due. If I read that the magnetic field is fluctuating and that it may reverse soon, then I'll start shopping for a Glock single-stack.

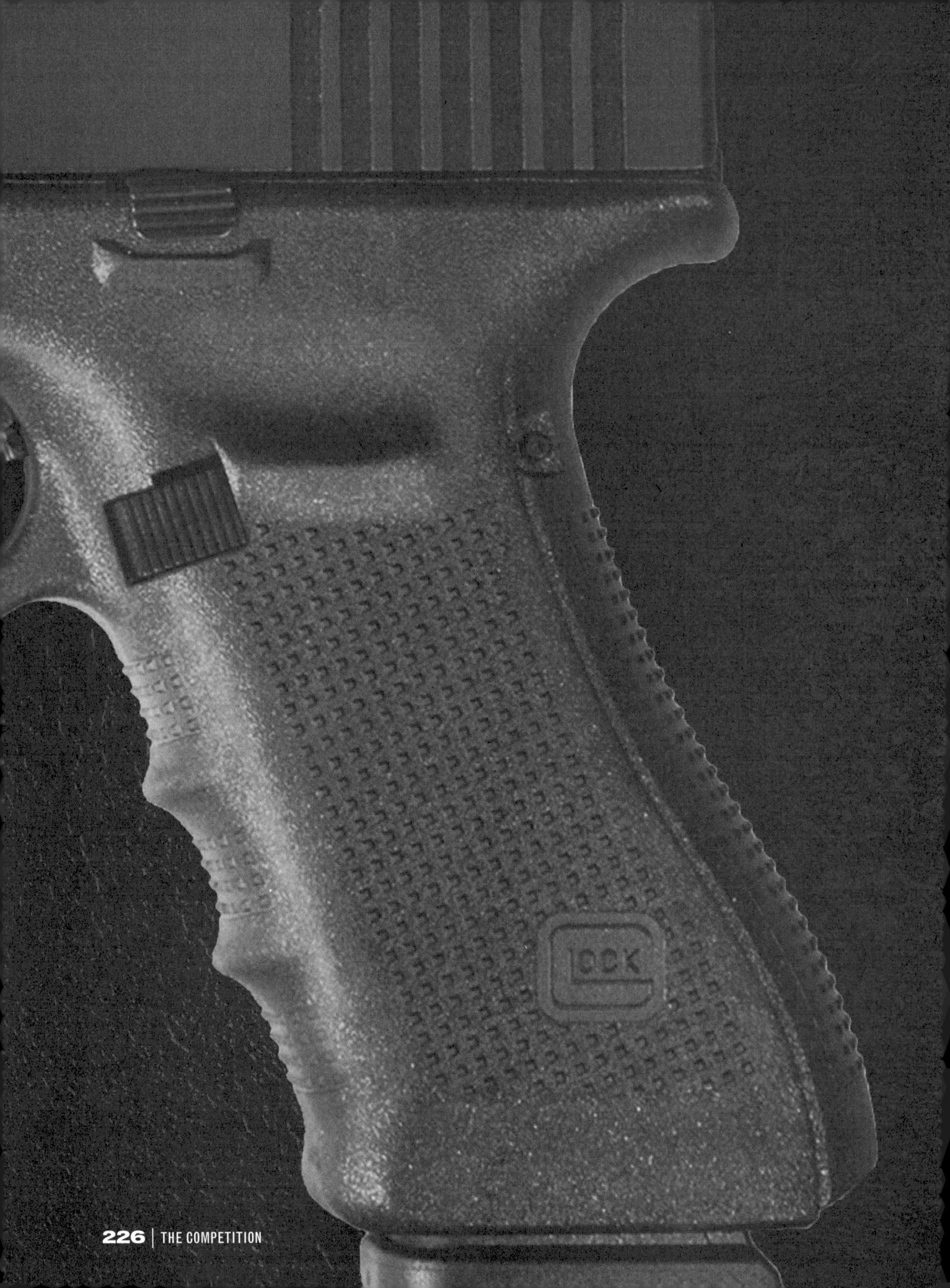

CHAPTER 15

The Competition

You say you love Glocks. You love them so much, you've risked the wrath of Gaston Glock and actually bought a pair of spandex short-shorts for your girlfriend, complete with the Glock logo silk-screened on them. (Good luck in getting her to wear them, by the way.) Do you really know what the others offer, have done with their copies, lookalikes, and variations on a theme? Do you know where they stand in comparison to the Glock? Have you shot them side by side or compared features? Or did you just "see the light" and have only ever owned a Glock?

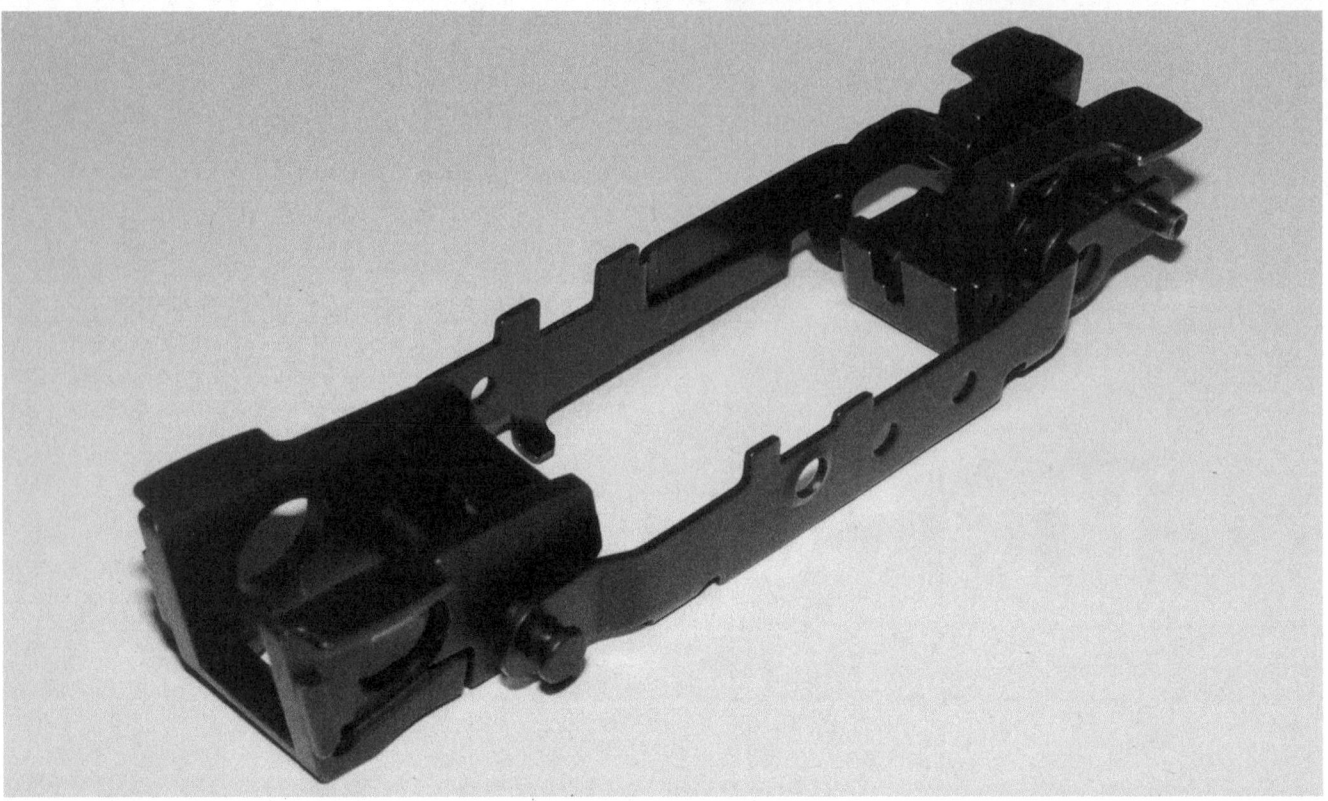

The S&W M&P uses an internal chassis, one that connects the trigger with the striker and not by means of a flexible polymer shell. *Photo courtesy S&W*

If you truly want to be informed and you're willing to risk your love affair with Glocks, then read on and see what your favorite blaster is up against.

Smith & Wesson

When Glock first appeared here in the U.S., in the 1980s, S&W owned the police market. It owned it in revolvers, as Colt's had long since bowed out of that segment, and Ruger, while working hard, was not able to make much of a foothold there. Smith & Wesson also owned it in pistols, as no one else had the volume, features, and history it had—that, and almost no one else had a double-action pistol, which police forces adamantly insisted on buying, were they to allow their officers to transition off revolvers and carry those "newfangled" self-loading pistols.

While SIG had a few under the Browning label, S&W dominated the burgeoning pistol market, and all of its semi-autos were variants of its SA/DA system. The exemplars here were the S&W M-39 and M-59. The M-39 was a single-stack 9mm that dated from the early 1950s. The 59 was the hi-cap (there was no .40 at that time, of course), that dated from the early 1970s and had the traditional double-action (TDA) trigger system. The slide on each had a hammer-dropping safety, a safety that also stayed down and locked the mechanism. Left down, you had to push it up to the fire position in order to get the pistol to work. Once you did that, your first shot was revolver-like, long and heavy in its double-action. Subsequent shots were short and light, like that of a 1911, in single-action.

The frames for both the M-39 and the M-59 were machined from aluminum or steel. In the mid-1980s, S&W went through a change, switching production over from the traditional rows of mills and lathes to a CNC-based system, and the number of models exploded. The quick reset time of a CNC machine made it possible to offer a *huge* number of variations. In the old system, to make a change you'd have to remove the "fixture," the specialized vise to hold a part, on each of 10, 20 or a hundred mills or lathes. Then you'd have to check the dimensions, make the parts, and swap them to something else. In a CNC machining center, all there is to do is swap out the "tombstone," load a different program, and get back to work. You could literally change models being produced during a lunch break.

The profusion of models got so intense that we at the shop (and many others, I'm sure), joked about the "S&W of the Month Club," and S&W even put out a circular slide rule, a model assignment system, where you could look up the features on any given model, just by turning the wheel—I kid you not. The numbering system was expanded first to a three-digit system (as in the M-439), and then to a four-digit system (for example, M-5906) and even that wasn't enough to track them all.

To give it credit, S&W tried. It worked the system hard for most of a decade, until it finally decided it just couldn't convince buyers that the TDA system and metal-framed pistols were what they wanted. So it came up with the Sigma.

I attended an S&W Dealers' Range Day where the Sigma was unveiled. Smith & Wesson's PR folks and such gathered a bunch of us at a range, feeding us coffee and doughnuts in the morning, while telling us about all the new models they had. After a quick lunch, they set us loose on the range with tables full of guns, ammo, magazines, and hearing protection. Boy, was I surprised when a significant percentage of the dealers simply faded off to the parking lot, fired up their cars or trucks, and left. Free ammo? Loaner guns? And when we're done we don't have to police brass, clean guns, or even box things up? Fine that they left. Simply meant there was more ammo for the rest of us.

The Sigmas were each attended by a stack of ammo—as in *4,000 rounds per pistol*. We lined up and waited our turn to load up. We'd each load a mag, wait in line to get to the firing point, shoot when we got there, then go back to the end of the line and repeat.

In short order, the slides of the Sigmas were so hot we could not touch them to work the action. When the slide locked back, each shooter would drop their magazine and put the Sigma down. The next shooter would pick it up by the polymer frame, slap in their magazine, and use the edge of the bench to push the slide back far enough to unlock and then close. The Sigmas were blisteringly hot and stayed that way until the ammo was gone. They did not malfunction. Oh, and these were all .40 Sigmas, not 9mm.

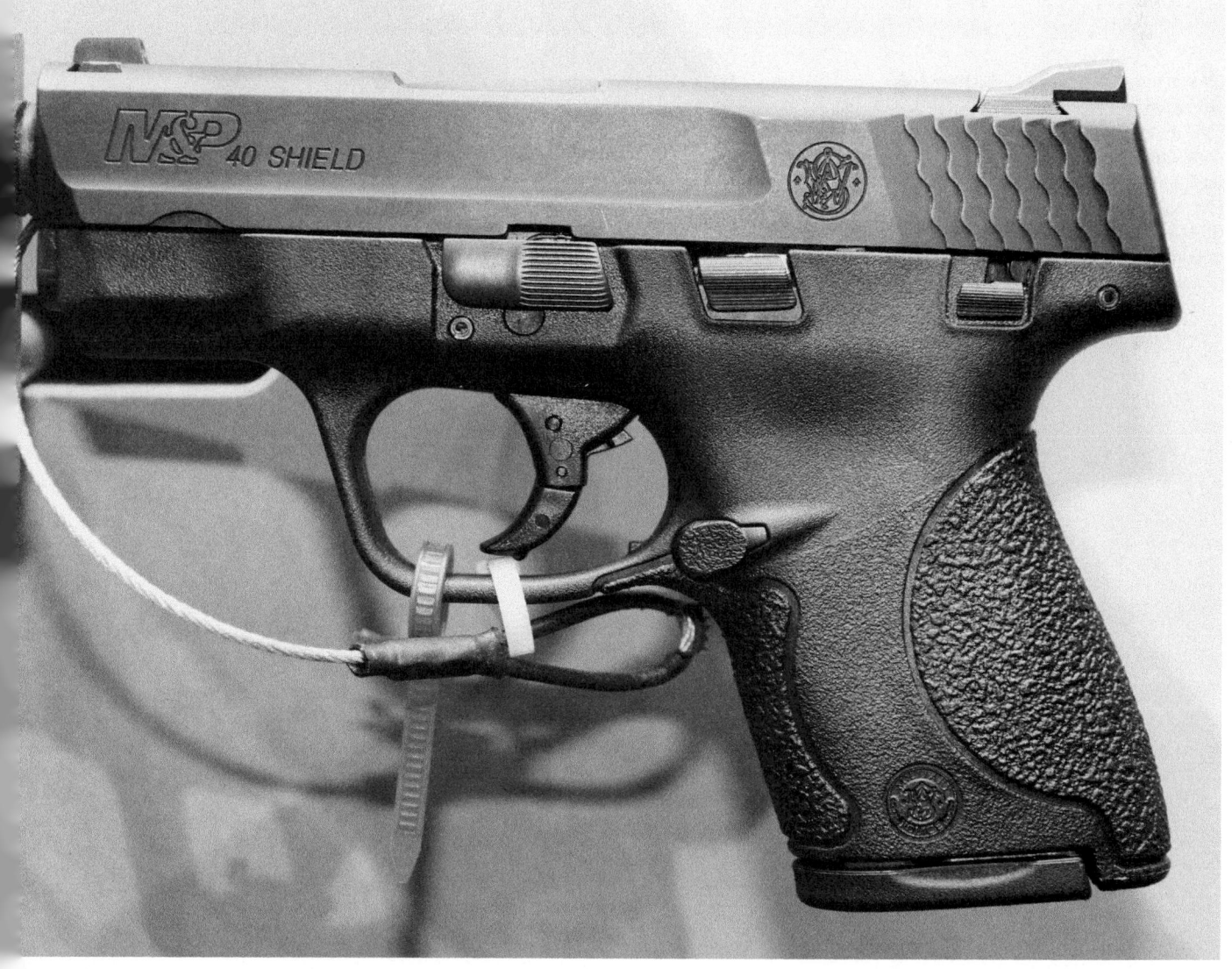

This S&W Shield is in .40, and it's a compact and powerful little carry gun.

FN has not only come out with the FNS, a striker-fired competitor to the G17, but also the FNS equivalent to the G34/35. Look for this one in Production Division and in 3-Gun matches.

There was a catch. The Sigma was a close copy of the Glock. So close, in fact, that, for a while, we gunsmiths amused ourselves by trying this or that part, swapping from Glock to Sigma and back. This close match got S&W into a bit of trouble, and Glock sued them. The suit was settled by S&W making some changes to the Sigma and paying out an undisclosed sum. What did it change? Heck if I remember. Again, there was a short, amusing time when we compared the "old" Sigmas to the new, trying to discover what had been changed, but once the thrill of that wore off, who bothers to keep track? The only way to know now would be to buy an early Sigma, one produced from 1994 to about 1996, and compare the dimensions with one after that, say from 1997 onwards. I'm not that bored.

One aspect I've learned from S&W Sigma detractors since then is that the trigger is apparently awful. That's news to me, but there are some who simply hate and cannot abide it. Heavy, yes, but it is, after all, a striker-fired pistol of the early era. You'd *expect* it to be un-fun. Me, I figure the more rounded grip contour of the Sigma is triggering some of that deep response, and they just can't help themselves. What really matters is that S&W has told me that the Sigma, by far, is the model with the lowest return rate. I don't know the actual numbers, but the differences between it and other modes are great enough that it is a point the company reps have mentioned without having to be prompted. I'm not sure if that is because it's such a close copy of the Glock and the Glock has had relatively trouble-free existence (as long as you stay in 9mm, and Gens 1 through 3), or if it's due to some extra that the S&W process and staff brought to the pistol.

One drawback of the Sigma is that the accessory rail is proprietary. You can't bolt any of the Picatinny rail-mount lights, lasers and such to it. For a lot of people (and agencies) who won't be mounting a light, that doesn't matter.

Another noteworthy bit of information: When you consider that S&W sells plane-loads of Sigmas to the armies and police forces of foreign countries, and those buyers would not be the least bit hesitant to send them back if they found a problem, that's interesting stuff. Still, S&W didn't stop with the Sigma.

Smith & Wesson M&P

I traveled to S&W to see the new M&P when it was unveiled in January of 2005. We got the

Springfield deserves credit for bringing a lot of heat to the "a better Glock than Glock" competition. The XDm, with as many shots and a grip safety to boot, is putting a lot of pressure on Glock.

rundown, we shot the guns, we toured the factory and saw how they were made, and we were all impressed. S&W started with the hard one, that is it made the first M&P as a head-to-head competitor to the Glock G23. The first M&P was a Commander-sized .40 pistol. Why? The S&W bosses were not forthcoming on this (who would be, really?), but the reasons are pretty obvious. By 2005, the world was clearly enamored with the .40 S&W cartridge. Carry guns were becoming the new normal. If a police department was going to be in the market for a pistol sidearm, then they were probably going to be looking for a .40 and probably for one compact enough for both duty and off-duty/plainclothes use.

Why else make the comparison to the G23? Well, making a reliable pistol in .40 is more difficult than doing the same in 9mm. Plus, the smaller size was more difficult to debug than the larger one. So, start with the hard one first, and life is easier when it comes time to make the rest. In due time, we had full-sized 9mms, .45s, and all the variants.

We also had design and manufacturing advantages in the M&P. In manufacturing, S&W through-hardens its slides and barrels. Then they get the Melonite treatment, that being the treatment that makes the surface file-hard. So the parts are both case-hard and through-hard—and tough.

The M&P design has three advantages over the Glock, two obvious and one not. The obvious ones are that the frame has replaceable backstraps and the slide stop is ambidextrous. In late 2005, Glock still didn't have a alterable backstrap. The M&P backstrap allowed owners to change the size of the grip so each could fit it to their own hands. An ambidextrous slide stop lets those who use this part to "slingshot" a slide that has locked back, to use either side. Lefties rejoice. The less obvious advantage? The internal chassis that is the skeleton of the M&P runs through the polymer frame at the magazine well and connects the trigger and the sear areas as a single unit. As a result, there is no flex or squish in the trigger linkage. The M&P can be built or tuned to a crisper, cleaner trigger pull than can Glocks. Since then, it has become a matter

As if the XDs in .45 wasn't enough, now Springfield offers the XDs in 9mm. Flat, compact, and with 7+1 magazines, you can bet Springfield will have an extended-on, making it a 9+1, in the near future.

H&K has worked hard to stay competitive. Even though it pioneered polymers in pistols, being too early cost them. The USP is a solid and dependable pistol, but it is blocky. Oh, heck, it's just plain big for its caliber and capacity.

of pride in some quarters that their M&P has a trigger almost like that of a clean 1911 trigger (and a lot closer than Glock's) . As a last bonus, the designers at S&W, when asked, found a way to build a thumb safety into the system. You can have an M&P with or without, and that matters to a lot of people.

Smith & Wesson SD VE

The SD is an amalgam of the Sigma and the M&P. The design takes the best of both; the low cost of the Sigma and the engineering advances of the M&P, and combines them into one. One big change is the accessory rail, which is now Picatinny-compatible and not the proprietary rail of the Sigma. The result? In 2012 dollars, the M&P MSRP runs $569, while an SD is $379. The Sigma is no longer on the S&W web page, but my recollection is that it was right between those prices. That makes the SD, available in 9mm & .40, a low-cost competitor to Glock, and one with many of the advantages of the M&P.

Ruger

Sturm, Ruger & Company started muscling into the police and defensive market in the mid-1970s, when it introduced a double-action revolver. Clobbering poor, tottering Colt's aside, Ruger went right at S&W. For all its efforts, though, it had a hard time dislodging S&W from the police revolver market. The main reason was that the S&W design lent itself to improving, and S&W was more than happy to teach police armorers how to do that. (Another benefit was that info trickled down to those of us who were not in PDs, but who had customers who wanted their S&W revolvers worked on.) The Ruger Security Six and the GP-100, while both amazingly durable, were not easy to "slick up." Even when worked on, they simply were not as smooth and light as a similarly and more easily 'smithed S&W. When the police market shifted to pistols in the early 1980s, Ruger shifted, too, offering up the brick-like P85. It kept at this market as well, just like S&W at that time,

"Only" a .22 LR, the ISSC fills a niche Glock has not yet addressed, that of being a smaller-caliber training pistol, one that costs less to shoot than a 9mm.

The S&W M&P, this one with an extended and threaded barrel for mounting a muzzle brake or suppressor.

and stuck with metal-framed pistols until the autumn of 2007, when it introduced the SR9. Oh, Ruger had made some polymer-framed pistols before, but those had been derivatives of the original metal-frame designs that simply had a polymer, or mostly polymer, frame as a replacement. The SR9, on the other hand, was built to be a direct, head-to-head competitor to the Glock—which, when you consider that the SR9 came out 25 years after the Glock was known, is quite a compliment to Glock.

I visited the Ruger factory, I saw the SR9s being made and, in due time, I received an SR9. I promptly thrashed it. I prevailed upon Magtech to send me a pile of ammo and, with a crew of volunteers, we put 6,800 rounds through it in one afternoon. We had one malfunction, which we attributed to the glove one of the shooters was wearing to protect his hand from the heat. I finished off the rest of the 10,000 rounds Magtech sent, then added another 5,000 rounds of miscellaneous factory and reloaded ammo and miscellaneous loads I had on my shelves.

When it came time to send it back, I phoned Robert Stutler, the vice president of the Prescott plant where my sample had been made. I told him that the engineers would have a fun time with it, as I'd put 15,000 rounds through it and, in the process, turned the barrel to a light "straw" color. I'd heated it up good. There was a pause and dead air from the other end of the line. "Uh, Patrick, why don't you just hang onto that one? There's nothing we can do with it now." Clearly, the accountants had been planning on scrubbing it up and sending it on to the next gun writer in line, and, so, here it stays.

The SR9 has advantages over the Glock, one of which is the magazine. Made of steel, by Mec-Gar, they are durable, easy to strip and clean, reliable, and common. The magazine is also the part that activates the magazine disconnect safety. In the minds of a lot of people, having a pistol that doesn't work when the magazine is out is a good thing. That way, those who know little about firearms are "safe" once they've removed the magazine. Opinions differ.

Opinions aside, Ruger was clever in the design of this feature. First, you have to know that the typical drop-magazine safety design is to put the magazine into the trigger system, where the extra parts and friction cause a less than stellar trigger pull. On the SR9, the top of the magazine pushes the block out of the path of the striker assembly, thus, the magazine safety has no effect on trigger pull.

As a bonus for those who want to do without it altogether, you can both easily remove the magazine safety and easily discern if the safety is there or not. To remove it, unload the gun, remove the slide, disassemble the striker system, and take out the bar that is the magazine safety. Then re-assemble without including the bar. To see if an SR9 has it, lock the slide to the rear and turn it over. You can plainly see if it is or isn't there.

Three more benefits of the SR9 are its ambidextrous magazine catch, an ambidextrous thumb safety, and a reversible backstrap. About where the mainspring housing is on a 1911, the SR9 has a rubberized section. You can remove it and turn it over; one side is arched while the other is flat. Not exactly the full-on replaceable backstrap of other designs, but enough to make a difference in feel. Since its introduction, the SR9 has become available in compact sizes and in .40 S&W.

FNH-USA

FNH-USA stuck with the hammer-dropping, traditional trigger longer than most. But, in the end, it offered what buyers seemed intent on owning: striker-fire. The origins are the FNP series, a TDA trigger system pistol that has a polymer frame, stainless steel slide and barrel, and holds a goodly number of rounds. While the magazine holds only 14 or so in 9mm, due to the angle the bottom of the magazine tube, that's enough, and it is a plenty reliable pistol. So much so that, when they sent me one to test, I bought it and stuffed it into my bug-out bag, the one ready to go if I have to race out the door.

FNH-USA has since improved it, changing the frame/barrel seat interface, which got the boreline lower to your shooting hand, and changed the magazine. The FNX, while still a TDA system, it held more rounds (16 to 17 in

S&W has offered the Sigma for many years now, but it is soon to be replaced by a new pistol, one with more M&P looks, but the Sigma's utter un-breakability—not that the M&P is fragile, mind you.

9mm), and with the lower bore line came less muzzle rise in recoil. The new magazines are not interchangeable with the FNP.

Last offered was the FNS. Here, the same pistol was altered to be a striker-fired system. It uses the FNX magazines, so you get lots of ammo, and it also features ambidextrous thumb safety, magazine release, and slide stop. There is an accessory rail, now common on pistols and, as a last bit of inducement to change, the frame rails, the part the slide rides on, can be replaced. If you wear the frame rails enough (and this would take a mighty shooting schedule), they can be replaced with new ones and off you go. It also has replaceable backstrap, It comes in 9mm and .40, but for those who want to go with a bigger hammer, one in .45, you'll have to use an FNX. At least for now, if the FNS sells in anything like the volume it deserves, the .45 version will be along soon.

Springfield XD & XDm

The XD comes to us courtesy of Croatia, with the folks at Springfield Armory being clever enough to see a good thing when it passed in front of them. The big deal with the XD is the grip safety.

While you can get an XD in four sizes and three calibers, the core of the model is an interesting mix of features. First, you have the polymer frame and striker firing system. Next there's the grip safety, which prevents it from firing unless you're holding the grip safety down. Then there are the steel magazines, which are nickel-plated for corrosion resistance. The barrels and slides are stainless steel, Melonite treated and, thus, super-hard and durable. The accessory rail is a Picatinny, so all lights lasers and such will fit. On some models, you can even have a thumb safety, if you wish.

As good as the XD is, there are some complaints, primarily that the grip angle was not all it could be, and that the bore was higher over the shooting hand than it should be. A more engineering- or gunsmithing-oriented complaint concerned the magazine design, which held down capacity. For instance, a full-sized XD in 9mm holds 16 rounds.

Enter the XDm. Springfield changed the grip, magazine, slide and bore height, and the texture of the polymer frame. Now, a 9mm 4½-inch model (comparable to a G17) holds 19 rounds. Where the XD looks a bit blocky or slightly clunky, the XDm is all aggressive angles, edgy grippy sections, and high capacity. You also get, a loaded chamber indicator, it retains the grip safety and, as a bonus, you can disassemble without having to dry-fire the pistol. Springfield also added a replaceable backstrap, one that fits below the grip safety.

This last feature was not accomplished without a certain amount of drama and hand-wringing. The change in magazines was a big deal, and it made the XD and XDm magazines incompatible. I've mentioned this before, but it's worth noting that Nikon and Canon went through the same thing, but with different decisions. When it became clear that auto-focus and electronic circuitry in cameras were going to be the future, Nikon stuck with its lens mount design and added to it. Canon said "frak it" and designed a new one. The old Canon cameras and lenses (known as the FD lens mount), are not compatible with the newer EOS line. Both Nikon and Canon paid for it, Nikon with successive generations of lenses that had more-or-less autofocus functions and various bodies with the autofocus motors in the body or not, while Canon incurred the wrath of its owners for forcing them to invest in a whole new setup of bodies and lenses.

Glock has continued with the same magazines and, until recently, did not have a replaceable backstrap. (Well, it still doesn't, but the flat goiter thing is a step forward.) When Springfield finally decided it couldn't take the capacity hit, it went with a new magazine. Which is the second curious thing—Springfield still offers the XD. Especially in the compact and sub-compact versions, I fully expected the XDm to replace the XD and the older model to be phased out. But no, the company has a large enough satisfied market for the XD that it remains in production, even in the compact versions, where a "compact" XD offers neither the ergonomics nor the capacity of the same compact XDm.

Then there is the XDs. When I first saw the XDs and laid hands on it, I thought, "This is a nice, compact 9mm pistol." Then I found out it was a .45. I was fully prepared to have my hand mangled from the recoil, but it is not at all unpleasant.

The really appealing things about

I love revolvers and I love engraved revolvers, but even I have to admit that the choice between five .38 Specials or 10 9mms is not a trick question. Ten is better than five.

the XDs are that it is flat and thin. It is thin, as in it's one-inch wide. It is flat, as in it feels like it is a board, not a broomstick. Now, if you like a fat grip on a compact pistol, no problem. You can use inner tube strips or a Hogue grip band and make it as portly as you want. The XDs holds five rounds in the mag plus one in the chamber, so it gives up one shot to the G36. I'm sure Springfield is working on that and, if it isn't, someone else is, because extra shots are always good.

The XDs is fractionally smaller, top to bottom and in length, than the G36, while being an ounce heavier. But the big difference is in the feel. Where the XDs makes the G36 feel just a bit bigger, the G30, the compact hi-cap, feels like Roseanne Barr. Let me amend that. I have no idea what Roseanne Barr feels like, but, as a mental picture, it should suffice.

SIG Sauer

Curiously, among the big-name defensive pistol manufacturers, SIG is one of the few that does not offer a striker-fired pistol. While a SIG P290 is a superbly built pistol and well suited

(top) Yes, Glocks are durable and they shrug off bad stuff. So do all its competitors. This S&W M&P survived a mud bath. *Photo courtesy S&W*

(above) The M&P chassis connects the trigger pivot to the sear block, another solid component; there's no squish in the trigger pull resulting from polymer flex.

to defensive uses, it is a hammer-fired DAO pistol. While SIG has a large list of hammer-fired, hammer-drop-safety pistols and satisfied customers (the Navy S.E.A.L.s, apparently, are much enamored of the P226, even to this day), we have to wonder how long it will be before this company offers a striker-fired pistol.

Beretta

The Beretta M-92 and Storm are both full-sized and compact pistols with an external hammer and a hammer-dropping safety. However, the Nano, a subcompact carry gun, is made as a striker-fired pistol. Is this the beginning of a Beretta stable of sub-, compact, and full-sized striker-fired pistols? Or is it just a grab at the compact carry market and the Italian manufacturer will stick with its proven external hammer TDA systems? Time will tell.

Taurus

Does Taurus make a striker-fired pistol? You bet. Which one? That, until recently, has been the problem. Taurus has had a reputation for having a catalog full of pistols, most of which were not available. Sorting them out was a major league task. Recently, Taurus USA hired itself a new CEO, Mark Kresser, and one of the first things he did was sit down with a catalog and a felt-tip pen. With that pen he started striking stocking numbers off the catalog. "Take this one out, this whole line goes, we aren't going to list that," and so on. I've seen the catalog.

The idea was to get a handle on stock numbers and inventory and start producing the ones people wanted in the kind of volume it takes to satisfy a volume of customers. What you can now get is what you want: full-size, compact, and sub-compacts pistols in .380, 9mm, .40, and .45, in blue and hard chrome, and all with polymer frames, hi-cap mags, and the Taurus 100-percent warranty.

Heckler & Koch

Heckler & Koch is the other big name holding out and not yet offering a striker-fired pistol. While there are many who complain about its customer service, when H&K comes out with something new, it sells boatloads of them.

Left in the driveway overnight in the freezing mud, it still works. *Photo courtesy S&W*

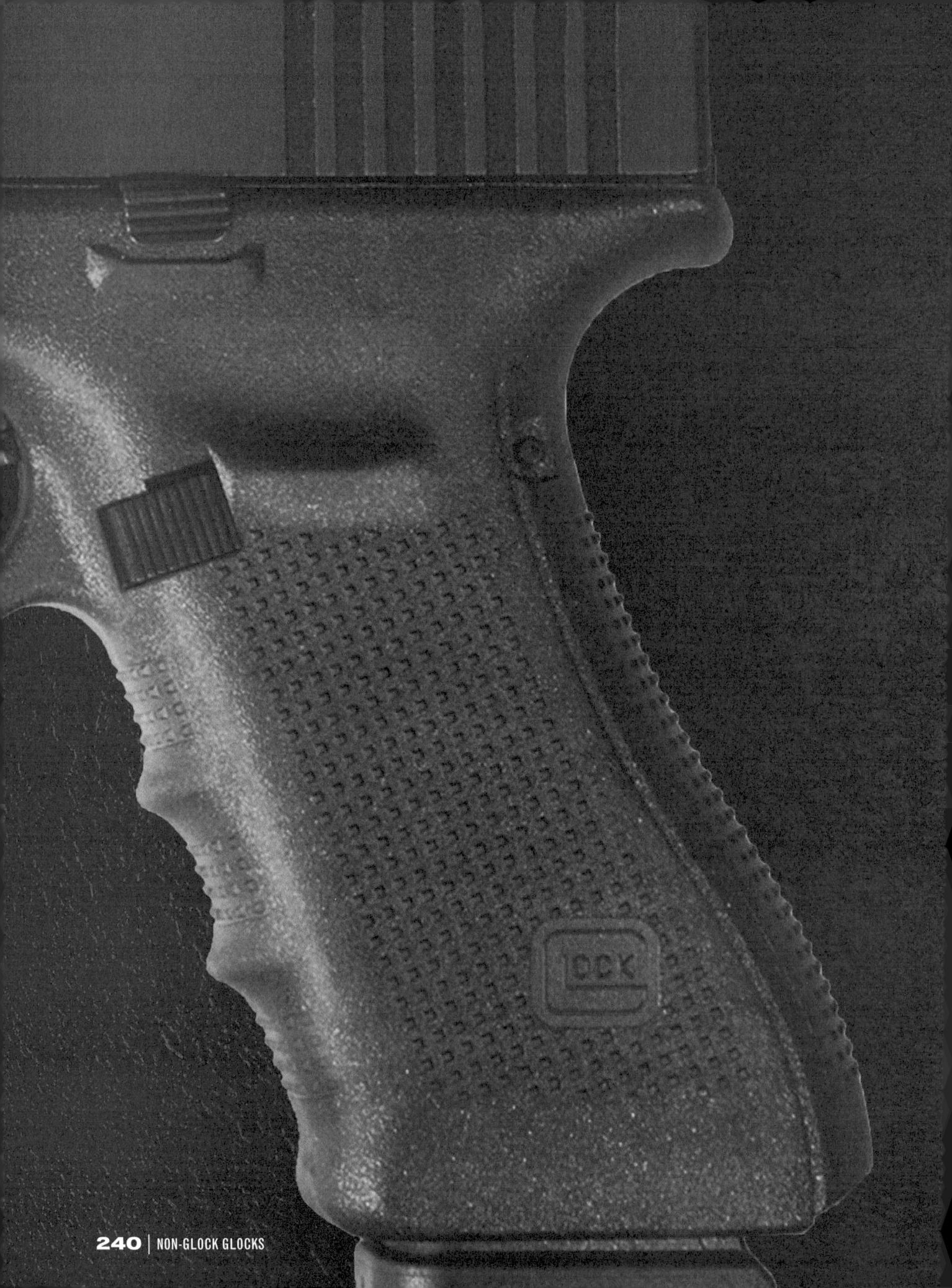

CHAPTER 16

Non-Glock Glocks

Back in previous Glock books I've written for Gun Digest, I had a chance to test CCF RaceFrames Glock offerings. The firm made Glock frames (well, to be technically and legally correct, Glock-*compatible* frames), out of steel and aluminum, and there was some talk back then of titanium. Well, titanium (chemical symbol Ti) proved to be ferociously expensive and the technical challenges were such that it has not been worth it for manufacturers or gunsmiths to work with it. I know a number of custom gunsmiths who were eager to try their hand at Ti and, once they got into it, decided, "No, this isn't fun."

I have a Ti-framed custom pistol, (not a CCF RaceFrame) which is now the third of the five that particular gunsmith will ever have worked on. Once he had a chance to get some practice working with Ti, he stopped accepting orders for it. Most everyone else in the custom gunsmithing arena have decided the same. But a steel or aluminum-framed Glock?

Cool. Except, it wasn't cool enough. The company CCF RaceFrames, LLC is now no more, the few remaining frames sitting on a shelf waiting for someone to come along and love them, assemble them, use them, and have fun with them. What happened? I have to think it was a situation of nothing-in-common meeting an interesting engineering advancement.

Glock made its name on polymer frames. In short order, it was "polymer frame equals Glock" in the minds of shooters. Competitive pistols with polymer frames were described as "Glock-like" or "polymer-made, but not Glock-shaped" in magazine articles, in gun shops, and on ranges across the country. For a while, Robbie Barkman, of Robar, did custom-built pistols on CCF RaceFrames and built them to spec. Made a few gun magazine newsstand covers, he did, and sold those custom pistols while the interest was there. But that's all done, I'm afraid. Making a Glock with a metal frame just didn't compute in the perspective of many shooters and would-be buyers.

What was a prospective firearms manufacturer wanting to get into this lucrative market segment to do? Easy. Make it polymer.

What CCF couldn't do, having already started down the metal-frame path, Lone Wolf could. Lone Wolf was begun and has grown, doing the things that Glock would not do, starting with replacement barrels that were kosher with lead bullets, then threaded barrels for suppressors, and on to carbines, custom guns, and more. Lone Wolf has shown the

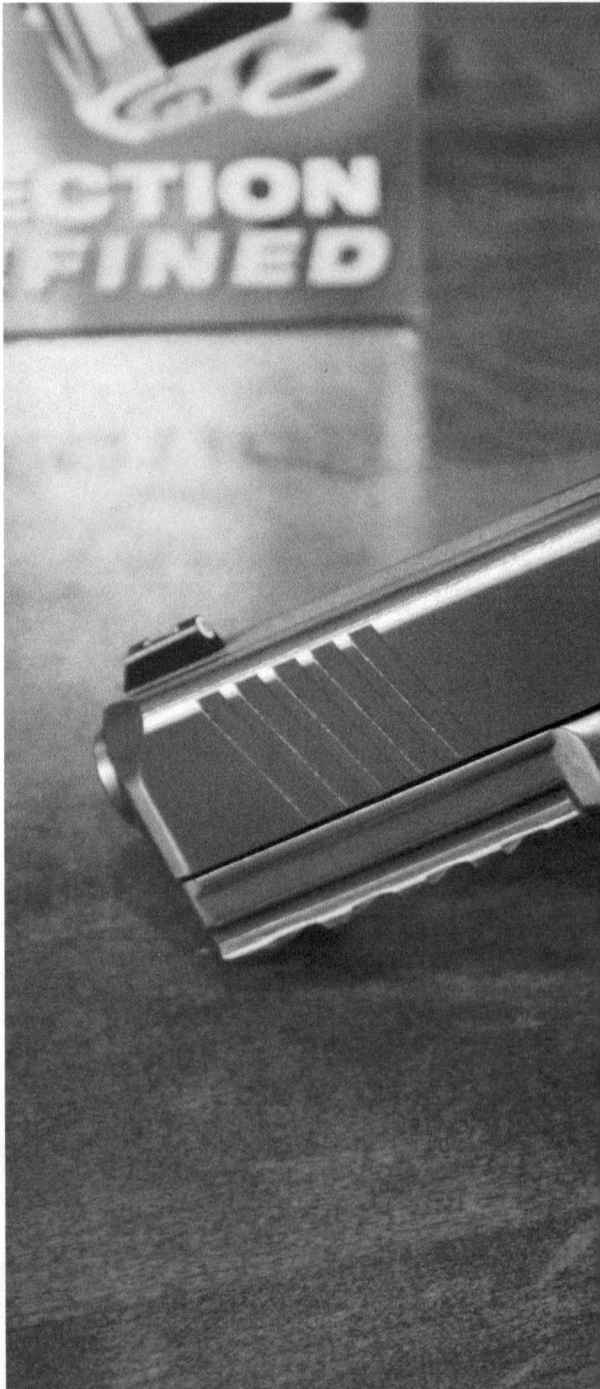

> Glock made its name on polymer frames. In short order, it was "polymer frames equal Glock" in the minds of shooters. Competitive guns with polymer frames were described as "Glock-like" or "polymer-made, but not Glock-shaped" in magazine articles, in gun shops, and on ranges across the country.

European gunmaker how things are done in America. And so, in due time, as it expanded the product line, Lone Wolf got to the point where it can make an entire pistol. It sent me one, so I could test it and report on it.

Make no mistake, you can have a Lone Wolf Glock in an assortment of sizes, calibers, options, and colors. So don't look this one over and say to yourself "Nice, but not what I need or want." The Open gun Lone Wolf sent me is a G17/22-sized pistol in .40 S&W, with red dot optic and muzzle brake. As such, it doesn't fit in a lot of competitions, but it's still way fun to shoot.

The frame is of a polymer that feels a bit harder than that used in Glocks. Perhaps it uses a bit more stiffening fiberglass or something (in this case, an approach not unlike rebar in concrete) or maybe the formula it uses simply pops out of the mold with a harder-feeling surface. The color is also a tiny bit more gray, which could be due to anything

For a while, Robar was building up CCF Raceframes as custom non-Glocks Glocks. Alas, this is no longer the case, which is too bad.

If you go the non-Glock route, you can get your pistols in colors.

from the amount of carbon black mixed in as a darkening agent to the formula, to the surface texture of the mold.

The dimensions, as far as I could tell, were the same as a Glock Glock, and all my magazines fit just fine. I tried swapping off the Lone Wolf slide assembly and trying my Glock slides, and they all fit just fine, too. So, there are no dimensional anomalies to worry about.

The slide is your normal-length G17 slide, with cocking serrations front and rear. The barrel is a Lone Wolf, which should not come as a surprise for a couple reasons. One, to get a Glock barrel longer than the slide is not easy and, on some caliber/models, not possible at all. Too, remember that Glock barrels hate lead bullets, whereas Lone Wolf barrels do not. On the end is the Lone Wolf muzzle brake of a very efficient design and one to scorch your arm hairs if you load light bullets fast.

The slide, while cut for iron sights (or polymer, if from Glock), has a red dot installed, in this instance a Burris Fastfire, a very compact red dot that is so durable it can be bolted

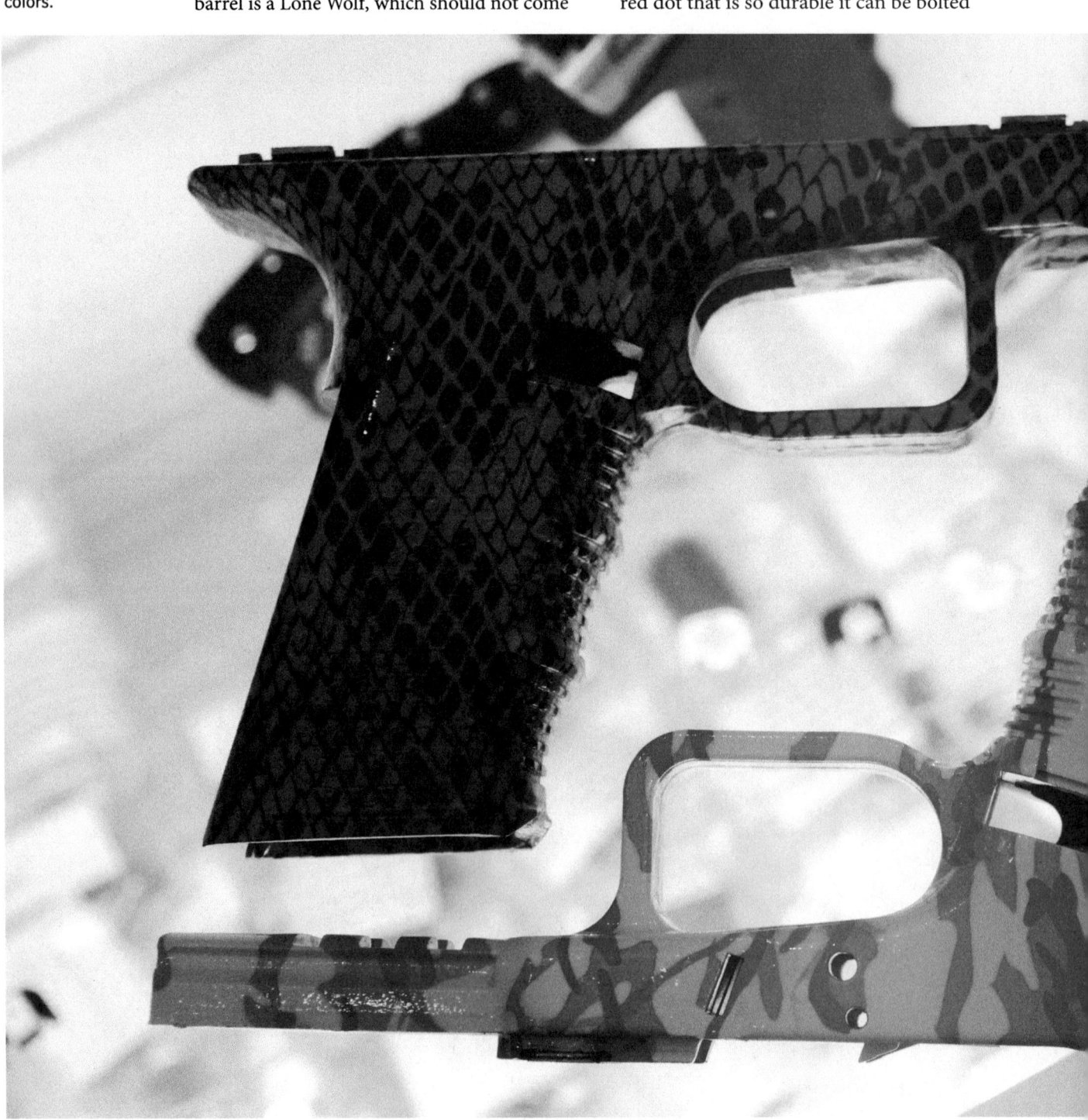

directly to the slide. (In the early days of red dots, we beat them to death regularly, even when bolted to the much more accommodating frame. On the slide, the old ones would have died right away, even if they stayed on.)

The Lone Wolf Open gun has a magazine funnel on the bottom, and the frame has a beavertail at the tang. Not that the recoil is going to be whipping the muzzle up so hard you need one, but, when it comes to the fractions-of-a-second scoring in Open, you want all the advantages you can get. Also, and unlike

Glocks, the Lone Wolf has a proper replaceable backstrap, a panel that you remove and replace to get the grip feel you desire.

In firing, the Lone Wolf Open is mild, even with regular .40 S&W ammo. The powder selection and bullet weight of standard .40 ammo is not tuned for best function in a comped pistol. The bullet is too heavy, the powder too fast. Still, it had mild recoil and the muzzle brake worked quite well.

For work in the Open Division, we generally test the pistol for proper function with off-the-shelf ammo. If it works 100 percent with that, then proceed to reload your own, where you'll look to build a combination of lighter bullet and slower-burning powder to get the recoil feel you desire. Some shooters want a gun that shoots "flat"—the comp works briskly, and the muzzle does not seem to come up. (It does, but is driven back down so quickly, it's hardly noticed.) Others want a pistol that shoots "soft," as in the comp reduces the hand impact, even though the muzzle rises in recoil. It is not possible to produce a comp/load combination that is both flat and soft. You have to have one or the other or a mix of them. What makes it flat makes the recoil brisker. What makes it soft causes muzzle rise.

A lighter bullet requires more powder to make "Major," as in post a Power Factor high enough to be scored with the big calibers. (Yes, I know this is a .40 and, as such, it is a big caliber, but most shooters shoot 9mm/.38 Super in Open, and the methods apply with all.) The increased powder is part of the "ejecta," the recoil-causing part of shooting, but the extra powder also creates extra gas, which, flowing through the comp, reduces recoil/muzzle rise. The task for each shooter is to find the combination of bullet weight/powder burn rate and volume that makes Major and produces the muzzle brake effect they desire. Some go for slower powders, others faster, and shooters can discuss bullet/powder combos with near-religious fervor.

Why not a .40 Open gun? Capacity. For any given magazine length (and the maximum length allowed in Open is 170mm), a magazine in 9mm will hold more rounds than one in .40. When a stage run is measured in single-digit times, a tenth of a second lost is bad. The time spent reloading can be too much to overcome, even when done during a non-firing movement on the stage.

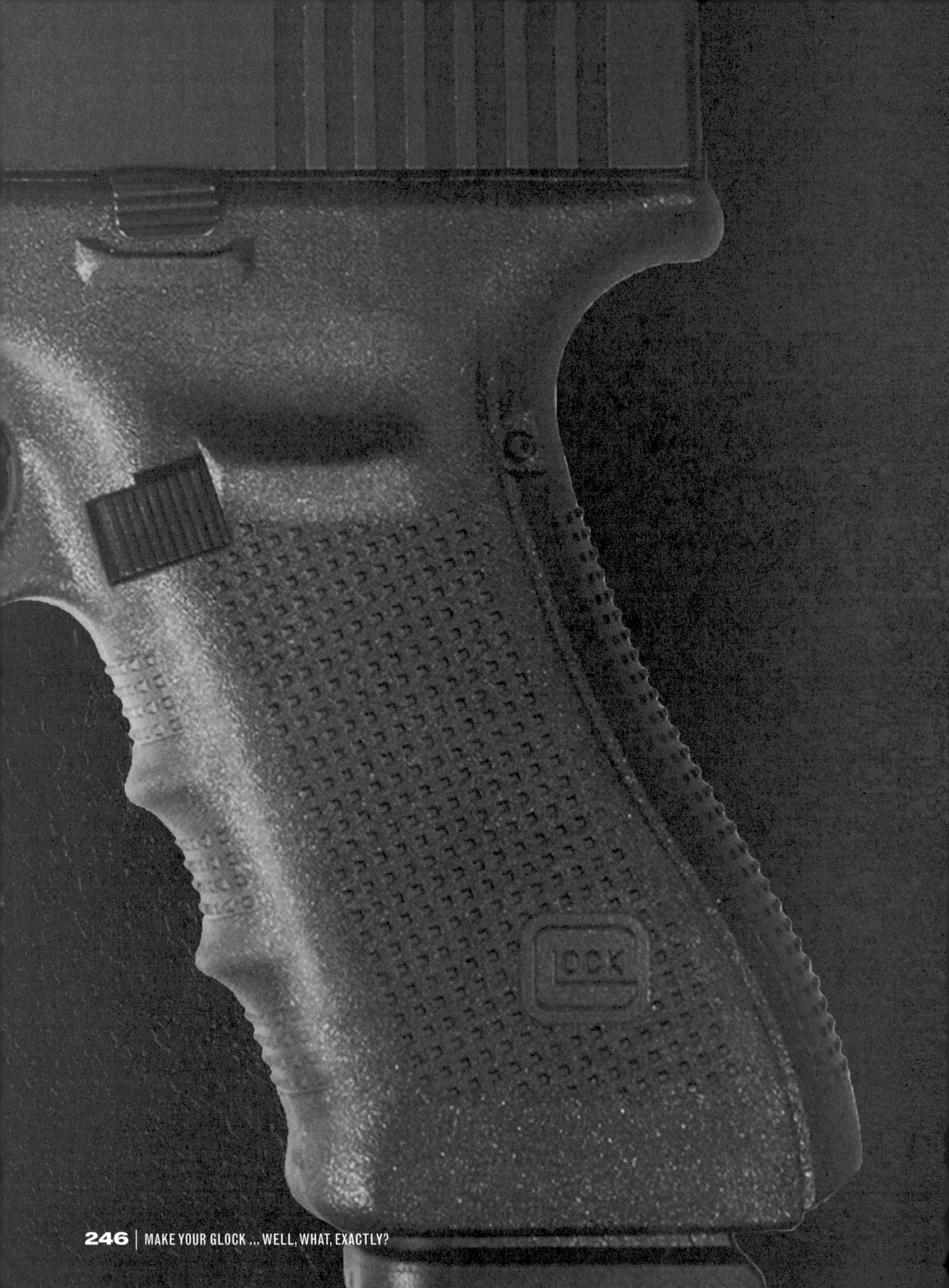

CHAPTER 17

Make Your Glock... Well, What, Exactly?

Let me shout this out. In my opinion, the Glock trigger is not my favorite. There, I've said it and, with that in mind, any improvement at all is cause for celebration in my eyes. And a significant improvement? That would mean that "Wow, we are *stylin'* and don't have to take a back seat to those 1911 guys anymore."

(below) The striker safety plunger head bears polishing. This one has been, but be careful not to over-round the edges or make it shorter.

(bottom) One of the places you can polish is the trigger bar tab that activates the striker safety. Take it out first, though.

Oh, if it were only so easy.

The idea comes up from time to time to do a book on gunsmithing the Glock. I patiently have to explain to the person who suggests it (sometimes an editor, sometimes a reader, sometimes a fellow gun writer), that the official Glock armorer's course takes eight hours. And the only reason it takes *that* long is that the instructor usually does it twice, once before lunch and once after. Having taken it a few times, invariably we spend the last couple hours of the day just doing a Q&A on all things Glock. Simply put, there isn't enough on Glock-wrangling to fill a book. So I'll just cut right to the chase: The trigger on a Glock can be improved.

Before we go any further, let's discuss just what it is that's wrong with the Glock trigger and why. I'll address this to three groups. Group 1 knows what a good trigger is and shakes their heads in disbelief every time they dry-fire a Glock. Group 2 are those who have fired nothing but Glocks and, thus, have no real frame of reference. And Group 3 are those who haven't done enough shooting with enough different or good-triggered firearms to do more than look on from the outside while we discuss this.

So, what *is* a good trigger? There are two kinds of triggers that are deemed to be good, the single-action and the double-action. In a single-action trigger, the trigger pull goes like this. There's initial contact, and then the slack and pre-load movement get "taken up," at which point (and at some significant fraction of the total pull needed), the trigger stops. Then, with additional pressure but no movement, the trigger "breaks" and the hammer falls. Some small movement post-break is

permitted (and is mechanically necessary), but the less the better.

That describes the perfect trigger pull, but sometimes that perfect is too good. If we take a bolt-action rifle, perfect is, well, perfect. After all, the shooter has to let go of the trigger completely to work the bolt, so the reset really doesn't matter. It could take the trigger a half a second to mechanically reset (basically forever, in firearms terms) and it wouldn't matter, because no one can work a bolt-action rifle anywhere near that quickly.

In handguns, perfect can actually be a hindrance. If the post-break movement, known as overtravel, is too short, then it is possible for a shooter who is trying to shoot at maximum speed to actually "tie up" the trigger mechanism. What happens is that, in the process of going faster and faster, the shooter "learns" to move his trigger a shorter and shorter distance to gain speed (this is pretty much a subconscious process, with little or no conscious input), until the shooter fails to move their trigger far enough. At this point, the pistol can't reset and there is no follow-up shot.

To shoot as quickly as possible, the mechanism has to have *some* overtravel and, thus, reset, enough that the shooter's brain (the actual trigger-pulling tool), can learn just how much is enough and not slip into too little. What makes this a difficult and messy process is that, if there is too much overtravel, accuracy suffers.

Firearms work in millisecond timeframes. In the time it takes your finger to push the trigger past the release point but before it stops at the limit of overtravel, the firing process has begun. The hammer is falling or the striker is moving forward. The impact of the trigger stopping at the limit of overtravel causes movement and vibration in the pistol as a whole. The greater that movement, the longer it takes for the system to stop moving.

If the hammer/striker strikes the primer (beginning the bullet's movement), and the firearm is still moving from the overtravel-induced motion, accuracy suffers. Obviously, if the firearm is still moving when the bullet exits the muzzle, the muzzle motion increases dispersion. Random movements of the muzzle at bullet release cannot increase accuracy. According to the Second Law of Thermodynamics, it can't even be a neutral effect. Movement is bad.

Short overtravel decreases the effect of such movement in two ways. By stopping over-

> The two examples of the "perfect" single-action trigger are those in tuned bolt-action rifles and custom 1911 pistols. There is a subset of rifle triggers known as "two-stage." There, the system uses (in the classic Browning design), a two-hook sear, one of which is spring-loaded. It, along with the Mauser bolt-action rifle, uses leverage and springs to create the take-up and then provide a clean break for the shot.

travel sooner, there is more time between the overtravel stop and the bullet's exit, thereby allowing the movement-induced wobble to be dampened. Also, by making the overtravel distance less, the impact is decreased, and the lesser impact means less movement to dampen in the greater time afforded. This entire process happens in such a short timeframe and is so subtle that many shooters simply don't realize that it happens.

As an aside, a perfect trigger need not be a *light* trigger. Yes, the current competition goal is a trigger of some two pounds in pull weight, but we're talking about the top shooters, the Masters and Grand Masters, who have shot a couple hundred thousand rounds in practice and competition and who do daily draw and dry-fire practice in addition to their practice maintenance and competition schedule.

In the course of investigating the early years of handguns, the beginning of the twentieth century, I came across an interesting situation: these early guns had heavy triggers. A typical WWI or earlier Colt 1911 had a trigger pull of seven or eight pounds—the trigger pull was amazingly crisp. You could take up the slack, then press until the pressure you were applying reached the seven- or eight-pound level (depending on the pistol you were testing), and then the hammer fell. As clean as those triggers were (and the pistols I checked, all collector's pieces or in museum collections), they had not been messed with since they'd left the factory.

Only the top edge, the long leg, and the top need polishing. The rest can be left alone, and should be.

The second perfect trigger is the double-action found on revolvers. Here, the intent is not to make a trigger that breaks cleanly, but one that releases without predictability. The perfect DA trigger has the same pressure all the way through the pull, that is, it doesn't start out with movement, then stop, and then require extra pressure.

The two examples of the "perfect" single-action trigger are those in tuned bolt-action rifles and custom 1911 pistols. There is a subset of rifle triggers known as "two-stage." There, the system uses (in the classic Browning design), a two-hook sear, one of which is spring-loaded. It, along with the Mauser bolt-action rifle, uses leverage and springs to create the take-up and then provide a clean break for the shot.

On a two-stage rifle trigger, the designer/builder can make it pretty much whatever they want it to be. Let's say you want a 4½-pound (total pull) trigger. You can build/design it so the take-up is one pound and the rest is 3½. Or the take-up is 3½ and the "break" is one pound. Obviously, you'd want a service trigger to be the former, while a competition shooter would want theirs built as the latter. But we're straying a bit from the Glock.

The second perfect trigger is the double-action trigger found on revolvers. Here, the intent is not to make a trigger that breaks cleanly, but one that releases without predictability. The perfect DA trigger has the same pressure all the way through the pull, that is, it doesn't start out with movement, then stop, and then require extra pressure. A DA trigger

A common trick in building a PPC handgun was to slick up the action and then put a rubber-backed stop screw in the trigger. The idea was to use the trigger to cock the hammer, and then finish the trigger pull in the last pound of pull, squeezing the rubber stop at the back, to wring the last bit of possible accuracy out of the system.

of, say, eight pounds, requires eight pounds of pressure to press it all the way through its stroke, but at no point can you tell there is any change beyond movement; clearly, it builds as it goes back, else it could not move. A trigger that requires eight pounds but doesn't move is *not* what we want. So, you press on the DA with one pound and it moves a bit. Up to two pounds, more movement. But the change is linear, that is without steps.

The process is simple. To shoot, you focus on the front sight and keep it on the target while you stroke through the trigger. Since you don't know in any precise way when the hammer will fall, all you can do is focus and press. You can't anticipate the shot, and that's good, for far worse than excessive overtravel is anticipation. Despite the assertions of Carly Simon, anticipation in shooting is a bad thing. It leads you to jerking, trigger-slapping, dropping the sights, and all manner of aiming buffoonery. A good DA trigger simply doesn't afford you the knowledge of when the firearm will go off and, thus, short-circuits the anticipation.

Most DA revolvers have pretty good double-action triggers. They have to. The market expects and demands it. Better yet is a trigger that has been slicked up by a compe-

If you over-polish, and shorten the height of the tip, you may run into striker and plunger conflict problems. An over-polished trigger bar and striker safety plunger might fail to lift the plunger enough, and the striker then binds, trying to make it to the primer.

MAKE YOUR GLOCK ... WELL, WHAT, EXACTLY? | **251**

(above) On the ejector block and the end of the trigger bar, polish only where they rub on each other. All other polishing is time wasted.

(right) You can polish the end tab, or tail, of the striker, but it is usually time wasted.

tent gunsmith, and there you will find a DA trigger that is a joy to use.

There are double-action triggers that are not anticipation-proof. Back in the Reagan era of PPC competition, revolvers were king and pistols were rarely seen. I was considered the range pariah on the sheriff's department PPC league for using a 1911A1, first in .45 (and that was considered a cannon, no matter how light I loaded it), and then .38 Super, loaded as lightly as I could and still get the pistol to function. These days, pistols are all over the place in PPC, simply because the pistol is now a common sight in police holsters.

A common trick in building a PPC handgun was to slick up the action and then put a rubber-backed stop screw in the trigger. The idea was to use the trigger to cock the hammer, and then finish the trigger pull in the last pound of pull, squeezing the rubber stop at the back, to wring the last bit of possible accuracy out of the system.

For those who have not done this, the indoor course had a maximum range of 50 feet and the "X" ring was the size of a playing card. Even in our friendly and small league, you had to shoot "clean," that is 600 points out of 600 points, to win. Ties were broken by "X" count.

With a .45, I averaged 596/600. With the Super, I upped that to 598/600. To shoot 600s I had to devote myself entirely to a DA revolver, .38 wadcutter ammo, and nothing but PPC. Since my aspirations were really in IPSC and bowling pin shooting, I accepted my "mere" 598 and used PPC to sharpen my ability to shoot accurately when needed.

The Glock Trigger

So, now that we know what the ideals are, where is the Glock in all this? The Glock trigger pull process is simple in description, if messy mechanically. To shoot a Glock, you press the trigger. This pushes the trigger bar back, compressing the striker spring until the connector cams the trigger bar down and off the striker tail. At this time, the trigger bar has also lifted the striker safety.

Let's start with the frame. Actually, we should call it what it is mechanically, the "enclosure." The shell of polymer is bendy/flexy and does not offer the support to the moving parts that a metal-frame pistol does. As you begin your trigger press, you also will be compressing the frame a bit, as the shell is non-rigid. I've had some try to argue that the trigger and the

Work on the frame, such as epoxying the rear and re-cutting it to a better shape, plus adding a tang such as this, are irreversible changes. Polishing the internals can always be undone by installing replacements, but these other modifications are permanent.

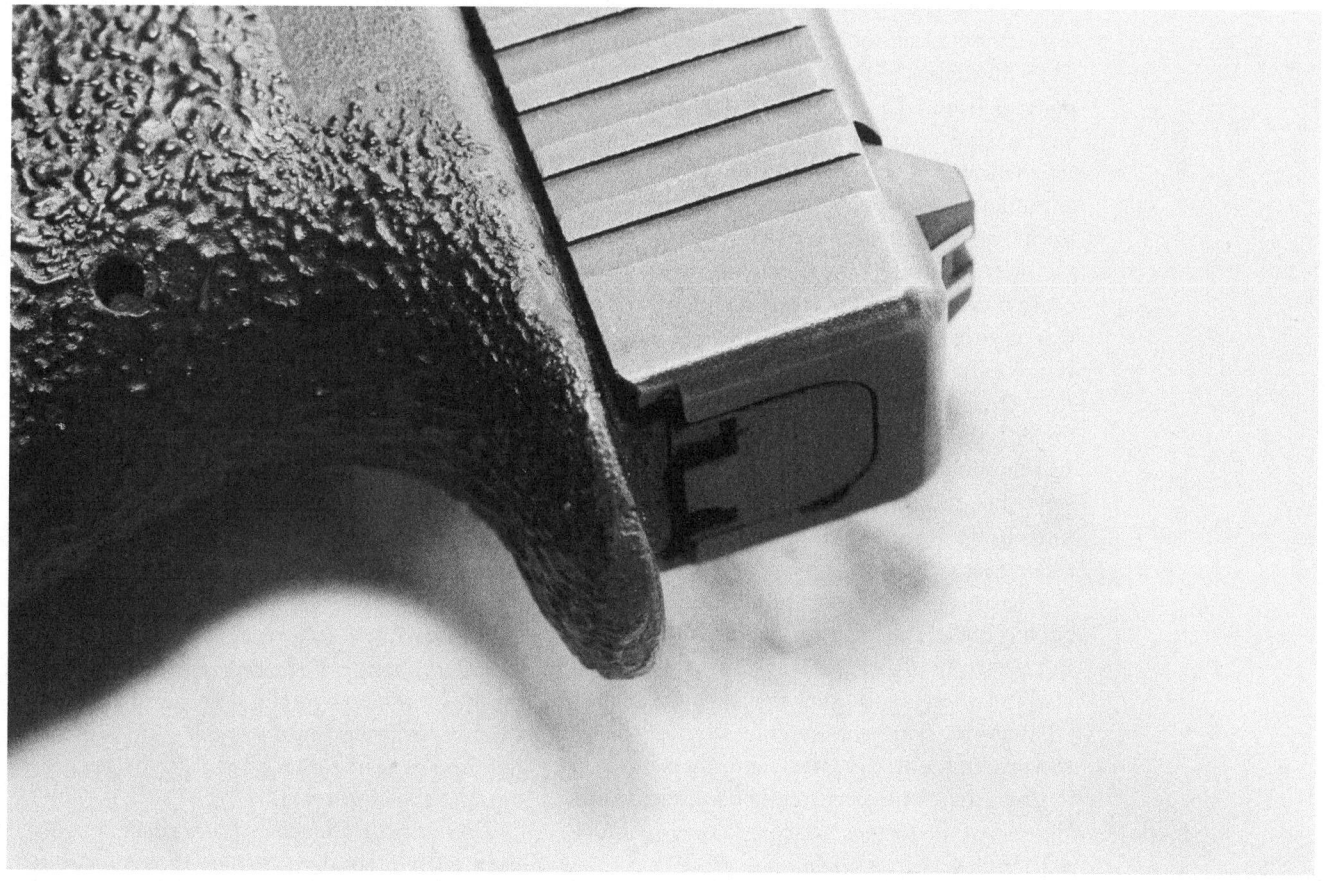

> Improving a Glock trigger is not going to be something you will do in the time between runs at a match. In fact, to do it right will probably take the better part of a weekend, a weekend not devoted to other work around the house. The job, at least as much as you can do, is mostly polishing.

trigger bar, moving in the shell, means that the shell does not flex. But the trigger pivots on its pin, and any pressure used to pivot the trigger also acts to press the pin towards the rear. (It is worth pointing out, at this juncture, that the S&W M&P uses a steel chassis inside of the polymer frame. The chassis is a rigid support for the trigger and striker connection, unlike the shell of the Glock design. That is one of the advantages of not being first, in that you can learn from your predecessors.)

The trigger safety itself probably doesn't cause much problem, as it pivots out of the way as your finger presses to the rear, and it is, theoretically, out of the way by the time the trigger begins its pivot. However, if your finger/hand is just the right (or wrong) size, you can be pressing on the trigger before the safety has fully cleared. That means a minor hitch in the trigger pull, until the trigger safety clears the frame.

The start of the trigger pull slides the trigger bar back. The bar rubs on the frame and the ejector block. While it is doing this, it is also compressing the striker against its spring. All these parts are rubbing on polymer or, in the case of the striker, steel rubbing on steel.

The process travels directly backwards until the end of the trigger bar comes in contact with the connector, the angled piece that diverts the trigger bar down. The trigger bar has to clear the drop safety slot in order to travel down, and any contact there adds to the rubbing. The connector increases the pressure needed to move the trigger bar. Also, as the bar is moving down, the end of the cruciform is sliding down off the striker tail. This is also about the time the trigger bar is lifting the striker safety. So, the trigger bar starts out crunching and grinding its way back, and then, just when you need things to be as stable as possible, the system throws three new sources of "noise" at your aiming process. At the end, the connector redirects, the striker tail adds drag, and the trigger bar must lift the striker safety. Yeesh. That's with the "3.5" connector. If you drink the Kool-Aid of the NYPD and add the extra/replacement trigger system that acts to eliminate the relatively easy slack take-up, you end up with a trigger pull that is just no fun at all. What to do?

Well, all the usual gunsmithing processes are of no avail. To make a trigger pull better on a pistol or a revolver, you polish the bearing surfaces, in some instances you'll correct geometry, and you can, in special cases, install replacement springs that ease the trigger pull. Ever polish polymer? It doesn't work that way.

Tools and Time

Improving a Glock trigger is not going to be something you will do in the time between runs at a match. In fact, to do it right will probably take the better part of a weekend, a weekend not devoted to other work around the house. An experienced gunsmith, with the tools at hand and a few (or a few dozen, hundred, whatever) Glocks under their belt, could probably whip through a Glock in an hour or two. The job, at least as much as you can do, is mostly polishing.

The Connector—Using Flitz, Simichrome, or some other metal polish and a felt wheel on a Dremel, polish the connector on the inside (outside of the frame) and angle face. The idea is to reduce any toolmarks the trigger bar could rub on.

Trigger Bar—Two places here. One is the rounded portion at the rear, the one that bears on the connector. Again, you want to reduce/remove toolmarks and provide a smooth surface and area of contact between the trigger bar and the connector.

Do not polish the end of the cruciform. Yes, there may be toolmarks there that you can remove, but, without the proper tools, you could change the angle of that surface. Removing toolmarks is good, but changing the angle is bad. Resist temptation and leave it alone.

Firing Pin Safety—The firing pin safety, as machined, has a sharp edge on it. To properly polish this, you need a power drill or drill press. Chuck the safety in the drill, turn on the drill at a low rpm, and use the polishing media you have selected to very slightly round the edge on the firing pin safety. You can use a fingertip loaded with polish, but a rubber eraser and the polish will save your fingerprints.

I've seen some who turned the stepped and angled head of the firing pin safety into a dome. This, along with changing the cruciform angle, is a bad thing. You want the trigger bar to lift the safety plunger, but you don't want there to be sharp edges to catch and cause trigger pull uncertainties.

Striker—Polish the tail of the striker where the cruciform bears on it. Unlike the cruciform tail, where the change is not apparent, it would be an obvious and egregious polishing job that changed the angle of the striker tail. You do not need to, nor should you, round the tail's surface. Just polish it to remove toolmakers and create a smooth surface. Once, done, clean the grit off, lube where appropriate, and reassemble.

If you make mistakes (and you'll know when you test-fire), you will be buying replacement parts and starting over. One of the good old gunsmith tricks is to start out R&D with new, replacement parts. Strip out the old and set them aside. Experiment on the new ones. If you mess those up, you can simply plug in the old parts and you are only out the time and parts cost.

"Competition" Parts

Can you replace the factory parts with better parts? That depends on your definition of "better." There are companies that make lighter strikers, for instance. A lighter striker takes less time, when hurled forward by the striker spring, to impact the primer and, thus, speeds up lock time. I see a couple problems with this, both somewhat theoretical, but still matters to be considered.

First, the lighter striker has less mass and, so, less ability to overcome problems such as gunk in the firing pin channel or a hard primer or one seated too deeply. Second, the lighter striker has less mass, thereby offering less resistance to primer blowback. In the course of ignition, the primer will experience the full force of chamber pressure. The primer is pushed back by this and transmits thrust to the striker. This pressure is the reason for pressure signs in excessive loads. The primer pushes back, *hard*, on the breechface, and then the case is slammed back over it. At a high enough pressure (or excessive headspace, not much of a problem here) the primer appears flattened.

So the firing pin is pushed back by the primer. What's the problem? Simple. The breechface on a Glock is very thin at the striker slot, so much so that the higher-brisance, lead-free primers can be an issue. Glock even tells users not to use lead-free primers. A lighter-than normal striker simply aggravates that concern.

These concerns affect several things. If you are using a Glock for defense and want 100-percent assurance that primers will do their job. So, for defensive use, don't use competition strikers.

For those using a Glock for competition, you'll be using reloads (tsk, tsk, says Glock) or factory-new ammo. Not much of a risk of failure to fire there, but what you will have to concern yourself with is that, after a couple hundred thousand rounds, your breechface may chip. I'd say, if you can afford that much ammo, you can afford a replacement slide, either Glock or aftermarket.

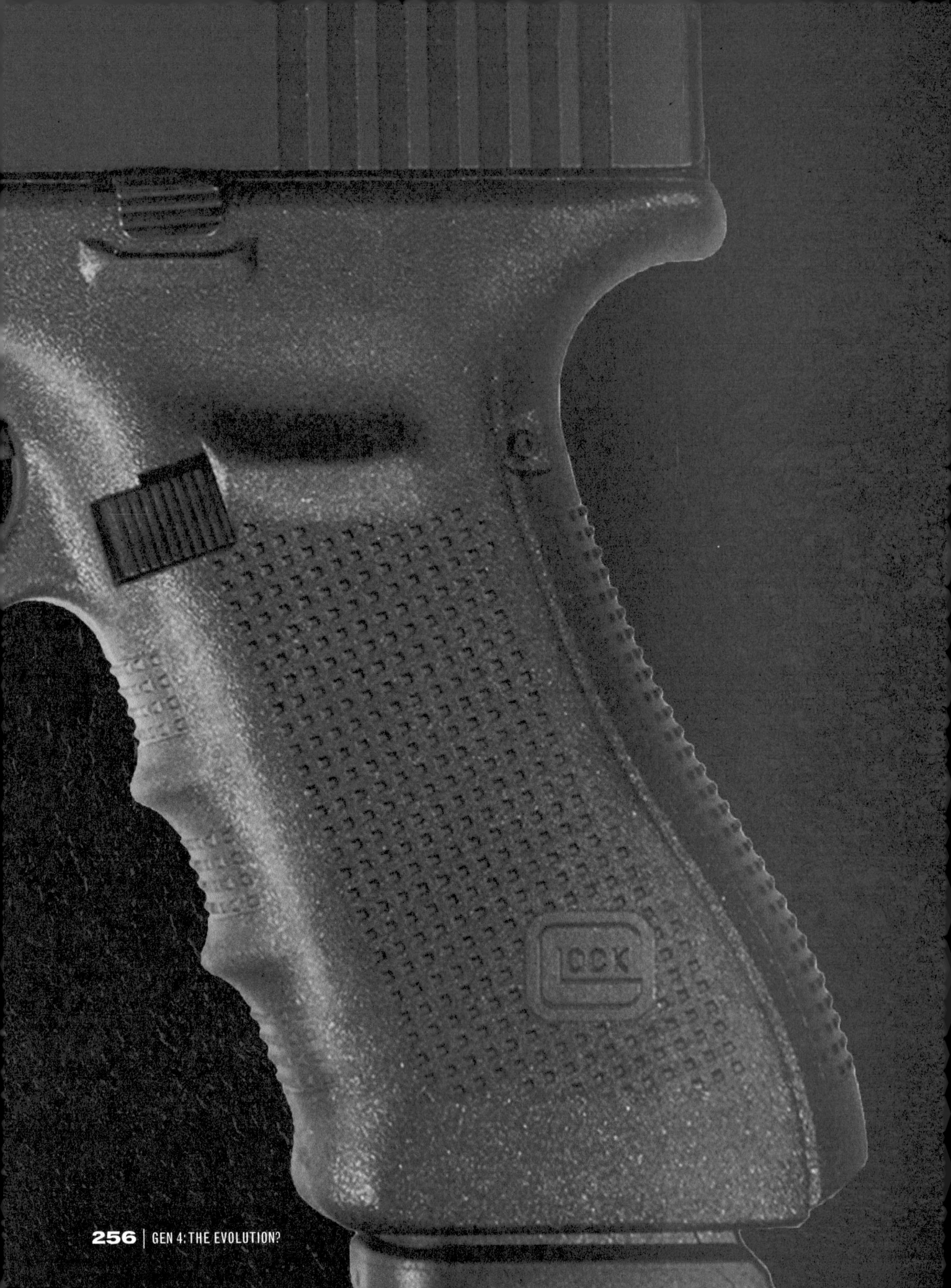

CHAPTER 18

Gen 4: The Evolution?

For those who haven't been running Glocks very long, and for those who need a quick reminder, here's the short story.

Glock makes the G17 and life is good. Soon, though, the G17 is "too big" for some, so Glock makes the G19 and life is good once again. Compact is good, two rounds less is no big deal.

Next come the Second Generation Glocks. These gain the frame surface checkering, which replaces the old pebble texture of the frames front and back.

The new recoil spring assembly required a change in the slide. If yours does not look like this, contact Glock to have it upgraded.

By the late 1990s, accessory rails, places to mount lights and lasers, are clearly going to be the future. Glock takes advantage of this knowledge to make some other changes and adds the "thumbrest." (This thumbrest is a vestigial part, not unlike a human appendix, and added, in this instance, solely to satisfy a moronic requirement for importation.) Glock also affixes a loaded-chamber indicator bump to the extractor, again to satisfy legislative buffoonery. Shortly thereafter, Glock changes the frame again and the "two-pin" frame becomes standard. Future collectors will obsess over transition-Gen frames with single pins and try to compile lists to show if the frame was a 9mm or .40. Along this road, the Glock gained a captured recoil spring assembly, so that, when you disassembled the pistol, you extracted the recoil spring and its guide rod as a single unit.

The Glock, by this time, had grown beyond the original boundaries. Where it had been a 9mm pistol, it was now available in 9mm, .40, .357 SIG, 10mm, and .45. It had a light rail, and when you put a light on it, things happened—basically, the .40 pistols became less reliable. In order to solve that problem, Glock made changes, specifically in a number of follower designs. Glock increased the magazine spring by a coil, increasing its strength but decreasing capacity by a round—this, though, became one great big wrangle that Glock was forced into, when various law enforcement customers complained.

It's one thing to ignore the protestations of individuals. But, when a large law enforcement agency tells you, in no uncertain terms, "Find a solution to this or we're sending these back for a refund," even the accountants have to take notice. To make things worse, as the word spread about the issues with .40s and using lights with them in the Gen 3s, lots more Glock law enforcement customers were more than a little ticked off at the prospect of a light-equipped Glock failing when they needed it most.

Glock also had to face another fact: its competitors were making inroads. In particular, the idea of replaceable backstraps had caught on, and Glock didn't have that feature. By the end of the first decade of the twenty-first century, every other maker of a polymer framed, striker-fired pistol had a replaceable backstrap. You could buy one from anyone else *but* Glock. Wait, amend that. You could not buy a S&W Sigma with a replaceable backstrap. However, where a G22 cost in the mid-$500 range, you could have had your choice of Sigmas for under $400. For lots of people, a $150-plus price difference went a long way towards salving the hurt of a stationery backstrap.

Glock had experimented a bit with the RTF surface for frames and the short-frame version of the G21. Still, these slight upgrades weren't gaining acceptance with the Glock masses. What to do?

Let's take a short step back and consider one aspect of firearms design: what caliber is a firearm made for? Consider the 1898 Mauser rifle. Designed for the 8mm Mauser (7.92X57) you can, with minor tweaks, chamber it in any other similar cartridge. The list is impressive and useful, but basically you can, without more than minor mods, make it in anything from .243 to .35 Whelen and be good to go. Something smaller in diameter, like a .223, requires a lot more of a change; magazine box, feed lips, bolt face, extractor, and ejector all have to change. At the other extreme, a Mauser in .375 H&H Magnum is mechanically possible, but, again, that conversion involves magazine box changes to include cutting into the front of the box, and mods to the feed ramp, which makes the bottom locking lug shoulder thinner (not a good thing, but the Mauser shrugs it off), as well as all the other changes mentioned.

A simple conversion, say to rebuild a military surplus Mauser from 7.92X57 to .30-06 or .270, was a piece of cake for a couple generations of gunsmiths. (To do so now would be a near-criminal act, as an unmolested military Mauser is worth more than the "sporter" it would become.) The conversions to .375 H&H involved a lot more work, and a lot fewer gunsmiths were willing to take the chance that

The Glock, by this time, had grown beyond its original boundaries. Where it had been a 9mm pistol, it was now available in 9mm, .40, .357 SIG, 10mm, and .45. It had a light rail and, when you put a light on it, things happened—basically, the .40 pistols became less reliable. In order to solve that problem, Glock made changes, specifically in a number of follower designs.

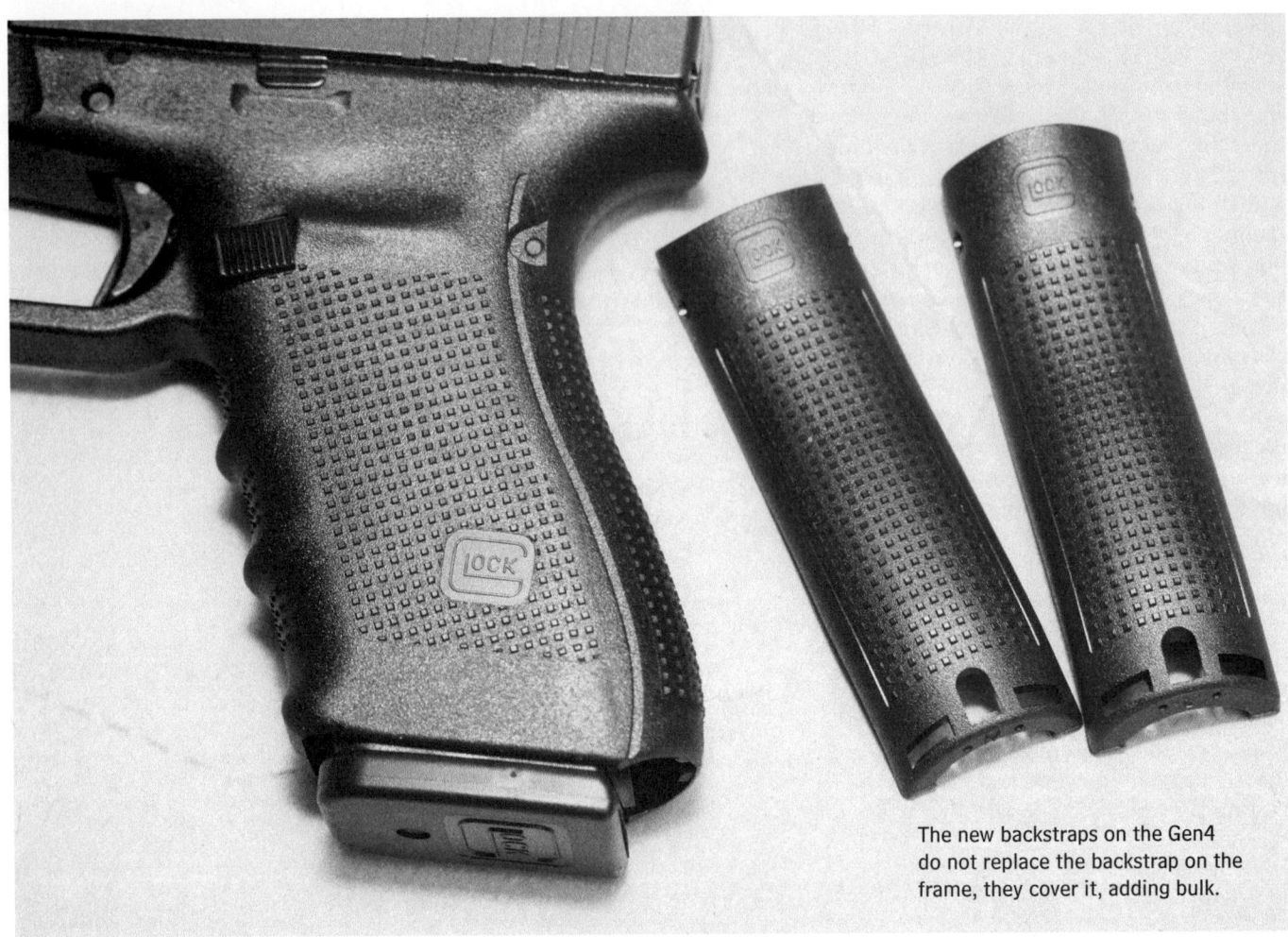

The new backstraps on the Gen4 do not replace the backstrap on the frame, they cover it, adding bulk.

The G17 was designed for the 9mm Parabellum cartridge. Lots of people seem to think the details of feeding, extraction, and ejection in any given pistol are of a minor nature. They are not. When Glock made the G22, it and everyone else back in 1990 who was frantically whipping up .40 pistols in their R&D labs were in the grips of "install a .40 barrel and a heavier recoil spring, and we have a 4.0 pistol" design mode. It didn't take long to find out that wasn't so true.

a marginal receiver, one that would otherwise withstand a lifetime of use as a .270 or .30-06, would bust itself halfway through a client's safari.

The point is, the more you deviate from the original cartridge, the more work you have to do to effect the modification and the less margin of error in design and fabrication you have. A blown case in an 8mm Mauser will blow the magazine internal off the receiver, maybe crack the stock and maybe not, but not much else. However, take that same receiver, re-barrel it to .375 H&H and make the needed modifications, and *then* blow a case, and the rifle will basically end up in two halves. Another thing to consider? The more suited to, the more specialized a firearm is to the cartridge it was made for, the more work it is to make it something else. There's a reason you see and saw a lot of sporters being made on Mauser actions and not on SMLE actions. The Mauser could be made into a lot of other calibers. With the SMLE, your choices were simpler. What diameter bullet did you want to be launching from a .303 British case? The SMLE was built for the .303 and anything else was out of the question.

Back to Glock. The G17 was designed for the 9mm Parabellum cartridge. A lot of people seem to think the details of feeding and extraction and ejection in any given pistol are of a minor nature. They are not. When Glock made the G22, it and everyone else back in 1990 who was frantically whipping up .40 pistols in their R&D labs, were in the grips of "install a .40 barrel and a heavier recoil spring, and we have a .40 pistol" design mode. It didn't take long to find out that that wasn't so true. It was, in some instances very *not* true. All other handgun manufacturers subsequently went through repeated design changes, evolving their .40s until they were true .40 pistols, with only the basic design in common with their similar 9mms. One maker, FN, even had to change the way it made the frames of its pistol, the Browning Hi Power (aka the P-35), in order to keep the pistol as it had been originally made from simply falling part under a no-sweat firing schedule.

Glock did not follow the crowd. I've talked to several former Glock employees who had the same reaction: "The G22 was, from the beginning, and still is, a 9mm pistol with a .40 barrel."

How does this mismatch manifest itself?

First, consider slide velocity. When the round goes off, the energy unleashed moves the slide and barrel back, though resisted by the spring. The more mass you hurl, and the faster you hurl it (don't forget the powder mass), the faster the slide and barrel travel. The spring can only do so much, when the mass comes back faster than it was originally designed to. Momentum and its law of conservation are described by the equation $P = mv$: momentum equals mass times velocity.

Let's take our basic G17, but we'll leave out most of the numbers for the moment. The bullet of 115 grains leaves the muzzle at 1,200 fps, that bullet propelled by less than five grains of powder. If we change the bullet to a .40, we now have a 180-grain bullet leaving at 950 fps, propelled by more than five grains of powder. I'm not going to do the messy arithmetic to convert them to actual mass. Instead, take a "back of the envelope" approach and compose a momentum equivalent, we'll call it ME, of 144 for the 9mm. For the .40, that ME

Numbers, numbers, numbers. Okay, these aren't numbers, but they are the sizes of the over-wrap backstraps.

is 176. If we take that as a ratio, then we arrange the formula to show velocity, which is $v = P/m$. The ratio of momentums are directly related to respective slide velocities, since the masses involved are so similar as to be trivially different.

Outside of recoil spring changes, the slide velocity of the .40-chambered pistol will be roughly 22-percent greater than that of the 9mm. Ouch. You know this to be true, as your hands tell it to you on every shot of .40 from your G22.

Left with a 9mm spring (it shouldn't be, but is, and I'm trying to illustrate the situation here), the 9mm-turned-.40 slide will move back faster and, having exceeded the limits of the spring, slam into the frame or whatever stops it with greater velocity. It will also snatch the empty case out of the chamber sooner and with more velocity. That is harder on the extractor, obviously from the higher speed, but also because, when the extractor snatches out the case sooner, the case has had less time to relax from the pressure of firing.

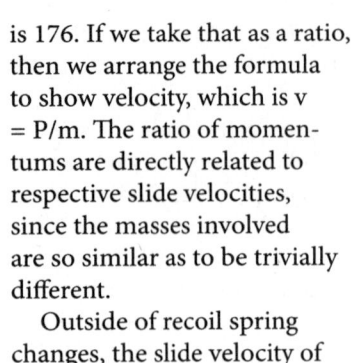

For some, the upgrades to the Gen4 weren't enough, as this is a Glock in the hostler of an officer who works a dangerous district in a tough town.

Clearly, the original spring won't suffice and, in many .40 handguns, you'll find that while the base pistol is much the same as the original 9mm it grew from, the .40 sports a stiffer recoil spring. I just checked, and the other pistol I compared it to, the Browning, has a markedly stronger recoil spring in a .40 configuration than it does in a 9mm—so much so that I was actually a bit annoyed at having doubted myself and subsequently had to wrestle the .40 spring back into place. (As a final comparator, peruse the Wolff spring catalog and compare the 9mm version of pistols to the .40.)

In the end, a stiffer spring can only do so much. Within those limitations, it also decreases the working margin available. Working margin? If the spring is too strong or a particular cartridge is a bit softer than designed, the stiffer spring can stall the slide and result in a malfunction. Also, a heavier spring can be made only with more steel. That means more coils or thicker wire, which means that a heavier spring can, when compressed, take up more space. As the Glock was designed with a flat coil (a very thin-stacking spring), adding in a heavier spring of regular music wire can take up too much space.

There's more. Even with a heavier spring, if *slide* mass is left the same, as the slide moves, it unlocks from the barrel and the barrel links down (in the Glock it "cams," same thing). The faster-moving slide will still unlock sooner in the cycle and with more velocity and it will slam the barrel down harder. On the Glock,

For those who are not enamored of the Gen4, and there are some, there are plenty of earlier Glocks to be had—or at least there were before the latest gun-control panic.

that means the barrel hits the barrel lock insert. The frame flexes, the barrel bounces up, and all the added friction wears on the inside of the slide. It also causes the locking block to bounce, and you can see that on the slide. Take your .40 apart, turn the slide over, and look at the bottom. If you've fired it for any volume, you'll see ding marks. Glock tells us this is a self-correcting problem, that once the dings get to a certain point they do not wear any more. I see it as a symptom that the system is not as balanced in .40 as it is in 9mm.

Things Learned Along the Way

In the course of researching this book, I did something that had not occurred to me to do before: I weighed the parts involved. Yes, yes, I know, I'm the expert, the guy shooters look up to, and I should have done this sooner. I have no explanation as to why it hadn't occurred to me before, but it hadn't. Regardless, this time around I took a sensitive scale with me and weighed things. Mine is not an industrial or scientific scale, just a common household kitchen unit, but it measures to tenths of an ounce. Close enough for our purposes and it's fast and easy to use.

What did I find? Well, I measured a pair of G17s, one from a few years ago and one from two decades ago. The difference was $^2/_{10}$-ounce, which could be the allowable weight difference in G17 slides, or it could be just that one was a bit more gunked up than

We found out about the Gen4 changes back in 2010, but it has taken some time to switch the models over in turn.

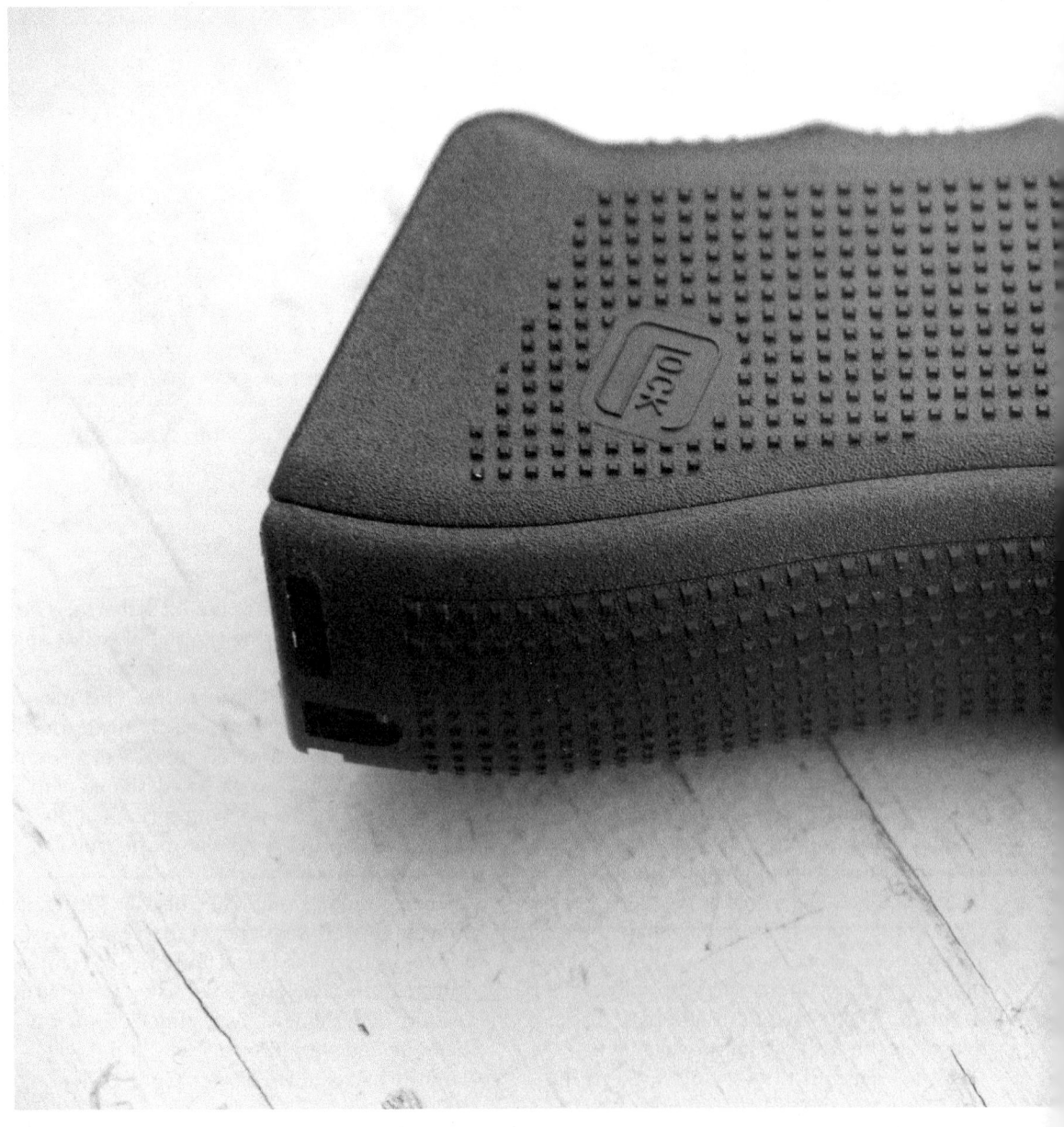

In the end, a stiffer spring can only do so much, and within those limitations it also decreases the working margin available. If the spring is too strong or a particular cartridge is a bit softer than designed, the stiffer spring can stall the slide and result in a malfunction. Also, a heavier spring can be made only with more steel, as in more coils or thicker wire, which means that a heavier spring can, when compressed, take up more space. As the Glock was designed with a flat coil (a very thin-stacking spring), adding in a heavier spring of music wire can take up too much space.

the other. As a percentage, they come in at just about a percent and a half of each other.

My G22 dates from the mid-1990s. It weighs 13.5 ounces, which puts it just about nine-percent heavier than the heavier of the two G17 slides. When you consider that the momentum equivalent of the .40 is some 22-percent greater than that of the 9mm, then the G22 slide is underweight. Also, there is no way of knowing where these slides fit in the Glock QC program. I may have the heaviest 9mm slide ever made and the lightest .40. Or it may be the other way around.

As a comparison, the G21 slide, chambered for .45 ACP and originally intended to handle the 10mm, is 16.5 ounces, a full 33-percent heavier than the G17 slide. The ME comparison there has the .45 ACP with a 27-percent advantage over the 9mm, so a 33-percent heavier slide is clearly overkill and shows its 10mm roots.

Another comparison. We can look at the G37, the .45 GAP equivalent of the G17. The frames are the same, but the magazines, slides, and barrels differ. The G37 I weighed has a slide that tips the scale at 16.6 ounces, $^{1}/_{10}$-ounce off the G21 slide weight. As the .45 GAP and .45 ACP are functionally equivalent, the weight of the G37 slide tells us that the G22 slide is underweight for its job.

As a capper to all this, consider recoil springs. Yes, I've already discussed this, but from the viewpoint of that the recoil spring should be stiffer. Well, in the G22 it isn't. Those who have been through the armorer's course or who go into the details of the parts lists would know that. Just to be absolutely

certain, at my most recent GSSF match, I asked the armorer, who was overhauling my G22, "So, the 9mm and .40 recoil springs are the same?" His reply, "Yep, same spring assembly for both."

So, we have the two cartridges with their ME disparity of 22 percent, which use the same-weight slide and the same recoil spring assembly. That means the only thing left to control recoil and slow unlocking is the angle of the cam surfaces of the barrel and locking block. Those surfaces are not long, they do not have a wide range in which they can work, and they are not efficient at handling the forces involved. Long story short: your G22 is working hard, since it is a 9mm pistol with a .40 barrel stuffed into it.

Other Issues

The magazine holds a round in a particular space in relation to the slide and barrel and at a particular angle. This location and angle are not chosen at random, but are, instead, specifically designed to make the trip from magazine to chamber as painless as possible. When the slide, moving forward hits, the round to feed, it hits so at the top center of the case rim, the resulting force tipping the round down as it begins to feed. The feed ramp has to be located forward of the magazine, under the feed lips and such that it "collects" the cartridge tip and guides it up to the chamber. The geometry of the system allows for a certain amount of tilting and rocking of the cartridge as it feeds—down, up, down, and up. A longer or shorter cartridge or one blunter than that of the original design may or may not feed, depending on how "forgiving" the particular design is.

Magazine feeding is also designed to work at a certain slide velocity. A faster-moving slide imparts more force to the cartridge, tipping it down faster and further and, thus, requiring a different feed ramp geometry with which to collect the round.

Let's take as our sample a same-length but blunter cartridge than the one originally intended. While the angles are all the same, the allowed "drift" of what works and what doesn't is smaller. A blunter cartridge doesn't have as much freedom to go off-line and still feed reliably.

We have the added problem of the slide speed really messing with magazine dynamics. The faster-moving slide spends less time cooling its heels behind the magazine, waiting while the top round lifts into place. Also, the added vibrations of the barrel slamming down harder and the slide bottoming out harder add to the troubles the magazine faces. "But wait," you say,

The first Gen4 Glock I laid eyes on, a G22, back in January 2010. I was underwhelmed.

GEN 4: THE EVOLUTION? | **267**

Gen4, .40 caliber, and still the same overly-large chambers.

"the slide can't go forward faster, it only has the temporarily stored energy of the compressed spring. It isn't like the reward motion, driven by higher bullet mass, etc." You would be correct about the compressed spring part of it. It *doesn't* matter (within the realm of time and energy we can measure), how fast a spring is compressed. Fast or slow, when it's compressed, it only has as much energy as it takes to compress it, no more. The extra energy? It creates heat, a minor portion of our exercise. However, in bottoming out, the slide also stores energy. The elastic collision between the slide and whatever stops it has energy, and the slide bouncing off of its stop adds to the slide velocity.

What does it all mean? The G22 second and third generations work just fine, as long as you change recoil springs as often as you do your oil. Forget all that bragging about going 10-, 15-, 20,000 rounds of 9mm from a G17 without so much as cleaning. The G22 wants a new spring at 3,000 rounds. Now, in a 1911 (and, yes, I know that the Glock-o-philes hate it when I mention the 1911), I don't worry about springs for most calibers. I'll replace a .45 spring when I feel like it, while a .38 Super being shot at Major will get a new spring in less than 10,000 rounds. A 10mm 1911 will get springs depending on its diet, and one that sees not much more than a .45-equivalent load will go to .45 schedules. A full-house 10mm gets the .38 Super Major treatment. But the G22 isn't a 1911. It once was a 9mm, and now it's a .40. It needs more TLC.

Look at it this way. Even if you reload (which Glock tells you not to do, but we all know you do anyway), 3,000 rounds of .40 is $400 to $500 in ammo costs. If you only shoot factory, it can be twice that. Are you really going to stand there and whine about a spring that costs you less than $10? And here's the best idea yet: shoot a GSSF match once a year. For the $25 entry fee, you get some practice and your friendly Glock armorer will swap out a recoil spring assembly if he has the slightest hint you need one. If your recoil spring assembly is an old number, you'll get a new one, even if your current spring is up to snuff.

It Doesn't End There

If you shoot your G22 on a range that has a large IPSC/USPSA presence and don't scrounge up your brass, the competitive shooters may come to hate you. The .40, with wider feed variables than the 9mm, had to be adjusted somehow. As a result, the G22 and other .40 Glocks have larger chamber dimensions than do many other .40 pistols. It is not uncommon to find .40 brass, fired from Glocks (the firing pin impression leaves no doubt), with swelling at the base. The base, being the part of the case that is outside the sizing die, doesn't get re-sized, so reloads in these over-sized cases can stick during feeding; they may not go in far enough to fire, or they may wedge so tightly that they cause extraction problems once fired.

The Gen4s

So, what did Glock do? It re-built the G17/22 frame and system to be a .40 and then swapped parts the *other* way in order to make a 9mm pistol. A Gen4 Glock is now built as a .40 and the 9mm is the modification.

What didn't Glock do? Perhaps not test the new model thoroughly enough. While not numerous, Gen4 malfunctions seemed to happen just about from day one. In the course of sorting things out, and without actually calling it a recall, Glock has gone through something like four different recoil spring assemblies on the 9mm, three on the .40, a couple ejector changes, and a magazine follower change.

An example of some of the struggles can be seen in the recoil spring assembly, a.k.a. the RSA. The Gen4 changed from the captured single-spring system to a captured dual-spring system. Glock also changed the clearance hole bored in the slide. Where the older holes had been smaller in diameter, the Gen4's is substantial. However, the initial production G17 and G22 slides were made with recoil spring clearance holes machined without some sort of bevel or recess. The larger RSA end could get out of alignment with the slide clearance, and then the RSA would then bind. This could happen under recoil or just from sustaining a blow. Gee, a pistol that can fail to work if it gets slammed into the floor in a fight. Where's the fun in that?

The slides, then, were redesigned to have a bevel, recess, alignment—whatever kind of ring you want to call it—machined into the slide. The change probably took a day of CAD/CAM and CNC programmer work, and the problem was solved. When was it solved? Good question, as Glock is mum on this subject. If you have a G17 or G22 with a prefix that begins with "Q" or you have one of the four-letter prefix guns, you're in the clear. Otherwise, take it apart and look. Those of you who have a non-recessed slide will need a special RSA that Glock will gladly provide.

The early guns (reports now are that the Gen4s coming out of the factory are much, much better), had failures to feed, failures to eject and, most annoying of all, erratic ejection—and by erratic I mean it tended to throw the empties into the face of the shooter. The problem? As mentioned above, the early 9mm (G17 & G19) Gen4 Glocks came with the same RSAs the G22s and G23s had, which

> Some of the struggles with the Gen4s can be seen in the recoil spring assembly. The Gen4 changed from a captured dual-spring system. Glock also changed the clearance hole bored in the slide. Where the older holes had been smaller in diameter, the Gen4's was substantial. But the initial production runs of G17/22 slides were made with recoil spring clearance holes machined without a bevel or recess. This means the larger spring end can get out of alignment with the slide clearance and then bind.

were too powerful. So Glock issued replacement RSAs; all you have to do is ask for one. If you want to look, the RSAs are marked. For G22s and G23s, you want RSAs that are marked 0-1. For the G17, you want 0-2 or 0-2-1 (for the non-beveled slides). For the G19, you want 0-3. In all instances, you can simply take your Glock to a GSSF match, show it to the armorer, and he'll figure it out. Once you have the proper RSA, you can replace with the same as needed when you wear one down.

As of the time this book goes to press, the current list of correct RSA and their codes is as follows:

Non-Recessed Slide G22 = Code 0 1-1
Recessed Slide G22/31/35/37 = Code 0 1-4
Non-Recessed Slide G17 = Code 0 2-1
Recessed Slide G17/34 = Code 0 2-4
G23/32 = Code 0 3-3
G19 = Code 0 4-3
G17T = 0 5-2
G21 = 0 7-2
G26/27/28/33/39 = 0-8

If yours doesn't match any of these, contact Glock, and it will exchange/replace your RSA with the correct one. Or, you could simply avoid the ammo that caused the problems, bulk, 115-grain FMJ ammo you buy at the lowest possible price. That's the stuff that causes failures to eject or tosses its brass in our face or down your shirt. Sure, that's all something to giggle about when it happens to someone else, but consider the consequences of having hot brass fall behind someone's (yours) shooting glasses. Burn? Yes. Worse are the gyrations of someone holding a loaded firearm, while they attempt to deal with the problem of hot brass and muzzles pointed in unsafe directions.

On the one hand, I really feel for the Glock engineers. They did their best, and they did as much testing as they could. But the expectations of the Glock shooters expecting an improved product could not have been lived up to. Even if the engineers had fired a bazillion rounds in testing, they still could have done only so much. Even if they'd taken every employee and made them test-fire the Gen4 R&D models, they could not have gotten the feedback of tens of thousands of customers, each using the Gen4 models in all situations, climates, day and night, etc.

Lesson to be learned? If you are buying a new Gen4 Glock and you intend to use it for daily carry or self-defense, you'd be wise to put a bunch of ammo through it, just to be sure. Not that Glocks aren't good, dependable pistols. They are. But it would be a bad thing to find out yours was the sole pistol made that year that needed just a bit more tweaking before it was ready to go.

Magazines

One aspect of the Gen4 that is an improvement, one area in which I give Glock some

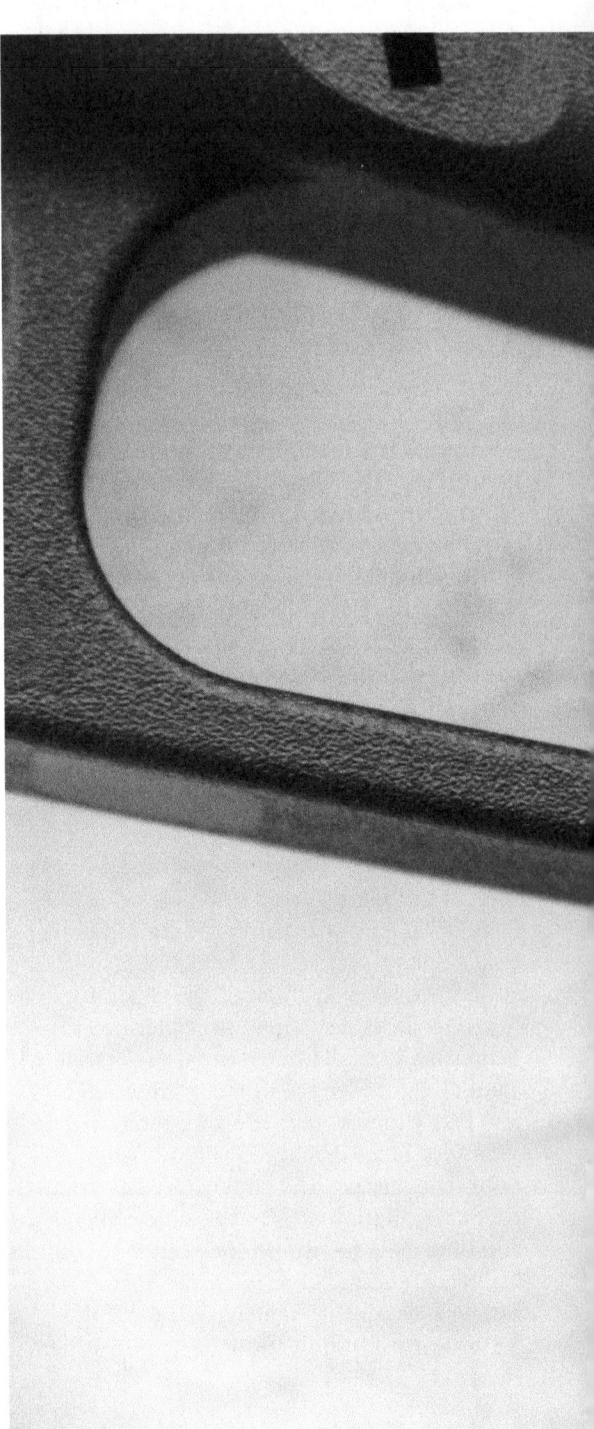

atta boys, are the magazines. The Glock magazine has always had a reasonably well-deserved reputation for durability and reliability. The construction of a steel stiffening shell encased in polymer means it is really, *really* hard to dent a Glock magazine.

A friend of mine is a police officer, and his family has owned a large gun shop in a suburb of a big city for decades. (Mitch, you know who you are.) He has a collection, not just a singular sample, of magazines that have been rendered unusable, simply by being in mag pouches. Those flapped, snap-closed magazine pouches you see on so many police officers belts, how are they made badly? Well, the magazine resides in the pouch, in some instances for years (you can't make this stuff up), and the steel snap continually presses on the magazine. Maybe the officer takes a fall or has a fight. Maybe it just gets dumped in a locker every night at the end of shift. Eventually, the snap

dents the steel magazine tube, pinching it just enough to prevent the follower from rising.

This does not happen with Glock magazines. What they *will* do, given enough time, is de-laminate. The polymer will separate from the steel, particularly at the feed lips. If the magazine still feeds and the dimensions are correct, Glock won't care. If it has been further damaged, Glock might offer a discount to replace it. Given the relatively low cost of Glock mags and the abundant supply, harassing Glock over something like this is unreasonable. So your 20-year-old Glock magazine, one you have used in countless practice sessions and matches, finally goes toes-up? Quit whining, ditch it, buy another, and get on with your life.

The Gen4 frame has an ambidextrous magazine catch, one switchable to work for either right- and left-handed shooters. You can swap the button from one side to the other, without tools, if you want. This did, however, require a change in magazines. The current crop of magazines now comes with three recesses for magazine retention, one on either side and one in the front of the magazine tube. One of the newest magazines will work just fine in an older generation Glock, but the older magazines won't work in the newest. That is the nature of improvements; sometimes going forward means leaving something behind. And, again, magazines are inexpensive, so buy more and keep them separated. If you have a rack of Glocks and use them regularly, you're already doing something to keep your 9mm, .40, and .45 magazines separated. Use a color code or painted dots in dimples, whatever, but keep the old magazines out of your new Glocks and you won't have a problem.

There is a drawback of the Glock magazine design, however, and that is its strength. The magazine's weight is retained only by a lip of polymer. That's why the magazine catch is also polymer. Given enough shooting, enough wear, and enough reloads, the shelf will wear and roll over. When that happens, it is done. What to do? Review a couple paragraphs back, where I tell you to buy more magazines.

Grip Size

If we all had hands the same size, glove makers would need to make only one size. We do not, and so glove makers go crazy trying to make gloves that are comfortable and useful on our hands. Pistols used to be a one-size-fits-all proposition, but the recent explosion of replaceable backstraps in pistol designs have made them a lot more adaptable.

The designs have varied in approach. At the big end, S&W uses a creation that wraps around the back and sides of the frame. The base frame is not intended to be used without a backstrap of one size or another on it, and the sizes range from small to large; their span is noticeable. At the other extreme, the Ruger SR9 design isn't even a backstrap. Ruger made the frame as slender as it could, and the replaceable part corresponds to the mainspring housing on a 1911. You want that flat or arched? If you need a frame/grip that is appreciably larger in diameter, then you have to use something like a Hogue Handall slip-over grip, one that adds finger grooves, increases size, and adds texture.

What did Glock do to accommodate so many different hands? It made the basic Gen4 grip size fractionally smaller than its previous frames. Then it designed a system that fits over the back of the grip, instead of replacing it. Now, there has never been a groundswell of complaints about the size of the G17 frame. In actuality, it is pretty well proportioned. The G20/21, on the other hand, has always been a fat-butted pistol.

Given the chance, Glock could have made the Gen4s smaller. If Glock had wanted to do that (and sticking it to the aftermarket modifi-

> **There is a drawback to the Glock magazine design and that is its strength. The magazine's weight is retained only by a lip of polymer. That's why the magazine catch is also polymer. Given enough shooting, enough wear, and enough reloads, the shelf will wear and roll over. When that happens, it is done. What to do? Review back a bit, where I tell you to buy more magazines.**

ers of Glocks), here's what it could have done: made the two frame sizes as small as mechanically possible; or made its frames sizes, like others, intended to be fired only with grip adapters.

By mastering these two things, the gun would be the smallest it could be, and there would be no real estate onto which an aftermarket modifier could attach their alterations. Then, Glock could offer a whole pantheon of grip adapters. Not just thicker and thinner, but tapered up or down, too. Offer them in colors. Offer them at low cost and even tell the owners how to modify them.

Glock didn't do that. It simply slimmed the grip down a bit, then offered three options to make it fatter. I grabbed the big one, the .45 ACP, to use as a test.

I used mine, which is an old, second-Gen G21, that has been subjected to grip modification by Robbie Barkman, and measured it. I then measured an original G21, a G21SF, and a G21 Gen4 with its slap-on plates. The measurements presented here are the distance from front to back, directly across the frame, immediately below the trigger guard.

RoBar-modified G2	2.120 inches
Stock G21	2.200 inches
Stock G21SF	2.080 inches
Gen 4 G21, bare	2.108 inches
Medium	2.170 inches
Large	2.26 inches

For those of you with gorilla-sized hands, the new G21 Gen4 with the large grip will be a boon. For the rest of us, the G21 Gen4 bare is in between a stock G21SF and the Robar-modified G21 I have.

Summary

What do we have after all this? We have a set of Glocks that have new roll marks, use the new ambi- magazines, and that's about it. Will there be a Gen5 series of Glocks? Probably, but not until after the issues with the Gen4 introduction have faded—faded quite a bit.

For those of you with gorilla-sized hands, the new G21 Gen4 with the large grip will be a boon. For the rest of us, the G21 Gen4 bare is in-between a stock G21SF and the Robar-modified G21 I have. As for Glock's new backstraps, they are different than those from other makers. Glock first slimmed the basic size of its grip frames, then created a backstrap system that fit over it.

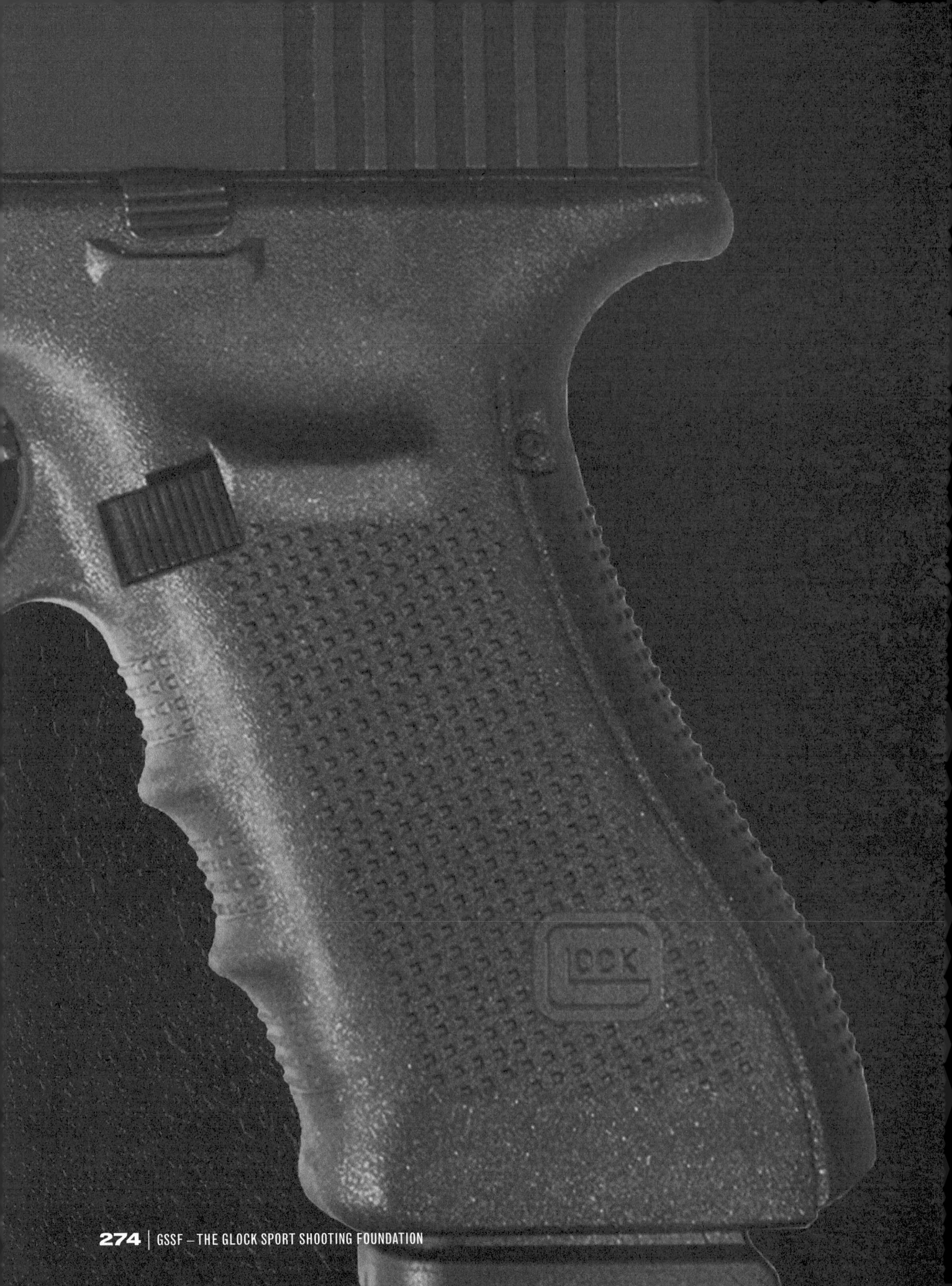

CHAPTER 19

GSSF—The Glock Sport Shooting Foundation

Here's a closer look at the rings with the scoring system and a new G30S to give you an idea of size.

I've talked before the benefits of competition. That you acquire skills you cannot get elsewhere. That, from competition, you gain familiarity with your firearm that you would not otherwise have, for example, by simply doing draw and dry-fire drills in your basement. That competition allows you to build "stress inoculation," learning how to deal with stress, function while stressed, and to test your limits when there are a timer and witnesses.

Here's the target, with the scoring rings highlighted. In the match, they will not have a nice black ring to denote them, so it is up to you to remember center of cardboard.

Still, many of you don't go to matches. This is, in part, due to a certain hesitation to look silly or less than spectacular on the range. It is perhaps unfortunate, but real, that a lot of shooters have more invested in their perceived skills than in their actual skills. This is not entirely the fault of the group as a whole. You may be influenced, unknowingly, by those who have too much invested in image to risk any dent in said image. In particular, I'm mocking the gun shop "experts" who tell you such things as "IPSC will get you killed" or "If you haven't gone through police training, you aren't really trained." But mocking the ill-informed is a fruitless task, and I should know better. So let's try a less-stressful approach: GSSF and loot.

The Glock Sport Shooting Foundation was founded to allow Glock owners a low-stress environment in which to have fun. Begun in 1992, the GSSF has always had, as its mission, a low-key approach to competition. Unfortunately for Glock, there were a bunch of shooters who didn't get the message, and it is entirely possible to find people who are just as pumped-up about competing in GSSF as in other shooting disciplines. Know that the structure of GSSF keeps a lid on those kinds of aspirations.

The GSSF structure arranged equipment divisions around the various Glock offerings, and you can only compete in a GSSF match while using a Glock. It doesn't matter how much "like a Glock" your other pistol is, if it didn't come from Glock, it isn't kosher to use. (That said, I'll bet there are a bunch of clubs that host GSSF matches that won't look too closely, so if you have an absolute Glock clone, they aren't going to kick up a fuss. That does not, however, mean you can stride to the firing line with your stainless steel-framed CFF Glock clone, and expect to be received warmly.)

Regardless which Glock you own, there is a category for it. An utterly box-stock G17? No problem. A souped-up, red dot-equipped G34 with a connector to lighten the trigger and a muzzle brake? Ditto. Your daily carry G23? Come on, you aren't paying attention. There are vertical and horizontal equipment separations. The heavy-hitter competitors are kept out of the common shooters' pool and are required to compete against each other. Basically, if you are ranked high enough in USPSA/IPSC, IDPA, Bianchi Cup, or other competitions, you have to shoot in the GSSF master categories. This does tend to splinter the entries in a match, since you can have a dozen different categories and skills class separations. The good news is that you can shoot in more than one of them. That's right, bring all your Glocks, shoot for the day, and get lots of fun in.

How did it end up this way? Let's step into the way-back machine and get ourselves to a less cynical time, one where the phrase "slick Willie" had not yet entered the lexicon, the period leading up to the summer of 1992.

For the entire decade of the 1980s, the big question on IPSC ranges had been about whether the .45 would be able to hold its own. Could it stave off the .38 Super as the competition caliber? In all that time, some things had remained the same. Competitors could choose between a .45 or a .38 Super. They could choose between a pistol with a muzzle brake or one lacking it. My home club, one of the biggest outside of California or Arizona, at the time, allowed you to do it all. You could shoot in Open or in Stock or shoot the match twice, once in each.

It was easy, because regardless the caliber or brake, you were shooting a single-stack, all-steel pistol, most likely a Colt 1911A1 or close copy. Your holster and mag pouches all worked just fine for both, so swapping classes was as easy as stepping over to the Safe Area and changing out guns.

What changed during the 1980s were the courses. They became more elaborate, involved, and lengthy. In the early years of IPSC, a stage could be 10, 15, maybe 20 rounds. A 20-round course in 1978 probably had several timed runs in it. By 1990, at least at our club, stages were 20 rounds minimum and each was a single run. You could find yourself having to engage a dozen or more targets (including one-shot-to-drop steel targets and two-hit papers), and run a goodly distance in the process. They were on the cusp of being described as "track meets with guns," and rightly so.

Then the wheels came completely off.

The .40 S&W was introduced in 1990. Jerry Barnhart used a red dot scope to win the 1990 USPSA Nationals, and Doug Koenig used a red dot scope to win the World Shoot that same year. A new pistol arrived, the CZ-75,

> During the 1980s, IPSC courses changed. They became more elaborate, involved, and lengthy. In the early years of IPSC, a stage could be 10, 15, maybe 20 rounds; a 20-round course in 1978 probably had several timed runs in it. By 1990, stages were 20 rounds minimum and each stage was tackled in a single run.

in the form of a Springfield offering and an EAA set of pistols. They were hi-cap, which meant a 9mm/.38 Super could now hold 16 to 18 rounds. The .45 shooters abandoned Open in droves. They could switch to Stock, but in short order the hi-cap 1911 frames arrived, and everyone realized that a hi-cap .40 held more rounds than a hi-cap .45.

GSSF matches have categories that encourage the use of all Glock models, with level equipment rules.

Since you need a bunch of magazines and you can only load 10 rounds, you now have a use for the 10-rounders we were saddled with back during the 1994 Assault Weapons Ban. A bonus? They cost less than the regular-capacity models, so stock up.

In all this churning, there was no place for the Glock. Oh, a G17 or a long slide, with a muzzle brake and red-dot would have been fabulous then, but the only Glock scope mounts available were clunky, bulky, and fragile. This was long before red dot optics became durable enough to mount directly to the slide. We were breaking these optics regularly, and it was common, until the mid-1990s, for a serious competition shooter to have multiple copies.

Actually, for a while, a serious competition shooter would have three competition guns. Each range bag of these shooters held a compensated hi-cap 9mm or .38 Super; one to shoot, one in the bag as a backup—and he had one in the shop getting repaired or overhauled. Each pistol had a couple red dots fitted to it. If a scope died in the middle of a stage, it was off to the Safe Area with tools to remove the old scope and install the backup, one that was already zeroed to that pistol and mount.

The equipment churning and arguing got so bad that some shooters split off and formed the IDPA, in reaction against the perceived excesses of IPSC. IDPA did have a place for Glocks, but if you take a really hard look at IDPA with regards to its stage designs, it is basically IPSC in the half-shell; no stage can be more than 18 rounds, but there's still a lot of running, hi-intensity adrenaline, and many props to encounter and problems to solve. The GSSF, formed in 1992, offered a safe haven for those who wanted to have some fun, but not be thrown into the bear pit.

GSSF Basics

You have a Glock and an interest in finding out how well you can run it. What will you be shooting at, what will you be shooting with, and what will you be feeding your Glock? And what do you get at the end of it?

Targets

You'll be shooting at falling steel plates, big falling steel plates known as "pepper poppers," and cardboard targets known as the NRA D-1 or Bianchi Cup target. Also known as "tombstones," they were specifically designed, in 1979, for the inaugural Bianchi Cup, to provide a target that was as inoffensive as possible, i.e., no head on top. The Bianchi Cup was intended to bridge the growing divide between the various handgun shooting competitions and find out who was the best of the best. It had aspects of IPSC, PPC, and bull's-eye, and the intent was to be origins-neutral. One facet, the falling steel, proved to be so attractive that the Steel Challenge, first shot in 1981, could be considered an outgrowth (though the intent was entirely different, but that's a subject for another book).

In the Bianchi Cup, the intent was to test accuracy. At close range, the target isn't so threatening, But consider that the paper portion has stages back to 50 yards, plus a stage where the target moves. GSSF matches don't have those, so don't panic.

The Bianchi Cup target is a rectangle of cardboard, with the top rounded and the scoring rings concentric to the center of the target. You have to know where the scoring rings are, because you can't see them in any but the best possible lighting.

The falling steel plates are eight inches in diameter and generally set to fall to any fair hit from a 9mm round. The setting will depend on the design of the plate rack and the diligence of the range crew setting things up, but, generally, if you hit the plate, it will fall.

Pepper poppers are steel plates that are 42 inches tall. The long part of it varies from six to eight inches wide. A foot or so down from the top there is a circular bulge, in effect a plate that is 12 inches in diameter. Where circular plates will fall to pretty much any hit, even a .22 LR, the design aspect of pepper poppers that matters is that by leaning them towards the shooter, the range officer can enforce power factor. In other words, when leaned properly, a pepper popper will fall to a full-power 9mm hit when that hit happens at the base of the "plate" or higher. A low hit won't take it down, nor will a hit from a wimpy reload.

Scoring

Scoring the steel is easy. If it falls, you get credit. If it doesn't, you'll have time added to the length of your shooting. Since your score is the time it takes you to mow down the rack of plates, four times, each timed by itself, the penalty can matter. And since a plate left standing costs you an extra 10 seconds for each plate, it is a good idea to hit them all.

For the paper, you are again scored on the time it takes you to shoot. However, hits outside the center two rings will incur added time. Hits in the "A" or "B" rings are known as "par" or "zero time" hits; they don't add time to your run. Hits in the "C" ring will earn you an extra

Here we see the falling plates and a shooter who has the idea right. If you miss, continue to the next plate, then pick up the standing one as you come back. Better yet, don't miss, but, if you do, don't thrash about.

On each run, you'll fire two shots on each of the cardboard targets and knock down one pepper popper. Pick which popper before you start and pick a spot on it. That's your aiming point.

second each, and hits in the "D" ring will get your three second each. A miss is good for 10 seconds. You can easily double your time, once the penalty seconds have been added up.

The Process

Let's say you've signed up for all the categories your gear, wallet, or time permit. What to do? Get yourself to the range and get in line. You'll need at least four magazines for each entry, because the Range Officers will not be happy if you have to reload your existing pair of magazines in order to shoot the stage your four times. Also, you can't load them up. You can have a maximum of 10 rounds in each magazine. Why 10? To keep a lid on the equipment race.

Once you get to the head of the line, you shoot the stage. For the stages with cardboard targets, you fire two rounds on each of the five targets. On the steel, you shoot until the plates are down or you are out of your 11 rounds (10 in the mag, one in the chamber). You may not reload to finish the plates or correct an error. There is also no reloading against the clock, no working from the holster. You'll start from low ready.

Once you're done, off to the next stage. Once you have finished all three stages, then you go back to your car, locker, or gear bag, swap your gear for the next category you've entered, and repeat. And repeat. And repeat, until you run out of time, ammo, entry money, categories, or the strength to pull the trigger.

GSSF Match Stages

There are three stages in a GSSF match, Five to Glock, Glock 'M, and Glock the Plates. Let's take Glock the Plates first, since it is the most straightforward and easiest to discuss. Not the easiest to shoot, mind you, but the easiest to explain.

Glock the Plates

In this stage, you have six, eight-inch plates set at 10 yards. The measurement method is involved, concerns itself with getting the firing point on the centerline of the plate rack, and is of concern only to the range crew setting up things.

You stand at the firing point, Glock in hand at low ready. On the buzzer, come up and mow the plates down. Easier said than done. I watched more than one shooter empty a magazine in a vain attempt at getting the rack cleaned, and one who failed to knock down a single plate.

How to improve the odds? The obvious retort is to practice more, but what kind of practice?

First, we figure out the sights. And you have to do this before the match, not during it. Assuming your gun club will let you, shoot your Glock from the bench at 10 yards. Your efforts are towards producing the smallest group of five shots you can. Shoot with a rest, not offhand or even two-handed. Use a small, defined aiming point. Consistently align your sights and place them in the same location vis-à-vis the aiming point and shoot a group. Done reasonably well, this should produce a group of five shots no more than an inch in diameter. Ideally, you should have all five shots touching.

Now, ask this: Where is your group, in relation to the aiming point? In relation to the sights? In your mind, overlay the sight picture you used and compare the location of the group with the sights. Is the group on the top center of the front sight? In the middle of the white dot? Someplace else? If you really want to drill this into your head, now draw an eight-inch circle around the group. Using the group as the center, in your mind, overlay your sight picture on the circle and group. This is the sight picture you want, when you are shooting Glock the Plates. You want the intended point of impact to be the center of the plate. That gives you the maximum wobble area for sight misalignment, trigger squeeze hiccups, etc. If the intent is to shoot the plate in the center and you have an "oops" of two inches, the plate still falls.

This is important, so pay attention. If the intent is to hit the plate and you have an "oops" of two inches, you missed the plate by two inches. Yes, this is the essence of the movie line "Aim small, miss small."

Now, when you go to shoot the plates, pick an individual mark on the plate. That is your aiming point. Pick one near the center. When bowling pin shooting was the all-consuming competition for many of us, we'd step to the line and pick an existing bullet hole on each of the five pins. That was our aiming point, not the pin itself. In the same manner, select a mark on the plate instead of settling for the plate as a whole as your aiming object. Miss the mark, you hit the plate. Miss the plate, you miss the plate.

The second part of the secret to being successful on Glock the Plates, if secret there be, is that you don't go to the next plate until you've shot the first one. It is common, when watching someone miss the plates again and again, to see the shot miss to the right of the intended plate, when they are shooting the plates from left to right. What's happening here is that the shooter gets right up to the point of crushing the trigger and, just as the action is about to start, they are like the dog, Doug, in the animated movie *Up* and his distraction of "Squirrel!" They're on to the next plate before they have finished shooting the first one. That said, as soon as you are certain the plate will go down, get on to the next one. Don't dawdle, don't stand there admiring your work, get on to the next one. Just not too soon.

As soon as you finish, sweep back across the plate rack, just to make sure. You'd be surprised at how many shooters, missing the plate but

In the third run, this shooter has knocked over his third popper. Wisely, he saved the farthest one for last, when he's warmed up.

On this range, there are two target arrays separated by the vision barrier of the barrels. Make sure you don't, in your eagerness, shoot the other guy's targets.

hitting the rack and hearing steel, stop at six and just relax. (Or maybe you aren't surprised.) Oops, time's a-tickin', and a miss costs you plenty. It costs you nothing to swing back and pick up and reshoot any plates that somehow missed your attention.

First run done? Good. Let the range crew reset the plates, while you swap magazines. Take a deep breath and exhale, and, when they ask if you're ready, give a nod. This time, shoot a bit faster. Not so much you lose track/sight of what you are doing, but be faster in between plates. Still make sure you hit each plate, but snap faster between plates to pick up time. By the fourth run, you should be as fast as you are going to get.

What if you miss? You lock the sights on the plate, break the shot and, as the Glock recoils, you switch to the next plate—and out of the corner of your eye you see the plate still standing. Don't stop. This is where a lot of shooters get themselves in a real mess. They stop the process on the plate they are moving to, swinging back and hurriedly trying to make up the miss. They get themselves so mentally and physically tangled that they miss it again, and again, have to stop, reset, then finish the plate rack.

Here's what you do instead. Continue. Shoot the next plate, and the next, finish the rack, and then swing back to finish the plate that so stubbornly refused to fall. This will get you in all kinds of trouble with the gun show commando types, who will tell you that missing and continuing on will let the tangoes get you, the zombies eat your brains, or the mutant biker gang overwhelm you. The heck with them, this is a learning experience.

Once you finish the stage, step off the line (under the Range Officer's commands, of course), and do some thinking. Run the "tape" of your recent stage through your head. Why did you miss? Did you leave the plate early? Slap the trigger? Did you shoot low, hit the frame, hear steel, and assume your plate was going to fall? Learn, adapt, adjust, and do better next time.

Cardboard

The other two stages in a GSSF match will feature cardboard, the NRA D-1 targets. Take a look at the target. See the rings? Good, because when the target is up on the frames and you are waiting for the beep, you won't. So find the horizontal line that goes right through the middle of the scoring rings. Where does it come to the edges of the cardboard? That is your aiming height. You want to be aiming at that level in the cardboard. This is important, as the center of the scoring circles is not the same as the center of the radius of the top curve of the target; aim there and you'll be too high. Mentally superimpose your sight picture test, the one you did with the 10-yard group, onto the cardboard at that horizontal line. That's your aiming point.

Five to Glock

Here, the only targets you'll see are cardboard. However, while some find steel intimidating, cardboard is unforgiving. If you miss steel, it's still standing, you know it, can see it, and can use some of your remaining ammo to correct that problem. If you miss cardboard, it won't tell you.

In shooting the Five to Glock, there are five targets and you'll fire two shots on each for 10 total. You shoot it three times for a total of 30 rounds and then your hits are recorded. No extra shots, no reloads against the clock.

The original Five to Glock had just one layout, but, after a few years, that got to be a bit routine, so the GSSF now has eight arrays, any one of which is allowed in a GSSF match. The furthest is 25 yards away, while in some arrays the farthest is "only" 20 yards off (not all clubs had the room for a full 25 yards).

There are a few versions, when it comes to shooting this stage. Left to right, right to left, near to far, far to near, and what I call the "bounce." Let's take a couple versions of the Five to Glock as our test, versions one and two.

Version one has the five targets arranged left to right and near to far. To shoot this setup the best, you bounce from left to right, near to far. To shoot version two best, you shoot it left to right, near to far. If you find that your fastest way to shoot is right to left, too bad. You'll have to change.

Now, in version three, you have a pair of targets at seven yards, two more, more widely spaced, at 13 yards and one foot (an even 40 feet), and one on the centerline at 20 yards. Hmm. Here you'll have to experiment. Is it faster to "bounce" the two close ones, slow down a bit and shoot the two outside, and then finish with precision shots on the far? Or do

> In shooting the Five to Glock stage, there are five targets and you'll fire two shots on each for 10 total. You will also shoot it three times for a total of 30 rounds and then your hits are recorded. No extra shots, no reloads against the clock.

Big-bore compact Glocks, 9mm compacts, Open guns ... there's room for all.

The firing pace is not warp speed, but proper form is proper form.

you simply sweep right to left or left to right? Only a timer, an afternoon, and targets will tell you.

If you are really intending to do well, you'll set up each version, practice, take notes, record times and scores, and see what works best for each array. Then, when you arrive at a match, you see what array they have, check your notes, and do your visualization for that array.

Glock 'M

Unlike the other two stages of GSSF, Glock 'M has both steel and paper. Here the steel consists of three pepper poppers, and you'll have four cardboard targets.

On the buzzer, lift your Glock and shoot two rounds on each paper target, but one and only one of the pepper poppers. You can use the extra shots in your Glock (remember, you started with 11 maximum) if you need them on the pepper popper, but you cannot use them on cardboard.

You have three runs of this for a total of 27 minimum rounds, and then your cardboard targets are scored.

That tactics question is, do you shoot the pepper popper as part of the cardboard target array, or do you shoot your eight shots on cardboard and then focus on one popper for your last three shots? The fast shooters have determined the quickest way to shoot each of the six versions of Glock 'M and will simply shoot the popper in the array as they go from one to the next cardboard target. If you are new at this, or

want to give yourself the best cushion, shoot cardboard, then steel.

Keep in mind through any of these stages that, with the paper targets, having your sights "on cardboard" is not enough. A trigger "slap" to the outside edge of the target will cost you three seconds of added time per hit. It is worth taking an extra second to make sure your sights are properly aligned and buried right in the middle of the target.

What Do You Get in GSSF?

A GSSF membership gets you a GSSF membership card, hat, patch, and a subscription to *The Glock Report*. A quarterly publication, it reminds you of the courses and rules and has scheduled matches listed, as well as results from previous matches. The match schedule gives the dates, club names, and for those programming their GPS navigation systems, both the club address and its latitude-longitude coordinates.

If you plan to get involved in GSSF, you really need the schedule, as the dates and approval of a GSSF match are controlled by Glock. A club can't just throw a match on the schedule, set up the GSSF stages, and call it a GSSF match. Yes, a club could certainly set up the stages on its own, but I'd bet calling them the GSSF stage names would be a violation of trademark protection, as would calling it a GSSF match without the correct endorsements. So, if the club schedule says "GSSF" in it, the match is Glock approved and sanctioned. And you know the full panoply of fun will be there, including a factory armorer who will overhaul your Glocks at no charge (well, they might grumble about a new barrel or slide, if it looks like neglect on your part), along with approved stages and procedures and wall-to-wall Glocks in use.

Why Do We Do This?

Why, for the practice, of course. Shooting improves skills, and shooting in competition, even a competition as mild as GSSF, improves your skills and your skills under pressure. But the best reason is loot.

If you do well in a GSSF match, you can win another Glock. Now, for those who are not into Glocks or guns, winning one of what you already have seems just a bit silly. But, if you practice (and have fun, too, let's not forget), you can shoot your vanilla-plain G17 and win a Glock that you could enter into another category of GSSF.

Fair warning, if you win too many, GSSF will bump you up into the Master category, where you'll then have to compete against those who also have won loot. But that's only fair. After all, you just demonstrated your ability to beat all the other guys who were starting out, so why not cut them some slack and throw in with the guys at your own skill level?

The loot comes with choices. You can select from a free Glock (some models are no charge, except for the sales tax in your state), and others are options at a small premium. In the last GSSF match I entered, I got the paperwork and opted for a Gen4 G34, which, with the premium, came to a cost of $142 plus tax. Now, I don't care how good a bargainer you are, you are not going to find a new-in-box Gen4 G34 for $142. (If you do find a Glock you can buy for that, it won't be new, and it may well need a trip to the next GSSF match for an overhaul.) Considering I had a day of fun, practice, and seeing the guys at the gun club (something I don't get to do much of these days) and I got to buy a Glock for a pittance, I have to mark that on the calendar as a really good day. You should give it a try.

Divisions

The USPSA and the IPSC (different organizations, one the U.S., the other the International), in the mid-1990s, finally got around to settling their equipment problems. In the process, they found room for Glocks. In USPSA, the division is known as "Production," and in it, you have to use plain sights (no red dots) shoot only a 9mm, no muzzle brakes are allowed, and you have to use a reasonably relevant holster. (As slight amendment, you don't have to use a 9mm, but you won't get to get the scoring bonus from using something

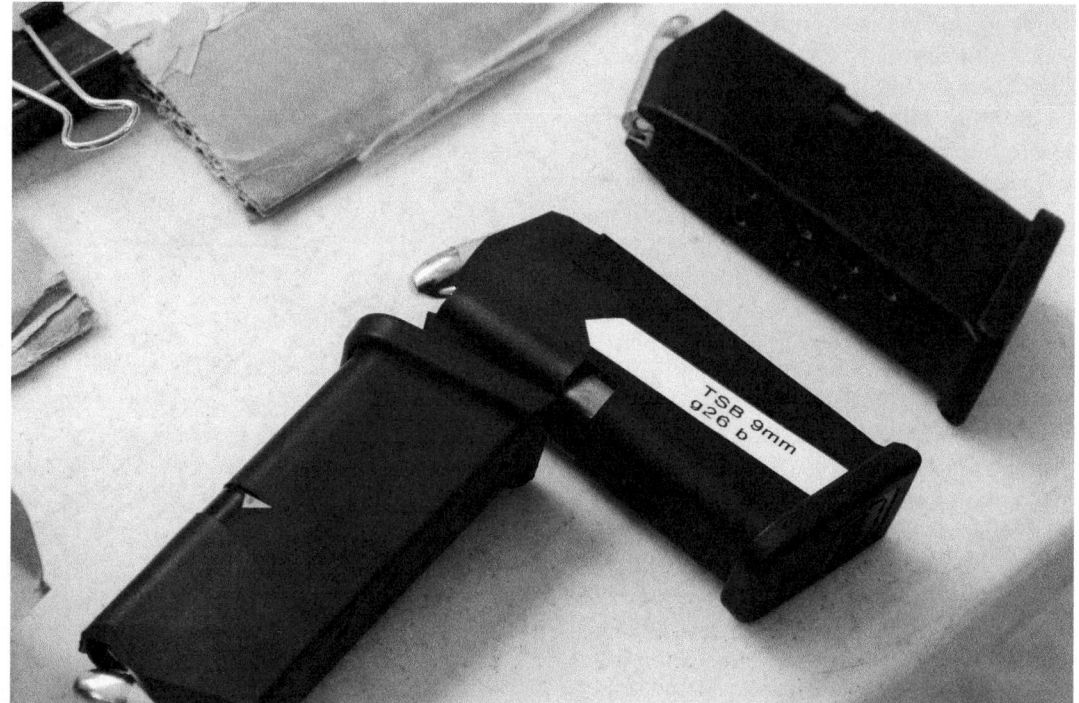

With a suitcase full of Glocks in various calibers, it is prudent to mark your mags. Otherwise, you may find you've loaded your .40 with 9mm ammo. That won't help your score.

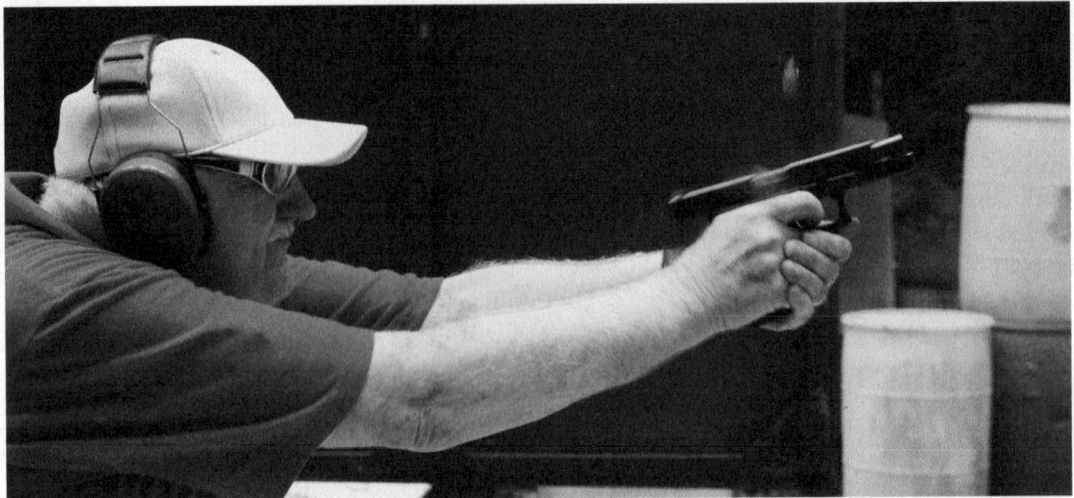

Young, old, working, or retired, if you have a Glock, there's a category in GSSF you can enter.

bigger. You shoot whatever you want, but you get scored as if you shot a 9mm, regardless.) You'll be limited to 10-shot magazines only, or loading only 10 in an otherwise higher capacity magazine. If you forget and load 11 rounds or more into your hi-caps, you'll find your entry has just been bumped to "Open." Open is the group of shooters with 30-round magazines, muzzle brakes, red dot sights, and very, very fast times. You don't want to be there with a G17 or G34.

The IDPA, formed prior to USPSA and IPSC creating their Production division, started out with a Production category. It has pretty much the same restrictions as the USPSA.

Glock has ruled the Production Division from the beginning (in USPSA, IDPA, and IPSC, there has been a lot of very serious competition), but, lately, other makers have been making inroads. What you won't see in Production is a laid-back, casual approach to the shooting. The guys who shoot Production and do well approach it pretty much as if they were using Open guns with red dots and muzzle brakes. Sometimes they even shoot as fast. If you ever start to feel like you're a big frog in GSSF, take a look at a USPSA match. If you find it interesting, dive in. If you find it too much, be glad Glock has created a place to have fun.

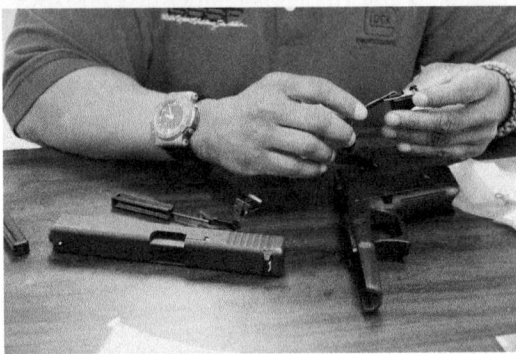

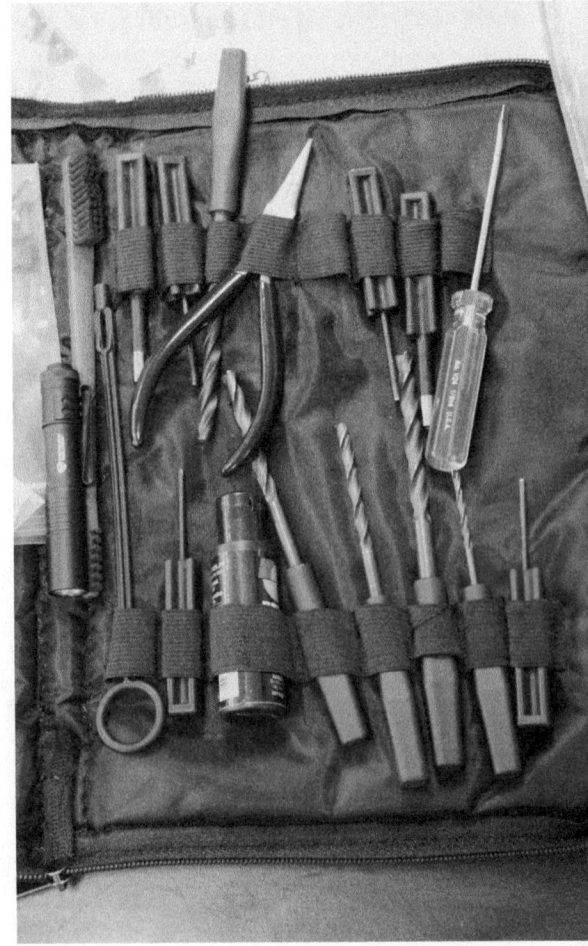

(middle) At a GSSF match, you can turn your Glock over to the care of a Glock factory armorer, who will update all the out-of-date parts, replace worn ones, and give it a clean bill of health. He won't actually clean it, that is still your job.

(right) For simple disassembly and cleaning, you need only one tool. But the Glock armorer shows up at a GSSF match with the full bundle of hand tools.

GunDigest
WE KNOW GUNS, SO YOU KNOW GUNS — THE MAGAZINE

ENTER TO WIN
NEW PRIZES BEING ADDED ALL THE TIME!

HIGH CALIBER SWEEPSTAKES

www.GunDigest.com

ENTER ONLINE TO WIN! CHECK BACK OFTEN!

NO PURCHASE NECESSARY TO ENTER OR WIN
Open only to legal residents of the United States and the District of Columbia age 18 years or older.
However, because of state regulations, this sweepstakes is not open to residents of Rhode Island.
All firearm transfers will be conducted in strict compliance with all applicable federal, state and local laws.
Limit: One online entry per person.

IMPROVE YOUR SHOOTING SKILLS

Handgun Training for Personal Protection is a must-read for anyone who is serious about maximizing their self-defense skills. This latest title from handgun authority Richard A. Mann teaches you how to get the most from your training.

> " This book belongs in every shooter's library. Mann provides a practical, hands-on guide to working with your handgun and the equipment that goes with it. Along the way, common misconceptions are corrected, and often neglected topics are explained. This book will become your go-to reference. "
>
> —Il Ling New, *Gunsite Instructor*

HANDGUN TRAINING FOR PERSONAL PROTECTION

Richard A. Mann

How To Choose & Use The Best Sights, Lights, Lasers & Ammunition

3 EASY WAYS TO ORDER

www.gundigeststore.com
(product U2147)

Download to your Kindle,
Nook or iPad tablet

Call (855) 840-5120
(M-F, 8-5 CST)